BUTTERFLIES
of the PACIFIC NORTHWEST

Robert Michael Pyle and Caitlin C. LaBar

Scientific Advisers: Jonathan Pelham, Andrew Warren, Jon Shepard,
David James, David Nunnallee, Paul Hammond, David McCorkle,
Dana Ross, Paul Severns, David Droppers, Norbert Kondla

TIMBER PRESS FIELD GUIDE

Published in 2018 by Timber Press, Inc.

This work is an updated and revised version of *The Butterflies of Cascadia*
© 2002 Robert Michael Pyle and Seattle Audubon Society.

Front cover photographs: top, Snowberry Checkerspot (*Euphydryas colon*); bottom left two, Sara Orangetip (*Anthocharis sara*) and Blue Copper (*Lycaena heteronea*); bottom center right, Oregon Swallowtail (*Papilio machaon oregonia*); bottom right, Red Admirable (*Vanessa atalanta*). Back cover: Northern White Skipper (*Heliopetes ericetorum*).

Interior photo and illustration credits appear on page 437.
Half title: Pale Crescent (*Phyciodes pallida*), male.
Frontispiece: Boisduval's Blue (*Icaricia icarioides pembina*), male.
Page 5: Oregon Swallowtails (*Papilio machaon oregonia*), pair.
Page 6: Purplish Copper (*Lycaena helloides*), male.
Page 8: Lustrous Copper (*Lycaena cupreus*), male.

Timber Press
The Haseltine Building
133 S.W. Second Avenue, Suite 450
Portland, Oregon 97204-3527
timberpress.com

Printed in China
Text design by Christi Payne
Cover design by Sarah Crumb
Serires design by Susan Applegate

Library of Congress Cataloging-in-Publication Data

Names: Pyle, Robert Michael, author. | LaBar, Caitlin C., author.
Title: Butterflies of the Pacific Northwest / Robert Michael Pyle and Caitlin C.
    LaBar; scientific advisers: Jonathan Pelham, Andrew Warren, Jon Shepard,
    David James, David Nunnallee, Paul Hammond, David McCorkle, Dana
    Ross, David Droppers, Norbert Kondla, Paul Severns.
Description: Portland, Oregon : Timber Press, 2018. | Series: Timber Press field
    guide | Includes bibliographical references and index.
Identifiers: LCCN 2017046297 (print) | LCCN 2017049482 (ebook) | ISBN
    9781604698619 ISBN 9781604696936 (flexibind)
Subjects: LCSH: Butterflies—Northwest, Pacific—Identification.
Classification: LCC QL548 (ebook) | LCC QL548 .P942 2018 (print) | DDC
    595.78/909795—dc23
LC record available at https://lccn.loc.gov/2017046297

To the memory of Thea Linnaea Pyle, John Hinchliff, Idie Ulsh,
and all other lovers and students of Pacific Northwest
butterflies who went before   —R M P

To Braden, Arthur, Jasmine, Rhiannon, Annabella, and all
my other butterfly-loving young friends, may this book
assist your future adventures   —C C L

CONTENTS

INTRODUCTION

In the summer of 1967, I was a 20-year-old undergraduate at the University of Washington. Instead of returning to a summer job as a Denver postman, I remained in Seattle to try to teach a class on the natural history of butterflies. In the half-century since, I have taught hundreds of such classes, but back then the idea was a novel one; no one knew what to make of it. At the first class meeting, only one student showed up: a rising Garfield High School junior named Jonathan P. Pelham. It soon became apparent that Jon knew as much about butterflies as I did, and much more about the local species. I dropped the pretense of the class, got a job with the Sierra Club, and became instant field colleagues with Jon—a relationship we have now enjoyed for 50 years.

Before long, we decided a Washington butterfly book was needed. Starting with Ben Leighton's 1946 checklist, and with the assistance of all the local collectors, we began the Northwest Lepidoptera Survey and a book project. Jon Shepard, then at the University of California at Berkeley, contributed his large set of records. Grant W. Sharpe, my postgraduate professor in the College of Forest Resources, enabled me to write an interpretive field guide to the state's butterflies as a master's thesis. Hazel Wolf and Earl Larrison paved the way for it to be published in Seattle Audubon Society's Trailside Series as *Watching Washington Butterflies* (wwb) in 1974.

Jon Pelham became Curator of Lepidoptera at the Burke Museum and proceeded to build a superb reference collection and data base. Not only wwb but also my 1976 doctoral thesis on the ecogeography of Washington butterflies and *Washington Butterfly Status Report and Conservation Plan* (1989) owed a great deal to Pelham's data and review. Around 1978, a group of lepidopterists (Jon Pelham, Jon Shepard, John Hinchliff, Dave McCorkle, and I, and later Paul Hammond) came together as the Evergreen Aurelians, with a view toward expanding the Northwest Lepidoptera Survey by assembling records from scores of collectors, and through further field work. The labors of the Evergreen Aurelians came to fruit in the form of atlases of Oregon and Washington butterflies, edited and prepared by master datakeeper and mapmaker John Hinchliff (1994, 1996). These works summarized the distributional knowledge of a century of butterfly study in the Pacific Northwest.

In the succeeding years, Ernst Dornfeld's classic *Butterflies of Oregon* (1980) and James R. Christensen's very useful *Field Guide to the Butterflies of the Pacific Northwest* (1981) both came into print and went out again, as had wwb. William Neill and Douglas Hepburn's *Butterflies Afield in the Pacific Northwest* (1976) helped to fill the gap. Demand for a new regional treatment led to my much-expanded *Butterflies of Cascadia* (boc) in 2000. Crispin Guppy and Jon Shepard's rich and detailed *Butterflies of British Columbia* (2001), Andrew Warren's brilliant and extremely thorough *Butterflies of Oregon* (2005), Jonathan Pelham's magisterial *Catalogue of the Butterflies of the United States and Canada* (2008), and David James and David Nunnallee's thrilling *Life Histories of Cascadia Butterflies* (2011) all pushed our knowledge of the region's fauna further.

In recent years, with the rapidly blooming clientele for butterfly watching, gardening, and study, Juree Sondker at Timber Press felt that it was time for a new field guide to succeed *Cascadia*, and the present book was born. Along with the same stellar cast of collaborators and advisers that had richly informed *Cascadia*, I recruited one of our most talented and well-equipped young butterfly scientists, Caitlin LaBar, as co-author.

David Nunnallee adapted the Hinchliff dot maps as shaded range maps for *Cascadia*. Since then, many new distributional records have come in, and the *Cascadia* maps have been modified to bring our picture of species distribution up to date. *WWB* (1974) was the first American field guide to use color photographs of butterflies from life, and I was one of the few people photographing butterflies in the region at the time. By the time Idie Ulsh, Dave Nunnallee, and I assembled images for *BOC*, we found there were many more photographers, and we had a surfeit of fine images to choose among. These were all still color slides, and *BOC* was one of the last major field guides to use them. Now, since the digital revolution, many people are photographing butterflies, and the choice is bewildering. Caitlin LaBar has wrangled, assembled, and curated the many new digital images submitted, along with some converted originals from *BOC*. Our scientific advisers have vetted our final selections for species identifications and gender assignments.

We have learned much in the years since *BOC* was published in 2002. The book you hold in your hands, *Butterflies of the Pacific Northwest*, follows on from that book, but it is more than a revision. We have attempted to gather the current state of our butterfly understanding in the region into a palatable, friendly, reliable, up-to-date, and highly usable form. It is intended for everyone who wishes to study, watch, collect, photograph, garden, or otherwise enjoy butterflies responsibly. While many questions remain about their exciting biology, I hope you will find what you wish to know about our region's butterflies in these pages, or at least enough to frame your questions and pursue your own answers in the field and in the literature. With care and attention, you should be able to identify most of the 200+ species of butterflies you might encounter between Canada and California, Idaho and the Pacific, with the tools provided here.

In 1974 (*WWB*), I wrote, "If the book helps you to see butterflies as necessary elements of an imperiled life matrix—or simply to see butterflies—it will have achieved its purpose." Now, with the deepened ecological crisis in mind, I can say nothing truer of my hopes for this Timber Press Field Guide, *Butterflies of the Pacific Northwest*.

—RMP, Gray's River, 2017

How to Use This Book

You should find *Butterflies of the Pacific Northwest* equally helpful in identifying and learning about butterflies you collect, photograph, or simply observe. In the latter case, you should be prepared to consult the book while you are watching, or to return to it with a sharp idea of what it was you saw. This means taking careful notes on size, color, pattern, posture, behavior, habitat, location, date—anything you think might be relevant. It's no good coming to the text with a vague recollection that you saw something orange and medium-sized. Books cannot substitute for careful observation. Canny naturalists find that a useful field guide is only as good as the information they bring to it.

First, when you spy a butterfly, try to get as close as you can, through stealth, binoculars, camera lens, or net. Then observe it attentively from all angles, noting the size, the color, and major markings on both the dorsal and ventral surfaces, and anything else that might help to distinguish it. Take notes or pictures. Then go to the book. Like everyone else, you will first flip through the pictures. If you recognize the family or group (hairstreak, swallowtail, etc.), that's a fine place to start. Chances are this is all it will take and you'll go right to it.

But if there is question between two or more candidates (or nothing looks quite like your butterfly), be sure to read through the **Recognition** section of the candidate species, to see if any definitive field marks eliminate or confirm their identity; and the **On the Wing** section, to see whether the season is likely. The list of **Host Plants**, including favored nectar plants, might provide additional clues. Finally, consult **Habitat and Range** (and the range map) without fail: many species can be virtually eliminated because they simply do not normally occur where your observation took place. That's not to say that species never occur out of range or in isolated, far-flung colonies, but you should first consider the kinds that may be considered usual where your butterfly flies. If you still think it is something else, perhaps it is—but be prepared to reinforce your conclusion with a voucher specimen, a photograph, or complete notes verified by a second observer, just as you would describe a rare bird out of range.

Once you have a tentative identification, sit back and read the rest of the entry so that you may begin to form a knowledgeable impression of your new acquaintance. Always remember that you will learn more from watching the animal carefully and at length than from any book. And I repeat, *take notes*: don't squander your original observations in the dimestore of your memory.

How Butterflies Work

In a field guide such as this, we are eager to get on to the species accounts, and there is too little space for a detailed discourse on these creatures and how they function. Several of the recent monographic books do contain excellent treatments of butterfly biology. I particularly recommend Sbordoni and Forestiero's *Butterflies of the World* (1998) and the introductory material in Scott (1986) and Guppy and Shepard (2001). Nonetheless, you should know a few basic things about these animals in order to put them into context with everything else you see out of doors.

Butterflies are an artificial subgroup of the large (perhaps a million species) insect order Lepidoptera, most of which we call moths. The order's name means "scaly wings," one characteristic that distinguishes butterflies and moths from other insects, along with their fused, sucking mouthparts, which operate much like a coilable drinking straw. The scales are shingle-like, hinged bits of cuticle covering the transparent membranes of the wings. The scales impart the color to the wings, either pigmented and reflecting "true" colors, or sculptured and refracting prismatic or iridescent colors. Though we might imagine this is for our benefit, it's really just our good luck. The colors are actually for birds and other butterflies, for purposes of defense, attraction, and identification. Butterflies see with large, spheroid, compound eyes composed of thousands of hexagonal lenses (ommatidia). Their messages flow to the optic nerve and brain, to be assembled into an integrated image that is probably considerably sharper than we once thought. A radical (=profound, complete) metamorphosis sees the fully sexually differentiated adults arise from eggs via several molts of the caterpillar followed by final transformation within the pre-pupa and chrysalis. Adults live an average of one or two weeks (with exceptions, noted below).

For butterflies to exist in a given area, certain needs must be met, and these differ from species to species. Most people, when asked about butterfly needs, would think first (or only) of flower nectar. Indeed, we idealize butterfly sustenance as the Nectar of the Gods. Edna St. Vincent Millay's poem "Mariposa" (*Second April*, 1921) reinforces this idea: "Mark the transient butterfly / How he hangs upon the flower." This image is true enough, to a point: flower nectar *is* the primary food source of adult butterflies, though far from the only one, and not all nectars are equal. Factors such as sugar type and density, freshness, quantity, flower UV reflectance and form, and individual experience all determine just which nectars a butterfly will tap. Both sexes take other forms of sugars as well, including rotting fruit, running sap, and the honeydew of aphids. Males evidently need to replenish supplies of nutrients that go into the production of their spermataphores

Red Admirable (*Vanessa atalanta*), close-up of scales

(seed packets of sperms and nutrient gifts for the females). They come to mud or damp sand, especially where some animal has urinated, for dissolved mineral salts. Mud-puddle clubs of male blues, skippers, and swallowtails congregated by the dozen on a damp trail, dirt road, or creekside will be a familiar sight to experienced butterfly watchers. But it doesn't stop there. Butterflies (both sexes) also throng to carrion and scat, attracted by the smell of decomposing materials rich in the amino acids and other organic compounds they need. The sight of ethereal butterflies sucking up to roadkill, bear poop, or horse pee turns Millay's verse on its head.

Then recall that these insects are two separate kinds of animals at different times of their lives. They begin active life

Close-up of a butterfly's head

as crawling, chewing, worm-like neuters, and finish as flying, sucking, highly sexual creatures. Thus they also count among their needs the green plants (usually leaves, sometimes flowers, buds, or fruits) that their larvae are adapted to consume. While a few types (e.g., Brown Elfin, Gray Hairstreak, Echo Azure) employ many species of host plants, most are much more specialized. Often this means just one family, genus, or even species of plant, as with the Monarch and milkweeds, or Johnson's Hairstreak and dwarf mistletoe. And the fodder must be succulent, causing some species (e.g., checkers) to swap hosts as the season dries out. All this greatly complexifies a given place's suitability as butterfly habitat.

Being mostly cold-blooded (some species, like Painted Ladies and Monarchs, can shiver to raise their temperature a little), butterflies depend upon solar radiation to make their flight muscles warm enough for flight (but not so hot that they perish, a real risk). Optimal body temperature is not far off our own. Not that the air must be that warm: butterfly wings serve as solar panels. Some species bask with their wings together and held close to the ground (lateral baskers), others spread their wings open (horizontal baskers), and still others pump them open and closed. The basal portion of the wings, nearest the body, is often darkly scaled, the better to absorb solar warmth for heating the muscles and ovaries—especially in high-altitude species like some parnassians and sulphurs. The fact that our region has a sunny side and a shady side reflects itself sharply in their relative abundance and diversity of butterflies.

And then come structural needs. There are exceptions to the short adult lives of butterflies; in our Northern Temperate region, that means the Monarch and the Mourning Cloak and its relatives. Monarchs migrate out of Cascadia in the autumn, the migratory generation spending the winter torpid on the California coast (and some, probably, in Mexico). When the fall migrants die on their spring return, they may have lived six to ten months. But they will not survive the winter unless they locate the proper type of forest to protect their clusters. Winter is the rub for our resident butterflies, too. Most species hibernate as egg, small caterpillar, or chrysalis, withstanding the cold through physiological adaptations. But at least eight species of tortoiseshells (*Nymphalis*) and anglewings (*Polygonia*), and, less commonly, ladies (*Vanessa*) undertake winter diapause as adult butterflies in Cascadia. They come out on warm days, so if you see a Mourning Cloak or Satyr Anglewing on New Year's or Valentine's Day, you won't be hallucinating. Andy Warren found six species of hibernators one early March day near Corvallis, in the advanced spring of 2006. The limiting factor for successful practice of this risky strategy is suitable shelter. Originally, these hibernators probably utilized caves and the same kinds of holes that cavity-nesting birds employ. Now, human structures often serve—tumbledown cabins, transmitter towers, woodpiles, outbuildings, birdhouses. A butterfly's needs may be far more than most people suppose. Our success in finding them depends in large measure on our awareness of these needs, and our ability to spot places where they are met.

Additional topics could be brought into this introduction to butterfly natural history, including courtship behavior, sex differences, and territoriality; migration and phenology (seasonal response); population biology, predators, parasitoids, and disease; mutualism with ants; mimicry, crypsis, and other defense mechanisms. Many of these subjects will come up now and then in the species accounts. The best way to raise questions and find potential answers is through your own careful observation. Now that you have a basic idea of what these sophisticated insects are all about, let's consider the nature of the region with which *The Butterflies of the Pacific Northwest* concerns itself.

Biogeography of Northwest Butterflies

Animals and plants occur where they do, and don't where they don't, because of particular characteristics of the landscape in concert with their own adaptations and ecological amplitude. "Rainfall, temperature, insolation (incoming solar radiation), soil moisture and topography [are] believed to be the main abiotic factors influencing the survival, growth and range limits of insects" (Singh Bais 2016). Our region has plenty of each.

Distribution is not random or arbitrary, and it is not always easily understood. Why the Woodland Skipper (*Ochlodes sylvanoides*)

and the Purplish Copper (*Lycaena helloides*) are nearly ubiquitous throughout Cascadia, while the American Copper (*L. phlaeas*) and the Mardon Skipper (*Polites mardon*) occupy minute portions of the region, can be answered only through close attention to these species' preferences, habits, and limiting factors alongside the region's ecological offerings, geological record, and human history. Biogeography, to me, offers one of the most engrossing and adventuresome avenues for butterfly study.

The natural subdivisions of the Northwest have been described geologically (McKee 1972) and botanically (Franklin and Dyrness 1988). In 1974 (wwb), I proposed

Astarte Fritillary (*Boloria astarte*) at Slate Peak (North Cascades)

a series of butterfly zones that roughly equated with geographic parameters. Later, I examined and tested a series of butterfly provinces based on analysis of some 10,000 distributional records (Pyle 1982). With the 50,000+ records on which the atlases of Oregon and Washington butterflies are based (Hinchliff 1994, 1996), and thousands more accumulated since, a reanalysis might suggest refined and somewhat altered patterns. But the general idea holds up: Cascadia consists of a mosaic of landscapes, each with its own particular face and influences in terms of butterflies.

Such studies reveal units of the countryside with distinctive, though overlapping, butterfly faunas. By picturing these, we can look for species that "ought" to be in a given area, or ask why expected elements might be missing, and thereby discern important conservation priorities. The makeup of a province's butterfly assemblage is determined by a delicate blend of adaptation, ecology, geology, and human use, which together constitute its biogeography. Therefore, the North Cascades will exhibit a fauna tolerant of high elevation, heavy precipitation, and a history of logging, fire, and grazing, with species drawn from Canadian, Far Northern, and to a lesser extent, Rocky Mountain and Sierran elements; whereas the Columbia Basin fauna tolerates drought, wind stress, and still more grazing and agriculture, and has a Great Basin complexion to its makeup. While they can be defined in various ways, here are the major ecogeographical provinces as envisioned in this book, with brief descriptions of their characteristics, adapted in part from Pelham (in Hinchliff 1994, 1996), Dornfeld (1980), and Pyle (1982).

Ecogeographic Provinces of the Pacific Northwest

Vancouver–San Juan Islands While northern Vancouver Island contains heavy forests and high mountains like the British Columbia Coast Range, the southern portion is similar to Washington's San Juan Islands. Lying in the rain shadow of the Olympics, these islands are much drier than surrounding mainland areas and proportionately more productive of butterflies. Garry oak, madrona, and Douglas-fir woodlands grow among extensive grasslands with mossy balds, floriferous headlands, and open summits. Elements largely extirpated around Victoria, such as the Island Marble (*Euchloe ausonides insulanus*), still survive in parts of the San Juans. Others, like the Great Arctic (*Oeneis nevadensis gigas*), persist on Vancouver Island but have not been seen in the San Juans for decades. With nearby Whidbey Island, these islands stand in need of further energetic survey.

North Cascades Beginning somewhat arbitrarily at Snoqualmie Pass and extending north beyond Manning Provincial Park in British Columbia, the North Cascades span the crest of the range into the foothills on both the wet west side and dry east side. Mt. Baker and Glacier Peak stand out as volcanoes in a region largely made of ancient sedimentary deposits, folded and metamorphosed, with intrusions. Mt. Stuart imposes a very large granitic batholith. The topography shows its age in the deeply dissected, low-gradient river valleys, with high relief all around. Extreme glaciation manifests in U-shaped valleys such as the larch-rimmed Methow, and scraped ridges ranging from 5,900 to 8,500 feet, with timberline reached between 5,500 and 7,000 feet. Douglas-fir/western hemlock forests underlain by salal on the west side grade into spruce/fir/whitebark pine highlands, then the rain shadow drops into ponderosa pine and eventually basin big sage on the eastern flank. Arctic-alpine habitats are narrow west of the crest, broader east. Northern elements absent elsewhere in the region come into the North Cascades, such as the Labrador Sulphur (*Colias nastes*), Astarte Fritillary (*Boloria astarte*), and Lustrous Copper (*Lycaena cupreus*). Slate Peak is well known, but vast areas (e.g., the Picket Range and most of the Pasayten Wilderness) remain unexplored by lepidopterists. West of the Fraser River rise the biologically similar Coast Range mountains of British Columbia, sharing Vidler's Alpine (*Erebia vidleri*) with the North Cascades.

Okanogan Valley and Highlands The Okanogan River makes a major corridor from the southern interior of British Columbia (where it is spelled Okanagan) into Washington. To the west, the land climbs into the Cascades. To the east rise the Okanogan Highlands, a mountainous expanse drained north-south by the Sanpoil, Colville, and Columbia rivers. Their valleys form aridland incursions into wetter uplands largely 3,000 to 4,000 feet in elevation, punctuated by a number of peaks over 7,000 feet. Partly Pre-Cambrian, outcrops are composed of a complex variety of volcanic, sedimentary, metamorphic, and intrusive rocks and their derivatives. Glaciation has been extensive. Ponderosa pine, lodgepole pine, and Engelmann spruce with true firs dominate the forested slopes, from bottom to top. Exotic species of weeds have overtaken many areas, but there is also much high country in largely natural condition. The extensive wildlands have been little explored for butterflies, which are particularly diverse and numerous in the province. Lake Roosevelt has flooded the riparian Columbia shores, but many canyons remain. Pale Crescents (*Phyciodes pallida*), Meadow Fritillaries (*Boloria bellona*), and Tawny-edged Skippers (*Polites themistocles*) are Okanogan specialties.

Pend Oreille–Selkirks From the northeastern corner of Washington and southeastern British Columbia to the Purcell Trench in the Idaho panhandle lies a lobe of the Selkirk Mountains drained by the Pend Oreille (Pend-d'Oreille in British Columbia) and Salmo rivers. This province has strong Rocky Mountain and Canadian associations both botanically and entomologically. Boreal meadows and forests feature the southernmost bog lemmings anywhere and the only caribou in Cascadia. Mount Spokane is the most prominent outlier of the Northern Rockies in the region. Riparian woodlands, meadows, and agricultural areas line the Pend Oreille River itself. Long Dash (*Polites mystic*) and Peck's Skippers (*P. peckius*) dwell here in the moist meadows, near Atlantis Fritillaries (*Speyeria atlantis*) in the fringing woodlands.

South Cascades (Washington) Roughly continuing southward from the North Cascades as a column down the spine of the range, and with similar tree cover, the South Cascades change character by becoming far more volcanic and less glaciated. Ash, lava flows, pyroclastics, and mudflows define much of the substrate. General elevations range from 4,000 feet in the south to 6,600 feet in the north, with Mt. Rainier reaching 14,410 feet and Mt. Adams, 12,470 feet. Noble fir dominates many of the higher forests, grand fir lower down. Arctic-alpine conditions are somewhat limited and depauperate compared to the North Cascades, but subalpine species such as Arctic Blues (*Agriades glandon*) live in isolated sky-islands deep into the region, as in the Dark Divide. Outliers extend onto the west side (Silver Star Mountain) and east side (Signal Peak) lowlands. The Big Lava Bed has Oregonian elements, such as Golden Hairstreaks (*Habrodais grunus*); and Mt. St. Helens, with its ongoing show of disturbance and recovery, dominates the province. Many east-side canyons from top to bottom are butterfly-rich, including Two-tailed Tiger Swallowtails (*Papilio multicaudata*), Great Arctics (*Oeneis nevadensis*), and many blues, coppers, and hairstreaks.

Columbia-Snake Basin Bounded by the Cascades on the west, the Okanogan Highlands on the north, the Blue Mountains on the south, and the Northern Rockies on the east, with the Columbia River running through it and the Spokane, Yakima, Snake, Deschutes, and John Day rivers feeding it, this great basinland contrasts greatly with all other provinces. A low plateau as much as a basin, it is underlain almost entirely by Miocene basalt flows up to a mile deep, from the great dike swarms in southeastern Washington and northeastern Oregon. The region is punctuated by dry ranges such as Horse Heaven Hills and Rattlesnake Mountain, and scored by deep coulees and channeled scablands gouged out by the Bretz floods released by the melting of Pleistocene ice dams of Glacial Lake Missoula. Once a rich mosaic of sage-steppe and bunchgrass prairie, the Columbia Basin has been transformed through irrigated agriculture, chemicals, grazing, and non-native plants such as cheatgrass. In preserves, rocky refugia, and pothole pockets, and along the Hanford Reach of the Columbia, one can still find characteristic species. The aridity (8 to 15

inches of precipitation per year) and wind create lithosols conducive to specialized plants and butterflies. The Juniper Dunes in Franklin County stand out in this largely treeless zone. Ruddy Coppers (*Lycaena rubidus*), Cedar Hairstreaks (*Callophrys gryneus*), Mormon Metalmarks (*Apodemia mormo*), Northern White Skippers (*Heliopetes ericetorum*), and Queen Alexandra's Sulphurs (*Colias alexandra*) live here, and both Monarchs (*Danaus plexippus*) and Viceroys (*Limenitis archippus*) patronize the riversides.

Palouse Hills A narrow and ill-defined province, this nonetheless distinctive district runs along the Washington-Idaho border between the Spokane and Snake rivers, blending into the Columbia Basin on the west and Snake Plains on the east. The Palouse is a rolling hilly region of deep loess soils (fine-grained, windblown glacial dust) that must have supported splendid prairies, now mostly converted to wheatfields. A few ponderosa pine and shrub-clad heights poke up from the Palouse, such as Steptoe and Kamiak buttes. Some of the butterflies recorded in the Palouse Hills (such as Meadow Fritillaries) haven't been found there in many decades and may be locally extinct, but renewed exploration is warranted.

Olympic Peninsula The complex and dramatic central massif of the Olympic Mountains is surrounded by the lowlands often described as the Maritime Northwest. Constructed largely of undersea basalts and marine sedimentary deposits, with extensive metamorphosis involved, the Olympics were elevated by crustal heaving and then heavily eroded by glaciation. Timberline comes at 5,500 to 6,000 feet, and summits exceed 7,000 feet. Habitats range from rain-shadow grasslands on the northeast (much affected by agriculture, then development) through Douglas-fir/western redcedar forests (heavily logged outside Olympic National Park, protected within), up to widespread alpine/subalpine meadows and ridges, and down on the west to temperate rainforest exceeding 200 inches of annual precipitation. The high Olympics share some species with Vancouver Island, others with the Cascades. They support high butterfly abundance and fair diversity, with endemics including the Olympic Parnassian (*Parnassius smintheus olympianna*), the Valerata Arctic (*Oeneis chryxus valerata*), and the Spangled Blue (*Icaricia acmon spangelatus*). West-side rainforests are among the most impoverished butterfly habitats in the world, but coastal bogs support Mariposa Coppers (*Lycaena mariposa*) and the maritime race of the Woodland Skipper (*Ochlodes sylvanoides orecoasta*). Rivers drain all sides, from the Hoh to the Hamma Hamma, the Skokomish to the Wishkah.

Willapa Hills–Oregon Coast Range Though separated by the Columbia River estuary, these segments run together ecologically. Lower and simpler than the Olympics, they consist largely of raised ocean crustal basalts and siltstone/mudstone sediments. They average 2,000 feet or so, with Coast Range prominences like Baw Faw Peak, Mary's Peak, and Saddle Mountain reaching 3,000 to 4,000 feet. Annual precipitation exceeds 120 inches in the Willapas, dropping to 80 (west side) and 50 (east side) in Oregon. The Coast Range supported some of the greatest coniferous forests anywhere, but the old Douglas-fir, western hemlock, western redcedar, and Sitka spruce forests have largely been replaced by short-rotation timber plantations. Red alders and bigleaf maples line the rivers. The small butterfly fauna increases southward to the Umpqua River; but the ridge-and-ravine topography supplies some interesting habitats on mountaintops and in valley bottoms, coastal meadows, and bogs. Pale Tiger Swallowtails (*Papilio eurymedon*), Margined Whites (*Pieris marginalis*), Echo Azures (*Celastrina echo*), and Western Meadow Fritillaries (*Boloria epithore*) typify the hill fauna. Oregon Silverspots (*Speyeria zerene hippolyta*) persist in a few remaining salt-spray meadows along the Pacific beaches with a few other cool-weather coastal specialists such as Greenish Blues (*Icaricia saepiolus littoralis*) and Hoary Elfins (*Callophrys polios*), all rare and highly restricted.

Salish-Willamette Lowlands The Puget Trough and Willamette Valley are often treated separately, but they have much in common. Both drain the Cascades and Coast Range on either side, exemplifying a lower, drier, partly grassland plain in the midst of wet forests. The biggest difference is that Puget Lobe glacial events scoured the Puget Sound (Whulge, to the Coast Salish) and Salish Lowlands; while the lowlands southward from Chehalis to Eugene were troweled by lava flows. The northern part of the province, therefore, is filled with mixed glacial, pluvial, and alluvial deposits, the southern with riverine clays and loams overlying Columbian basalts. Both sections have been largely deforested and heavily impacted by human uses and towns but contain interesting habitat remnants and attendant butterflies. In the north, for example, are the Puget Prairies, where you'll find Mardon Skippers (*Polites mardon*), Hoary Elfins (*Callophrys polios*), and Valley Silverspots (*Speyeria zerene bremnerii*);

and the Kitsap shrub-heaths, with Bramble Green Hairstreaks (*C. dumetorum*) and Northern Cloudywings (*Thorybes pylades*). Farther south are wet prairies, Garry oak, and Oregon ash glades, with Fender's Blue (*Icaricia icarioides fenderi*) and Propertius Duskywing (*Erynnis propertius*). Taylor's Checkerspots (*Euphydryas editha taylori*) and Eunomia Ringlets (*Coenonympha tullia eunomia*) link the Salish Lowlands to the Willamette Valley.

Oregon Cascades These are quite different in character from the Washington Cascades, still more influenced by volcanic activity and pumice-tuff soils. Technically they run from the Columbia River to Mt. Shasta, though the southern portion tangles with the next province south of Crater Lake. The side lying east of the Pacific Crest Trail is arid, high, and young, mostly Pliocene and Pleistocene. The wet western slope is made of dissected Oligocene and Miocene lavas. Arctic-alpine habitats are much more limited in extent and even more butterfly-poor than in Washington, occurring on upper Mt. Hood and Mt. Jefferson. The several other volcanoes run to subalpine at best among the cinderfields where the Volcano Blue (*Icaricia* sp.) occurs. Mid-montane canyons, such as the Santiam and Metolius, are prolific in wildflowers and butterflies such as sulphurs, coppers, hairstreaks, fritillaries, checkers, and anglewings. The forest gains incense cedar; rhododendrons proliferate in the understory. A unique assemblage has arisen on the volcanic sand plains east of Crater Lake, including Moeck's Fritillary (*Speyeria egleis moecki*) and Leona's Little Blue (*Philotiella leona*).

Blue-Wallowa Mountains Occupying the southeastern corner of Washington and a larger area of northeastern Oregon, the Blue Mountains complex is largely basaltic and sedimentary with flattish tops mostly under 6,000 feet. The most prominent subrange, the Wallowas, runs down to the mile-deep Hells Canyon at the Snake River, and up to 9,500-foot limestone and granitic peaks, glaciated into cirques and horns. High, rather dry meadows are common, but the true arctic-alpine habitat where the Beartooth Copper (*Lycaena phlaeas arctodon*) flies is quite restricted. The forest cover resembles that of the Cascades, but Rocky Mountain elements enter as well, giving both the flora and fauna a character distinct from the rest of Cascadia. The butterfly component changes to the west through the Strawberry and especially the Ochoco ranges, which could well be considered a province of their own. Big Summit Prairie in the Ochocos is a famously rich butterfly Valhalla for fritillaries, sulphurs, and others. The Touchet, Tucannon, Crooked, John Day, Powder, Grande Ronde, and Imnaha rivers drain the Blues. Look here for Edith's Coppers (*Lycaena editha*) and Great Basin Fritillaries (*Speyeria egleis*).

High Lava Plains Located in central Oregon and extending about 130 miles east from the Cascades into the Malheur Basin, this province is a high plateau (about 4,000 feet) interrupted by cinder cones and lava buttes. Most of the terrain is covered with porous pumice soil, and dry or ephemeral lakebeds outnumber surface streams. Juniper forest separates the ponderosa pine belt to the west from the sage- and rabbitbrush steppe to the east. One of the driest parts of Cascadia, the High Lava Plains receive 7 to 12 inches of precipitation in an average year, with butterflies typically following rainfall. Butterfliers here will see Desert

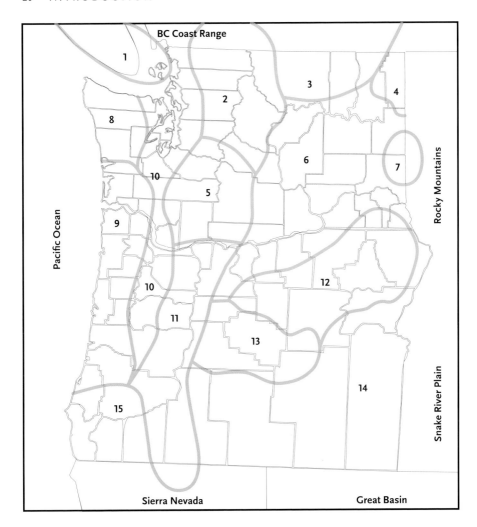

1 Vancouver–San Juan Islands
2 North Cascades
3 Okanogan Valley and Highlands
4 Pend Oreille–Selkirks
5 South Cascades (Washington)
6 Columbia-Snake Basin
7 Palouse Hills
8 Olympic Peninsula

9 Willapa Hills–Oregon Coast Range
10 Salish-Willamette Lowlands
11 Oregon Cascades
12 Blue-Wallowa Mountains
13 High Lava Plains
14 Basin and Range
15 Klamath-Siskiyou

Ecogeographic Provinces of the Pacific Northwest

Marbles (*Euchloe lotta*) and Dark and Great Basin Wood Nymphs (*Cercyonis oetus* and *C. sthenele*).

Basin and Range This large and inchoate province reaches from the "Oregon Lakes District" (Klamath, Summer, Abert lakes) and the Warner Mountains on the west, the country of Mountain Mahogany Hairstreaks (*Satyrium tetra*); up into the Malheur Basin and the Owyhee Uplands, and eastward across Idaho, south of the Snake River Plain. It is the northern extension of the Great Basin, with shallow saline lakes enclosed by fault-block mountains such as Winter Ridge, Abert Rim, and the spectacular Steens Mountain, where alpine meadows host distinctive subspecies of several fritillaries between 7,000 and 10,000 feet, and Shasta Blues (*Icaricia shasta*) and Skinner's Sulphurs (*Colias skinneri*) on top. A different, equally distinctive fauna haunts the Alvord Desert below Steens on the southeast. The highly fluctuating Malheur Lake and the Owyhee River are the main water systems. Sagebrush and rabbitbrush run into greasewood, shadscale, and saltbush, and one can see Mojave Sootywings (*Hesperopsis libya*), Western Pygmy Blues (*Brephidium exilis*), and Leanira Checkerspots (*Chlosyne leanira*). Weidemeyer's Admirals (*Limenitis weidemeyerii*) also enter the region here.

Klamath-Siskiyou The most divergent montane province, in its geology, floristics, and faunistics, is the globular range in southwestern Oregon known variously as the Siskiyous, the Klamath Complex, or both. Bounded by the Pacific Ocean and the Warner Mountains west and east, and more or less intruding between the Cascades and the Sierra Nevada, these rugged mountains have such a complicated history they were called "The Klamath Knot" by writer David Rains Wallace. Extensive serpentine and granite outcrops intrude among sedimentary and volcanic deposits. Numerous California plants and insects show up here, including endemics such as kalmiopsis (a heath that gives an important wilderness area its name) and Sternitsky's Parnassian (*Parnassius smintheus sternitskyi*). Moist near the coast, arid on the east side, the Siskiyous are incised by the Illinois, Chetco, and Rogue rivers. Distinctive butterflies abound in many places, such as 7,000-foot Mt. Ashland and serpentine Eight Dollar Mountain. Species to be sought here especially include the Gorgon Copper (*Lycaena gorgon*), Sierra Nevada Blue (*Agriades podarce*), California Crescent (*Phyciodes orseis*), Columbian Skipper (*Hesperia columbia*), and Lindsey's Skipper (*H. lindseyi*). Across I-5 to the east, the Cascade-Siskiyou National Monument is rightfully famous for its butterfly diversity.

Maps and Mapping

Naturalists have always enjoyed transforming their findings in the field into maps, and lepidopterists have been no exception. Range maps give us a chance to see how a given organism has adapted to and colonized the landscape, show where we may expect to see it, and suggest where we might seek extensions of its known range. Accurate mapping also aids conservation and management for rare species and their habitats: you cannot conserve something unless you know where it is. By updating range maps periodically, we can see not only where an organism has been known to occur in the past but also where it appears to have dropped out; then we can take a close look to find out why, and whether steps can be taken to bring it back. Pioneered in Great

Britain, this approach has been emulated in the Northwest.

There are several ways to represent species occurrence on a flat map, none of them perfect. As one outspoken lepidopterist put it, when it comes to maps, "there are lies, and then there are damn lies." He was right: no mapping scheme reflects reality on the ground with exact precision. In most field guides, butterfly records are generalized into shaded shapes to show the range of the animal or plant across large areas, such as a whole state or country. Shaded range maps, abstracted from the actual records, are handy for gaining a quick impression of a species' whereabouts on the land. Invariably, however, they give an exaggerated impression of its occurrence, since large areas of unsuitable habitat intersperse the sites of actual presence. Shaded range maps can be hand-drawn at a scale almost as elegantly detailed as point maps, or as crudely general as the shaded whole-county maps some books use. Counties are handy units for recording occurrence but can be misleading, as when a dot in one end or corner of a long or large county suggests that the organism is generally distributed there.

Other books, such as *Butterflies of British Columbia* (Guppy and Shepard 2001), map the point location of each record. Such maps are more accurate than shaded range maps because they show the actual spot where a butterfly was observed or collected. These "dot maps," as they are often called, have the virtue of denoting specific episodes of occurrence; if there are many records, patterns emerge that help characterize habitat and range, as well as hotspots— areas with high densities of individuals or species. A single point situated away from the main cluster of points might indicate a stray from its normal range, pinpoint a disjunct population, or identify an area that is under-sampled and should be surveyed to determine whether the butterfly is more widespread than thought. Issues with mapping point locations include loss of detail at large scales, and the difficulty of mapping records (especially historic ones) that lack precise location information. And the absence of a dot, due to collector bias or bad weather, may wrongly suggest absence. Absence of evidence never equals evidence of absence.

To use records without precise data, and to reduce errors made when drawing generalized range maps, many biologists use a standard grid to map records. In Great Britain, butterfly mappers employ the UTM grid of ten-kilometer squares to survey and map species' locations, while many lepidopterists in the United States traditionally used the township, range, and section (T/R/S) method on which the Public Land Survey System (PLSS) is based to record their field data. The PLSS, used in much of the United States, involves a grid of six-mile-square townships, numbered north-south and east-west, based on regional meridians of longitude and circles of latitude. Townships are divided into square-mile sections that may be further subdivided, which you may know if you have ever purchased property. One square-mile section equals 640 acres, a quarter section is 160 acres, and a sixteenth (or quarter-quarter) is 40 acres. Positions on the grid are indicated by metal tags on witness trees and posts. This system allows mapping of records that lack specific point locations yet are detailed enough to be assigned to one of its subdivisions. Since the advent of easily acquired personal GPS units, the PLSS is rapidly being supplanted by latitude/longitude coordinates that anyone can generate. Still, facility with T/R/S is a valuable skill to have, and handy too, as U.S. Forest Service, BLM, and many other maps are based on the PLSS. A GPS addict without his unit is up a creek, but a map-and-grid user will never lose her way.

I was fortunate to study with John Heath, Director of the Biological Records Centre at Monks Wood Experimental Station, and originator of the British Butterfly Recording Scheme, in 1971–72. This experience inspired the Northwest Lepidoptera Survey, managed by the Evergreen Aurelians. Our large legacy database presented a challenge for visual representation. This was solved by John Hinchliff, who meticulously recorded the many thousands of records by hand, and then transferred them dot by dot onto base maps, using the PLSS. These maps were published in his *Atlases* of Oregon and Washington butterflies (Hinchliff 1994, 1996). The data have been managed subsequently at the Oregon State Arthropod Collection at OSU and the Washington Department of Fish and Wildlife. Additional records are constantly being collected. In order to be useful, each record should be backed by a voucher specimen, a good photograph, and/or unequivocal field notes. To prevent misidentification, sight records are seldom accepted except for obvious species and from experienced observers. Every record must include the name of the recorder, the date, and the locality as specifically described as possible, whether by T/R/S, latitude/longitude, or a clear map description.

Going out to hunt for new distributional records provides a fine excuse for a field trip and a means of contributing to our understanding of butterflies in the region.

Each novel locality record constitutes a fresh quantum of scientific knowledge. Recording is also fun. John Heath called it "square bashing," since the records were recorded by ten-kilometer squares, and he used it to escape the office into the field of a sunny afternoon. Butterfliers vie in friendly fashion to secure new county records, and making a first state record is a thrill for any naturalist. Several of these are ripe for the finding in Cascadia, and a few national records (either for Canada or the lower United States) are possible along our shared borders. Making your mark on the map, you also advance the science.

For this field guide format, we elected to use shaded range maps drawn from John Hinchliff's dot maps augmented by more recent records. While they are up-to-date as of the 2016 field season, *you should not assume that the butterfly will be present in every part of the shaded area!* Even so, these maps should allow you to see clearly where a species has been found or might be expected to occur. Start here to ask whether a suspected species is likely to be present where you saw your butterfly. But don't rule out the possibility of finding a species outside its shaded area, since new records turn up every season. Shaded hemispherical areas on the borders of maps indicate that the species occurs not too far off the map in that direction.

Your careful observations will help us to refine these maps in the future. If you think you have a range extension, backed up by a voucher specimen or good photograph and full data, by all means turn it in (see "Data Banks: Where to Send Your Records" in References and Resources). The importance of accurate, reliable butterfly range maps for conservation purposes should make it abundantly clear why butterfly transfers and releases are ill-advised. Whether for weddings, schools, or other purposes, *butterflies should never be released far from their point of origin*, unless part of a planned and monitored conservation scheme. Once the trustworthiness of the individual dot on the map has been lost, we will no longer be able to say with any confidence where our butterflies actually occur in nature.

Ecology and Conservation of Cascadian Butterflies

We are fortunate in Cascadia to have a diverse set of ecosystems overlain by a lot of public land. We also suffer from certain conditions inhospitable to butterflies, heavy extractive land uses, and dramatic population growth in some areas. With habitats ranging from sage-steppe grasslands to temperate rainforest, from arctic-alpine highlands to basin deserts, with mid-montane canyons in between; with biogeographic exposure to many mountain ranges; and with penetration by several major river corridors, the Northwest fauna expresses a remarkable degree of diversity. However, the combination of cool, damp conditions near the coast and heavy coniferous forest cover (mostly under industrial management) with location in the far corner of the continent works to depress the total number of species and individuals.

Particularly in western Cascadia, we commonly encounter sunny, flowery, promising conditions, only to find butterflies all but absent. Butterfly-finding in the Maritime Northwest requires persistence and hopefulness. It helps to be able to enjoy few or individual animals fully, in the absence of abundance (see my essay "I, Clodius," in Pyle 2015b, about being a butterfly lover in the rain world). Jon Pelham refers to the species I study along the maritime edge as "mold butterflies," and surviving winter molds is indeed one of the major limiting factors for butterfly abundance on the wet West Side.

Good places to seek and find butterflies include open, well-flowered spots such as meadows, fields, and pastures; forest clearings and glades; mud puddles and riverbars; unsprayed roadsides, trails, and powerline rights-of-way; parks, yards, gardens, and nurseries; canyons, mountainsides and summits, and rocky knolls and prominences. Many butterflies seek mates around hilltops, others patrol ravines and sunny swales. Above all, look for the creatures where they find their own sources of livelihood: around larval host plants, adult nectar flowers, sap flows, damp earth, carrion, scat, and fallen fruits. Your own experience will soon begin to suggest the sorts of localities that will reward. Habitat is everything: you'll learn to expect Greenish Blues (*Icaricia saepiolus*) in damp meadows, Coral Hairstreaks (*Satyrium titus*) around cherry scrub, fritillaries and swallowtails at thistles, three species of bright nymphs around stinging nettles, and Dun Skippers (*Euphyes vestris*) in certain seeps and woodland coves.

More and more, as our own numbers and needs proliferate, we find our favorite places altered beyond pleasure or recognition. This is particularly true in the Seattle-Bellevue and Greater Portland areas: witness the sacrifice of Sara's Orangetips (*Anthocharis sara*) for warehouses in the formerly verdant Kent Valley. When near-urban habitats drop out, we lose our opportunities to encounter common species close to home. I call this condition "the extinction of experience" (Pyle 2011).

When such losses occur within our "radius of reach" (much smaller for the poor, old, young, or disabled), the opportunity for refreshment from nature flees and alienation sweeps in. Since childhood epiphanies are more often based on face-to-faces with insects than anything else, the loss of "vacant" lots and surprise-filled green space is serious business. Butterfly gardens, parks, and nature reserves take up some of the slack, but nothing substitutes for a patch of "waste ground" close to home, where a child can jar a bee, swing a net, or wonder at a spider's webworks. Grassy fields where Ochre Ringlets (*Coenonympha tullia*) can be found in town, such as Portland's Oaks Bottom, have grown scarce; while Margined Whites (*Pieris marginalis*) and Clodius Parnassians (*Parnassius clodius*) have disappeared from our cities' woodlands.

Urban growth is only one of the ecological challenges faced by Northwest butterflies. Intensive, industrial forestry clearly affects woodland species, especially our few old-growth-dependent types such as Johnson's Hairstreak (*Callophrys johnsoni*). Managed woodlands, however, can be friendly to adaptable species such as the Margined White (*Pieris marginalis*), Echo Azure (*Celastrina echo*) and several fritillaries, but not when aerially sprayed with herbicides that destroy their cardamines, red osier dogwoods, and violets. Defoliants zealously applied to our roadside verges by state and county agencies ruin much potential habitat. Irrigation of shrub-steppe aridlands, such as occurs wholesale in the vast Columbia Basin Project, has converted immense tracts of rich natural grasslands to crop circles. Many lepidopterists believe that the single greatest impact on butterfly habitats in the intermountain West comes from overgrazing by cattle and sheep. We have all returned to formerly productive sites only to find them devastated by "hooved locusts and mountain maggots," in John Muir's colorful terms. Elsewhere, grazing can benefit butterflies, by arresting shrub succession that can overwhelm violets or other host plants. Responsible grazing policy and practices protect the full array of rangeland organisms, from the cow/calf units to the cryptogram layer of lithosol soils and the violets and fritillaries they support, to the ranching families themselves.

Since 1974 (wwb), many new threats to our Lepidoptera heritage have arisen. One of the most alarming among these is the aerial application of the bacterium *Bacillus thuringiensis kurstaki* (Btk) to combat gypsy moths (*Lymantria dispar*), spruce budworms (*Choristoneura* spp.), Douglas-fir tussock moths (*Orgyia pseudotsugata*), and other lepidopterous competitors for food or fiber. Studies at Oregon State University suggest widespread susceptibility among non-target butterflies and moths to this pathogen, raising the specter of large-scale butterfly barrens on the public and private forestlands and in our cities. Large tracts of our national forests have been sprayed with Btk, along with neighborhoods in Seattle and Salem and even Forest Park in Portland. Guppy and Shepard (2001) have an excellent discussion of this subject. More selective strains of Btk might help reduce mortality.

Exotic plants such as spotted knapweed, yellow star-thistle, and Scotch broom take over many acres of native habitat annually (while providing some nectar service for pollinators: bull thistle and purple loosestrife are favorites for swallowtails, fritillaries, and Monarchs). Certain nonnative plants have become important host plants for butterflies, such as the plantains that Taylor's Checkerspots (*Euphydryas editha taylori*) favor. At Mima Mounds, an important DNR state Natural Area Preserve and butterfly habitat in the Puget Prairies south of Olympia, managers fight Scotch broom with fire. But too much burning, too fast, has proved lethal to populations of rare butterfly species. Here and elsewhere, scarce skippers are caught in the crossfire as ecologists seek regimens to suppress brush while not eradicating protected insects on grassland preserves.

Three federally listed species of butterflies reside in Cascadia. The Oregon Silverspot (*Speyeria zerene hippolyta*) dwells in certain salt-spray meadows on the coast, where development, the spread of scrub, and a hostile climate all jeopardize its existence. It is surviving in some Oregon locales through combined efforts of The Nature Conservancy, the U.S. Forest Service, the National Guard, the Oregon and Woodland Park zoos, and others. In southwest Washington, where I rediscovered it in 1975, a series of cool, wet summers and coastal development caused its apparent extinction. Habitat has been acquired and managed, and violets planted for it on the Long Beach Peninsula, however, and reintroduction from Oregon may be a future option.

The endangered Fender's Blue (*Icaricia icarioides fenderi*) was named for the late McMinnville lepidopterist Kenny Fender. Long thought to be extinct, it was rediscovered by Paul Hammond and Paul Severns in remnants of Willamette Valley grassland. Listed as federally endangered along with its host plant, Kincaid's lupine (*L. oreganus kincaidii*), it has become the subject of intensive ecological studies (e.g., Schultz 1997). And the endangered Taylor's Checkerspot

Oregon Silverspots (*Speyeria zerene hippolyta*)

(*Euphydryas editha taylori*) is the subject of vigorous management actions at Joint Base Lewis-McChord and other grassland restoration sites on the Puget Prairies and in the Willamette Valley, where it too was thought to be extinct until rediscovered by Andy Warren. Both native paintbrushes and naturalized plantains are propagated for the larvae, the better to ensure their survival. Rearing programs for reintroduction of several of these rare species have been undertaken at zoos and corrective facilities around the region.

The remarkable rediscovery of the Island Marble (*Euchloe ausonides insulanus*) at San Juan Island National Historic Park by John Fleckenstein in 1998, 90 years after its presumed extinction on Vancouver Island, has led to a robust program of research and conservation measures by state and federal agencies to maintain it. The National Park Service has a challenge on its hands here, since its primary host plants are exotic mustards that had been a target of eradication. Such are the conundrums that can arise when one tries to put the pieces of disturbed ecosystems back together, while saving all the surviving parts.

Butterfly conservation is not the oddity it was in 1967, when I first published on the subject. In recent years Jon Shepard has conducted numerous rare species surveys in British Columbia for the provincial government, and Ann Potter coordinates similar activities for the Washington Department of Fish and Wildlife. Dana Ross, Candace Fallon, and colleagues with the Xerces Society have surveyed many Oregon butterflies of concern. Sadly, though, as willingness to conserve butterflies has grown, so has the need. My survey of Washington butterfly conservation needs highlighted many

Orson Bennett ("Bug") Johnson, for whom Johnson's Hairstreak (*Callophrys johnsoni*) is named, afield with Maude Parker and Adella Parker Bennett of the Young Naturalists' Society, Seattle

populations that should be monitored for their ecological status, and a few in more or less urgent need of outright protection efforts (Pyle 1989). The Mardon Skipper (*Polites mardon*) has been listed as endangered in Washington, and the Golden Hairstreak (*Habrodais grunus*) and several others are candidates for listing.

All these cases of jeopardy relate to habitat issues rather than collecting. Insects reproduce very effectively, and butterfly collectors are both exceedingly inefficient predators and generally responsible in their actions. While it is extremely difficult to make a dent in most mobile insect populations with a net, the bulldozer, the cow, and the plow eradicate whole butterfly colonies in no time (New et al. 1995). The proliferation of insecticides and herbicides threatens our own health as well as that of beneficial insects. Dams inundate riparian habitats along with salmon beds. Introduced parasitic flies and predatory wasps are cause for concern. Global warming will likely affect our alpine, desert, and water-limited butterflies for the worse, even as it enables the expansion of southerly species into our territory.

While much of the story is negative and admonitory, it is good to note some positive signs concerning the impact of agricultural reforms on butterflies. David James' research on butterfly conservation in vineyards attracted much media and peer attention and showed the possibilities for combining butterfly conservation with habitat restoration for biologically based pest management (James et al. 2012). His and others' work in the Pacific Northwest is at the forefront of research on the benefits of low input agriculture and butterfly/nature conservation. The Xerces Society, named for the extinct Xerces Blue, has also been tilling these fields of reform. Since 1971, the society, headquartered in Portland, Oregon, has been working internationally to conserve invertebrate habitats and populations, including butterflies.

From the butterfly houses in Victoria and Seattle to Willamette Valley Fender's Blue reserves to collaborations between zoos, prisons, military bases, and scientists both citizen and university, butterfly stewardship is spreading across Cascadia. Maintaining our fauna and the flora it depends upon will cost a lot of work and attendant frustration, especially as our population burgeons. Even so, I believe that

with care, effort, and attention, we should be able to sustain a rich natural butterfly heritage in the region once hopefully called Ecotopia.

Enjoying Butterflies

Traditionally, most people who have purposefully gone forth to enjoy butterflies have done so as collectors. As Morton Elrod wrote in *The Butterflies of Montana* (1906): "Love for the humble little creatures of the air, love for the beautiful in nature, love for nature itself . . . making him more appreciative, more happy, and more contented, will be the final reward of the young collector." Butterfly collecting, even in this time of nonconsumptive resource use, has its appropriate place, a subject we will return to. But these days, the relatively small number of collectors must share the butterfly fauna with many new enthusiasts with objectives other than—and sometimes directly opposed to—the taking of specimens and assembly of a collection.

The first book explicitly devoted to spreading the practice of butterfly watching as an outdoor activity in this country was my WWB (1974). Since then, my *Handbook for Butterfly Watchers* (1992) and other resources have found a receptive public ready to broaden their outdoor repertoire. The North American Butterfly Association (NABA) arose particularly to cater for the growing body of butterfly-watching naturalists. Many birders have shifted to or added butterflies in order to maintain the novelty and discovery that drew them outdoors in the first place, or simply because they have discovered the accessible beauty of butterflies. Now, especially in the East, the number of people pursuing butterflies through binoculars (in Jeff Glassberg's

Arctic Fritillary (*Boloria chariclea*) alights and delights

phrase), or "butterfliers" as they call themselves, has begun to rival that of birders in some localities. As natural history devotees discover the ubiquity, approachability, and ease of acquaintance of our butterfly fauna, not to mention the brilliant riches of foreign locales, they will surely multiply like Cabbage Whites on broccoli.

However, watching is far from the only way to take pleasure from butterflies. Indeed, I know blind butterfly lovers who enjoy their smells, touch, and metamorphosis with windowbox rearing chambers. Rearing butterflies from egg or larva through the pupal stage to the flying adult has long been one of the richest experiences available to the young or impressionable, and no elementary or biology classroom should neglect the first-hand lesson of profound metamorphosis—the pixels on a flat screen are no substitute for the glittering scales on a butterfly's wing. Nor are Painted Lady kits purchased from afar—what kind of a lesson is it for children that butterflies come in a box and may be released willy-nilly, regardless of their natural whereabouts? Industrial Painted Ladies may be better than nothing in the classroom. But it is far more satisfying and instructive to go out yourself to bring back wild larvae (woolly bear caterpillars are great for this). Or cage gravid females with their host plants—nearly all females you catch will be fertile, and they are much easier to find than eggs, larvae, or pupae. Purchasing Monarchs for release is both unethical and illegal unless the source is local and Monarchs naturally breed in the area of release, which leaves out most of western Cascadia. If you wish to tag and release Monarchs to enhance our understanding of the species' remarkable and poorly grasped migration patterns, work instead with native Monarchs in their usual range, through the Facebook group run by David James of wsu (facebook.com/MonarchButterfliesInThe-PacificNorthwest). Elsewhere, rear the species at hand, whether swallowtails or handsome orange-and-black Isabella Moths (=woolly bears).

Butterfly gardening means cultivating plants selected to enhance the numbers and variety of butterflies in your own home environment. At the alpha level, this merely involves growing nectar plants for attracting adults. The more satisfying beta level will lead you to include caterpillar host plants, in hopes that your garden will actually provide breeding habitat for visiting species. Several fine books are available on this subject, including the beautiful *Gardening for Butterflies* (Xerces Society 2016).

A little tolerance for larvae on your plants, a bit of curiosity about who eats what, and a suitable rejection of chemical

management around the home will give you a safer, brighter, better understood, and infinitely more interesting setting. You will find that a little effort expended in this direction will reward you with wonderful opportunities for observation and study right in your own yard, and a much more interesting, holistic approach to making a garden. Even your lawn can be butterfly-friendly if you don't spray or mow too close, supporting Woodland Skippers (*Ochlodes sylvanoides*) on the west side, or Sandhill Skippers (*Polites sabuleti*) on the east, and furnishing fine nectar for visitors in clover and dandelion blossoms. My lawn is full of veronica, and to see an Echo Azure (*Celastrina echo*) visiting its blossoms, blue on blue, subverts the stereotype of lawn-as-barren. I mow to let the hawkbit and dandelions bloom for the skippers and coppers, but not go to seed or crowd out the skippers' and wood nymphs' grasses.

A special moment comes when a sought-after or unexpected species shows up. Portland butterfly gardener and habitat consultant Maurita Smyth celebrated when the first Cedar Hairstreak (*Callophrys gryneus*) arrived in her yard one spring. I will never forget a lunch break during one Fourth of July Butterfly Count when a very rare California Sister (*Adelpha californica*) appeared on our butterfly bushes in full view of all the participants; or when Echo Azures first turn up at damp wood ash, breaking wet winter's hold, soon followed by Brown Elfins (*Callophrys augustinus*) on rhododendrons and Two-banded Checkered Skippers (*Pyrgus ruralis*) buzzing around volunteer large-leaf avens. Even in wet Wahkiakum County, the native Douglas asters are thronged in late summer with Mylitta Crescents (*Phyciodes mylitta*) and Woodland Skippers (*Ochlodes sylvanoides*), and sometimes American Ladies (*Vanessa virginiensis*) and Pine Whites (*Neophasia menapia*) come to the Mexican sunflowers.

Butterfly counts, just mentioned, are becoming more popular every year. Charles Remington, Ray Stanford, Jerry Powell, Paul Opler, and other lepidopterists had long urged annual one-day counts. These were begun formally in 1975 by Sarah Anne Hughes as the Xerces Society Fourth of July Butterfly Counts, modeled after the National Audubon Society's Christmas Bird Counts. Numbering in the hundreds nationwide, the counts are now coordinated by the North American Butterfly Association, and several take place routinely in the Pacific Northwest and northern California (for a location near you, check with naba.org). These activities, in addition to providing a delightful day out for like-minded folk, are beginning to give a meaningful sense of the fluctuations in butterfly numbers year-to-year, while acquainting counters with habitat issues in their vicinities. Taking part in a count is a great way to shorten the learning curve; on our annual Chumstick Mountain count, we know we will have a vigorous day afield while meeting 30 to 60 species.

Another quick way to enhance your knowledge, especially about behavior, is to take pictures of butterflies. Patience, stealth, and great watchfulness are at least as important as fancy equipment and lots of pixels. As the images in this book show, compared to the adequate but simple shots in wwb (and better but still film-based portraits in boc), we have come a long way with digital butterfly photography. The number of contributors further suggests the growing devotion to this sometimes frustrating, always challenging sport. If you avoid

the temptation to stun, chill, or otherwise manipulate the insects, you'll find the pursuit immerses you in the most careful kind of attention—and that's what naturalists do: *pay attention.* An examination of the pictures in this book will reveal the kinds of places pictures may be sought, at flowers, mud puddles, basking spots, rotting fruit, sap, carrion, or scat. By combining careful rearing with acute observation and fine photography, David James and Dave Nunnallee secured the first images of many of our species' immatures, few of which had been well documented before. Photographs of adult butterflies in the wild are being accepted as data records more and more, alongside voucher specimens. But for images to have such value, they *must* be accompanied by detailed data (where, when, and who, precisely recorded), and it helps to take several views, especially both dorsal and ventral when possible, to facilitate reliable identification. Some species just cannot be determined beyond doubt without a specimen in hand, but many or most can, given good enough photos with solid information.

Modern photography equipment rapidly changes with advances in small-camera technology in cell phones, smaller and lighter pocket cameras, and increasing affordability of professional-quality digital SLR cameras. All have increased the availability of high-quality photography equipment to the average user. There will always be discussions about Nikon versus Canon, point-and-shoot versus SLR, and any number of camera accessories, but the key is to find a camera that fits your situation. Do you like to hike and don't want to pack a lot but can't bear to leave home without a camera? Consider a new smart phone with the latest camera technology, or a lightweight pocket camera with close-up capabilities. Are you a serious photographer or do you aspire to be? Consider investing in a digital SLR camera with changeable lenses and an adjustable, external flash. The greater the resolution you are able to capture, the higher the chance of getting pictures that will be acceptable for publication. Most images in this book, for example, contain at least two megabytes of data.

The key to capturing high-quality images of live butterflies is to have a camera with a lens that allows you to be close enough to the butterfly to produce a detailed shot but that doesn't require you to be so close that you risk scaring it away. Most serious butterfly photographers use digital SLR cameras such as the Nikon D300, D5000, or D7000 series, or the Canon EOS 5d Mark III and other Canon EOS models. Caitlin uses a Nikon D7100 with a variety of Nikon lenses, primarily an AF-S VR Micro-Nikkor 105mm macro lens, AF-S VR Micro-Nikkor 60mm macro lens, and an AF-S DX Nikkor VR 18-200mm all-purpose zoom lens, usually with the added boost of a Nikon SB-700 Speedlight Flash, which mounts into the shoe above the built-in flash. While not always necessary, using an external flash with adjustable flash options allows for added flexibility and greatly helps reduce unwanted shadows. Rapid-fire repeat shooting helps too, the multiple images yielding one or more that are just right, and sometimes even catching good pictures of butterflies in flight.

The images that follow show the wonderful results that can be obtained by serious hunters with big lenses and the knowledge of how to use them. But it is surprising to see how well casual photographers can do with their cell phones or point-and-shoots.

Equipment aside, the most important things are to watch closely, move slowly, and learn to think like a butterfly.

Don't forget a good, close-focusing pair of small binoculars, a useful tool for all field work. Lepidopterists vary in their habits, preferences, and equipment, and fewer collectors than watchers have adopted field glasses into their kit. But I have considered mine to be a vital part of my body for most of my life, whether watching or catching or both. Turned upside down, binoculars also substitute as another essential item for entomology: the hand lens. Many birding binoculars work all right for butterflies at a bit of a distance. But for near observation, it is necessary to have binoculars that truly focus closely. Several models from most makers are now available that bring subjects into sharp focus anywhere from one to five feet from the watcher. Six- to eight- power magnification and as much light-gathering as possible complete the specs.

The most valuable tool for butterfly study is the good old-fashioned butterfly net. It is also the cheapest and most effective antidote to Nature Deficit Disorder— give a curious kid a net, and watch her go! Good, inexpensive nets may be purchased from BioQuip Company (bioquip.com), or you can make your own from available materials, as kids have done from time immemorial. I have carried a Colorado cottonwood-limb-based net, dubbed Marsha, for more than 40 years.

While most readers will want to enjoy their butterflies alive, some will still prefer collecting as their approach of choice. Many books (e.g., Winter 2001) give the specifics of technique and equipment. Moving slowly and fluidly, gently tracking the quarry before springing catlike with the net, serves the collector as well as the watcher and photographer. Go easier on females than males, especially for rarities, and always keep detailed data (where, when, who) to dignify your prey as scientific specimens rather than mere curios. Be aware that regulations must always be followed (you may not collect in national parks or wildlife refuges, state parks, or Nature Conservancy lands without a permit, but national forests are open to non-commercial collectors, as well as most BLM and DNR lands). Always respect private property as well as those who might be trying to watch or photograph the same insect you hope to net. Report your finds to the Northwest Lepidoptera Survey to be a part of our growing regional data base, and always be ready to cheerfully explain your activity to the curious. Feel free, if the situation warrants, to say that you are collecting moths, wasps, or flies, or studying pollination biology. Illogically, these pursuits are far less likely to incur righteous wrath than "butterfly collecting."

For those who feel antagonistic toward collectors, we want you to know that butterflies, like other insects, are great reproducers most of the time. It is usually very difficult to do direct damage to an insect population with a hand-held net. Imagine controlling mosquitoes with a fly swatter. Far more damage accrues to beneficial insects through bug zappers, autos, and pesticides than all the collectors of all time could ever account for. Habitat loss, of course, is the great source of mortality, and the records provided by collectors over the years have helped us to pinpoint habitats of significance and patterns of distributional decline or expansion. Making a reference collection remains the speediest, most thorough way to learn the local

insects, and the main route through which youngsters gain a serious interest in biology. When you see a butterfly net, be aware that it probably signifies learning rather than an act of willful destruction. Nor must a net necessarily be a lethal implement. I have used catch-and-release techniques for many years to allow students to see the creatures up close, then watch them fly free, unharmed. The only trick in doing this is to employ tweezers (smooth, spade-tipped stamp tongs work best) to gently but firmly grip all four wings, near their base, as you remove the insect from the net to examine it up close. Don't let it get too hot in direct sunlight, be careful of legs, wings, proboscis, and palpi, and you can have a richly rewarding face-to-face with no harm to the subject. Practice this with larger butterflies first. Afterward, release the butterfly gently on a nearby flower or nose.

Above all, I urge tolerance and mutual understanding among all users of the butterfly resource. For we all *use* butterflies, even if our interest is purely aesthetic. Butterfly-based recreation has come a long way since 1974 (WWB), as shown by the growth of the butterfly clubs in the region. Butterfly watchers already outnumber collectors and may someday swamp them overall. But it is important to remember that our basic knowledge of butterflies, their ecology, whereabouts, and conservation needs, is based on those who have swung nets in previous years. *None of our butterfly references, including this book, would be possible had it not been for the collectors.* Until fishing, hunting, and the swatting of mosquitoes are all considered out of bounds in some future Schweitzerian society, the preserving of voucher specimens will remain a useful and legitimate purpose in lepidopterology.

Now—when our need to understand biodiversity in order to conserve it is greater than ever—is no time to terminate the scientific sampling of insects, which begins with a kid with a net.

Watchers and catchers, gardeners and photographers, all share a passion for these remarkable animals as living, reproducing, enchanting, and eternally fascinating organisms. We hope you will do the same, and however you choose to approach butterflies, we wish you success in the search.

About Names

Names signify the subdivisions of the animal kingdom our butterflies belong to. Throughout the species accounts, brief descriptions introduce the families, subfamilies, tribes, and major genera of butterflies—in other words, the groups to which they are seen by specialists as being most closely related by descent. Naturalists often find themselves frustrated by changing names of organisms as applied by specialists, and by the lack of agreement among various texts and field guides. In this book we use names in the following manner.

Spelling By zoological convention, family and higher category names are capitalized but not italicized (Pieridae). Genus names are italicized and capitalized (*Colias*); species epithets are italicized and lower case (*eurytheme*). English names are in Roman type. We employ the convention of capitalizing all common species names of butterflies (Orange Sulphur), but not group names (sulphur, white); and lower-casing all other animals and plants (except proper nouns) for purposes of ready distinction.

The Linnaean system of binomial nomenclature (genus and species) has been in use for more than 250 years. Like every

other organism, each butterfly belongs to a kingdom (Animalia), subkingdom (Invertebrata), phylum (Arthropoda), class (Insecta), order (Lepidoptera), suborder of convenience (Rhopalocera), superfamily (Hesperioidea or Papilionoidea), family, subfamily, tribe, genus (and sometimes subgenus), and species (and often subspecies).

Family We accept the modern concept of six families of butterflies: skippers (Hesperiidae), parnassians and swallowtails (Papilionidae), whites, marbles, and sulphurs (Pieridae), gossamer wings (Lycaenidae), metalmarks (Riodinidae), and brushfoots (Nymphalidae). All six families occur in Cascadia.

Genus and Species We employ the names that best reflect our understanding of relationships, as based on recent revisions, current research, and the studied opinions of Northwest lepidopterists. In this book, we follow Jonathan P. Pelham's *Catalogue of the Butterflies of the United States and Canada*, as revised periodically online (butterfliesofamerica.com/US-Can-Cat. htm). When the *Catalogue* genus or species epithets differ from names used in Pyle (1974, 1981, 2002), Opler (1999), or other standard sources, we give the equivalent names in the Aka section so they may be recognized. For example, *Boloria chariclea* used to be known as *B. titania*, what we formerly called *Parnassius phoebus* in the Northwest is now understood to be *P. smintheus*, and so on.

Subspecies Because of their number, often poor definition, flux, and limited utility to many users, we are not routinely treating subspecies in this guide; we do, however, mention certain well-known, highly distinctive, threatened, or otherwise notable races or varieties. The photographic images, both from life and specimen plates, seek to show the range of variation expressed by many of the named subspecies.

Common Names There have been two strong efforts to bring order to vernacular butterfly names in North America, first the Xerces Society/Smithsonian common names synonymy (Miller 1992), then the NABA (1995, revised 2001) prescriptive checklist of English names. While uniformity has its merits, imposed uniformity for its own sake can violate both regional color and good sense, as well as personal volition. Generally, the common names we use correspond with the NABA list. But in a few cases, where Northwest usage or other good arguments favor another name, we use it instead, e.g., Western Meadow Fritillary (NABA: Pacific Fritillary). In such cases we give the NABA name in the Aka section. Likewise with the Xerces/Smithsonian names and other traditional (e.g., Alfalfa Butterfly for Orange Sulphur) and common names coined by Scott (1986) or used in any recent texts Cascadians might use. As with longstanding ornithological practice, we seldom give common names for subspecies, unless they have special regional or conservation significance. Very few new common names are introduced in this book. Every name appears in the index. You should easily be able to find any Cascadian butterfly in these pages, regardless of what it might be called in any other source.

Why Names Change

Amateur naturalists love to joke among themselves about the evil machinations of the taxonomists, who get their kicks by changing the scientific names of plants and animals as soon as we have become familiar with them. Some actually seem to believe

this is done out of spite for amateurs. In reality, those who describe and revise scientific taxa (named categories of organisms) are as interested in stability as anyone. But they are bound to present the truth as they see it, and this sometimes necessitates changing a well-known or well-loved name.

The main ways this happens for scientific names are these: a) New discoveries: species or subspecies new to science are found, necessitating a new name; this may alter previous arrangements. b) Lumping: taxa previously thought to be separate are judged to be conspecific, thus sinking the younger of the two names. c) Splitting: one species is separated into two or more distinct entities, thus raising subspecies names to specific status. d) Historic adjustments: taxonomic researchers find that an older valid name exists that supersedes an existing epithet, that a current name is a synonym of another, older one, or that an error exists in application, gender, or other condition. Neither random nor arbitrary, these changes are ruled by the *International Code of Zoological Nomenclature*, overseen by a commission. Such changes may be irritating, but in the long run they help to bring coherence and order to our picture of an exceedingly complex living world that doesn't easily fit into boxes.

Remember that the history of speciation doesn't necessarily accommodate a simple system of naming, and there are still no easy ways to determine genetic distance between populations. What makes a species or a subspecies, even a genus or a family, is ultimately a judgment call. Those who make these judgments do so based on the best, most recent data from mitochondrial DNA, allozyme sequences, protein electrophoresis, and other molecular studies; hybridization experiments; and comparison of traits such as genitalia and markings, behavior, ecology, and life history, not to mention hunches, assumptions, and informed guesses drawn from extensive field observation.

Specialists often disagree in their interpretation of data and information. Some practice a "typological" species concept through the application of cladistics, the rigorous testing and portrayal of relationship involving statistical character analysis; others prefer a "biological" species concept, using all available evidence to infer degree of genetic separation. The latter may result in a more "natural" set of species, but the former is more objective. Most specialists actually consider both lines of reasoning. I have had to make judgments, especially where one colleague believes two taxa blend together, and another feels they are genetically separate. In some cases, as with certain checkerspots, both facts may be true in different places, as odd as that may seem. Since nature is dynamic, science imperfect, and inquiry constant and ongoing, there will continue to be changes in the names we use. Unfortunately, we will probably never see a permanent checklist for our butterflies. But that is doubtless preferable to repressing new information in order to maintain a rigid system of names based on artificial or easy distinctions.

Butterflies Vary!

Remember, and remind yourself often, that butterflies are living, sexually reproducing organisms whose genes are constantly scrambled and who therefore *vary*. Variation furnishes the grist for natural selection. If every individual exactly resembled the pictures in field guides, they would all be

Aberrant Taylor's Checkerspot (*Euphydryas editha taylori*)

clones. Butterflies are neither minted like coins nor printed like stamps: they are the products of parents with differing traits, and therefore each one is an original. In field seminars, I ask my students just how diverse *we* are, for our species. First they say a lot, because we differ in gender, age, and looks. But when I point out that we have very little ethnic range, they see that our range of variation is minor. Then I ask which of us they would choose for field guide portraits of the male and female *Homo sapiens*, by which a Martian could identify humans from all over the earth, Swede or Masai. This dramatically makes my point about variation.

Some species are relatively constant, like Mourning Cloaks and Painted Ladies. Others, such as checkers and sulphurs, vary quite a lot. None of our butterflies is as dramatically polymorphic as the dog or the human, but they all range more or less away from whatever we consider the "norm." They can experience gigantism, dwarfism, albinism, melanism, gynandry, and environmental influences. Furthermore, they fade and fray with age and exposure to sun, weather, birds, and brush, so they vary still more with freshness and experience.

Get used to it! As Norbert Kondla puts it, "People who look at multiple individuals will encounter butterflies that have not read the field guides and don't agree with published descriptions and available pics on the Internet, just as a matter of individual

A not-so-familiar Monarch (*Danaus plexippus*), displaying albinism

A melanic Chalcedona Checkerspot (*Euphydryas chalcedona*), minus white spots

variation." Always compare various illustrations in your search for an insect's identity. Build a better butterfly library, both wide and deep. Frequently visit the website of Butterflies of America (butterfliesofamerica.com), with its many photographs of our butterflies both from the field and set as museum specimens. And if you will follow and study the next section with care, you will have more success than if you simply try to match butterflies to pictures in the expectation that they should be identical. Thank goodness, they never will be all the same.

BUTTERFLIES
of the PACIFIC NORTHWEST

SPECIES ACCOUNTS

Here we give our basic understanding about each species in our region in a standard form. We have omitted descriptions and illustrations of life history stages other than the adult, referring users instead to the comprehensive *Life Histories of Cascadia Butterflies* (James and Nunnallee 2011); all serious butterfly lovers in our ecoregion should have that book, too. Each account is ordered as follows.

Names Our preferred common (English, vernacular) name, the genus and species, followed by the author, the person who first described the species in the scientific literature (in parentheses if first assigned to a different genus), and the year of publication of the original description.

Type Locality The place of origin of the specimen on which the species' original description was based. Older type localities were often vague, recent ones more specific. If a type locality has been restricted by a later worker, it is listed here as if original.

Aka "Also known as," giving other English and scientific names, if any, under which you are likely to find the butterfly listed in relatively recent literature. *The Aka section does not constitute a formal synonymy*: an entry under Aka does *not* mean it is equivalent, only that the species has been called by that name at some time. These names should help you cross-reference resources.

Legal Conservation Status, if any, is given in red. Note: sgcn = Species of Greatest Conservation Need.

Recognition The usual size, general looks, and specific distinguishing traits of the butterfly. The most important field marks are bold-faced, and comparisons are often given to similar species with which it might be confused.

Variation The range of phenotypes (="looks") to be encountered in the species within our territory, including geographical, seasonal, and sexual variation, sometimes naming subspecies.

Host Plants Preferred or required caterpillar foodplants; favorite nectar plants for the adults.

On the Wing Earliest and latest periods for which we have records, and peaks of activity. Flight period varies dramatically with altitude, latitude, and annual snowmelt. Also given here is the number of broods (=generations) per year, and the usual overwintering stage.

Habitat and Range The kinds of landscapes where the butterfly may normally be found, and the distribution of the species in the world, the continent, and the region.

Remarks Ecology, behavior, conservation status, personal experience, etymology, history, aesthetics, lore, and/or anything else that we want you to know about the species.

Symbols and Abbreviations < , > = less than, greater than, referring to average wingspan (atypically small or large individuals may occur, and females are usually larger than males). dfw, vhw, etc. = dorsal (topside) and ventral (bottom side) of forewings or hindwings. (The terms "upperwing" and "underwing" are ambiguous; they can refer either to dorsal or ventral surfaces, or to primary or secondary wings, and are not used

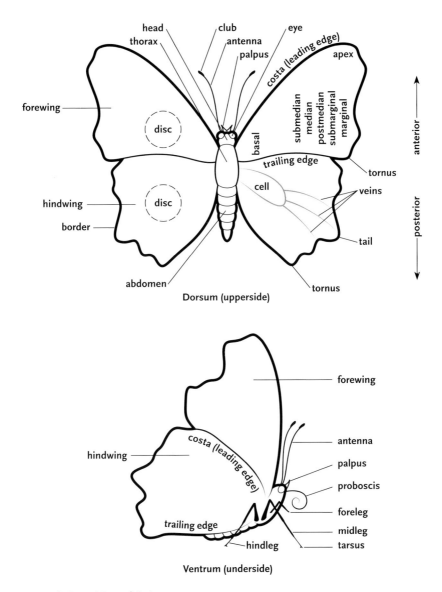

Diagram of a Typical Butterfly's Anatomy

here.) "Upperside" and "underside" are okay, as are "above" and "below." The forewings are also called primaries, and the hindwings are the secondaries. sp./spp. = species, ssp. = subspecies, singular and plural. (Note that the singular of the word "species" is species.) Standard abbreviations for states, provinces, and directions. Co/cos = county, counties.

ORDER LEPIDOPTERA: Butterflies and Moths

Lepidoptera, the fourth-largest order of insects, may comprise as many as a million species. Moths account for most of these. The name (*lepido*, "scale"; *ptera*, "wing") refers to the scale-covered or shingled wings of butterflies and moths. They are further distinguished by their sucking mouthparts (a curlable, drinking-straw like proboscis) situated between a pair of fuzzy labial palpi. Lepidopterans undergo a profound metamorphosis from the egg (ovum, ova), through the wormlike caterpillar (larva, larvae), and chrysalis (pupa, pupae) to the adult (imago, imagoes). There are three body parts (abdomen, thorax, head), with large compound eyes on the head, four wings and six legs attached to the thorax, and fully differentiated male and female genitalia in the last abdominal segments. The wings are supported by stiffened veins whose branching pattern is distinctive for each family. Pigmented (reflecting) and structural (refracting) scales furnish the colors and patterns, which fade as the insect ages and wears. Adult longevity varies from a few days to nearly a year, usually lasting a week or two. Winter diapause may take place in any stage, depending on the group (e.g., chrysalides for swallowtails, adults for anglewings). Butterflies, and some moths, are diurnally active and dependent on solar warming; most moths are nocturnal, and many can generate some body heat, as can a few butterflies.

RHOPALOCERA: Scudders and Skippers

The old term "Rhopalocera" used to be considered a suborder of Lepidoptera containing the true butterflies (or scudders) and the skippers, jointly called butterflies in English. It was opposed to "Heterocera," supposed to contain the moths. Now there are usually considered to be five to eight suborders and 23 or so superfamilies of Lepidoptera. What we call "butterflies" is really an artificial grouping of two of the superfamilies belonging to suborder Dytrisia, all the other superfamilies being moths. Rhopalocera no longer has any scientific standing, but as a category it is still useful for conveying "scudders and skippers considered together." The two lineages involved may have common origins, or may have arisen from separate moth ancestors. There may be some 18,000 species in the world, more than 800 in North America, and about 200 in Cascadia. All members have clubbed antennae, as do a few odd groups of moths that do not occur in Cascadia.

Propertius Duskywing (*Erynnis propertius*) crashes a puddle party of Anise Swallowtails (*Papilio zelicaon*).

SUPERFAMILY HESPERIOIDEA, FAMILY HESPERIIDAE: SKIPPERS

Usually considered butterflies, yet distinctive, skippers tend to have compact bodies and short, heavily loaded wings that must flap rapidly to gain flight. One Australian species retains the hook-and-eye (frenulum and retinaculum) that link the fore- and hindwings in many species of moths. In North America, skippers are mostly duller than the "true" butterflies, but this is not true in the tropics. Daunted by their complexity, confounded by their general similarity and fleetness, many butterfly enthusiasts ignore skippers, but this is their own loss. Skippers' behavior, beauty, and natural history prove highly rewarding when attended to with patience, and their lack of popularity means that many discoveries await. And most of them really can be readily discerned, with a little familiarity and practice.

We in the Northwest are far less rich in skippers than is Texas, where the 200 or so species exceed the tally for true butterflies.

The yucca- and agave-boring giant skippers (Megathyminae) do not reach Cascadia. We have 39 species (about one percent of the world's fauna) belonging to four subfamilies. Old books often said that skippers are "halfway" between butterflies and moths. While skippers arose from moths and might or might not have given rise to true butterflies, they are not today any closer to moths than other butterflies. Wings tend to be proportionately short and broadly triangular, thoraxes broad, heads seemingly large. The antennae may be short, and their clubs are sharply curved or slightly hooked. Most skippers are fairly small and fly in the speedy, skipping, stop-and-go manner that gives them their popular name. Overwintering usually occurs in the larval stage, and the chrysalides are sometimes enclosed in loose silken cocoons. Our four subfamilies differ greatly in several characteristics.

Subfamily Eudaminae: Dicot or Spread-wing Skippers I

Like the pyrgines, these have broad, squared-off wings often held flat to the side when perched—hence, "spread-wing." Many of the tropical eudamines are large for skippers, dramatically tailed, and iridescently colored. Their colors tend toward grays, browns, and blacks here, and cloudywings look very much like most people's idea of moths. But the first species listed is by far our most spectacular skipper in both coloration and size.

Pacuvius Duskywing, male

Comparison of Dicot Skippers (Subfamilies Eudaminae & Pyrginae)

Specimens are shown approximately at life size

Northern Cloudywing
Thorybes pylades

Western Cloudywing
Thorybes diversus

Mexican Cloudywing
Thorybes mexicana

Dreamy Duskywing
Erynnis icelus

Persius Duskywing
Erynnis persius

Propertius Duskywing
Erynnis propertius

Pacuvius Duskywing
Erynnis pacuvius

Alpine Checkered Skipper
Pyrgus centaureae

Common Checkered Skipper
Pyrgus communis

Two-banded Checkered Skipper
Pyrgus ruralis

Northern White Skipper
Heliopetes ericetorum

Northern White Skipper
Heliopetes ericetorum

Silver-spotted Skipper   *Epargyreus clarus* (CRAMER) 1775

Dayton, VA

RECOGNITION > 2 in. Chocolate-brown, **long DFW crossed by brassy gold patches**, bluntly tailed **VHW with large, jagged, bright silver marks** across their discs. No other NW skipper approaches its size or dramatic markings. **VARIATION** Highly variable but always easily recognizable. W-side individuals, closer to CA, often smaller and darker with less brassy sheen above and violet overscaling below. **HOST PLANTS** Many kinds of legumes, incl. ornamental locusts (*Robinia*), wisteria, and wild licorice (*Glycyrrhiza lepidota*) esp. along the E Columbia R. *Hosackia crassifolia* commonly used W of the crest. Nectars on spreading dogbane, dame's rocket, thistle, clover, and many other flowers; males mudpuddle. **ON THE WING** E April to E September, peak in June. A single generation, pupae overwinter. **HABITAT AND RANGE** Watercourses, parks, gardens, afforesting cuts, heath-like Christmas tree farms, and other open, flowery places at lower to middle elevations. Most of the US and S Canada; irregular in the W, omitting the Great Basin. Much of the E side of Cascadia, far less common on the W side; barely in SW coastal BC and S Vancouver Is.; Puget Trough in WA, more abundant south-

ward in Coast Range and Siskiyous of OR.

Our largest skipper, this is also the most dramatically colored. From the glassy golden spots on the forewings and the big silver patches on the ventral hindwings, its rapid, herky-jerky flight alloys a brilliant metallic streak. In Great Britain, the name Silver-spotted Skipper applies to what we call the Common Branded Skipper (*Hesperia comma*); ours has the greater claim, with much larger silver spots. In boyhood, I pretended that these common neighborhood habitués of honeysuckle bushes were giant skippers of the desert Southwest. Unlike the yucca- and agave-burrowing megathymines, which do not make it north to Cascadia, *E. clarus* is a generalist on many kinds of peas. In the Southeast it has adapted to feed on kudzu, and become enormously abundant in places because of it. It occurs regularly in unsprayed Christmas

Male, dorsal

Ventral

tree plantations above Hood Canal, but unpredictably elsewhere in western Washington. Silver-spotted Skippers like hot and sunny country as well as moisture, so they become more common in eastern and southwestern Cascadia. It may follow the wild licorice that is advancing westerly along the Columbia River. Males perch well above the ground, from late morning through early afternoon, alert for interloping males and passing females.

Northern Cloudywing *Thorybes pylades* (SCUDDER) 1870

Massachusetts

RECOGNITION < 2 in. Muddy dark brown dorsum, lighter outward. Two hyaline white bars run into the FW costa, a loose clump of white dots between and below them, all these small to prominent and showing through below. Brand new individuals can look very black-and-white. VHW **dark brown shading into hoary gray, crossed by two bands of irregular, connected darker spots**. Fringes brown, lightly checked on fresh individuals, can appear whitish in the right light. **Males have a conspicuous costal fold on FW**, lackin in females and the next two species. Mexican Cloudywing is smaller, finely striated, with larger white spots; Western is in between in size, under cell-spot slender and elongated. Duskywings are smaller, more complexly marked. **VARIATION** According to Warren, "Phenotypic variation among populations of *T. pylades* is not great, and a careful review of populations throughout the species' range is needed before confidence can be placed in the use of trinomials to describe variation." I find the fringes on W-side individuals lighter than E-side, sometimes approaching white. **HOST PLANTS** An array of legumes (vetches, locoweeds, clovers, alfalfa) and likely lupines. Known PNW hosts incl. *Hosackia crassifolia* and *Acmispon nevadensis*. Caitlin LaBar found an egg in Klickitat Cyn on fewflower pea (*Lathyrus pauciflorus*) and reared it through. Males visit mud with duskywings. **ON THE WING** L April to M July, peak in June. A single generation, full-grown larvae overwinter. **HABITAT AND RANGE** Canyons,

clearings, and flowery flats. Most of N Am, spotty in Great Plains and Great Basin. S BC, Cascades and NE mtns of WA, N Cascades, Blue Mtns, Ochocos, and Siskiyous in OR. Missing from much of C OR, and very sparing around S Puget Sound and S Vancouver Is.

Male, ventral

Female, dorsal

Male, dorsal

A biggish skipper giving the impression of darker-on-dark will likely be this. Fairly wary, but easy to follow in flight and quick to re-alight after disturbance. The rare west-side Washington population, smaller, darker, and lighter-fringed, sometimes flies among blooming camas on prairies. Also occurs on the Hoosport Heaths, where Christmas tree plantations above Hood Canal support many ericaceous and other native plants, approximating a presumed vanished heath-like community, perhaps a remnant of a postglacial period in which such habitats were widespread. Throughout the West, the distribution of this butterfly is curiously patchy. Warren has found it common in Oregon only in oak habitats in the Siskiyous and northeast Cascades.

Western Cloudywing   *Thorybes diversus* BELL 1927

Plumas Co., CA

Aka California Cloudywing, Bell's Cloudywing, Diverse Cloudywing

RECOGNITION < 1.75 in. Similar to Northern, **but sub-cell white bar is longer and narrower,** and **male lacks costal fold**. Differs from Mexican by an absence of striations on the outer portion of the wings beneath. Fringes dark-checkered until worn off. **VARIATION** OR individuals are a little darker below than those in CA. **HOST PLANTS** Clovers incl. *Trifolium wormskioldii* (in CA) and perhaps American vetch and other legumes. Warren reported a female nectaring on a native rhododendron in late afternoon. **ON THE WING** M May to E July. One brood, presumably overwintering in the pupal stage. **HABITAT AND RANGE** Damp glades and small clearings among coniferous woodland. Its entire range is from C to N CA, extending into the Siskiyou Mtns in Josephine and Curry cos, OR, and the Cascades and Warners farther E.

This narrow endemic is more a Sierran than Cascadian butterfly, an example of the high degree of California speciation that barely

Male, dorsal

Ventral

makes it into our territory. Careful attention to detail should distinguish it from the former species, with which it overlaps. I have seen it only once, beside a serpentine pitcher plant bog along the Wimer Road, a historic cross-border stage route in the Siskiyous. In the same area, Warren found

males territorial from late morning to mid-afternoon around moist areas on dirt roads, males returning to the same elevated rock. The flight is characteristically speedy, much faster than Northern Cloudywings in the same habitat.

Mexican Cloudywing   *Thorybes mexicana* (HERRICH-SCHÄFFER) 1869

Mexico
Aka Mountain Cloudywing, Nevada Cloudywing, Dobra Cloudywing, *T. mexicanus*

RECOGNITION <
1.5 in. Dark brown, paler on the outer HW, with darker bands across the HW below. **FW light spots are longer and larger** than on *T. pylades*, the one below the cell often full and offset, and these spots are rimmed with dark scales. **The ventral surface is distinctively and darkly striated**, there is no costal fold on the male, and the **buff fringes are checkered when fresh. VARIATION** The OR Cascades and Sierra Nevada race, described from Fort Klamath, OR, in 1893, tends

Female, dorsal

Female, ventral

Male, dorsal

to be larger and more two-toned below, with bigger FW spots than the species has farther S. **HOST PLANTS** Various legumes, incl. vetches, locoweeds, and clovers. Opler reports nectaring on pussytoes, wild onion, and iris. **ON THE WING** L May to M August. A single generation, presumably overwintering in the pupal stage. **HABITAT AND RANGE** Montane and subalpine meadowlands, often near streams and seeps. Rockies from S ID to S Mexico; Sierra Nevada; S Cascades. OR Cascades from Summer and Crater lakes N to Mt. Jefferson, mostly around 5,000 feet, but known from 3,000 to 6,000+.

Dornfeld found the species abundant in Three Creek Meadow, south of Sisters in Deschutes County, Oregon, at 6,300 feet. At the same locality, on 1 July 2001, Warren observed over 300 in four hours, and I have watched it near there mudding about lakeshore meadows. According to Comstock, in his 1927 classic *Butterflies of California*, the abundance dropped off toward the north in California, which does not seem surprising for a butterfly of Mexican affinities. Scott says the males nectar, puddle, and perch on high points to investigate potential females.

Subfamily Pyrginae: Dicot or Spread-wing Skippers II

The pyrgines tend toward broad, squared-off wings that they commonly hold flat to the side when perched—hence, "spread-wing." Many species are colored in grays, browns, and blacks, often checkered or mottled with white or pale patches of scales. Duskywings are moth-like and often fly with a very similar moth. If in question, look for the hook-clubbed antennae.

Certain pyrgines can be very challenging to identify, in some cases requiring dissection for certainty. The fuzzy labial palpi point forward from the face. Males may have androconial scales set in conspicuous costal folds on the forewings. Pyrgine and eudamine larvae feed on a variety of dicotyledonous (net-veined) plants such as mallows, lupines, and willows rather than grasses, so I call them dicot skippers. Their flight may seem "buzzy" or rushed, but some of them are also capable of gliding, unlike hesperiines. Of some 1,100 species in the world and a tenth that many in North America, we have a tenth again in our fauna, or one percent of the total.

Common Sootywing *Pholisora catullus* (FABRICIUS) 1793

"Indiis," prob. Georgia
Aka Roadside Rambler

SPECIAL CONCERN IN BC

RECOGNITION < 1.25 in. **Shiny coal-black with rows of tiny white dots near the wingtips, white head**. Can have a bluish or dull brassy cast below. Very small, wings narrow and rounded. White spotting variable. Males have costal fold on FW bearing yellow-brown sex-scales. Fringes dark, unchecked. Flies near the ground. A minute, dark skipper in our territory will be this species or a Common Roadside Skipper, which is brown, not black, with a checkered fringe. The next species, which occurs in the Great Basin, has very distinctive markings. Dun Skippers are larger and lighter, with pointed wings. **VARIATION** Nothing significant, except more or less white dotting, and fading iridescence with age. **HOST PLANTS** Weedy chenopods (lamb's quarters, goosefoot, pigweed, Russian thistle), amaranths (cockscombs), and mallows (cheeseweed). NW records incl. *Atriplex rosea*, *Chenopodium rubrum*, *C. fremontii*, *C. album*, *Amaranthus retroflexus*, *Salsola tragus*, and *Malva neglecta*. Nectars on garden thyme, mallows, and many other flowers. **ON THE WING** L March to E September, peaks in May and August. Two generations, larvae overwinter, forming the chrysalis in spring. **HABITAT AND RANGE** Banks of watercourses, lanes, parks, waste ground, ditches, field edges, foothills, alkali flats, shrub desert, and other open and disturbed sites where the adaptable hosts thrive. Most of the US to S Canada, N Mexico. Throughout the lower, drier portions of E-side Cascadia but scarcer toward the NE.

Male (above) and female (below), ventral

Like the Common Checkered Skipper, the Common Sootywing haunts vacant lots, rural roadsides, ditchbanks, alleys, and other secondhand lands rich in weeds and children. These are often two of the first species to turn up in insect collections, since kids are close enough to the ground to spot them and fast enough to catch them. Rare west-side records, such as one

Dorsal

Male, dorsal

that came to a night-light in Pacific County, Washington, might result from introductions of pupae in hay loads; this is definitely a butterfly of the dry, hot country. The males patrol gullies and roadsides, prepared to engage other males or court females.

Lepidopterists have a sense that it has been diminishing in recent years, perhaps in response to neonicotinoid insecticides, but I found it abundant along the lower Grande Ronde River in Asotin County, Washington, in 2016.

Mojave Sootywing   *Hesperopsis libya* (SCUDDER) 1878

Mohave Co., AZ
Aka Great Basin Sootywing, Lena Sootywing, *Pholisora*

RECOGNITION < 1.5 in. Brassy black or brown above with small light spots, more developed in females. Goldish near the VFW tip and below, glossy black basally. **VHW sooty, crossed by a median row of bright white spots, with one more near the base**. No costal fold on males, margins not checkered. **VARIATION** OR individuals average larger than populations to the S, and have less pallor above and sometimes larger white spots below. **HOST PLANTS** Shrubby chenopods such as common saltbush (*Atriplex canescens*). Nectars esp. on rabbit-

Female, dorsal

Female, ventral

Male, dorsal

brush (*Chrysothamnus*). **ON THE WING** L July to E August. One generation, larvae overwinter. **HABITAT AND RANGE** Hot, dry, sage and saltbush landscapes. "One of the common skippers of the southern deserts" (Comstock), extending N to E MT, SE OR, and S ID.

Hart Mountain National Antelope Refuge in July, though perhaps not comfortable, is a good place and time to find this butterfly. Dornfeld, speaking of Oregon, calls it "a butterfly of the desert . . . whose center of distribution lies in the Great Basin." The Saltbush Sootywing (*H. alpheus*) is still smaller, with noticeably rounded wings and brown-checked fringes, and mottled rather

than spotted. Grazing the northwestern counties of Nevada, it should be sought in the same southeastern Oregon counties that host *H. libya*—Lake, Harney, and Malheur. Few people venture afield in this territory during a season that can shift from frigid to blazing in a day or two. Some watchful person with a net and quick reflexes against the spring wind may eventually establish this state record. Warren urges searching for the Mojave along the Snake and Burnt rivers in Hells Canyon country; Ferris and Brown suggest collectors "check *Atriplex*-covered shale beds in early-to-mid summer." Both species of *Hesperopsis* may be expected to expand toward the north as the climate warms.

Genus *Erynnis*: Duskywings

In 1974 (*WWB*), I wrote: "Like the Short-eared Owl, Dusky Wing Skippers appear to flap their wings only in an axis above the midlines of their bodies. Also, their wingbeats are very fast. These two characters give one the impression that they are flying with their wings in the resting position, without effort, rather like a witch on a broom stick. Couled in black with hoary highlights,

they fit the image. Only their sunny haunts among bright flowers give them away as butterflies, after all. But when the clouds shroud the sun and the dusky wings settle among withered weeds and shriveled leaves, their dun wings draped like a grim and tattered cloak, the simile is restored." This still seems appropriate. Beyond the metaphorical, the genus *Erynnis* seems to be under a spell of inscrutability for the collector and more so for the watcher. The species are similar, variable, and subtle in their distinctions. Dissection reveals diagnostic differences in the valvae of the male genitalia. Otherwise, all duskywings are dark, more or less marked with lighter and darker spots (sometimes hyaline near the forewing apex), and remarkably moth-like. It is no disgrace to conclude that one has seen a duskywing, and leave it at that. But with careful attention to appearance, range, habitat, and ecology, careful observers will be able to identify many individuals to species. The genus name commemorates the Erinyes, or Furies, the "ministers of justice" in the underworld according to Heraclitus. Certainly they exact a stiff penalty from all who attempt to understand their nuances. Nineteenth-century lepidopterists, possessing classical educations and little knowledge about the new species they were describing, often gave them names from the Classics, adopting a theme for a given genus. For example, Pacuvius, Propertius, Afranius, and Persius were all Roman poets—dedications made for no obvious reason.

Dreamy Duskywing   *Erynnis icelus* (SCUDDER AND BURGESS) 1870

"New England"
Aka Aspen Duskywing

Male, dorsal

DFW. Grayish brown forewings crossed by darker chain-like spots and **pale frosty scale-rows** (esp. in males, distal to the cell), HW by small buffy spots. Antennal clubs, palpi, and hindleg tibial tufts are all prominent. **VARIATION** Very little, over its large range. Males frostier than females, and light banding varies with age. **HOST PLANTS** Chiefly willows and aspens, perhaps other poplars and birches. Nectars on composites and clovers, among other flowers. **ON THE WING** E April to L July, peak in June. Larvae hibernate in the final instar, pupate in spring, one brood. **HABITAT AND RANGE** Northern and montane N Am. In Cascadia, occurs across S BC, and from sea level to mid-elevations in the Cascades, Okanogan, Selkirks, Blues, and OR Coast Range, but so far missing from maritime WA, W of Puget Sound.

RECOGNITION < 1.5 in. Small for a duskywing with rather **stumpy wings, humped along the leading edge** (costa) in males by the prominent androconial fold. May have small light skipper-spots near apex, but **no hyaline spots on**

Male, dorsal

Male, ventral

The Dreamy Duskywing is a boreal animal. Its compact, short-winged, and silvery-furry appearance suggests northern affinities and makes it the most recognizable of the smaller duskywings. Seek it in spring in cool, montane places, basking at the sun, and farther uphill as the season progresses.

An old campfire ring in the Okanogan attracted several males to the cold damp ashes, nicely contrasted with Persius Duskywings sunning and sipping ashy salts side-by-side. Icelus was the son of Hypnus (=Somnus), the winged Greek god of sleep. This association led Scudder to call it Dreamy.

Propertius Duskywing   *Erynnis propertius* (SCUDDER & BURGESS) 1870

California
Aka Western Oak Duskywing

SPECIAL CONCERN IN BC; SGCN IN W WA

RECOGNITION < 1.75 in. This is our largest duskywing, and the most strongly marked. **Alternating pale and dark spot-rows on the FW give a banded look**, esp. on females. Much whitish "furry" scaling on DFW, more so on males, which have costal folds as well. **Hyaline spots prominent, quite large on females**, fringe brown. Other duskywings smaller, darker, less contrasty, and not associated directly with oaks. **VARIATION** Though individuals may vary and males and females are sexually dimorphic, no

geographic variation has been noted or described. **HOST PLANTS** Garry oak (*Quercus garryana*) in BC, WA, and most of OR; other species of oaks farther S in OR and into CA. At higher elevations in OR, golden chinquapin (*Chrysolepis chrysophylla*). Possibly others in S-C BC. Nectars variously but frequents camas lilies (*Camassia*) where present, as on San Juan

Female, dorsal

Male, dorsal

Male, ventral

ls. **ON THE WING** L March to M July, peak in May-June. One staggered brood, with larvae hibernating in nest of oak leaves; early spring pupation in a vague cocoon. Sometimes a partial second generation. **HABITAT AND RANGE** Oak openings, glades, nearby grassy spots, hilltops, mud puddles, and wildflower stands from S BC to Baja California, E to Nevada. Follows the range of Garry oak almost exactly, from E-side Cascades to Puget Trough and Coast Ranges and Siskiyous. Records far from oaks represent wanderers or perhaps a different host.

Even small stands of Garry oak, sometimes a single tree, may support populations of Propertius. The fragmented and discontinuous distribution of oaks in the Salish Lowlands test this trait, and will do so more severely as the oaks continue to diminish along with the western gray squirrels that likewise depend on them. Oaks alone are not enough, as the skippers require dead leaves and understory for hibernal sites. Although they are abundant in the Columbia Gorge, still common in the Willamette Valley, and present in the Puget Trough, I have been unable so far in many searches to find them in five oak-bearing counties in between: Columbia in Oregon, and Clark, Cowlitz, Wahkiakum, Grays Harbor, and Lewis in Washington. The reasons are a mystery to me. Propertius looks like a giant at mud among the other duskywings. Warren saw hundreds at wet rock faces along roadsides, and I've encountered scores on old lilacs in Klickitat Canyon. They are wonderfully cryptic among last year's oak leaves.

Pacuvius Duskywing   *Erynnis pacuvius* (LINTNER) 1878

New Mexico
Aka Dyar's Duskywing, Buckthorn Duskywing

RECOGNITION < 1.5 in. A dark duskywing, mottled with black and gray on brown, with small hyaline spots in the dark bands. DHW and V lighter brown. **Males** distinguished from the often sympatric *E. persius* by **absence of tibial tufts on the hindlegs** (or by genitalic dissection); females by **having gray scaling only outside the dark discal bands**, on both sides in *E. persius*. **DFW (when fresh) has mottled brown patches** in, below, and distal from cell, absent on *E. persius* and *E. icelus*. **VARIATION** Farther S the wings become white-fringed and the dark markings less contrasty, but the dark-fringed NW population is relatively consistent across our region. **HOST PLANTS** Various *Ceanothus* species. In WA, strongly associated with snow-brush ceanothus (*C. velutinus*). Males hilltop and visit mud. **ON THE WING** L April to E August, peak in May-June. One brood, last-instar larvae overwinter. **HABITAT AND RANGE** Transition zone scrublands, chaparral, and ponderosa pine/Douglas-fir forest clearings dominated by *Ceanothus* shrubs and thickets, in many W mtn ranges ringing the Great Basin, from S-C BC to Baja and Veracruz. BC-WA borders to Selkirks, Cascades, Blues, most OR ranges.

Male, ventral

Male, dorsal

Male, dorsal

Because this species often flies with the Persius Duskywing, it is risky to record it without genitalic dissection, careful examination of the tibiae, or voucher specimens, unless fresh with stand-out brown patches. I have found the two together hilltopping in the Pend Oreille, looking very similar. Two related white-fringed species occur up to north-central California and should be sought along the Oregon border. The Mournful Duskywing (*E. tristis*) has the ordinary isosceles-triangle shape of most duskywings, while the Funereal Duskywing (*E. funeralis*) has long, narrow forewings. Ray Stanford reported an *E. tristis* collected by Chuck Sekerman from Siskiyou Pass, Oregon, but the specimen has not been located and the record needs confirmation. The Afranius Duskywing (*E. afranius*), browner and paler with more contrasting markings than *E. persius* and lacking its pelt of long hair-scales but bearing tibial tufts, may barely occur in our region. Records in western Idaho and extreme southeastern British Columbia, where it is considered endangered, suggest it should be looked for in northeastern Oregon and southeastern Washington. Previous records in Washington and Oregon have been determined by Warren to refer to *E. persius* after all.

Persius Duskywing   *Erynnis persius* (SCUDDER) 1863

New England
Aka Hairy Duskywing

RECOGNITION < 1.5 in. The usual duskywing pattern of alternating black and buff patches against the dark brown background. **DFW overlain by heavy gray hair-scaling on the basal half of males; females have patches of gray on both sides of the dark FW band.** Hyaline spots appear in the FW band, and **tibial tufts prominent on males' hindlegs**. **VARIATION** Individuals average progressively smaller and darker from inland mtns to the Coast Ranges, but can vary widely in size within a single population. **HOST PLANTS** Lupines (*Lupinus latifolius, L. sericeus*) fide Pelham, goldenbanner (*Thermopsis*), *Astragalus*, and *Lotus*. In the E, rarer and thought to feed on willows and poplars. Nectars on yellow daisies, bleeding

Male, dorsal

Male, ventral

Female, dorsal

heart (*Dicentra formosa*), and many other flowers. Males hilltop and visit mud. **ON THE WING** M April to M August, peak in June. **HABITAT AND RANGE** Various open, sunny places, such as meadows, glades, and mountaintops. Watch for it in moist forest clearings, but not in wet forest or desert. Montane and boreal W well into AK, almost to Mexico; NE and Great Lakes states. Occurs in all mtn ranges of Cascadia, E of the maritime edge in WA but W to the coast in Curry and Tillamook cos, OR.

By far the most common and widespread Northwest duskywing, it is the default identification for any duskywing encountered, until proven otherwise. Persius is a frequent sight at puddles and flowerfields across much of montane Cascadia throughout spring and into summer. In the Coast Ranges it favors south- and southwest-facing slopes where

oaks, balsamroot, goldenbanner, and other drier-soil plants occur like western outliers of more easterly floras. Scudder named it after third-century Roman poet Persius, not Perseus, the son of Danae and Zeus, the slayer of Medusa, and the great-grandfather of Hercules, as is sometimes stated. Why Scudder attached such literary monikers to these subtle butterflies we may never know, since the etymologies were seldom explained by their authors in those days.

Genus *Pyrgus*: Checkered Skippers

About 30 species of these black-and-white skippers occur in the world, mostly in the northern hemisphere with a few in the American tropics. In English-speaking Europe, they are known as grizzled skippers, and our Arctic Skipper is called the Chequered Skipper. American species of *Pyrgus* have been called checkered skippers—for their obvious pattern—at least since W. J. Holland referred to them thus in the 1898 edition of his *Butterfly Book*.

Alpine Checkered Skipper   *Pyrgus centaureae* (RAMBUR) 1842

Dalarna, Sweden
Aka Grizzled Skipper (NABA)

RECOGNITION < 1.25 in. Black-brown above crossed by bands of white spots, less distinct on HW. **Pair of small white spots nearest the body on DFW are adjacent and do not reach cell. No white spot at base of DHW.** Beneath, white patch-band crosses an olive field. Fringe boldly checkered. **Strongly limited to alpine habitat. VARIATION** Our PNW *P. c. loki* tends darker below than the trans-Canada *P. c. freija*. **HOST PLANTS** Elsewhere, a variety of rosaceous herbs incl. strawberries and cinquefoils. Reared in PNW by James and Nunnallee on *Fragaria virginiana* and *Potentilla fruticosa*. **ON THE WING** E June to L August, peak in July, depending on snowmelt. Possibly biennial. One summer brood, grown larvae overwinter. **HABITAT AND RANGE** Occurs above timberline in moist alpine and subalpine heaths and swales. In Cascadia, it is known only from the

Female, ventral

Male, dorsal

N Cascades N of Lake Chelan, WA, and higher elevations in S BC. Occupies hard-to-reach arctic-alpine heights and appears only sparsely and sporadically. More records will be found when more backpackers watch for butterflies in the N Cascades and Okanogan Highlands.

Its common name situates this species both with its near relatives and its habitat. NABA's common name may cause confusion with the widespread European species *P. malvae*, known as the Grizzled Skipper in Great Britain. *P. malvae* overlaps in many places with the Holarctic *P. centaureae*. Loki, the namesake of our subspecies, was the son of a giant in Norse mythology and a tricky, troublemaking rascal, sort of a nordic Till Eulenspiegel whelped of Coyote.

Two-banded Checkered Skipper   *Pyrgus ruralis* (BOISDUVAL) 1852

Plumas Co., CA

RECOGNITION < 1 in. Tiny, black-brown banded with white spots in two parallel rows. **White spots nearest body are not adjacent, uppermost runs along cell. White spot at DHW base.** Underside variegated with white, olive, chestnut-reddish. Fringes checkered. Looks gray on the wing. **VARIATION** Slight tendency of specimens to be smaller and darker with darker wing fringes toward the E. **HOST PLANTS** Mallows (*Sidalcea*) and rosaceous herbs, such as cinquefoil (*Potentilla*) and strawberry (*Fragaria*). In SW WA, large-leaf avens (*Geum macrophyllum*) and dewberry (*Rubus ursinus*) are likely used. Reared on *Vaccinium scoparium* by James and Nunnallee. Nectars on dandelions, strawberry, toothwort, and other early bloomers. **ON THE WING** E March to E September, peak in May–July, depending on altitude. Pupae overwinter, one spring brood. **HABITAT AND RANGE** Montane edge-meadows, burns, and glades, roadsides, unsprayed rights-of-way, herbaceous hillsides, from maritime forests to the subalpine. Much of the moister W, S BC to S CA/C CO; nearly all Cascadia except for the dry basinlands.

One of the earliest emergers in spring, *P. ruralis* appears when little else is on the wing besides Echo Azures and Sara's Orangetips. With these it flies among last year's coltsfoot stalks and nectars on dandelions. The butterfly is not shy and the flight is slow, gray,

Dorsal

Male, ventral

a large cinquefoil; individuals may show up some tens of yards or more from the nearest stand of it. Since emergence occurs later at higher altitudes, lepidopterists sometimes think they have discovered a colony of the Alpine Checkered Skipper when in fact they have this species. This possibility got me excited in a subalpine meadow above the Skykomish River in the southwest Olympics many years ago, far removed from the only Washington records of *P. centaureae*. I've found it abundant around Klickitat County mud-slicks and vernal pools surrounded by strawberries, and around dewberry swales on San Juan Island. Another species, the Small Checkered Skipper (*P. scriptura*), has not yet been found in Cascadia but should be sought in the northernmost California and Nevada counties and adjacent Oregon; it will not be mistaken for the region's other diminutive *Pyrgus* species, since the Two-banded occurs in moist, green places in spring and the Small flies in hot, arid sites in summer.

and "buzzy," and often taken for that of a moth or a large fly, or overlooked altogether. I've found Willapa Hills populations closely associated with large-leaf avens, a handsome, native rosaceous plant that resembles

Common Checkered Skipper   *Pyrgus communis* (GROTE) 1872

Demopolis Co., AL
Aka Tesselated Skipper

SPECIAL CONCERN IN BC

RECOGNITION < 1.5 in. Larger than the other checkered skippers, with **bigger, more angular white spots that sometimes dominate the dorsum**, although some (usually females) may be quite black, esp. at the base of the wings. **Grayish scaling makes it look quite blue in flight. The eggshell-white ventrum is crossed by black-rimmed, tan to olive bands.** Fringes lightly checkered with gray. Female Northern White Skipper can be very similar but is bigger, lacks black at the base of the wings above, and the bands below are muddier and lack black outlines. **VARIATION** Little to no geographic variation through most of its range, according to Warren, though individuals tend to be darker toward the coast.
HOST PLANTS A wide variety of malvaceous herbs, incl. cheeseweed (*Malva neglecta*) in towns. Pelham records *M. neglecta*, *M. parviflora*, *Malvella leprosa*, and *Sphaeralcea munroana*. James and Nunnallee add *Iliamna rivularis* (streambank globemallow) as a "highly favored host" on the E flank of the Cascades. Nectars on marigold,

Female, dorsal

Male, dorsal

Male, ventral

thistle, knapweed, alfalfa, and many annuals. **ON THE WING** M April to M September, peaks in June and August. One to three generations here, full-grown larvae overwinter. **HABITAT AND RANGE** Flies in a great variety of open spaces, from alleys and vacant lots to basinlands, foothills, and pastures to headlands. Throughout much of the US and S Canada; in Cascadia, SE BC, WA E of the Cascade Crest, and most of OR from the coast (very few sites), Siskiyous, and Willamette Valley E.

When children spot these skippers in vacant lots around the cheeseweed, they think they're blue; then, catching them in a jar or net, they see that checkered skippers are really scaled in patterns of black and white and gray. Long body scales like fur refract sunlight so as to look blue, and the whir of the wings contributes to the effect. Along with Common Sootywings, these proliferate in weedy, disturbed situations and towns. Why they fly in western Oregon, even to the coast at grassy Cascade Head, then retreat east of the Cascades farther north, is probably a combined function of moisture and warmth. The only records west of the crest in Washington are near the Columbia Gorge. A habitué of low, warm, arid places, the Common Checkered Skipper overlaps very little with *P. ruralis*; but where it co-occurs with the Two-banded, *P. communis* usually appears later and in drier, sunnier sites. A butterfly of even hotter climes, the White Checkered Skipper (*P. albescens*) was formerly considered a subspecies of this one but has been shown conclusively by John Burns to be a separate species. It should be sought in the southernmost counties of Cascadia. Genitalic dissection will be necessary to be certain of any potential records.

Northern White Skipper   *Heliopetes ericetorum* (BOISDUVAL) 1852

Butte Co., CA
Aka Large White Skipper, Great White Skipper

RECOGNITION < 2 in. A **big, oystery-pale** skipper. Males are clear pearly white above with gray toward the base and **black chains of chevrons along the margins**. Above, darker females look like giant Common Checkered Skippers, but with the variable gray-black checkers separated by broad white bands, and the bases of the wings grayish. **Below, both sexes clouded with poorly defined areas of straw, pinkish brown, or mustard. VARIATION** No geographic variability, but sexual dimorphism is profound.

HOST PLANTS Globemallows (*Sphaeralcea*), hollyhock (*Alcea*), *Iliamna rivularis*, *Malva sylvestris*, *M. parviflora*, and *Malvella leprosa*; in CA, uses *Fremontia* and other malvaceous herbs. **ON THE WING** E May to E October, peaks in June-July and August-September. Two or three broods, larvae overwinter. **HABITAT AND RANGE** *Ericetorum* means "of the heath" or "of the hedge," and the butterfly does frequent strips of vegetation in arid country: riverbanks, canyons, and weedy field margins, as well as

Female, ventral

Male, dorsal

lower forest openings, roadsides, and alfalfa fields. Great Basin and most of CA, greater Columbian and Snake basins and the Snake R. Plain. NE OR, lower ⅔ of E WA, and W-C ID. Not yet found in BC. Opler indicates that the species is resident only in the deep SW, spreading occasionally to the NW; but we consider the disjunct Columbia Basin population is well established as a permanently resident butterfly.

Noticeably larger than the checkered skippers, especially in the more heavily marked female, this skipper suggests impressive bulk for a temperate pyrgine. The male's white wings flash in the sunshine, exactly as the genus name ("sun-flier") implies; they shimmer opalescent when spread for basking or nectaring. It is frequently taken for a species of white on the wing, until one notes that it flies like a skipper. Like the Mormon Metalmark and the Pale Crescent, it appears sporadically and in some of the same places, and can seldom be predicted: search for all three species in arid east-side

Puddle party, males

Female, dorsal

canyons. And like the metalmark, it is the only northwest-temperate representative of its group; several other white skippers occur in Mexico and barely into the United States. Ed Gage, an erstwhile Washington lepidopterist, once wrote me that he found it common in alfalfa fields near Tri-Cities: "Very nice to watch as you're mowing hay," he wrote.

In Ben Leighton's pioneering *Butterflies of Washington*, a record of Don Frechin's for this species is given from "Ruby, Eastern Washington." Hinchliff's Washington atlas placed this at Ruby, Pend Oreille County, a major northeast range extension. Guppy and Shepard felt the dot should have applied to Ruby, near Conconully, Okanogan County, an extension north but not east. Parsimony suggests a third Ruby, in Benton County, Washington, near Richland, in the heart of the species' range. Other Frechin "Ruby" records—Lorquin's Admiral, Pale and Two-tailed Tiger Swallowtails—could have come from either site. However, Frechin's report of the Clodius Parnassian from Ruby clinches the Okanogan Ruby. Frechin probably caught the skipper below Ruby and the parnassian above, and then, as was the custom then, just listed the nearest town for both. This tangled allegory points out the importance of keeping complete records!

Subfamily Heteropterinae: Different-winged Skippers

The next species and its relatives are sometimes lumped with the next subfamily, the Hesperiinae. Members of this small subgroup lack an apiculus (the recurved hook on the knob of the antenna) that other grass-feeding skippers possess, and their palpi protrude forward as in the Pyrginae. The name implies a difference in the wings as well, and our single representative certainly displays utterly distinctive speckled patterning on the wings.

Arctic Skipper *Carterocephalus palaemon* (PALLAS) 1771

Leipzig, Germany
Aka Arctic Skipperling

VARIATION E Arctic Skippers tend to be smaller and lighter, most W populations larger and darker, esp. on the VHW. Those of the Klamath

RECOGNITION < 1 in. Absolutely distinctive. Brownish black above marked with crisp tawny to yellow spots; VFW orange, **VHW tan studded with bright creamy or pale yellow ovals**.

are an exception; yet W and S into the redwood country, *C. p. magnus* is described as "larger . . . clearer, brighter, bolder, with more expanded dark and orange patterning than in all others" (Emmel et al.). **HOST PLANTS** Grasses, incl. *Calamagrostis purpurascens* (purple reedgrass) in CA, and false brome, tor-grass, and purple moorgrass in the UK. Nunnallee found a fifth instar on reed canarygrass (*Phalaris arundinacea*) in Chelan Co., WA. Nectars on composites, iris, Jacob's ladder, large-leaf avens, among others. Males visit mud, seeps, and trickles.

Female, dorsal

Male, dorsal

Male, ventral

ON THE WING M April to E August, peak in May-June. One brood, larvae overwinter. **HABITAT AND RANGE** Forest openings, grassy breaks, streambanks, montane meadows, and moist lowland pastures, sea level to mid-montane. Circumboreal, S into the US in mtns to the Tetons and N CA. In Cascadia, present across S BC, the Selkirks, Okanogan Highlands, Cascades, NE Olympics, Willapa Hills, and Salish Lowlands of WA, and Blue Mtns, Cascades, Coast Range, and Siskiyous in OR.

Arctic Skippers are more boreal than truly arctic. Called the Chequered Skipper in Great Britain, it is recently extinct in England and endangered in Scotland. A fully diagnostic portrait (dorsal and ventral, wrought in copper and brass nails) appears on the sign of The Chequered Skipper public house in biologist Miriam Rothschild's village of Ashton Wold in Northamptonshire, where the beer served is Skipper Ale. The northern California population has been reduced by logging of redwoods and overgrazing of coastal meadows. I have watched Arctic Skippers hanging like nuggets from Jacob's ladder in the wet meadows of Katmai National Park, Alaska; ducking out of hardwood forest edges just off I-5 in southwest Washington; and basking in the last sun of warm May days on long grass-heads in tall pastures of the Salish Lowlands, where they like to zip about courting shortly before sunset. Its striking pattern, shining with bright orbs like a tiny fritillary, prevents confusion with any other butterfly. Palaemon, a mortal from the Royal House of Thebes, became a lesser deity of the sea.

Subfamily Hesperiinae: Monocot or Folded-wing Skippers

The majority of the 2000+ species of these generally tawny, brown, or golden skippers (aka grass skippers) dwell in the Neotropics, two dozen of them in Cascadia. Their caterpillars consume monocotyledonous (parallel-veined) plants, including palms and bamboos, or in our latitudes mostly grasses and sedges. They frequently curl the blades with silk to form nests, in which they feed, overwinter, and pupate. Adults "skip" rapidly in flight, seeming almost to bounce on the air; and when they perch, they often hold their wings at distinctive angles, with the hindwings near 90 degrees to the body and the forewings closer to 45 degrees. While dicot skipper males may produce their pheromones in forewing edge-flaps or on leg tufts, monocot skippers commonly possess velvety black streaks or patches on the forewings, called sex brands or stigmata. Within each stigma, special androconial scales make the sexual identity-cum-readiness hormones in glands at their bases. Their labial palpi point upward along their faces. Hesperiines are big nectarers and puddlers, and are not as hard to tell apart as they seem.

Juba Skipper, female

Comparison of Monocot Skippers (Subfamily Hesperiinae)

Specimens are shown approximately at life size

Garita Skipperling
Oarisma garita

European Skipperling
Thymelicus lineola

Fiery Skipper
Hylephila phyleus

Sachem
Atalopedes campestris

Woodland Skipper
Ochlodes sylvanoides sylvanoides

Woodland Skipper
Ochlodes sylvanoides orecoasta

Sachem
Atalopedes campestris

Woodland Skipper
Ochlodes sylvanoides sylvanoides

Woodland Skipper
Ochlodes sylvanoides bonnevilla

Yuma Skipper
Ochlodes yuma

Yuma Skipper
Ochlodes yuma

*O. sylvanoides
bonnevilla*

Rural Skipper
Ochlodes agricola

Dun Skipper
Euphyes vestris

Dun Skipper
Euphyes vestris

Comparison of Monocot Skippers (Subfamily Hesperiinae)
Specimens are illustrated at 200% of life size

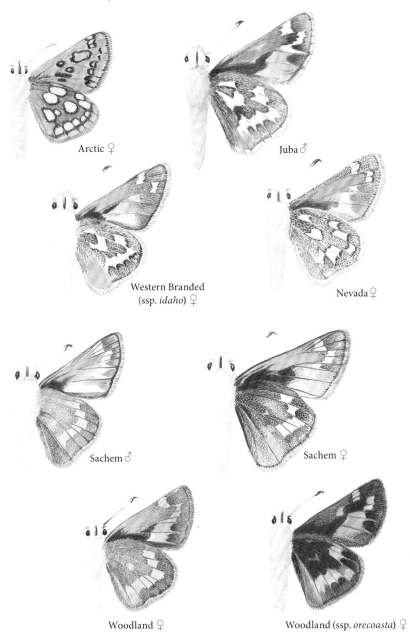

Arctic ♀

Juba ♂

Western Branded
(ssp. *idaho*) ♀

Nevada ♀

Sachem ♂

Sachem ♀

Woodland ♀

Woodland (ssp. *orecoasta*) ♀

Comparison of Monocot Skippers (Subfamily Hesperiinae)

Specimens are illustrated at 200% of life size

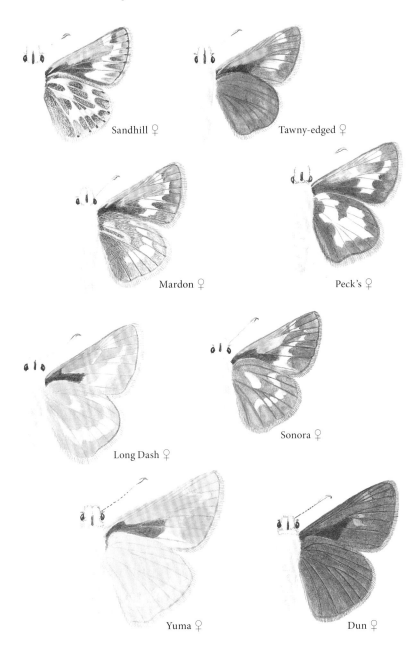

Sandhill ♀

Tawny-edged ♀

Mardon ♀

Peck's ♀

Long Dash ♀

Sonora ♀

Yuma ♀

Dun ♀

Comparison of Monocot Skippers (Subfamily Hesperiinae)
Specimens are shown approximately at life size

Uncas Skipper
Hesperia uncas

Juba Skipper
Hesperia juba

Common Branded Skipper
Hesperia comma manitoba

Common Branded Skipper
Hesperia comma manitoba

Common Branded Skipper
Hesperia comma hulbirti

Western Branded Skipper
Hesperia colorado idaho

Western Branded Skipper
Hesperia colorado oregonia

Western Branded Skipper
Hesperia colorado oregonia

Columbian Skipper
Hesperia columbia

Lindsey's Skipper
Hesperia lindseyi

Lindsey's Skipper
Hesperia lindseyi

Nevada Skipper
Hesperia nevada

Nevada Skipper
Hesperia nevada

Nevada Skipper
Hesperia nevada

Comparison of Monocot Skippers (Subfamily Hesperiinae)

Specimens are shown approximately at 125% of life size

Peck's Skipper
Polites peckius

Sandhill Skipper
Polites sabuleti

Mardon Skipper
Polites mardon mardon

Peck's Skipper
Polites peckius

Sandhill Skipper
Polites sabuleti

Mardon Skipper
Polites mardon mardon

Sonora Skipper
Polites sonora

Sonora Skipper
Polites sonora

Mardon Skipper
Polites mardon klamathensis

Draco Skipper
Polites draco

Tawny-edged Skipper
Polites themistocles

Long Dash
Polites mystic

Draco Skipper
Polites draco

Tawny-edged Skipper
Polites themistocles

Long Dash
Polites mystic

Garita Skipperling *Oarisma garita* (REAKIRT) 1866

"Rocky Mtns, Colorado Terr."
Aka Western Skipperling, Garita Skipper

RECOGNITION > 1 in. Very small, triangular, and **square-cut-looking, dark brown with a brassy sheen.** Above, the veins look darker than the wings; below, they stand out as lighter. Trailing edge of the VFW is black, anal fold of the VHW is bright tawny. Darker than European Skipperling, and male lacks the fine stigma on DFW. **VARIATION** Individuals vary from oranger to browner or almost blackish gray, but not much geographically. **HOST PLANTS** Scott lists 12 species in nine genera of grasses and one sedge; he considered it the most polyphagous skipper in CO. Caterpillars probably employ some alien grasses as well as natives, judging from exploited habitats. Nectars on composites and other flowers.

ON THE WING E June to E August, peak in July. A single generation, last-instar larvae overwinter. **HABITAT AND RANGE** Montane and transition grasslands, moist pastures, weedy marshes and fields. Rocky Mtns, to NE OR, E/N-C WA, SE BC in Blue Mtns, Palouse Hills, Selkirks, and Okanogan Highlands.

Either this species has been wildly overlooked in past years, or it is dramatically expanding its range. Though it was formerly thought to be a denizen of wetter meadows dominated by native grasses in the northeastern part of the region, I have recently found it widespread throughout the Palouse in many kinds of grasslands, including weedy habitats. For example, it was abundant on The Nature Conservancy's Rose Creek Preserve, eight miles from Pullman, though WSU entomologists had never reported it from Whitman County over the

Male, dorsal

Male, ventral

preceding century. Warren has similarly found it expanding in northeastern Oregon, even into mowed lawns and along roadsides. It flits among grasses, perches and basks, and visits flowers. The flight is usually low, slow and "moth-like," although it can accelerate when alarmed. The species' name recalls the La Garita Mountains, west of the Sangre de Cristo range in Colorado, the state from which it was described. But James Ridings collected the type material considerably north of there, in Clear Creek County. *Garita* means "little hut" in Spanish, so when Tryon Reakirt named it, perhaps he had a rustic Colorado cabin in mind.

European Skipperling *Thymelicus lineola* (OCHSENHEIMER) 1808

"Germania"
Aka European Skipper (NABA), Essex Skipper

RECOGNITION < 1 in. A tiny skipper with a **bright tawny orange upperside** and plain buckskin underside. Inside the pale fringe on DFW, the **black border invades the veins**. Males

have **thin black stigma** along the bottom of the discal cell on DFW, which darker, browner, light-veined Garita lacks. **VARIATION** No geographic variability recognized here. **HOST PLANTS** Grasses, incl. orchard grass (*Dactylis glomerata*) and couch grass (*Elymus repens*), with an apparent preference for timothy (*Phleum pratense*). Nectars prolifically on vetches, clovers, dogbane, and various composites (incl. orange hawkweed). Scott reports 24 individuals trapped and perished in the slipper of a cypripedium. **ON THE WING** E June to E September, peak in July. Single-brooded, eggs overwinter. **HABITAT AND RANGE** Hayfields (esp. timothy), meadows, pastures, grassy waste ground, margins of corrals, roadsides. Holarctic, introduced into ON about 1910, and perhaps separately in BC at a later date. Now spread throughout E US and here and there in the W. Known NW range so far limited to several locations in S BC from Victoria to Nelson, W Whatcom Co., WA, several sites in Okanogan, Ferry, Stevens, and Pend Oreille cos, WA, and W-C ID.

Group

The Essex Skipper, as it is known in England, expanded across the continent in the last century. It and the Cabbage White are our only introduced butterflies. Since the eggs overwinter in hayfields, they can easily

Male, dorsal

Male, ventral

be shifted about with bales of timothy hay and waste from seed-cleaning operations. Thea Pyle found the first Northern Rockies specimens near McCall, Idaho, and Big Sky, Montana, in the summer of 1991, and the first in Washington in 2002, near Blaine. It has since spread widely into both natural montane meadows and disturbed habitats, becoming enormously abundant in the Rockies states. From the Green Mountains of Vermont to Wisconsin pastures on Lake Michigan to the Little Bigfoot in Montana, I have never seen a butterfly more numerous, with the exception of Mexican overwintering Monarchs and Pine Whites erupting along the Payette River. In Whatcom County, it hasn't yet spread far beyond our original find (James and Nunnallee) and has not been found in Oregon, but both are to be expected. Sightings of Garita account for false reports of European Skipperling, but Garita has light veins on dark wings, and European dark veins on light wings. That trait, and the merest eyelash of a stigma on the golden males of European Skipperlings, will tell them apart.

Common Roadside Skipper *Amblyscirtes vialis* (W. H. EDWARDS) 1862

Mercer Co., IL
Aka Black Little Skipper

RECOGNITION < 1 in. **Tiny, dark brown, with violet or frosty scaling on the outer VHW** and a cluster of minute white skipper-spots near the FW apex. **Fringes checkered light and dark.** Can suggest the Dun Skipper or Common Sootywing, but smaller, with more marking and a strikingly different shape, forewings like long, narrow isosceles triangles with the short side convex. **VARIATION** No geographic variability named or described. Sexes are similar. **HOST PLANTS** Many grasses accepted, incl. *Poa*, *Agrostis*, *Avena*, and *Uniola*. Nectars prefer-

Dorsal

Ventral

entially on ground ivy (*Glechoma hederacea*) and verbena among others. Males visit mud. **ON THE WING** L April to L August, peak in June. One PNW generation. Fed-up caterpillars likely overwinter. **HABITAT AND RANGE** Roadsides, as advertised, as well as other warm, sunny, exposed locations: gullies, trails, streambanks, and hillsides, moist aspen meadows, sea level to subalpine. W of the mtns, where more restricted, outcrops with S exposure. Often limestone-associated (Stanford). Much of N Am, but highly discontinuous in the W. All across S BC, almost entirely E of the Cascade Crest in WA, avoiding both the damp W side and the dry Columbia Basin. Farther W, S of the Columbia, incl. Willamette Valley and

OR Coast Range. All major mtn ranges in Cascadia except Olympics, and scarce in Siskiyous.

Many species of roadside skippers occur in the Southeast and Southwest, but this is the only one that reaches the Pacific Northwest—hence, the only one we have to try to identify. You have to look closely to see it, as it is small, dark, and skips close to the ground. A classic locality for it is Swakane Canyon, near Rocky Reach Dam in Chelan County, Washington. There, along the lower stream, it may be reliably found in June when the Greenish Blues are flying around the rare endemic Thompson's clover. But I have seen it more often on dirt roadsides than anywhere else, making definite sense of both the English name and the Latin, which means "highway." I've passed the time watching this lively little butterfly while on the road, thumbing for a ride.

Fiery Skipper   *Hylephila phyleus* (DRURY) 1773
Antigua

RECOGNITION < 1.25 in. **Very short antennae.** Above, male is clear orange with large black stigma; female long-winged with clear tawny spotbands on dark brown, both with **very toothy, jagged border.** Underside variable; male VFW yellow-orange, female browner with orange along VFW costa; male **VHW tan with scattered brown or black dots** ranging from vague to sharp, minute to small. Female VHW tends toward brown, with paler spotbands and darker dots. **VARIATION** In S-C CA, lighter and oranger than in the SE and Caribbean, with smaller, peppery spots; in NW CA described as olivaceous below with bold black markings. **HOST PLANTS** Various grasses in S; in N CA, most likely species of bentgrass (*Agrostis*) and bluegrass (*Poa*). Nectars on a wide variety of garden and weedy flowers, incl. lantana and pansies. **ON THE WING** April to October in N CA, with as many generations as the season allows, prob. two or three there. No winter

Female, ventral

Male, ventral

Male, dorsal

diapause in any stage. **HABITAT AND RANGE** Unsprayed lawns and parks, grassy verges, vacant lots, weedy fields, dikes, ditches, and airfields. Argentina N to S US (breeding) and C US (migrating). Resident along CA coast and deserts N through frost-free latitudes.

You know the bright, speckled little Fiery right away by its dark dots and super-short antennae. Females, with their long wings, can suggest female Sachems, but lack their glassy forewing spots and usually have distinctive ink-spots below like the males. One of many species that expands its range in the summer, contracting only when the cold insists. Not yet found in Oregon, but it probably will be soon. It is a highly adaptable and mobile butterfly that may expand farther into Cascadia as the climate further ameliorates.

Genus *Hesperia*: Branded Skippers

These tawny grass skippers illustrate the overall group name with their rapid, skipping flight. They are small to robust, most have long, narrow triangular forewings, and nearly all exhibit rows of silvery white spots on the ventral hindwing running together into a bright chevron or circlet. Hindwings are often drawn out near the abdomen, giving them an eccentric shape. Males have sharp black stigmata on the dorsal forewing housing the woolly androconial scales; females are larger and more heavily spotted. The species can be very challenging to distinguish, but our assemblage is small and reasonably straightforward. The 20 or so species are mostly Nearctic. They resemble the genera *Polites*, which flies earlier on the whole, and *Ochlodes*, whose common member flies later, lower, and in more generalized and disturbed habitats.

Uncas Skipper *Hesperia uncas* W. H. EDWARDS 1863

Vic. Denver, CO
Aka White-vein Skipper

RECOGNITION < 1.4 in. Tawny orange above, dark-bordered and basally, with white apical spots (larger on female). Male has black stigma on DFW, female dark patch in cell. VFW duller with increased white spotting. **VHW has light silvery veins against olive-tinged ground color**, extending from the silvery basal chevron out through the **bowed, continuous spotband** to the light margin. Inner HW fold is ochre. Sandhill Skipper has light veins below, but they (like the spotband) are yellowish, not silvery. *H. nevada* lacks light veins and has final silvery spot sharply offset. **VARIATION** Males of OR Uncas vary in size and brightness, smaller ones often darker too (Warren). Females bright and big, almost as large as Juba. VHW veins are fairly well marked on OR specimens. **HOST PLANTS** Warren suspects Indian ricegrass (*Achnatherum hymenoides*) in OR. **ON THE WING** L May to L June. One generation, prob. overwintering as eggs or young larvae. **HABITAT AND RANGE** Sage-steppe, plains, alkali basins, arid canyons.

Female, dorsal

Male, dorsal

Male, ventral

W N Am between SK and C Mexico, W Great Plains to Sierra Nevada; NE NV to SW ID and SE OR in Harney and Malheur cos, where

Warren found it faithfully frequenting *bajadas* (linear, sandy bluffs) running out from the bases of mtns into the Alvord Desert in Harney Co., OR, with Juba on nearby rocky hilltops. Also C OR in Deschutes and Crook cos, where somewhat different Uncas occupy flat pumice; and from the Pueblo Mtns, and the Owyhee River Cyn, between 3,600 and 4,200 feet.

Uncas enters the Basin and Range and Owyhee Upland provinces of southeastern Oregon. First found in that state by Stanley G. Jewett, Jr., at Frenchglen, it was redis-covered by Christy Galen, Carolyn Bohn, and Mark Smith, biologists performing rare plant surveys for the Oregon Natural Heritage Program in 1978–79. Dan Thack-aberry found a big population at the north end of the Alvord Desert, and Erik Runquist pushed the known range west to Pine Moun-tain in Deschutes County. This progression shows the cumulative effect of field work by pros and amateurs working together.

Juba Skipper   *Hesperia juba* (SCUDDER) 1874

"neighborhood of Salt Lake City, UT"
Aka Yuba Skipper, Jagged-border Skipper

RECOGNITION > 1.5 in. Females can be very large and bulky for a grass skipper. Males tawny orange above with black DFW stigma, females ochraeous with brown DFW bar and on DHW. Both sexes have pale apical spots on DFW and **strongly toothed black margins, pointing inward, scalloped by orange veins running to margin**. On VHW the large, chunky spotband stands out sharply against olive background, and tends to show through the slightly translucent HW to the upperside. Hindmost spot in VHW band is connected more or less in a curved line with the others, or a little offset inwardly, but not strongly as in *H. nevada*. Silvery basal chevron often in two parts. Antennae half as long as FW, with small clubs. **VARIATION** Size varies. Females can be considerably larger and brighter overall. **HOST PLANTS** Various bunchgrasses incl. *Poa pratensis* (Kentucky bluegrass), *Bromus*, and *Deschampsia*. Not to my knowledge recorded on *Bromus tectorum* (cheatgrass), the alien species that dominates much of the NW steppe. Nectars esp. on rabbit-brush and many other composites (e.g., Barnaby thistle, balsamroot) as well as alfalfa, lilac, milkweed, mints, and others. Males visit mud. **ON THE WING** M April to E October, peaks in May and September in two generations, but see remarks. May overwinter as eggs or early instar larvae. **HABITAT AND RANGE** Sagelands, canyons, roadsides, drier woodland openings throughout much of W N Am. S BC, most of WA, OR, and ID, sea level to 10,000 feet. Far less common in W OR and Pugetopolis, and absent from Olympics and maritime WA and BC.

Female, dorsal

Male, dorsal

Male, ventral

Juba shows up both spring and fall in many kinds of grassy places. Berkhousen and Shapiro (1994), detecting autumn pollen on spring individuals, hypothesized that univoltine adults overwinter in California; but rearings by James and Nunnallee demonstrated bivoltinism in Washington. Juba Skippers can be numerous in autumn, on rabbitbrush in particular, where you can spot the giant females from a distance.

Adults disperse, showing up as singletons on isolated clumps of chrysanthemums. Such wanderers may account for the occasional records in western Washington and Oregon. A big female Juba gives the impression of a bumblebee with colored wings, or a standard *Hesperia* species on steroids. The name probably comes from the Yuba River with the English Y replaced by the Latin J.

Common Branded Skipper   *Hesperia comma* (LINNAEUS) 1758

Sweden
Aka Comma Skipper, Holarctic Grass Skipper, Silver-spotted Skipper (UK)

RECOGNITION < 1.25 in. Medium-sized reddish orange or tawny, male with prominent dart-like stigmata on DFW, **broad dark borders not extending inward in tooth-like pattern** as in *H. juba*. Gray or greenish VHW with crescentic row of sharp, variable, yellowish or silver-white spots, **basal one not offset**. Thoracic hairs shine green. Antennae < ⅓ wing length, with long clubs. Distinguished from *H. colorado* primarily by its highly restricted occurrence in PNW. **VARIATION** Extremely variable throughout its Holarctic range. Two well-separated ssp. in WA and BC: *H. c. hulbirti*, endemic race to high Olympics, is large (females can be as big as *H. juba*), has dull brassy olive or orangish VHW disc (MacNeill calls it "rather shaggy"), large, bright pearly white or yellowish VHW spots, light patch on VFW, and a hairier head than other ssp. *H. c. manitoba* occurs in the subalpine and arctic-alpine zones of the N Cascades of BC and WA, is darker, with large white spots below and short wings. **HOST PLANTS** Grasses, incl. *Festuca ovina*, *Muhlenbergia*, *Stipa*, *Andropogon*. Nectars on chokecherry, gayfeather, goldenweed, yellow yarrow, and many other composites. **ON THE**

Male (left) and female (right) (ssp. *hulbirti*)

Male, ventral (ssp. *hulbirti*)

Male, dorsal (ssp. *manitoba*)

Male, ventral (ssp. *manitoba*)

WING E June to L August, peak in July-August, depending on snowmelt. One flight, spring in W valleys, summer to fall in highlands and deserts. One brood, eggs overwinter. **HABITAT AND RANGE** Subalpine meadows, arctic-alpine tundra and fellfield. Circumpolar; in N Am, ranging across Canada and S into the Great Lakes states, N MT, N ID, and N WA in Clallam, Jefferson, Whatcom, Okanogan, and Chelan cos. To 8,000 feet on Cascade summits.

All the skippers formerly included under *Hesperia comma* may represent one "super-species" or several closely related species. Guppy and Shepard maintain *H. comma* as an umbrella species. We consider the paler lowland populations to be *H. colorado*, with *H. comma* restricted to alpine populations in northern Washington. The center of diversity of *Hesperia* is North America, so Eurasian *H. comma* probably represents a Beringian incursion westward from Alaska. Males are big hilltoppers. At peak bloom in Olympic meadows, cumbrous mating pairs of *H. c. hulbirti* flop among the alpine grasses by the dozens.

Western Branded Skipper   *Hesperia colorado* (SCUDDER) 1874

Lake Co., CO
Aka Common Branded Skipper, *comma, harpalus, oregonia*

Female, dorsal (ssp. *idaho*)

Female, ventral (ssp. *idaho*)

SALISH SEA SEGREGATE SPECIAL CONCERN IN BC, SGCN IN WA

RECOGNITION < 1.25 in. Medium-sized reddish orange or tawny, male stigmata prominent with silvery black interior felt, **broad dark borders not extending inward in tooth-like pattern** as in *H. juba*. **VHW gray or greenish, spotband sharp, variable, yellowish or silver-white, large to almost absent; spots in-line**, not basally offset as in *H. nevada*. Sometimes white scaling extends slightly into veins, but all along them, as with *H. uncas*. Thoracic hairs shine green. Antennae < ⅓ wing length, with long clubs. Best distinguished from *H. comma* in PNW by range. **VARIATION** *H. c. idaho* is gray-green below with the spots quite silvery. It occupies all our area E of the Cascade Crest, up to the edges of the alpine. *H. c. oregonia* has been used for those that fly from the Siskiyous N through W OR Cascades and Puget Sound lowlands sparingly to Vancouver Is. and the San Juans, but see remarks. In SW OR, it is warmly reddish above and has an olive disc with light yellowish spots (or white on the females) without a pearly luster, smaller and darker to the N in W OR. Rich golden to ochre on VHW with little or no light spotting in Del Norte Co., CA, and serpentine ridges of SW Curry and SE Josephine cos, OR. **HOST PLANTS** Grasses, incl. *Lolium, Festuca idahoensis, Achnatherum, Bouteloua, Andropogon*, and *Bromus*. Nectars on composites

Male, dorsal (ssp. *idaho*)

Female, ventral (ssp. *oregonia*)

and many other flowers. **ON THE WING** E May to L September, peak in July-August. One staggered flight, spring in W valleys, summer to fall in highlands and deserts, fall in the Klamath. Overwinters mostly as eggs. **HABITAT AND RANGE** Broad range of grasslands, Puget Prairies to alpine meadows and fellfields to desert and basin steppe; E Vancouver Is., San Juan Is., but much rarer W of the Cascade Crest until S OR; W states into S BC and AB.

Our most abundant branded skipper in the Cascades and in many interior habitats, rarer on west side. Layberry et al. separated ten subspecies of the *H. comma* complex into *H. colorado*. San Juan Islands *H. colorado* resemble *H. comma* from the nearby Olympics. Populations in Oregon north of the Siskiyous and in western Washington and British Columbia that have traditionally been called *H. c. oregonia* do not actually resemble that subspecies and are currently referred to as "nr. *oregonia*" (western Oregon) and "Salish Sea segregate" (western Washington). Males hilltop on prominences ranging from six-foot Mima Mounds on the Puget Prairies to 6,000-foot Slate Peak in the North Cascades, and higher.

Columbian Skipper   *Hesperia columbia* (SCUDDER) 1872

"California"
Aka Columbia Skipper, Chaparral Skipper

RECOGNITION < 1.4 in. Bright or dark tawny orange above, with brown running inward from deeply toothed dark border. Male stigma broad with yellow interior felt, female has brown patch in same location. VFW oranger toward costa, greenish tip; VHW greenish ochre. Silver-white spotband reduced to a short basal arm and longer, separated distal arm, both of them narrow and straight; basal band reduced to one or two spots, not a crescent. **VARIATION** No ssp. described; OR individuals larger and darker than those in CA. Females

Ventral

Male, dorsal

Male, ventral

paler than males. **HOST PLANTS** In Marin Co., CA, the main host is *Koeleria macrantha*, a low bunchgrass of arid edges among chaparral. *Danthonia californica* also suggested. Nectars on *Allium*, *Epilobium*, *Eryngium*, and *Polygonum douglasii* (Warren). **ON THE WING** E May to M October, peaks in May and September. Warren suggests two generations in S OR, one above 5,000 feet. Prob. overwinters in the egg. **HABITAT AND RANGE** Closely tied to chaparral communities on the Pacific slope, from Baja to SW OR. Brushy spaces and grassy forest clearings in Siskiyous and S Cascades in Klamath, Jackson, and Josephine cos, OR, where males may be found hilltopping, visiting mud and flowers, and behaving territorially.

Nearly a California endemic, the Columbian Skipper is distinctive. Since it does not occur near the Columbia River, its name must have come from some vague idea of the region held by Scudder, a New Englander. Males perch on hilltops among scrublands and open oak woodlands where females might best be encountered. Warren found it common at Eight Dollar Mountain and Erik Runquist in the Cascade-Siskiyou National Monument. Confusion with the Western Branded Skipper or Lindsey's Skipper, at least for males, can be settled by examining the stigmata; those of *H. colorado* and *H. lindseyi* are narrow and black, with black androconial felt inside. The Columbian has a matte black patch beside the shiny brand, and yellow felt within the slit.

Lindsey's Skipper   *Hesperia lindseyi* (HOLLAND) 1930

Ukiah, Napa Co., CA
Aka Lindsey's Branded Skipper, Lost-egg Skipper

RECOGNITION > 1.25 in. **Bright orange above.** Little marking on females; vague black border on males, thinner and more discrete on females. Male has narrow stigma with black felt. **VHW yellow-brown to greenish**, light spotband creamy or yellowish in male, white in female. **Individual spots angular; veins lined with pale scales**, tipped in black in the light fringe. Other grass skippers with light veins: Uncas Skipper does not overlap in range; Sandhill Skipper smaller, larger light areas below, different habitats. Western Branded Skipper overlaps

but lacks the whitish veining except for slight projections from the spots. **VARIATION** The Siskiyou-Klamath population differs from the type, farther S, by its washed-out upperside and white-spotted-and-veined, "shaggy" appearance below. Warner Mtns individuals are greener below, and a population in the S Umpqua drainage is darker than others. **HOST PLANTS** Females often

Male, dorsal

Female, dorsal

Female, ventral

Male, ventral

oviposit in clumps of an arboreal frondose lichen, *Usnea florida*, "whether on a fence post or forty feet up in a tree" (MacNeill); elsewhere, lupines, fescues, or oak leaves. From there, the young larvae must find host grasses, which in Marin Co., CA, incl. fescues and *Danthonia californica*. Nectars esp. on *Apocynum* and *Allium*. **ON THE WING** E June to M July. One brood. Fully formed caterpillar diapauses through much of the summer and all winter, until temperature, moisture, and day length are all right for emergence and pupation. **HABITAT AND RANGE** Grassy chaparral and oak woodland. S-C CA/SW AZ, N through the CA Coast Ranges and Sierra foothills to SW OR and Warners; from Siskiyou and Lassen cos, CA, to Washoe Co. in NW NV, and N into Curry, Josephine, Jackson, Klamath, Lake, and Douglas cos, OR.

Lindsey's Skipper was one of the last American branded skippers to be distinguished and named. W. J. Holland, author of *The*

Butterfly Book, the most widely used text and guide for several generations, named comparatively few taxa. He honored Arthur W. Lindsey, an important student of the North American skippers, with the patronym. We owe our knowledge of this species' extraordinary host plants (and much of our understanding of the genus) to C. Don MacNeill, whose 1964 UC Berkeley Ph.D. thesis and subsequent work remain the major studies on the western American species of *Hesperia*. Lindsey's Cascadian occurrence virtually overlaps that of the Columbian Skipper, extending a little farther east and west in southwestern Oregon. Scott says the males patrol over grass, sometimes perching on ridges, in search of females. I watched one in the Applegate watershed, skipping from flower to stake, alternately nectaring and perching, and sometimes flying through a sprinkler's spray. Warren found it the dominant butterfly in the Cascade-Siskiyou National Monument, nectaring on spreading dogbane.

Nevada Skipper *Hesperia nevada* (SCUDDER) 1874

Nr Fairplay, South Park, CO
Aka Montane Skipper

RECOGNITION > 1.25 in. Bright tawny. Easy to tell reliably from other *Hesperia* spp. with a look at the VHW, where in the silvery spotband, **the ultimate basal spot (nearest the tail end) is dramatically offset inward from the others**—still touching, but **obviously out of line**. Western and Juba may have this spot slightly offset, but not as radically; Nevada is brighter than the former, FW tips blunter than in the other species, and dark margin fades into the wing unlike the usually well-defined border of *H. colorado* or the dentate border of *H. juba*. **VARIATION** Populations in Blue Mtns of OR and WA-BC Cascades are paler than the CO topotypes. Those in S Lake Co., OR, are distinguished from the type by being deeper orange above and darker olive-brown beneath with smaller light spots, and with more distinct borders. **HOST PLANTS** Grasses, incl. western needlegrass (*Achnatherum occidentale*) and prob. several others. Larvae make shelters, then pupate, at the bases of the grasses (Pelham). **ON THE WING** E May to L July, peak in L May. Single-brooded, mid-size larvae overwinter. **HABITAT AND RANGE** Associated with lithosols and high, windswept sage-steppe plateaus and summits of ridges and peaks, usually above 4,500 feet (Warren), often dominated by basin big sage. Seldom far from ridgelines and hilltopping rocks; females nectar below. W states and provinces, fairly continuous around the Rockies and patchy in the Great Basin. S-C, C, and NE OR, S-C and N-C WA, S-C BC in Similkameen and Okanagan valleys.

Male, dorsal

Female, ventral

For a long time the only Washington records were Newcomer's from the Yakama Indian Nation and Shepard's from the Okanogan Highlands. Abundant concentrations have since turned up on Manastash and Umtanum ridges and other high shrub-steppe expanses on the Yakima Firing Range between Ellensburg and Yakima. In Oregon it was known only in the southern Blue Mountains, Lake County far to the south, and not in between, until Andy Warren found it flying together with *H. uncas* on pumice plains in Deschutes and Crook counties. One of our patchiest butterflies, the Nevada Skipper is often considered rare but can occur in abundance when conditions are right. Overgrazing (and bombardment?) on its native grassland habitats may affect its numbers.

Genus *Polites*: Golden Grass Skippers

On the whole, *Polites* species are smaller than those of *Hesperia*; they have rounder hindwings, their male stigmata are more wavy with gray velvety patches next to them, and their spot-crescents on the ventral hindwing are often composed of more or less discrete yellowish ovals rather than a connected row of pearly white checks. Cascadia enjoys one of the highest concentrations of *Polites* species anywhere: our fauna includes seven of the world's 12 species, all of which occur between northern Mexico and southern Canada. Scudder had their fleetness in mind when he named the genus for Polites, swift-footed brother of the weakling Paris.

Peck's Skipper   *Polites peckius* (W. KIRBY) 1837

"Lat. 54°" ("NE US or SE Canada")
Aka Yellowpatch Skipper, *P. coras*

RECOGNITION < 1.25 in. Dark brown above, with tawny restricted to the leading edge of the FW beyond the stigma in males and discrete patches in females. Yellow apical spots. On VHW, both sexes have big yellow spots in an irregular band, the middle one long, set into a chestnut-brown background, and more yellow spots at the base of the wing, together eclipsing most of the wing's brown. The yellow patches appear on the brown DHW also, but not as large. **VARIATION** Variable, but not consistently in our region; yellow patches smaller in Great Plains than W. **HOST PLANTS** Grasses, incl. Kentucky bluegrass, saltgrass, and bromes. Nectars on vetches and gayfeather but will also use oxeye daisy and other meadow flowers. **ON THE WING** L June to E August, peak in July. A single generation, both grown larvae and pupae may overwinter. **HABITAT AND RANGE** Wet montane meadows, marshy edges of potholes, roadsides, riparian habitats. Much of N US and Canada, sparsely in Okanogan–Pend Oreille of NE WA, Blue-Wallowa Mtns of NE Oregon, SE BC, and N ID.

Common, weedy, and expanding in the East, even a lawn skipper, this species (like *P. themistocles*) is much more sparse, patchy, and specialized in the Far West. This may represent a very old distribution, whereas

Female, dorsal

Male, dorsal

Male, ventral

recent arrivals are colonizing parts of the Rockies, and perhaps one day they shall meet. Males perch in grassy swales, watching for passing females. One July day in the broad, mid-elevation Tiger Meadows of Pend Oreille County, Peck's Skippers flew along with Long Dashes and Garita Skipperlings—a dizzying medley of bright golden flickers. The name has gone back and forth between Yellowpatch and Peck's, *P. coras* and *P. peckius*, with the latter currently recognized. By any name, it is easy to identify by its distinctive yellow fleur-de-lis outlined in chestnut. Perching head up on a grassblade with its hindwings held out in the characteristic hesperiine posture, the butterfly displays this trait boldly.

Sandhill Skipper   *Polites sabuleti* (BOISDUVAL) 1852

San Francisco, CA
Aka Saltgrass Skipper

Female, dorsal

IMPERILED IN BC

RECOGNITION < 1.2 in. Small, bright tawny or brassy yellow, male with black stigmata, female with light yellow spots, both rimmed with broad, deeply dentate black borders. **VHW has a yellowish or ivory-colored spotband and basal crescent with elongated middle spots that run out along the veins** against a lighter or darker olive background, giving a stripy effect. Veins black-tipped in yellow fringe below. Pale pattern can occupy most of the VHW in some individuals or populations. **VARIATION** A dozen ssp. have been described around the W. Ours range from smaller and very pale in the Great Basin to large and chocolatey in the Siskiyous; generally lighter S and E and darker N and W. **HOST PLANTS** An array of grasses, among them Idaho fescue, Kentucky bluegrass, and Bermuda grass. *Distichlis* (saltgrass) is a common host in the Snake Basin and other alkaline areas. Nectars on clover, alfalfa, weedy composites, and marigolds and other summer garden annuals. **ON THE WING** E May to L

October, peaks in May-June and August. Two broods at lower elevations, one summer brood at higher elevations. Pupae overwinter. **HABITAT AND RANGE** Lawns, parks, ditchbanks, marsh edges, alkali flats, and (farther S) mountain and subalpine meadows. W basins and ranges, S into Baja. Okanagan Valley of S BC, E of Cascades in WA and OR from Lake Chelan to Spokane R. S, from Columbia-level to 8,000+ feet in OR Cascades. A SW WA (Wahkiakum Co.) record is either a wanderer or mislabeled.

Of three Pacific Northwest skippers with a "cobwebby" pattern on the VHW (the others being *Hesperia uncas* and *H. lindseyi*), this is the only one common in much of our area. Like other species in *Polites*, it behaves adventitiously in some parts of its range and as a sedentary colony-dweller in others. For example, Thea Pyle found the first Chelan County individuals in the early 1980s in vacant lots, a double-brooded generalist; while in midsummer 2000, it abounded in Tuolumne Meadows, Yosemite National Park, as a single-brooded alpine specialist. These differences may depend on both environment and genetics. A weedy species expanding in the lowlands of the Columbia Basin, the Sandhill Skipper should be

Female, ventral

Male, dorsal

sought wherever rivers and other corridors extend beyond its known range. It is colonizing westward in Klickitat County along the Columbia River. Shepard found that the species' adaptation to diffuse knapweed

(*Centaurea diffusa*) for autumn nectar in southern British Columbia enabled a second generation farther north than usual. Sabulet was a friend of the Parisian first describer, Boisduval.

Draco Skipper   *Polites draco* (W. H. EDWARDS) 1871

Twin Lakes, Lake Co., CO
Aka Rocky Mountain Skipper, Dragon Skipper

SPECIAL CONCERN IN BC

RECOGNITION 1 in. Narrowly tawny above between broad dark borders, esp. females. Distinguished by the **VHW spotband being sharply yellow or white with the central spot or two elongated into a spike that protrudes into the cell**, but not much light veining such as *P. sabuleti* has. This punctuated pattern shows through to the upperside in the tawny DHW spots. **VARIATION** No geographic varieties have been described. **HOST PLANTS** Grasses. **ON THE WING** E June to L July, peak in E July. Single-brooded. **HABITAT AND RANGE** Alpine and subalpine meadows, dry grassy

slopes, avalanche chutes, creeksides. Yukon, far NW BC, Rocky Mtns from AB to NM; in Cascadia, W-C ID.

Included on the strength of its occurrence in Valley County, Idaho. Field collectors should be on the lookout for it in the high Pend Oreille and Selkirk country of northeastern Washington and the Wallowa Mountains of northeastern Oregon. Noted skipper revisionist W. H. Evans considered

Female, ventral

Female, dorsal

Male, dorsal

it a subspecies of *P. sabuleti,* and Scott thought it was probably an altitudinal form, replacing the Sierra Nevadan *P. s. tecumseh* in the Rocky Mountains, but has since accepted its specific status. Theodore Mead collected the types in the San Juan Mountains of Colorado in 1871. He sent them to his future father-in-law, William Henry Edwards of Pennsylvania, who named the butterfly either for Draco the dragon or the merciless Athenian bureaucrat who inspired the term "draconian." F. M. Brown found Draco the most abundant *Polites* species in Colorado.

Mardon Skipper   *Polites mardon* (W. H. EDWARDS) 1881

Tenino Prairie, Thurston Co., WA
Aka Cascades Skipper, Little Oregon Skipper

ENDANGERED IN WA, IMPERILED IN OR, FEDERAL SPECIES OF CONCERN

RECOGNITION < 1 in. **More compact, with shorter, rounder wings** than other *Polites* spp. Orange and brown above, females lighter than other species, males' stigma small and bent, border dentate. **VHW yellowish, grayish, or brownish olive, coarsely scaled, with discal band of prominent, longer than broad, and often diffuse yellow to off-white spots** giving an overall muddy impression. *P. sonora* tends to

Female, dorsal

Male, ventral

have smaller, more discrete yellow spots below and longer, narrower wings. **VARIATION** The type tends toward a concolorous olive-brown, grizzled VHW; it occurs in Thurston, Yakima, and Klickitat cos, WA, and (maybe) NW Del Norte Co., CA. *P. m. klamathensis* averages shorter, less rounded wings and is more two-toned in appearance, oranger below; it flies in Jackson, Klamath, and Curry cos, OR, and Siskiyou Co., CA. **HOST PLANTS** Idaho fescue (*Festuca idahoensis*), red fescue (*F. rubra*), California oatgrass (*Danthonia californica*), sedge (*Carex*) in WA, Roemer's fescue (*F. roemeri*) in SW OR. Nectars preferentially on blue violet (*Viola adunca*), common vetch, prairie lupine, and Idaho blue-eyed grass on the Puget Prairies, and dandelion, wallflower, vetch, sego lily, and penstemon in the mtns. **ON THE WING** M May to E August, peak in May (Puget Prairies), June-July (montane habitats). A single generation, chrysalides overwinter. **HABITAT AND RANGE** Undisturbed glacial-outwash mounded prairies in S Puget Trough; ponderosa pine woodland openings, *Ceanothus* breaks, and grazed meadows in S WA Cascades from 2,000 to 5,000 feet. Serpentine, rhododendron heath meadows, and a few other kinds of sites in SW OR and NW CA.

Male, dorsal

Mardon was once considered Washington's only endemic butterfly. Then Sterling Mattoon found it on serpentine outcrops in northern California, and occurrences were confirmed in several southwestern Oregon locations. While the original Tenino Prairie populations in the Salish Lowlands direly contracted before human expansion, colonies have been managed on Joint Base Lewis-McChord, the Glacial Heritage Preserve, and elsewhere in Thurston County. Xerces Society, Washington Department of Fish and Wildlife, and other surveys found additional colonies in the southwestern Washington Cascades; and the Cascade-Siskiyou National Monument protects some habitat of the recently discovered Klamath subspecies in southwestern Oregon. Threats include wildfires, overgrazing, and spraying for forest insects. The origin of the epithet remains a mystery, but it is *not* the MarDon Resort in Adams County, Washington.

Tawny-edged Skipper *Polites themistocles* (LATREILLE) 1824

"l'Amerique méridionale"

SPECIAL CONCERN IN BC

RECOGNITION < 1 in. Short, triangular wings. Mostly dark tan, esp. females, but both sexes have a **bright tawny leading edge above and below** (sometimes vague in female). Stigma twice-bent like a long S on male's DFW, female has bright light spots on DFW. No other monocot skipper has **unmarked, olive-drab DHW**. Dark mustard VHW sometimes has a vague paler spotband but is more commonly plain. Fringes light. **VARIATION** Cascadia has its own ssp., *P. t. turneri*, described from Jesmond, BC. It is supposed to differ from the type by being smaller and darker overall, with its light patches brownish orange rather than yellowish. Guppy and Shepard feel this ssp. is sound and that the type enters BC in the Rocky Mtn Trench. **HOST PLANTS** Grasses, incl. Kentucky bluegrass (*Poa pratensis*) in Denver, and *Panicum, Dicanthellum, Digitaria,* and *Koeleria macrantha*. Nectars on alfalfa, red clover, dogbane, and thistles, among others. **ON THE WING** L May to E August, peak in June. **HABITAT AND RANGE** Grassy spots of many types, but in Cascadia seemingly limited to the edges of mountain marshes,

Female dorsal

high valleys, and the margins of ponds in dry grasslands. Most of the NE ⅔ of N Am, S interior of BC, Okanogan–Pend Oreille in WA; disjunct in N CA and possibly NE OR.

Most regions in North America have one or more species of hesperiine that adapt to townscapes and become what I call "lawn skippers." In much of Cascadia, this would be the Woodland Skipper, or on the dry side of the Cascades, the Sandhill Skipper. Growing up in Denver and suburbs, my common lawn skipper was *P. themistocles*. It has since dropped out of the city almost completely, a probable casualty of lawn chemicals, according to Ray Stanford. Yet, while the Tawny-edged thrives in unsprayed urban localities from the Great Plains east, it becomes a rare denizen of wild habitats in its northwestern reaches. More widespread in British Columbia, it dips into Washington in only a few locations in the Okanogan Valley and Highlands and Pend Oreille, such as Moses Meadows, Okanogan County. The northern California records come from south-southeast of Mt. Shasta, around Mc-Cloud, where a large colony is reported, and adjacent Siskiyou County. This seems to represent an indigenous occurrence, and therefore an old disjuncture. It should be sought in the southernmost Oregon Cascades. A 1925 record from Corvallis probably represented an introduction associated with the railroad or the osu Turf Grass Unit. Andy Warren examined a specimen collected along railroad tracks at Minam, Wallowa County, at 3,000 feet, in 1945. A distinct phenotype, it was probably not a railroad introduction. If these Tawny-edged Skipper colonies indeed represent native relicts in the mountains of both northeastern California and Oregon, they would closely parallel the American Copper—common in the lowlands of the East, rare and isolated in western ranges. Apropos of absolutely nothing,

Male, dorsal

Male, ventral

Themistocles (527–460 bce) was an Athenian physician and statesman and reputedly a friend of the father of Hippocrates.

Long Dash   *Polites mystic* (W. H. EDWARDS) 1863

Hunter, Greene Co., NY
Aka Long-dash Skipper, Mystic Skipper

RECOGNITION < 1.25 in. Females more tawny above than males, with broad black border. **Males have blunt-tipped stigma connecting with black dash running toward apex**; females also have dark bands from base to tip of DFW, and **black base of VFW**. Both **DHW** and **VHW have arcs of long yellow spots, concentric with border, enclosing a light basal spot**. Above, these spots diffuse against brown, below may be more discrete against rusty gold ground. Females' wings are broad, males' narrower, both pointed and longer than on Woodland Skippers, which also have a long dash. VHW spots longer and more distinct on Long Dash, more nebulous on Woodland, which is also smaller and shorter-winged and tends to fly later in the year in lower, weedier places. **VARIATION** Ground color of VHW varies from golden through various browns. MacNeill (in Howe) suggested that an unnamed NW ssp. exists, differing from the yellow, less contrasty CO prairie ssp., *P. m. dacotah*. He doesn't mention how they differ, but Warren has seen this ssp. from SW BC (Mt. Fernie ski area) and says they are basically intermediate between *P. m. dacotah* and the richer-colored and more strongly marked type. **HOST PLANTS** Various grasses (e.g., *Poa*, *Agropyron*, *Phleum*). Seen nectaring on oxeye daisies on forest roadsides in NW MT and NE WA. **ON THE WING** E June

Female, dorsal

Female, ventral

Male, dorsal

to E August, peak in June-July. Single-brooded. Third- or fourth-instar larvae overwinter. **HABITAT AND RANGE** Wet meadows, streamsides, marshes, grassy swales, meadows, and prairies. Widespread across N US and Canada, in Cascadia restricted to SE BC, N ID, NE WA in Selkirks and Okanogan Highlands, and into NE OR.

In the southeastern Rockies, dramatically spreading into suburban and secondary habitats; formerly absent on the eastern edge of Denver, it is now common there. Farther west in more "original" conditions, such as a high bullrush marsh east of Yellowstone and boreal grasslands in northeastern Washington. We should keep an eye out for all tawny skippers in the spring and summer to see if our *Polites* species too begin to spread. The epithet might come from Mystic, Connecticut, but that is some distance from the type locality. The common name is a reference to the extended stigma and apical bar of males, and parallel marks on females. Some putative specimens from the Blue-Wallowa Mountains in northeastern Oregon were found by Warren to be Sonora Skippers, but Long Dashes do occur to the east in Idaho and west beyond Baker City.

Sonora Skipper   *Polites sonora* (SCUDDER) 1872

Tenino Prairie, Thurston Co., WA
Aka Sonoran Skipper, Western Long Dash

CRITICALLY IMPERILED IN BC; _P. S. SIRIS_ SGCN IN WA

RECOGNITION < 1.25 in. Tawny and brown above with dark rusty border and vague lighter spotband across the DHW. Male stigma appears fairly long and broad, extended by dark patches beyond and below; but not as long as on Long Dash nor as square as the Sachem's. Female has yellow dots around dark DFW patch. **VHW tan, olive, or brown, with distinct small creamy spots in a connected semicircular band enclosing a basal spot**. Long Dash and Woodland Skippers both have vaguer bands beneath, Mardon has shorter, stubbier wings and granular appearance below. **VARIATION** VHW disc brownish in the Cascades and Olympics; darker overall and tan-rusty on the Puget Prairies, SW WA, and the Willamette Valley, OR; and oranger above, yellower below far to the SE in Lake Co. A type much resembling *P. mystic* below flies in the Blue-Wallowa Mtns. **HOST PLANTS** Various grasses. Nectars abundantly on legumes such as red and white clover and birdsfoot trefoil (*Lotus corniculatus*), and on thistle, hawkbit, sneezeweed, penstemon, and cinquefoil. **ON**

Female, dorsal

Male, dorsal

Male, ventral

THE WING L May to L August, peak in June-July. A single generation, fourth-instar larvae overwinter. **HABITAT AND RANGE** Flowery meadows, clovery pastures, forest lanes and roadsides, stream banks, grassy clearings in woodland, and swampy springs. Occurs spottily through montane W, sea level to 6,500+ feet. Cascades, Blue-Wallowas, Ochocos, Willapa Hills, Willamette Valley, Siskiyous; absent from the drier basinlands and steppes, and the Selkirks.

Sonora Skippers are adaptable, colonizing boggy edges of logging roads near Humptulips, anthropogenic meadows, roadsides, and abandoned logging camps in the southern Willapa Hills, and in unusually warm summers, even my back yard. They move on or die out as conditions change through succession. More stable populations occur higher up and in natural areas. Recent discoveries in the northeastern Olympics and on the Conboy Marshes of Klickitat County show how a butterfly can be easily overlooked even in a well-sampled area. It shares some spots with the rarer *P. mardon*, but flies later, and seems to be replaced by *P. peckius*, *P. themistocles*, and *P. mystic* in northeastern Washington east of the Okanogan River, and by *P. sabuleti* in the Columbia Basin. Their bright legions are something to see in irrigated pastures of the Klamath Basin in early July.

Sachem   *Atalopedes campestris* (BOISDUVAL) 1852

Sacramento, CA
Aka Field Skipper

RECOGNITION < 1.5 in. **Noticeably larger and longer-winged than most other tawny skippers** it might be consorting with, esp. Woodland Skippers. Male bright, female browner above. **Male has a big, rectangular black patch around** the stigma; female has a glassy spot just beyond a black patch in the **DFW** cell. Both have black vFW "armpits," **yellow spots on olive vHW**—smaller spots against a purply background on the female, and often larger, filling

Female, dorsal

much of the dusky disc, on the male. Only Juba and Yuma Skippers are as large; Juba has silvery spots below while Yuma is plain. Lacks peppery dots of the smaller Fiery Skipper. **VARIATION** Highly variable, esp. in the VHW ground color and size and brightness of its spotband. Smaller, darker, and sharply marked on N CA coast, mossy to yellow to amber below. **HOST PLANTS** Numerous grasses such as crabgrass, goosegrass, and bluegrass; said to be a pasture pest on Bermuda grass (*Cynodon dactylon*) in the S. **ON THE WING** M May to L October, peaks in June and October. Successive generations as the conditions permit. Thought not to overwinter N of frost line, but see remarks. **HABITAT AND RANGE** Pastures, old fields, gardens, lawns, parks, cemeteries, canalsides, road verges, and open prairie. Brazil to C US, expanding N seasonally and perhaps permanently. Patchy in S BC, Columbia-Snake-Yakima drainages in WA, most of N and W OR.

The Sachem began turning up in the Willamette Valley in the mid-1960s; Maurita Smyth found it in her Portland butterfly garden in 1986. After several autumns' searching, I found the first specimens on the Washington side of the Columbia River in a garden near the Vancouver Mall in 1990. Soon it turned it up in the Gorge and Tri-Cities, where it is now common. Lisa Crozier's doctoral research, "Winter warming facilitates range expansion: cold tolerance of the butterfly *Atalopedes campestris*," was one of the first studies to demonstrate butterfly response to warming trends, and it should be expected to expand farther north. David James showed larvae successfully overwintering in Tri-Cities temperatures

Male, dorsal

Male, ventral

as low as -25C (-13F). Sachem remains on the wing when most other species have passed from the autumn scene; watch for it on frost-free marigold beds up to Thanksgiving. The exaggerated badge of the male's stigmata recalled Native American regalia for Scudder, who called it the Sachem, an Algonquin word for "chief."

Woodland Skipper   *Ochlodes sylvanoides* (BOISDUVAL) 1852

Plumas Co., CA
Aka Western Skipper

RECOGNITION > 1 in. Often the only tawny skipper about. Both sexes have dentate dark margins and a **long, wavering dark-scaled streak running diagonally across the DFW from base to somewhat rounded tip**, darker in male due to black stigma forming the inner half of it. VHW pale tan to dark brown with chunky yellow spotband (see ssp.). Smaller than Juba Skipper or Sachem, the other late-flying species.

Regardless of ground color, **VHW spots usually squarer, larger than in most other tawny grass skippers**. *O. s. bonnevilla* has been mistaken for the similarly immaculate and sympatric *O. yuma* by experienced lepidopterists, but Yuma is much larger and flies earlier. **VARIATION** Highly variable everywhere. The typical race, with the VHW warm tan and the spotband creamy and continuous, occupies most of the montane and moister lowland parts of the region. Ranges to the richly colored maritime race *O. s. orecoasta* with chocolate-and-butter-colored VHW at the NW coast, and to the very pale, washed-out tan *O. s. bonnevilla* in the

Male, ventral

Female, dorsal

Male, dorsal

Columbia and Snake basins, often lacking any discriminable spotting on the vhw. *O. s. omnigena*, smaller and paler/yellower than the type, may be applicable to all WA material E of the Cascades that is elevationally above (and darker than) *O. s. bonnevilla*. **HOST PLANTS** Pelham lists these for WA: bluebunch wheatgrass, bearded wheatgrass, colonial bentgrass, common wild oats, Siberian wildrye, giant wildrye, and reed canarygrass. Nectars

Ventral *(ssp. orecoasta)*

on mints, garden herbs such as thyme and lavender, alyssum, fireweed, butterfly bush (*Buddleia*), heather, phlox, selfheal, pea, oxeye daisy, pearly everlasting, hawkbit, thistles, gumweed, yarrow, and both tansy ragwort (*Senecio jacobaea*) and tansy (*Tanacetum*). **ON THE WING** M June to E October, peak in August. One brood, first-instar larvae overwinter. **HABITAT AND RANGE** All PNW except W Vancouver Is., almost every open, grassy habitat in Cascadia, from tidewater saltmarshes to montane meadows, vacant lots to freeway median strips, forest roadsides to sage-steppe desert, and unsprayed lawns. Throughout the W, plains to coast, S Canada to N AZ.

This rapid golden darter is the constant companion of late summer and fall days in most of Cascadia. From late July until early October, it may be the single most abundant butterfly. The appellation "woodland" comes from the European *O. sylvanus,* which our species resembles (*-oides* = "like"). It haunts all sorts of open areas, often in company with Mylitta Crescents and Purplish Coppers—sometimes a goldenrod or tansy ragwort drips with all three. Gardeners throughout the region note these numerous, "friendly" nectarers with pleasure. Frequently they appear in dry, grassy spots with a flower or two where you expect no butterflies at all, and may be found almost anywhere but the deep forest and high arctic-alpine. In my maritime valley, when hundreds of Woodlands throng the butterfly garden in late August and bask on Asian pear leaves in late sun, I find individuals resembling almost every named variety.

Rural Skipper   *Ochlodes agricola* (BOISDUVAL) 1852

Sausalito, Marin Co., CA
Aka Farmer, California Skipper

RECOGNITION > 1 in. Small, tawny orange above with a diffuse dark border. Male DFW with prominent black stigma, female with a black patch in the same place, **both sexes with a white glassy spot between the cell patch and tip, repeated below. VHW clear bright tawny on male, dusky purplish brown on female**, with vague row of light spots more pronounced on female. **VARIATION** Rural Skippers in SW OR are somewhere in between two CA ssp. in appearance, tawnier than the topotypic Marin Co. skippers, darker than those described from Plumas Co., and larger than either. The VHW markings tend to be poorly expressed. **HOST PLANTS** Grasses. Nectars on California buckeye (*Aesculus californica*), coyote mint (*Monardella villosa*), dogbane. **ON THE WING** L May to L

Male, dorsal

July, peak in E July. Prob. overwinters as young larva. **HABITAT AND RANGE** Forest openings and edges along streams and cooler slopes. N Baja through Alta CA in foothills, Coast Ranges to SW OR. Siskiyous, S Cascades in Curry, Josephine, Jackson, and Klamath cos.

Shapiro calls this a species that "eschews civilization." The old vernacular, the Farmer, is suitable both to its scientific name and its habitats. The Rural Skipper is a glassy-spotted, early summer species that barely reaches southern Oregon from California, much of which it occupies. Opler comments that these small, bright skippers congregate around California buckeyes for nectaring, courting, and mating, and Dornfeld reported it perching on shrubs along mountain roads in the Siskiyous. Rarer Rurals prefer more wooded habitats than the very common Woodland Skippers, and fly earlier in the season.

Male, ventral

Yuma Skipper   *Ochlodes yuma* (W. H. EDWARDS) 1873

Owens Lake, Inyo Co., CA
Aka Giant-reed Skipper

CANDIDATE IN WA, IMPERILED IN OR

RECOGNITION < 1.75 in. **Large, overall bright tawny with few obvious markings**. Male has narrow black margin, a **long, slender stigma**, and **bright, immaculate** vhw; the female may have pale spotbands D and V and black basal smudges on DFW. Not confusable with any other except the basin race of the Woodland Skipper (*O. sylvanoides bonnevilla*), similarly hued and plain, but Yuma averages 1.5 to 2 times larger and is finished flying before *O. s. bonnevilla* emerges most years. **VARIATION** Warren finds our NW specimens larger, the males darker orange, with less distinct black borders, than either the AZ-CA or paler NV populations. **HOST PLANTS** American common reed (*Phragmites australis* ssp. *americanus*). I found a small colony associated with variegated eulalia grass (*Miscanthus*) at

Male, dorsal

Maryhill State Park in E Klickitat Co., WA, the first record on anything other than *Phragmites*, and David James then reared it on *M. sinensis*. Nectars on thistles and yellow composites at marsh edges; in UT, visited Joe Pye weed, knapweed, and *Peritoma serrulata*. **ON THE WING** E July to E September, peak in August.

Male, ventral

A single NW generation, first-instar larvae overwinter. **HABITAT AND RANGE** Restricted to stands of reeds in low-elevation alkaline aridlands, usually around marshes, seeps, canals, rivers, and ponds. Great Basin from C-W AZ to SE (Lake Co.) OR, with N records in Hood River, Wasco, Sherman, and Wallowa cos, OR, and Grant, Klickitat, and Asotin cos, WA.

This large golden skipper typically restricts itself to far-flung *Phragmites* reedbeds. While the European form of the reed is widely

naturalized, Yuma occupies disjunct stands of the alkali-loving, native giant reed in the Great Basin and southwest deserts. Small colonies can occur many miles from the nearest stronghold, probably the result of post-glacial relictualism. Yuma can be abundant: I've seen hundreds on the wing in Dinosaur National Park, Utah; other times, only singletons show up, such as an old female I found where the Grande Ronde River enters the Snake. The species was known no farther north than Nevada until 1984, when Jonathan Pelham discovered a substantial colony at Sun Lakes–Dry Falls State Park, Grant County, Washington; this colony was almost lost to herbicides when spray crews mistook the native reed for the European. Ray Albright found the first Oregon records near Imnaha (Wallowa County) and Summer Lake (Lake County), and Ray Stanford has reported several sites along the Columbia. As yet, there is no sign that this handsome animal is spreading on miles of introduced reeds that line canals throughout the Columbia Basin Irrigation Project in Washington, but the Columbia and Snake River specimens might have leapfrogged on them.

Dun Skipper   *Euphyes vestris* (BOISDUVAL) 1852

Meadow Valley, Plumas Co., CA
Aka Sedge Witch, Dun Sedge Skipper, *E. ruricola*

RECOGNITION < 1.4 in. Dull (=dun) but **warm moleskin or violet-brown all over**, a little darker above, aging to plain dark tan. White "skipper marks" in the FW apex, and sometimes a vague vHW spotband, are more or less pronounced on the female. Male has dark-on-dark DFW stigma, edged with rusty scales, and often no other markings on longish, quite pointed wings. **Face, head, and thorax often furred with rusty red.** Common Sootywing is coal-black, the Common Roadside Skipper much smaller, other hesperiines more or less tawny; duskywings

mottled and broader-winged. **VARIATION** Most Cascadian Dun Skippers look much like the CA type, except for NE WA (Pend Oreille Co.) and ID records, which resemble Rocky Mtns *E. v. kiowah*—smaller, nearly devoid of light markings in both sexes, with little rust or purplish glossiness below. **HOST PLANTS** Sedges; Scott observed oviposition on *Carex heliophila* in CO. Nectars on fireweed, dogbane, lotus, horsemint, goldenrod, sweet William, thistle, and many others. **ON THE WING** L May to E September, peak in July. One generation in

Female, dorsal

Female, ventral

Male, dorsal

N, two or more farther S. Caterpillars hibernate in third instar. **HABITAT AND RANGE** Sedgy edges of woodland roads and watercourses, meadows, canyons, seeps, various wetlands and grasslands. W Coast and most of US from the Rockies E, and S Canada. In BC, WA, and OR, almost entirely in or W of Cascades except for a few records in Kittitas, Yakima, Klickitat, and Pend Oreille cos; rare in NE ID.

Several eastern members of this dark genus are known as "the witches." We have only this, often as singletons. Dun Skippers seldom achieve the great abundance here that they do in the Rockies and farther east, but they occupy a wide range of sites. In southwestern Washington, I have found them in my backyard in the Willapa Hills, on logging roads among second-growth hemlocks, at the head of a small tidal slough, and perching in "coves" or clearings among scrub alder in managed forest. One of the few butterflies that proliferates west of the Cascades and is almost absent on the east side, reversing the common pattern. Pelham found stable colonies along small seeps in cattle country around the Ellensburg valley, and a handful of sites in Pend Oreille County. Why should a butterfly so well adapted to the Rockies (and much of the country) absents itself from most of the Selkirks, the Okanogan Highlands, the Blues, and the Wallowas?

SUPERFAMILY PAPILIONOIDEA: SCUDDERS

The Latin *Papilio* (cognate of the French *papillon*, "butterfly") gave its name to Linnaeus' first butterfly genus in 1758; 44 years later, Latreille extended the name to the branch of the Lepidoptera containing the insects we all recognize as butterflies. These have long been called (rather unfortunately) the "true" butterflies, as opposed to the skippers. Scott coined an excellent punning name for the superfamily, the scudders. This name describes their scudding (as opposed to skipping) flight, while simultaneously commemorating the greatest lepidopterist of an earlier era, Samuel Hubbard Scudder, author of *The Butterflies of the* *Eastern United States and Canada with Special Reference to New England* (1889), a monumental work. Scudders are distinguished from skippers by having unhooked antennae, generally longer wings, and slenderer bodies, and therefore less wing-loading, enabling them to soar (or scud). All scudders share certain traits of wing venation, beyond which a wide array may be found in the details of branching, wing color, pattern, and shape. Most authorities recognize five families of scudders, all of which are represented in Cascadia. Perhaps 13,000 to 15,000 species occur worldwide.

FAMILY PAPILIONIDAE: PARNASSIANS AND SWALLOWTAILS

The largest butterflies in the world belong to this family. The biggest of all are the birdwings of New Guinea, occasionally reaching a foot in wingspan; our grandest species, the Two-tailed Tiger Swallowtail, might reach near half that in a very big female. Of the 550 or so species worldwide, most occur in the tropics. Cascadia has ten of these, two parnassians and eight swallowtails. Their three pairs of legs are all approximately the same size. The family is distinguished in the larval stage by the caterpillars possessing an eversible orange prong behind the head. When this osmeterium is projected, a strong, citrusy odor is given off. Predators are supposed to find this unappealing, but to many a person who has reared swallowtails, the scent is evocative of youthful days in the presence of caterpillars.

Papilionids are great nectarers and very strong flappers and gliders, frequently patrolling canyons or hillsides. Many species take part in mimicry complexes, either as models or mimics, or both. Of the three subfamilies, two follow, with summaries of their characteristics; the third consists of a single odd, primitive southern Mexican species, *Baronia brevicornis*.

Subfamily Parnassiinae: Parnassians and Festoons

These big white butterflies, dotted with scarlet and ebony, grace many of the alpine heights of the northern hemisphere. Only five species occur in North America, around 50 in about a dozen genera in the Old World. Their unlikely-seeming relationship to swallowtails is confirmed by elements of wing venation and larval morphology. They have long captured the imagination of lepidopterists and collectors, who have named a near-infinitude of local races. The type species, *Parnassius apollo* Linnaeus 1758, is the largest of all, with great red spots, but it is endangered in most of its Eurasian habitat from afforestation and other agricultural changes. The recent substitution of "apollo" for "parnassian" as the generic common name, by Scott and Canadian authors, is regrettable. These butterflies have been known as parnassians in North America for more than a century, and it would be sad to lose the English association with their mythic headquarters—Mount Parnassus, home of the gods—in favor of just one of those gods. Festoons are fancy, pinked Old World relatives belonging to the tribe Zerynthiini.

Parnassians exhibit a highly visible female sphragis. Some other butterflies possess this "biological chastity belt," but none so visibly. During mating, males exude a fluid and mold it into shape with their genitalia. This becomes the sphragis, a vaginal cap or plug that prevents any subsequent matings by the female, though it leaves her ovipositor free and clear. This ensures the passing of the first male's genes. In species of high places with unstable weather and short seasons, in which the males emerge a week or more before the females, this could be an adaptation to limit the amount of egg-laying time lost to successive matings, while ensuring gravid females will probably encounter fit, surviving males. The courtship itself is aggressive, the males simply taking the females down from the air and abruptly copulating with them. Males try to mate with capped females but almost never dislodge the plug.

McCorkle and Hammond (1986) showed that the larvae probably mimic cyanide-producing, black-and-yellow millipedes of the family Polydesmidae. In much of western Cascadia, Clodius Parnassian larvae coexist with polydesmid millipedes of the genus *Harpaphe* in large numbers. Since parnassians themselves are thought to be toxic to predators (hence the red spots in the adults), this may be a case of Müllerian rather than Batesian mimicry.

Clodius Parnassian (*Parnassius clodius*), newly emerged

Clodius Parnassian   *Parnassius clodius* MÉNÉTRIÉS 1855

Bear Valley, Marin Co., CA
Aka Clodius Apollo, American Apollo

P. C. SHEPARDI **CANDIDATE IN WA;** *P. C.*
ALTAURUS **SPECIAL CONCERN IN BC**

RECOGNITION < 3 in. **Large, milky to smoky
white**, with rounded, gray-black and red or
pink spots. **Red spots only on HW, not on FW;
antennae entirely black. FW bars gray,** black
in *P. smintheus*; wings of males substantially
transparent, females more so. Male abdomen
cream-furry, female shiny black with **big white
sphragis.** Ventrum often yellowish, with red
spots expanded. **VARIATION** Lots to do with
elevation, latitude, and moisture, with many
names applied. Large, bright, variable ssp.
occurs throughout W Cascadia, incl. the Coast
Ranges. High-elevation populations flying in
the N Cascades of WA and BC are smaller and
grayer with somewhat heavier HW markings.
Selkirk and Blue Mtns populations have
reduced red and black spotting. A very large

and lightly marked expression flies in the basalt
canyons of Garfield, Columbia, and Asotin cos,
SE WA, and Nez Perce and cos S in ID. In the
Siskiyous may be found the also large, very
white *P. c. sol.* A big, light Santa Cruz Mtns race,
P. c. strohbeeni, is thought to be extinct. **HOST
PLANTS** Bleeding heart (*Dicentra formosa*) in
W part of range, *D. uniflora, D. pauciflora,* and
D. cucullaria farther E and in drier habitats; a
population on Wizard Island in Crater Lake uses
stunted bleeding heart on basalt rubble. *Coryd-
alis* suspected but not demonstrated. Nectars
on candyflower (*Montia*), fireweed (*Epilobium*),
blackberry, Columbia lily, tansy ragwort, and
hawkbit, lower down; dogbane, red clover,
pearly everlasting, asters, marsh marigold,
and grass of parnassus in montane meadows
and roadsides. **ON THE WING** E May to M
September, peak in July. One generation, eggs
overwinter. **HABITAT AND RANGE** Open wood-

Male, dorsal

Female, dorsal

Female, ventral

Male, ventral

lands, roadsides, forest parklands, subalpine edges and chutes, riparian canyons, sea level to 7,000 feet. Absent from urbanized part of former range. NW N Am, SE AK to C CA, WY, UT. Montane and maritime Cascadia, absent from arid lowlands except for Hells Canyon region.

Clodius is one of the most conspicuous and common butterflies of the Northwest summer countryside, wherever wild bleeding hearts grow. People are often amazed by its beauty when they view it closely for the first time, with its cherry-red and inky spots on chalky, semi-transparent wings. The name was inspired by Clodius and his sister Clodia, less-than-admirable Roman citizens whose only virtue was such beauty that they were surnamed Pulcher. The European practice of naming every local population of parnassian as a different subspecies, carried to ridiculous lengths for *P. apollo* with hundreds of named varieties, extended to North America but with a little greater restraint. I am not at all sure that most of the named races mean very much, but as points on a continuum of variation they have some usefulness. The "shepardi" race, not currently accepted as a distinct subspecies, is one of the most interesting. Pioneer naturalist C. V.

Piper found it first at Wawawai in 1894, and Jon and Sigrid Shepard rediscovered it in the 1960s. The type locality and much of its habitat were inundated by controversial Snake River dams, but it survives in remote parts of Hells Canyon National Recreation Area. High-elevation Oregon parnassians, in *P. smintheus*-like habitats, always turn out to be Clodius. One male I netted in Three Sisters Wilderness had affixed to furry scales on its thorax a viable egg, which I took home and reared to the third instar.

Mountain Parnassian   *Parnassius smintheus* DOUBLEDAY 1847

Rock Lake, nr Jasper, AB
Aka Phoebus Parnassian, Rocky Mountain Parnassian, Smintheus Parnassian, Small Apollo, Rocky Mountain Apollo, *P. phoebus*

P. S. OLYMPIANNA IMPERILED IN BC

RECOGNITION < 2.5 in. **Large, white to dusky-transparent** with black and red spots, dark near body. **Red to pink spots often but not always on both FW and HW; antennae barred**

black and white. FW bars black, not gray as on *P. clodius*. Little or no transparency on male, more on female. Male abdomen creamy-furry, female shiny light or black with **small dark brown hooked sphragis.** Wings and fur of fresh adults, esp. males, can be quite yellowish

Female, dorsal

Male, dorsal

Male, ventral

Female, ventral

into Josephine and Jackson cos, OR. Highest colonies are the darkest. **HOST PLANTS** *Sedum lanceolatum* (Chumstick Mtn, Chelan Co., WA); *S. divergens* (Olympics), *S. stenopetalum* (Cascades), and *S. oreganum* (BC Coast Range); *Rhodiola integrifolia* (Sunrise Peak, Skamania Co., WA). Nectars on sedums, yellow composites, and lewisias. **ON THE WING** L April to M October, peak in July. One brood, but biennialism may occur, eggs spending the first winter, older larvae hibernating a second time. **HABITAT AND RANGE** Upper elevations to the highest arctic-alpine, where sedums grow. Generally flying higher than Clodius, though they overlap in the mid-montane. Dry rocky ridges, summits, fellfields, tundra, S slopes and meadows; 1,000 to 8,500+ feet, N AK to NM and CA, all higher BC, WA, and ID ranges, but in OR, only the NE and SW, strangely absent from OR Cascades.

below. **VARIATION** *P. s. olympianna* (Olympic Parnassian) in the Olympic and Vancouver Is. mtns is small and dark, esp. females. *P. s. magnus* is the biggish, variable ssp. of the BC and WA Cascades and Okanogan Highlands and the Blue-Wallowa Mtns in SE WA and NE OR, with spots ranging from almost absent to pronounced. *P. s. sternitskyi* (Sternitsky's Parnassian) of the Siskiyous has big red spots, the lower one on the HW white-centered; it nips

Parnassians are frequent companions of hikers in the mountains and forests, Clodius earlier and lower, Mountain higher and later. Females are reminiscent of smoked glass. The red spots fade with age from deep scarlet to pale salmon, and vary from big and striking to almost missing on some montane individuals. Mountain Parnassian flies in great numbers across the highlands of the region but drops out of the Cascades south of the Columbia, perhaps due in part to recent volcanic history. This species flies in colder places and temperatures than most butterflies, sometimes in falling snow. First described as *P. smintheus*, it was later lumped with the Holarctic *P. phoebus*; Shepard resurrected *P. smintheus* based on structure of the micropyle of the egg and other traits, with *P. phoebus* restricted to Alaska. Phoebus ("brilliant," "shining") Apollo was the son of Leto and Zeus. In the *Iliad*, Homer called Apollo "the Sminthian" (the Mouse-god "but whether because he protected mice or destroyed them no one knows," according to Edith Hamilton.

Subfamily Papilioninae: Swallowtails, Kites, and Birdwings

These are the classical butterflies of most people's common conception. Many species possess hindwing extensions, or "tails," as distractive targets for predators; many others do not. Their hosts are umbellifers or *Artemisia* for the black swallowtails, broad-leaved trees and shrubs for the tigers. Both subgroups begin larval life as a saddled black imitation of a bird dropping, then molt into a handsome, smooth-skinned creature, green with false yellow and blue eyes in the tigers, dramatic rings of black, orange, and sometimes pink in the blacks. Their chrysalides hang diagonally upright, anchored by a silk posterior button and a silk strand or "girdle" around the thorax, and generally spend the winter. The three tribes are Papilionini (most of the North American species belong

here); Troidini, an *Aristolochia*-feeding group including the birdwings, and of which we have just one, the Pipevine Swallowtail; and the Leptocercini or Graphini, containing the fast-flying, long-tailed kites. No kites occur in Cascadia, but our Pale Tiger is sometimes confused with one, the Zebra Swallowtail of the eastern states.

Pipevine Swallowtail   *Battus philenor* (LINNAEUS) 1771

"America"
Aka Blue Swallowtail

RECOGNITION < 4 in. Long, narrow black wings, dorsum coal-black (male) to dark slate (female), **glazed and shot with brilliant metallic blue** esp. on male HW; dorsal submarginal row of blue-green to yellow spots much more pronounced on female. Dark gray **VHW with Mylar-blue outer half, ringed by big, black-rimmed, persimmon-red spots. VARIATION** W Coast *B. p. hirsuta* is somewhat smaller than the type, and has longer scales on the thorax, abdomen, and wing bases, giving it a slightly hairy (hirsute) look. The amount and shade of blue varies with individual, gender, age, angle, and intensity of the light. **HOST PLANTS** Aristolochiaceae: native and ornamental pipevines (*Aristolochia*); *A. californica* used in N CA. Tilden and Smith report wild ginger (*Asarum caudatum*), and Scott adds that females and larvae usually refuse *A. canadense*. **ON THE WING** L April to L July. Multiple generations S, one in N, chrysalides overwinter. **HABITAT AND RANGE** Canyons, desert washes, scrub, fields, and parklands where the host grows, though adults may wander, esp. males. S Mexico to S US, spreading N with season and incidence of ornamental pipevines; breeding resident in N-C CA, coincident with *Aristolochia californica*. OR records from Coos, Jackson, and Klamath cos.

Female, ventral

The extraordinarily beautiful, iridescent blue Pipevine Swallowtail, which occurs in a resident population north of Sacramento Valley, has been found just four times in southwestern Oregon. The first I found in the collection of Angus Hutton in Papua New Guinea! He had struck it with his car at North Bend in southwest-coastal Oregon,

Female, dorsal

Male, dorsal

and saw others. Subsequent finds have come from Ashland and Klamath Falls. Our sole West Coast member of Troidini, the essentially tropical tribe containing the giant birdwings. If it indeed uses or adapts to wild ginger, a common Cascadian woodland plant, or if *Aristolochia* moves northward as the climate warms, this species might spread farther into Cascadia. Pipevine renders the adults distasteful, so its looks (and range) are copied by several mimics in the heart of its range, including females of several swallowtails, the Red-spotted Purple, and the female Diana Fritillary.

Male, ventral

Oregon Swallowtail   *Papilio machaon* LINNAEUS 1758

"Europae"
Aka Old World Swallowtail (NABA), Baird's Swallowtail,
Artemisia Swallowtail, *P. oregonius/-a, bairdii*

RECOGNITION < 4 in. **Large, broad-winged, with broad bands of cheesy yellow bars across black background,** with lots of yellow dusting in basal black of DFW, even more below. Blue postmedian HW spots lined with orange; caudal orange-red spot has **clubbed black pupil eccentric and touching outer rim,** centered in Anise. **Abdomen yellow with narrow black stripes on top and sides;** Anise abdomen is black with narrow yellow stripes. **VARIATION** The Eurasian type and *P. m. aliaska* quite different with orange caudal patch orchid-rimmed and black pupil at edge. *P. m. oregonia* quite constant in Cascadia. *P. m. bairdii,* of the SW and Great Basin, comes in both black and yellow forms, but ours are always yellow. **HOST PLANTS** Umbelliferae in Europe; Oregon Swallowtail restricted to tarragon (*Artemisia dracunculus*) in the wild, though it can be reared on carrot or parsley. Both umbels and *Artemisia* incl. the feeding-cue chemical anisic aldehyde. Nectars on thistles, rudbeckia, balsamroot, zinnia, petunia, phlox, *Vicia cracca,* milkweed, and wild roses. Males hilltop avidly. **ON THE WING** M March to

Female, dorsal (ssp. *oregonia*)

Female, ventral (ssp. *oregonia*)

Male, dorsal (ssp. *oregonia*)

M October, peaks in May-June and August-September. Two broods, pupae overwinter. **HABITAT AND RANGE** Basalt canyons, shores, and slopes in arid interior where the host plant grows, and the cliffs, plateaus, and mtns above. Holarctic; in NW, C-S BC, most of WA E of the Cascade Crest, C, NE, and SE OR, and W ID.

The Oregon Swallowtail was designated the official Oregon State Insect in 1979. Based on differing views of genetic data, some swallowtail researchers place it in the Western Black Swallowtail (*P. bairdii*), while others conclude that both *bairdii* and *oregonia* are subspecies of the circumpolar and probably ancestral Old World Swallowtail (*Papilio machaon*). The first butterfly Linnaeus described, he named after the physician to the Greeks at Troy. *P. m. bairdii* honors Spencer Fullerton Baird, the celebrated secretary of the Smithsonian Institution who greatly furthered biological exploration in the 19th century. *P. m. oregonia* was described from The Dalles in 1876 by W. H. Edwards. L. I. Hewes, in a 1936 *National Geographic* portrait, wrote that "*Oregonia* is a crisp, sharply marked denizen of the arid wind . . . utterly devoid of leisure," living among "terraced basalt and . . . blistering rocks." That pretty much describes how one must approach it. It does not seem to use Suksdorf's wormwood (*Artemisia suksdorfii*), common all the way to tidewater on the Columbia, thus limiting its downriver range; but this may change with warming.

Anise Swallowtail   *Papilio zelicaon* LUCAS 1852

"Californie"
Aka Zelicaon Swallowtail, Western Swallowtail

RECOGNITION < 3.5 in. Medium to large, broad bands of lemon- to butter-yellow bars across background. Base of DFW mostly black, FW shorter, less drawn out than on Oregon Swallowtail. **Caudal red-orange spot has free, round black pupil. Abdomen black with yellow side-stripes**, unlike Oregon. **VARIATION** Other ssp. and/or forms occur elsewhere, but the main CA type flies in Cascadia. Varies significantly in size, ranging from small alpine males to big maritime females; the ground color too varies from pale to bright yellow, and some are much blacker than others. **HOST PLANTS** Wide range of native and introduced umbellifers (Wehling listed 69 host plants in 39 genera), incl. desert parsleys (*Lomatium*), inland, alpine; cow parsley (*Heracleum*) and sea-watch (*Angelica lucida*), coastward; and fennel (*Foeniculum*), urban. Nectars on lilac, lupine, beach pea, camas, pink allium, yellow mustard, azalea, columbine, fireweed, coltsfoot, balsamroot, gumweed, yarrow, pearly everlasting, hawkbit, thistles, manzanita, and penstemons. **ON THE WING** L February to L September, peaks in May and July-August. One brood in higher and drier locations, oppor-

tunistic second (and third?) generations in urban or coastal sites where growing season permits and moisture maintains succulent forage. Pupae overwinter. **HABITAT AND**

RANGE Almost every habitat, from saltmarsh to urban parks, gardens, and weedy alleys, to deserts, forest clearings, canyons, and alpine summits. Throughout W N Am from Baja to N BC, potentially everywhere in Cascadia but deep woods. Males puddle and hilltop ferociously on mountaintops, looking for females; females frequent slopes and bottoms in search of umbels.

This common but beautiful swallowtail possesses one of the broadest ecological amplitudes of any of our butterflies, meaning it prospers in a remarkable array of places and conditions. At Leadbetter Point, in Willapa Bay National Wildlife Refuge, the butterfly has two distinct broods on angelica growing right down to tidewater; 40 miles southeast, on the Julia Butler Hansen Refuge for the Columbian White-tailed Deer, cow parsnip is the provender of choice; and up the Columbia Gorge at Catherine Creek, it is Gray's lomatium. In the Central District of Seattle, the abundance of escaped sweet fennel in vacant lots and alleys permits a fall

Female, ventral

Male, dorsal

brood. The larvae feed happily on garden anise, but the common name comes from a frequent California host, *Perideridia*, which grew prolifically in wetlands; it was a winter staple for the Miwok, who called it yampah, but it was known as wild anise to Europeans. An easy guest for butterfly gardens.

Indra Swallowtail   *Papilio indra* REAKIRT 1866

"Pike's Peak, Colorado Terr."

Aka Short-tailed Black Swallowtail, Short-tailed Swallowtail, Cliff Swallowtail

---

CRITICALLY IMPERILED IN BC

RECOGNITION < 2.5 in. Indra is our only black swallowtail that is really mostly black. Small for a swallowtail, with **very short tails. Coal-black with bands of small yellow spots** across wings, broader on the HW. Blue submarginal spots on HW, larger on female, and red-orange caudal spot with black pupil. Anise has much broader yellow bands, even in dark individuals. **VARIATION** Of the many W ssp., two fly in our bioregion. The type covers most of the range. *P. i. shastensis* extends from Napa Co., CA, N into the Siskiyous and S Cascades of Josephine, Jackson, and Klamath cos, OR. The authors characterize it as darker than the type, with the postmedian yellow bands being narrower by about half. **HOST PLANTS** Umbels, mostly in the genus *Lomatium* in Cascadia (Newcomer recorded it on *L. papilioniferum* in Yakima Co.). Seldom seen nectaring, but females sometimes visit mints and composites, and males frequently mudpuddle, sometimes with as many as five other species of swallowtails. **ON THE WING** L March to M August, peak in May. The single brood overwinter as pupae. **HABITAT AND RANGE** Dry ravines, canyons, riverbanks and roadsides, hilltops, and rocky desert washes. Many W ranges, from S BC to Baja. In WA, E Cascades and the Columbia, Okanogan, Palouse, and Blue Mtns; mountainous N-C, NE, and SW OR, Steens Mtn, and W-C ID.

Male, dorsal

Male, ventral

The Indra Swallowtail is particular about location, and seldom especially numerous. Sometimes you can find males mud-puddling in some numbers. At canyon seeps in the Colorado Front Range and lakeshores in the Okanogan, we have seen mud-puddle clubs involving dozens of swallowtails of five or six species, including a good smattering of Indra. In Icicle Canyon near Leavenworth on a day in May, fresh, jet-black Indras and lemony Anises studded the damp riverside mud as harlequin ducks took their rest in the sun on mid-river boulders. The Oregon distribution is odd, with Indra flying in the Siskiyous and on Steens Mountain but seemingly skipping the whole of the Cascades between Mt. Jefferson and the California border.

Canadian Tiger Swallowtail *Papilio canadensis*
ROTHSCHILD & JORDAN 1906

"Newfoundland"
Aka Eastern Tiger Swallowtail, Tiger Swallowtail, *Pterourus*, *glaucus*

RECOGNITION < 3.5 in. Medium-large, bright yellow with medium-width black border and tiger-stripes across all wings. Unlike on Western Tiger, **uppermost DHW crescent is orange**, and there is some or much **orange on VHW marginal crescents**. Orange flushing and blue spotband on VHW more intense than on the usually larger Western. **VARIATION** No ssp. The orange on the VHW is both the most variable and distinctive trait. **HOST PLANTS** Salicaceae, incl. willows, birches, poplars, and alders. Nectars on spreading dogbane and groundsel along forest edges; males puddle. **ON THE WING** E April to E August, peak in June. A single generation, chrysalides overwinter. **HABITAT AND RANGE** Open woodland glades, roadsides, and streambanks, edges of meadows, and lightly wooded slopes; boreal conifer and aspen groves. All across subarctic Canada, dipping into N MT, ID, and WA in Ferry and Okanogan cos.

Male, dorsal

Male, ventral

Wesley Rogers first found Washington specimens referable to this species (then considered a subspecies of the Eastern Tiger) near Oroville, Okanogan County. Some have suggested that Cascadian individuals represent introgression of Canadian genes into Western Tiger populations through hybridization. As well as hybrids, Guppy and Shepard record *P. canadensis* in the Ashnola River Valley near the Washington border, collected by Norbert Kondla. Layberry et al. show the species' range all along the northwestern U.S. border. Hybrids occur, but tigers vary in the diagnostic traits, and determining hybrids reliably is difficult. In British Columbia, this is the more common butterfly where both Canadians and Westerns fly; south of the border, the reverse is true, as if they could read their own names. I have yet to find a good example in Washington, but I have seen it in the Yaak Valley of northwestern Montana. Tiger swallowtails are so common in summertime that most lepidopterists take them for granted. Careful sampling of yellow tigers in northern locales, such as the birchwoods of Pend Oreille County and forests above the Columbia and Okanogan rivers, might show that *P. canadensis* is more abundant south of Canada than we have hitherto appreciated.

Western Tiger Swallowtail   *Papilio rutulus* LUCAS 1852

N Fk Feather R., Plumas Co., CA
Aka Tiger Swallowtail, *Pterourus, glaucus*

RECOGNITION > 3.5 in. Large. **Bright yellow with medium-broad black border and tiger-stripes** across wings; submarginal metallic blue zones on HW, expanded below. Caudal red-orange crescents at the inner angle of the single-tailed HW. From the tail up, **marginal HW crescents are yellow; upper one on DHW never orange** as on Canadian. Pale Tiger has broad black stripes and is nearly white; Two-tailed Tiger has narrow bands and

Female, dorsal

double-tailed HW. **VARIATION** Females are larger, lighter, broader-winged than males; yellow varies from rich to pale. **HOST PLANTS** Broadleaved trees incl. bigleaf maples, willows, aspen, black cottonwood, and plane trees in cities. Nectars on blackberry, thistles, helianthella, hawkbit, yarrow, balsamroot, teasel, alfalfa, sweet William, red columbine, phlox, lilac, rhododendron. Males mudpuddle. **ON THE WING** M April to L September, peak in June. One generation in N, successive broods farther S; extended emergence period and longer life than smaller butterflies. Pupae overwinter. **HABITAT AND RANGE** Riversides, canyon streams, woodland glades, parks and gardens, many others. W of the Great Plains from S BC to N Mexico, throughout Cascadia.

Without doubt the Western Tiger is the most familiar butterfly to Cascadians, who more often than not think they are Monarchs. Having adapted to a wide array of trees and human habitats, *P. rutulus* makes one of the best all-round urban butterflies. Though they browse in numbers insufficient to damage ornamentals, they are susceptible to tree-spraying, including the Btk bacterium sprayed against gypsy moth infestations. Such eradication zones may end up without

their swallowtails and other butterflies for years. Occasional hybridization occurs between Eastern and Western Tigers. Human settlement doubtless brought the two species together through irrigation and shade-tree planting. Where several kinds of swallowtails mudpuddle together, this species is usually more abundant than the others, though sometimes that distinction belongs to Pales or Two-taileds. Male Western Tigers seek females by flying up and down corridors such as creekbeds or canyons. Stand in a likely canyon or along a woodland edge and you'll see the same ones patrol back and forth again and again. Females may be seen around the foliage of their host trees, often flirting among the leaves high up in the woodland canopy. The epithet comes from the Rutulians, a fierce Italian tribe opposed to the Trojans settling in their territory.

Female, ventral

Male, ventral

Pale Tiger Swallowtail   *Papilio eurymedon* LUCAS 1852

N Fk Feather R., Plumas Co., CA

Aka Pale Swallowtail (NABA), Pallid Tiger Swallowtail, *Pterourus*

RECOGNITION > 3 in. Large. Ground color **chalky white or creamy with very broad black borders and tiger-stripes**. Little or no yellow scaling. Band width distinguishes it from washed-out Western Tigers that lose most of their yellow. Shiny blue HW areas reduced except on brighter females, but the red-orange caudal spots can be extensive. **VARIATION** No named geographic races. **HOST PLANTS** In the NW, chiefly *Ceanothus cuneatus* (buckbrush) and *C. velutinus* (snowbrush ceanothus) E of the Cascades, red alder and cascara on the W side; oceanspray, serviceberry, bitter cherry, and hardhack (*Spiraea douglasii*) are also used. Nectars on chokecherry, mints, Columbia lilies, sweet William, penstemons, toothwort, lilacs, and phlox; visits sprinklers. **ON THE WING** M April to E October, peak in May-June. One generation, chrysalides overwinter. **HABITAT AND RANGE** Open woodlands and chaparral, or the Cascadian equivalent, broadleaved scrub in hilly, open terrain; montane canyons and slopes, ocean bluffs, and shrubby/flowery spots from sea level to high summits. Intermountain W from S BC to Baja and NM, all our region except driest basins and deeper forests.

Female, dorsal

Male, dorsal

Midwesterners come west often mistake Pale Tigers for Zebra Swallowtails (*Eurytides marcellus*). That species, which feeds on pawpaw E of the Great Plains, has much longer tails and even whiter wings with long red slashes below. The Pale Tiger is a versatile butterfly—I've seen it sailing over the Dungeness Bluffs, lined up at mud like frigates at anchor in the Chumstick Mountains, lingering over sweet Williams in my butterfly garden, gracing every pendent head of Columbia lily in a Mt. Adams woodland, and jousting with four other papilionids at the summit of Rattlesnake Mountain above the Hanford Reach.

Not as common overall as *P. rutulus* nor as ubiquitous as *P. zelicaon*, it nonetheless fairly swarms over dry-side slopes of snowbrush ceanothus along with California Tortoise-shells, and at damp spots on the floors of Cascadian canyons such as Tumwater, Icicle, or Santiam, in the company of duskywings and blues. Pale males hilltop to find females, and patrol like the other tigers. They may hang around for a while on one summit, then move far along the ridge to try another spot. Like Western Tigers, these frequent road-sides—who has not tried to dodge swallowtails while crossing Cascades passes in June! The resulting roadkills, though sad, offer an opportunity for obtaining study specimens, since close encounters with windshields often leave the wings unblemished.

Male, ventral

Two-tailed Tiger Swallowtail *Papilio multicaudata* W. F. KIRBY 1884

"Mexique"
Aka Two-tailed Swallowtail (NABA), Doubletail, *Pterourus*, *multicaudatus*, *daunus*

RECOGNITION < 5 in. **Very large.** Bright warm yellow with **black border, tiger-stripes noticeably narrower** than on the Western Tiger. **HW has two tails rather than one,** and the nub of a third. Submarginal metallic blue patches extensive around posterior orange spots on DHW and running up VHW and VFW, esp. in females. **VARIATION** Ours are smaller, paler, narrower-striped, and straighter-winged than those in SW US/N Mexico. **HOST PLANTS** In Cascadia mostly western chokecherry (*Prunus virginiana* var. *demissa*) in natural areas, green ash (*Fraxinus pennsylvanica*) in E-side towns. Pelham found that larvae feeding on chokecherry would not change to bitter cherry (*P. emarginata*) or ash. Nectars on cherries, columbine, larkspurs, thistles,

teasel, knapweed, mints, soapwort, and scarlet gilia. **ON THE WING** L March to M September, peak in June. A single generation, but occasional autumn emergents appear. Pupae overwinter. **HABITAT AND RANGE** Canyons and

Female, dorsal

watercourses, parks and gardens, shrublands, backyards, shady streets, E of the Cascades in BC, WA, to SW OR, and S throughout the W.

The butterfly affectionately called Double-tail (whose scientific name means "multiple tails") is the second biggest butterfly in North America; Cascadian females may exceed five inches in wingspan. Only the Giant Swallowtail (*P. cresphontes*), a southern citrus-feeder, sometimes has a broader wingspread. For such a grand butterfly, it is also common, gracing city streets from Kelowna to Guadalajara, where it soars abundantly over dense urban traffic. Having adapted to feed on green ash, one of the commonest shade trees in aridland towns, the Two-tail thrives in places like Othello, Washington, and Burns, Oregon. W. D. Wright (1905) wrote that this tireless species "seems never to stop to feed or to rest, but is always in rapid flight." Males course up and down canyons after females.

Male, ventral

Male, dorsal

FAMILY PIERIDAE: WHITES, MARBLES, AND SULPHURS

More than a thousand species make up this cosmopolitan family, ranging from smaller than a copper to swallowtail-sized, and many of them capable of vast abundance and mass movement. Yellow and white colors predominate among most of the species due to pteridine pigments in the scales; bright orange wingtips and striking black marginal patterns are common. Pierids are fairly closely related to swallowtails and share with them the silken girdle that holds the chrysalis upright at a cant from a vertical surface. Though present almost everywhere, pierids thrive especially in two districts that exclude many other butterflies: the High Arctic and intensively man-made environments. Having adapted to weedy crucifers and legumes, they proliferate in many agricultural fields and cities. The first butterfly one sees upon visiting a new region is usually some sort of pierid, comfortably situated among the weeds and fumes of the airport runway apron. Others are at home in high, clean, wild places, more in keeping with their namesake, the Pierides. The daughters of Zeus and Mnemosyne, the Pierides (aka the Muses) lived in Pieria, in Thessaly.

Subfamily Coliadinae: Sulphurs, Yellows, and Oranges

Some 300 coliadines occur around the world, including some of the most northerly, truly Arctic species as well as many torrid-zone specialists and pantropical generalists. Many genera, in fact, dwell chiefly in the tropics and deserts, but our major genus, *Colias*, penetrates south of the Tropic of Cancer (as in the Andes) only in montane habitats. Most species feed as larvae on the foliage of legumes (Fabaceae), with a few boreal exceptions on heaths (Ericaceae) and willows (*Salix*).

Orange Sulphur puddle party

Comparison of Sulphurs (Subfamily Coliadinae)
Specimens are shown approximately at 60% of life size

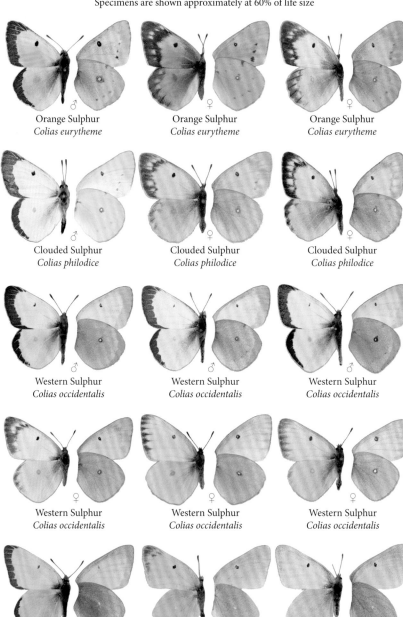

Orange Sulphur
Colias eurytheme

Orange Sulphur
Colias eurytheme

Orange Sulphur
Colias eurytheme

Clouded Sulphur
Colias philodice

Clouded Sulphur
Colias philodice

Clouded Sulphur
Colias philodice

Western Sulphur
Colias occidentalis

Western Sulphur
Colias occidentalis

Western Sulphur
Colias occidentalis

Western Sulphur
Colias occidentalis

Western Sulphur
Colias occidentalis

Western Sulphur
Colias occidentalis

Queen Alexandra's Sulphur
Colias alexandra

Queen Alexandra's Sulphur
Colias alexandra

Queen Alexandra's Sulphur
Colias alexandra

Comparison of Sulphurs (Subfamily Coliadinae)
Specimens are shown approximately at 60% of life size

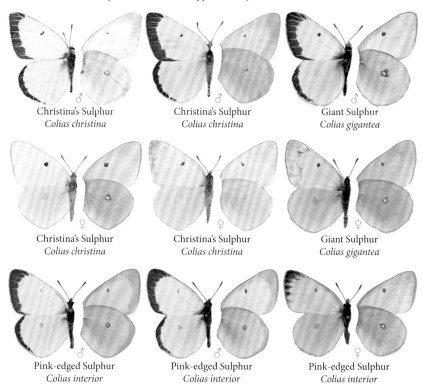

Christina's Sulphur
Colias christina
♂

Christina's Sulphur
Colias christina
♂

Giant Sulphur
Colias gigantea
♂

Christina's Sulphur
Colias christina
♀

Christina's Sulphur
Colias christina
♀

Giant Sulphur
Colias gigantea
♀

Pink-edged Sulphur
Colias interior
♂

Pink-edged Sulphur
Colias interior
♂

Pink-edged Sulphur
Colias interior
♀

Specimens below are shown approximately at 80% of life size

Skinner's Sulphur
Colias skinneri
♂

Skinner's Sulphur
Colias skinneri
♀

Skinner's Sulphur
Colias skinneri
♀

Labrador Sulphur
Colias nastes
♂

Labrador Sulphur
Colias nastes
♀

Dainty Sulphur *Nathalis iole* BOISDUVAL 1836

"Mexique"
Aka Dwarf Yellow

RECOGNITION < 1 in. Unmistakable—and **tiny. Butter-yellow above with broadly black DFW tips** and diffuse black bars along trailing edge of FW and leading edge of HW, more extensive on **female, which may also have black borders** and orange DHW. Yellow and black below with orange FW costa, HW more or less olive. **VARIATION** Highly variable, with spring emergers much darker olive below. Females darker overall. White males occur in some populations. No ssp. are recognized. **HOST PLANTS** A great generalist, feeding on a wide variety of weedy and garden composites incl. sneezeweed (*Helenium*), beggarticks (*Bidens*), marigolds, and cosmos, often nectaring on

Male, ventral (spring)

Male, ventral (summer)

same. **ON THE WING** Sole Cascadian record: 31 July. In CO: E May to E December. Multiple generations irrupt toward the N; no stage over-winters in the N. **HABITAT AND RANGE** Weedy and disturbed locations, grazed aridlands, parks and gardens, urban-edge abandoned agricultural fields, esp. along watercourses such as irrigation ditches and creeks, and beside roadsides, railroad lines, and rights-of-way; but found at high elevations also in the Rocky Mtns. Resident from S US/N Mexico and S. Migrates in summer throughout C US and S Canada, rarely reaching NW and NE. Very rare in SE WA, SW ID, NW NV, W MT.

The only really tiny sulphur outside southern climes. In late July 1975, my party found seven fresh males of the Dainty Sulphur near the confluence of the Grande Ronde and Snake rivers in southeastern Washington. That same year, Steve Kohler caught one near Missoula. Later, an older record emerged from Gibbonsville, Idaho. These are still the only Northwest records for the smallest American pierid. When spring conditions in the South favor an extravagant growth of host plants and nectar, and weather favors travel, great but dispersed cadres of Dainty Sulphurs advance northward out of the deserts. During the best years for *N. iole* migrations, modest numbers sometimes reach beyond mid-continent and make it into the Northwest and Northeast. These occurrences are recorded many years and miles apart, but always along watercourses such as the Snake and the Shenandoah. The Dainty Sulphur infiltrates the North for the season, colonizing weedy habitats and bringing off successive, rapid generations. Whether many individuals travel great distances themselves, or each brood hopscotches northward a bit at a time, is not certain; a Monarch tag would cover their whole wings. The presence of those seven on the Grande Ronde, probably siblings, indicates that a gravid female likely made it there from some distance away. When you encounter a Dainty Sulphur, there is no doubt about what you are seeing. Keep a lookout, as there are bound to be additional occurrences along Cascadian watercourses as the climate warms.

Male, dorsal; pair, ventral

Other Immigrant Sulphurs

Certain species of tropical and subtropical sulphurs conduct northward migrations, seldom as dramatically as *Nathalis iole*, but in many years contributing individuals far beyond their usual range. A couple of species have nipped into the Northwest and been noticed, and others might be seen by collectors and watchers willing to look carefully at solo sulphurs in disparate localities. Here are six possible vagrants to keep in mind.

Cloudless Giant Sulphur / *Phoebis sennae* (Linnaeus) 1758 / "Cassia Americes." Paul Hammond sighted one on 23 May 1992, on the Willow Creek Preserve near Eugene, Oregon, and one other has been seen in Douglas County, Oregon. This powerful sulphur with bright, plain, greenish yellow wings, mottled with reddish below, is as gigantic as the Dainty Sulphur is tiny. Great movements occur in the East, but western sightings are dispersed.

Tailed Orange / *Pyrisitia proterpia* (Fabricius) 1775 / "Jamaica." The only one ever found in our region was taken by Jon Pelham at his grandmother's house in Stayton, Oregon, on 12 August 1964. There was a cannery in Stayton, and the butterfly might have been a stowaway in a boxcar. Whether it arrived as a hobo riding the rails or as a chrysalis on a travel trailer we will never know, but its natural arrival cannot be ruled out, since it is a famous long-distance disperser. Males are brilliant citrus-orange with black leading edges, females ochre with black tips, both possessing longer or shorter pointed tails depending upon the season.

The following species of wandering yellows have been found in surrounding states, just a few counties from Cascadia, at least once.

California Dogface / *Zerene eurydice* (Boisduval) 1855 / Marin Co., CA. The California State Butterfly. Large,

A pair of Cloudless Giant Sulphurs (*Phoebis sennae*)

orangey-yellow with orchid overtones and a broad black border indented like a poodle's profile with a black eye. Recorded north to Shasta County.

Southern Dogface / *Zerene cesonia* (Stoll) 1790 / Georgia. Light yellow with the same poodle-face design. Recorded to northwest Nevada (Washoe County) and Mariposa and Mono counties, California. On the wing, it looks like a great big sulphur, which it is.

Mexican Yellow / *Eurema mexicana* (Boisduval) 1836 / "Mexique." Pale yellow and poodle-faced, smaller, with short tails, in any habitat. A record from Eureka County, Nevada, begins to approach Oregon. In Colorado it often ends up at high altitudes.

Sleepy Orange / *Abaeis nicippe* (Cramer) 1775 / "Virginien." Resembles the Tailed Orange's intense orange above, but duller, with black border on all four rounded wings, and no tails. A single occurrence in Flathead County, Montana, places the species near our territory.

Tailed Orange (*Pyrisitia proterpia*)

Genus *Colias*: Sulphurs

Throughout their circumpolar range fly some 70 species of *Colias*, almost all with a similar pattern. This overall similarity creates difficulties when it comes to identification, exacerbated by the facts that species very similar in appearance may be biologically distinct, while species that seem different may hybridize. These problems are highly evident in Cascadia, with some taxonomic relationships (and many individual specimens) still unclear; and a revision of the genus, not reflected here, has been proposed (Hammond and McCorkle 2017). Even so, many of our Northwest sulphurs (aka sulfurs) sort out reasonably well by wing features, range, and habitat.

The important characters are 1) the ground color of the dorsal surface of the wings, which is some shade of yellow, orange, grayish green, or (in form "alba" females) whitish; 2) the presence, absence, and nature of the black border on the upperside; 3) the color and density of dark scaling on the ventral hindwing; 4) the presence or absence and distribution of brown spots on the ventral hindwing ("eurytheme spots"); and 5) the structure, shape, and color of the discal spot on both dorsal and ventral hindwings. Most of the underside characters are easily seen, since the adults perch with their wings closed over their backs, and sulphurs readily pause to nectar and mudpuddle. However, photographers will be frustrated trying to shoot their uppersides, and no butterflies lead netters on a merrier, more often futile chase than sulphurs.

Clouded Sulphur *Colias philodice* GODART 1819

Virginia
Aka Common Sulphur

RECOGNITION < 2.5 in. Pale butter-yellow above, yellow or lime-green below (or may have significant orange). Males have pure charcoal or black border on dorsum, yellow-spotted on females. Many females lack yellow pigment and are white (form "alba") but still have border. DFW has oval black cell-spot, DHW round orange central spot. **VFW with a few blackish submarginal spots; VHW with up to six vague or prominent brown "eurytheme" spots in a submarginal row and a prominent dark spot at the costa; VHW discal spot pearly with double, concentric (not fused) red rings, usually with a satellite spot** of the same sort. Fringes pink. Western Sulphurs have fewer, less prominent, or no "eurytheme" spots. Orange Sulphur "alba" females may be indistinguishable, but tend to be larger and have the dark border better developed on the DHW. **VARIATION** Compared to the E type, our W *C. p. eriphyle* trends smaller and paler with reduced spotting and ringing on ventrum, often lacks the satellite spot, and has pointier FW. Spring individuals are smaller yet, more heavily dusted with dark scales, and greener than the yellower, larger

Female, dorsal

Female, ventral

Male, ventral (spring)

Male, ventral (summer)

Pair, dorsal

summer hatchers. Rarely orange individuals occur, some of which are hybrids with *C. eurytheme* and some not, but these cannot readily be told apart. **HOST PLANTS** Many recorded, all Fabaceae, incl. *Astragalus* (milkvetch), *Oxytropis* (locoweed), *Lathyrus* (pea), *Medicago sativa* (alfalfa), *Melilotus* (sweetclover), *Trifolium* (clovers, esp. red and white), *Vicia* (vetch), *Hedysarum* (sweetvetch), *Lupinus* (lupine), *Thermopsis* (goldenbanner), and garden peas. Nectars briefly on alfalfa, asters, and many other flowers rarely visited by butterflies, incl. serviceberry. Males visit mud. **ON THE WING** E April to M October, peaks in May, June, and August. At least three broods in warmer, drier parts of the region. Broods overlap in summer as individuals move up and down in elevation, so it is possible to see Clouded Sulphurs any time after L June in C Cascadia. Third- or fourth-instar larvae overwinter, giving them an early spring start. **HABITAT AND RANGE** Many types, wild and agricultural. Frequent in alfalfa fields with the Orange Sulphur. Found along forest roads and edges of meadows, not in deep forest. N Am except W Coast strip. Resident throughout most of basin and E montane Cascadia up to about 4,000 feet, expanding its range in summer to incl. alpine habitats and crossing the crest to occupy Salish Lowlands and Willamette Valley, but far less so than Orange Sulphurs.

The appearance of the Clouded Sulphur in Cascadia seems less a case of "everywhere" than "anywhere," except along the Pacific Coast strip. *C. philodice* is resident in areas where Orange Sulphurs seldom survive the winter, but yellows show up on the West Slope in summer much less frequently than do oranges. Though the two often hybridize in alfalfa fields, Clouded Sulphurs with orange on them also occur naturally, and cannot readily be told from hybrids or early season Orange Sulphurs. Therefore the only records we accept for *C. p. eriphyle* are pure yellow individuals. Few summer drives through the irrigated Columbia Basin fail to spatter the windshield with smeared yellow wings, smooshed hemolymph, and clear nectar spills, from the clouds of Clouded Sulphurs. Their mud-puddle clubs are famous on hot days in dry places, especially where an animal has urinated on a dirt road. The Pale Clouded Yellow (*C. hyale*), a ubiquitous, butter-colored European insect much like this one, was the original "butterfly" (*buttorfleoge* in Old English). The epithet *philodice* means "summer-lover" (more or less); and Eriphyle was the wife of Amphiarus, a seer and a warrior against the royal city of Thebes in Sophocles' tale of Antigone.

Orange Sulphur   *Colias eurytheme* BOISDUVAL 1852

Sacramento, CA
Aka Alfalfa Butterfly

RECOGNITION < 2 in. Dorsal ground color ranges from **rich, deep golden orange to pale orange to warm yellow with orange patches in the central portion of each wing.** Otherwise similar to preceding species, with many females white (form "alba") but often larger, "eurytheme" spots more pronounced. *C. christina* in NE WA may be flushed with orange but lacks brown "eurytheme" spots and pink rings around VHW spot; *C. occidentalis* in SE WA/NE OR has orange suffused over the yellow ground color, but more golden yellow VHW with discal spot simple-ringed, not dou-

Female, dorsal, ventral

Female, ventral

Male, dorsal

ble. Occasional yellow individuals have been reported. **VARIATION** No ssp. Spring individuals are smaller and more heavily dusted with dark scales over VHW, with orange restricted to patches; summer sulphurs are larger and brighter with fully orange uppersides. Hybrids with Clouded Sulphurs have smaller, but still noticeable, orange patches, resembling spring hatchers and naturally orange Clouded Sulphurs. **HOST PLANTS** Alfalfa and many of the same plants used by the Clouded Sulphur, as well as *Lotus corniculatus* (birdsfoot trefoil). Pelham has reared it from *Sphaerophysa salsula* (swainson-pea) and *Thermopsis rhombifolia*. In lawns not cut too near or sprayed, clovers furnish both oviposition and nectar. Nectars on hawkbit, fleabane, asters, marigolds, calendula, red clover, blackberry, and, of course, alfalfa. **ON THE WING** L March to E November, peaks in July and September. Two or three

Pair, ventral

summer. I've watched this brilliant creature locate a minute patch of purple flowers in a vast barren rockpit with ease, and zero in on the last red clover in our yard on a lowering Thanksgiving Day. It is an irony that one of the toughest late-season butterflies cannot pass the winter routinely in the North; we have very few spring records, even in the southern Oregon counties. As the climate warms further, the Orange Sulphur might become a regular year-round resident. Due to their exaggerated abundance in alfalfa fields, it and Clouded Sulphurs sometimes hybridize. Separate pheromones and the presence (*C. eurytheme*) or lack (*C. philodice*) of ultraviolet reflection in the males' wings usually allow females to choose correctly. But freshly emerged females, less able to select, are vigorously courted by males of either species and thus mis-mate. A large alfalfa or red clover field in midsummer may display thousands of orange and yellow sulphurs dancing over the sweet purple blooms, nectaring, courting, spiralling, rejecting, mating, and ovipositing. The introduction of alfalfa and forage clovers from Europe doubtless aided these species' successful spread far beyond their original, more southerly range. Sometimes they are considered pestiferous and sprayed for, but usually do little harm, and provide pollination that farmers often pay for by renting bees.

broods after arrival from farther S or E. No diapause, so does not overwinter successfully in the N except in mild conditions. **HABITAT AND RANGE** Alfalfa fields, montane meadows, yards, parks, open sunny places. All N Am S of NWT, resident below an uncertain longitude, infiltrating N in summer; expands to most of Cascadia (except extreme NW) by late summer.

This is the most abundant butterfly in the higher Cascades in the fall, often seen moving uphill along mountain roads and on high mountaintops, and some years see great numbers all over western Cascadia in late

Western Sulphur   *Colias occidentalis* SCUDDER 1862

"Gulf of Georgia" (Jefferson Co., WA)
Aka Golden Sulphur, Intermountain Sulphur

RECOGNITION < 2 in. Dorsum male clear lemon-yellow, female yellow to light cream, black-dusted at base. FW tips pointed. DFW margin narrow, solid black in males, smudgy/broken or absent in females. FW discal spot round, oval, or crescentic, and small; DHW discal spot light to bright orange; wing fringe pink. **Ventral ground color usually a golden yellow or almost burnt-orange, heavily dusted with black scales over yellow.** Often a few light "eurytheme" spots on VHW, esp. at costa. **VHW discal spot large, pearly, encircled by a single red rim,** sometimes with a satellite. Orange forms have few or no "eurytheme" spots below.

Female, ventral

Male, ventral

Clouded Sulphurs have heavier "eurytheme" spots, double pink rim on VHW spot, and fly in more habitats. Queen Alexandra's Sulphurs usually lack the pink spot-rim and are greener below. **VARIATION** Highly variable. The main Cascadian race, as just described. A very golden and undusted form ranges S from the OR Siskiyous. Several ssp. and segregates in E OR (Ochoco, Steens, Blue Mtns) and E into ID often have bright orange males and pale yellow or white females. **HOST PLANTS** Peas (*Lathyrus lanszwertii, L. nevadensis, L. pauciflorus*) and lupines (*Lupinus latifolius, L. sericeus*) *fide* Pelham. Newcomer reported spring vetch (*Vicia sativa*) and white sweetclover (*Melilotus alba*) in Yakima Co.; Hardy thought *Lathyrus nevadensis* likely on Vancouver Is. Nectars on Columbia lily and others; males mudpuddle. **ON THE WING** E May to L September, peak in June-July. One generation, third-instar larvae overwinter and feed for another month in spring. **HABITAT AND RANGE** Meadows, roadsides, dry steppe slopes, and glades in forested settings. Streamsides from mid-montane down to foothills; sea level manzanita heath and timberline in the Olympics. S BC S to C CA and W-C ID. Lee side of Coast and Cascade ranges in S BC, seemingly absent from N Cascades until S of Lake Chelan; common again S to the C OR

Cascades, then another gap until Siskiyou/ Sierra; S-C Vancouver Is. and Olympic Peninsula, several isolated ranges in C and E OR.

Alexander Agassiz first collected this species during the northwest boundary survey between the United States and British Columbia. Agassiz, a marine ichthyologist for the U.S. Coast and Geodetic Survey, sent the specimens to his father, the pioneering Harvard naturalist Louis Agassiz, who gave them to Scudder to describe. The type locality has long been assumed to lie in British Columbia; but as H. A. Hagen's 1883 commentary on the expedition makes clear, Agassiz collected his material near Port Townsend, Washington. A colony I found in 1975 on manzanita heath above Dungeness Spit may have been the sole surviving remnant of the type population, but it hasn't been seen since. Westerns proliferate in the Cascades between Stevens Pass and Santiam Pass but, strangely, not much north or south of those points. Dominantly orange populations east and south of the Ochocos have been attributed to both this and the next two species by different authors.

Christina's Sulphur   *Colias christina* W. H. EDWARDS 1863

Slave River, NWT
Aka *C. occidentalis christina*

RECOGNITION < 2 in. Dorsum male butter-yellow to often bright orange, or a patchy blend; female yellow to light cream to milk-white, with little to no dark scaling on margins, esp. HW. FW discal spot oblong; DHW discal spot big and bright orange; wing fringe pink. **VFW often clear orange, VHW ground color often greenish. No "eurytheme" spots on VHW.** VHW discal spot round, encircled by a single, smeared red rim. Orange forms have little or no eurytheme-spotting below. Clouded Sulphurs have heavier "eurytheme" spots, double pink rim on VHW spot, and fly in more habitats. Queen Alexandra's Sulphurs lack the pink spot-rim and are greener below. **VARIATION** Highly variable, oranger to the N and E, yellower W and S; females vary from apricot through pale yellow to dominant clear white. Six ssp. define regional distinctions, which run together at edges. MT race *C. c. sacajawea* is dramatically yellow and orange in patches. *C. c. columbiensis* occupies the Chilcotin District of BC, while *C. c. pseudocolumbiensis* applies to the population in S BC and NE WA from the Okanogan to the Selkirks and S to the Spokane R. It has more rounded wing tips and edges; can be orange-flushed above, is yellower beneath, usually with thin pink rim around VHW cell-spot and light pink fringe. It is large and may be taken for the Giant Sulphur, which lives in willow bogs and has thick pink rings.

Female, ventral

Male, ventral

Females of both ssp. pale or bright yellow, very seldom whitish. **HOST PLANTS** Legumes, incl. *Vicia*, *Lupinus*, *Hedysarum*, and *Thermopsis*. Nectars on native and exotic thistles and many other forest flowers. **ON THE WING** E May to L September, peak in June-July. One generation, third-instar larvae overwinter and feed for another month in spring. **HABITAT AND RANGE** Montane forest roads, trails, glades, and clearings. *C. c. pseudocolumbiensis* flies in forested habitats, meadows, on roadsides, and hillsides, and pioneers recently burned-over areas in NE WA, S BC, and N ID/MT.

Other ssp. to NE OR and points N, E, and SE.

Classic Christina's is citrus-orange, especially in the northern part of its range, while the beautiful Montana race along the Rockies Front resembles orange juice poured over eggs, sunny-side up. The status of this species is in flux, as it relates to the previous and following species. Almost everyone who studies it in detail comes to a different conclusion as to where it belongs. Its great beauty, however, is uncontested.

Queen Alexandra's Sulphur   *Colias alexandra* W. H. EDWARDS 1863

Foothills W of Denver, CO
Aka Alexandra's Sulphur, Ultraviolet Sulphur

RECOGNITION < 2.75 in. Biggish. Most individuals in PNW are larger than most other sulphurs, esp. the desert-steppe populations. Dorsal ground color of *C. a. edwardsii* butter-yellow, warmer toned on outer third. **FW fairly pointed**, outer margin usually straight. FW discal spot round or oval. Black borders of males often narrow as in preceding species; on females, incomplete, faint, or absent. DHW discal spot small and variable, pale yellow to bright orange. **Wing fringe often completely white or yellow**, sometimes pale pink. **Ventral ground color lime-green to**

Female, ventral

Male, ventral

yellowish gray, always with a heavy dusting of dark scales, esp. in early spring individuals. **HW discal spot white**, not pearly, never with a satellite, and usually unrimmed. Seldom has "eurytheme" spots. Clouded Sulphur can be green below but has double pink-rimmed pearly VHW spot. Western has pink rim and dusky yellow VHW color. Pink-edged has rounded wings, yellow ventrum, and is brightly pink-fringed. **VARIATION** The NW *C. a. edwardsii* looks somewhat like the type but is larger and lives chiefly in sage-steppe, is less densely green beneath, and sometimes has pink fringes and spot-rims. It occurs in E Cascadia from C WA south. **HOST PLANTS** Pelham has recorded WA ovipositions on milkvetches (*Astragalus canadensis, A. filipes, A. obscurus, A. purshii,* and *A. lentiginosus*) and on *Medicago sativa* (alfalfa). **ON THE WING** L April to E September, peak in July. The long flight period suggests two broods. **HABITAT AND RANGE** Steppe and semi-desert habitats and adjacent forested uplands, where it is usually seen flying in dry canyons and draws, and over rolling terrain. W Great Plains to E Cascades and Sierra, NM-AZ to C WA. Columbia, Snake, and Great Basin drainages in Cascadia, essentially all E OR and SE portion of WA.

Adults in the desert fly strongly and disperse widely, aided by the strong steppe winds, and are most often seen flying rapidly at a distance; forest dwellers are more leisurely in flight, pausing often to visit nectar. At mud or damp sand after summer rains, the males resemble fleets of green sails beached by a receding tide. When William Henry Edwards named the Northwestern race *C. a. edwardsii*, it was not after himself but in honor of his friend Henry Edwards, a California lepidopterist, actor, and entrepreneur. Two northern subspecies previously assigned to this species are now considered races of *C. christina*. Some workers consider them all a single species, others would split them into several species. Stay tuned (see Hammond and McCorkle 2017)—sulphur systematics are a work in progress.

Labrador Sulphur   *Colias nastes* BOISDUVAL 1832

Nain, Labrador
Aka Arctic Green Sulphur, Arctic Sulphur, Nastes Sulphur

RECOGNITION < 1.75 in. **Small** for a sulphur. **Greenish above and below**, or upperside can be a dingy yellowish or dirty white. **Both sexes have light spots in the black border**: our only sulphur whose males have fenestrated borders. VFW whitish; **VHW olive-green peppered with black**. Often "eurytheme" spots on VFW; VHW cell-spot may be thinly rimmed with pink, often smeared distally. Pale pink fringe. **Occurs only in the northern arctic-alpine** in the region. **VARIATION** The amount of green, yellow, or white on the upperside varies with gender, age, and individual. **HOST PLANTS** Alpine milkvetch (*Astragalus alpinus*) and other legumes. Pelham found it strongly associated with *Oxytropis* *campestris* (slender locoweed) at Horseshoe Mtn in the Pasayten Wilderness. **ON THE WING** E July to E September, peak in July-August, depending on snowmelt. Single-brooded. First- to fourth-instar larvae overwinter. May be biennial, spending two winters as a caterpillar. **HABITAT AND RANGE** Windswept tundra ridges, often where pink mountainheath (*Phyllodoce empetriformis*) grows. Screes, fellfields, and summits. Circumpolar. Arctic Ocean S to S BC, N WA (Okanogan Co., 6,000 to 8,000 feet), along the Rockies in AB, and NW MT.

Writers (Jack Kerouac and Gary Snyder among them) and lepidopterists have spent

Female, ventral

Female, ventral

Male, ventral

summers in remote high-country fire lookouts, scribbling or collecting between fire-watch duties. In this way Jon Shepard discovered the Labrador Sulphur in the Lower 48 in 1961, on a north-facing cliff of Bunker Hill at 7,000 feet, deep in what is now the Pasayten Wilderness. Since then

it has been taken at a few other stations including Windy Peak at 8,300 feet, and Horseshoe Basin, all in a narrow strip along the Canadian border in the western Okanogan Highlands. Shepard found it "alert and difficult to approach," liable to fly on approach and blending into the dry tundra when it lands. Scarce and elusive, it darts low over the stony terrain, dropping moth-like to take shelter. Perhaps no other Cascadian butterfly presents such a difficult challenge to find, watch, catch, or photograph. A vast area of potential habitat for it remains unexplored.

Giant Sulphur   *Colias gigantea* STRECKER 1900

Fort York, MB
Aka Great Northern Sulphur, Large Willow Sulphur, *scudderiv*

Female, ventral

Male, ventral

RECOGNITION > 2.5 in. **Large and robust.** Males bright yellow, females variably pale yellow or white. Yellowish beneath, more or less dark-scaled. Male border usually narrow and complete, female's varies from absent to apically pronounced on the FW. **VHW pearly discal spot has a heavy and smeared or simpler rose ring, often with a satellite; VFW orange spot large**. Pink fringe. *C. christina pseudocolumbiensis* can be similar in size and looks but prefers forest clearings. **VARIATION** *C. g. harroweri*, smaller than the Hudson Bay type, is likely to graze Cascadia; its borders are a little wider, ventrum greener and less dark-dusted. **HOST PLANTS** Bog willows (*Salix*). Females nectar on the edges of wetlands early in the morning. **ON THE WING** E June to E August, peak in July. One generation. **HABITAT AND RANGE** Dwells in and around willowy fens, carrs, and basic (but not acid) bogs from N AK to W-C WY, S-C BC.

Among the most habitat-limited species in the genus, the Giant Sulphur may give you wet feet (and legs, and more) in the search for it. Ferris writes that females remain in the deep habitat most of the time. Unlike many sulphurs, these do not wander far from home, but Norbert Kondla finds that they do fly out of their breeding habitat at times. The nearest occurrence to Cascadia is in British Columbia. Suitable willow bogs occur in certain Pend Oreille valleys, and it might turn up in northeastern Washington. The largest one I have ever seen was a white female, fully three inches in wingspan, found by Megan Vogel on 4 July 1976, at 10,000 feet on the Beartooth Plateau in south-central Montana. Scott lumps the Giant Sulphur under *C. scudderi*, another willow-feeding sulphur that replaces this one in the southern Rockies.

Skinner's Sulphur   *Colias skinneri* BOISDUVAL & LECONTE 1830

NE coast of Labrador
Aka Pelidne Sulphur (NABA), Blueberry Sulphur, Labrador Sulphur, *pelidne*

RECOGNITION < 1.5 in. Smallish. Male pale yellow above with black border entire, females often white with border jagged and merely hinted. FW rounded. DFW, VFW cell-spots small if present. **Base of wings above, FW disc below, and VHW dusted with black scaling.** VHW cloudy olive, with cell-spot small but **thickly rimmed in rose**, often crowding out pearly center. Pink fringes. *C. interior* is yellower below, larger, and has more pink on the edges and less around the VHW cell-spot. **VARIATION** Southern races (Rockies, PNW) differ from the arctic type by being more heavily dusted with black scales on the VFW disc, more so yet on the VHW at Yellowstone. **HOST PLANTS** Heaths, notably huckleberries (*Vaccinium*) and creeping wintergreen (*Gaultheria humifusa*). **ON THE WING** L June to E September, peak in July. The single flight stretches toward fall in a year of late snowmelt. **HABITAT AND RANGE** Arctic tundra, high forest clearings, forest roads and rights-of-way, moist meadows; here, high mountain cirques and slopes, 6,000 to 9,000 feet. E and W High Arctic, but not in between; and a disjunct population down the Rockies from mid BC and AB to MT, WY, ID, and OR. In Cascadia, Steens and the Wallowa Mtns of OR.

Dornfeld called this sulphur one of the rarest of Oregon butterflies, and wrote: "Unless settled at wet places to sip moisture, Skinner's . . . is a difficult capture as it is a rapid and erratic flyer over the rough terrain of boulder-strewn mountain slopes." He knew it only from the high Wallowas, but it was later discovered on Steens Mountain, where most lepidopterists go to encounter it now, near the summit. Chasing Skinner's is a challenge that requires great care not to break a leg or a neck while swinging your net. The butterfly should be sought on the

Male, ventral

Male, ventral

Variation between females (left) and males (right)

few high peaks in southeastern and north-eastern Washington. This and the next belong to a guild of northern sulphurs that

have adapted to heath host plants instead of the usual legumes or the less-frequent willows.

Pink-edged Sulphur   *Colias interior* SCUDDER 1862

Nr Grand Rapids, Lake Winnipeg, MB

RECOGNITION < 2 in. Bright sunny yellow with noticeably rounded wings and FW margin, and **bright pink fringes**, esp. when fresh. Male with complete, sharp, black borders broadened inward at the tip; female light yellow (rarely white) with sooty vestiges of an apical border. Small

black FW cell-spot, orange DHW cell-spot, and VHW pearly cell-spot simple-rimmed in pink, lacking a satellite. Ventrum clear yellow without brown spots and little black scaling. Clouded has "eurytheme" spots and double pink rim to VHW cell-spot; Western has dark scaling beneath and pointed FW; Queen Alexandra's is greenish below without pink fringes; Christina's is bigger, fringes much subtler; Skinner's has VHW olive cellspot with smeared

red rim. **VARIATION** No ssp., and the animal is quite consistent across the N. **HOST PLANTS** Various blueberry heaths incl. bog bilberry (*Vaccinium uliginosum*) and dwarf bilberry (*V. cespitosum*). Nectars frequently at meadow composites, and males mudpuddle. **ON THE WING** E June to M September, peak in July. **HABITAT AND RANGE** Mid-elevation forests, esp. in clearings, burns, marshes, and meadows, along roadsides, and heathlands. Between 2,600 and 6,000 feet in OR. Subarctic Canada, extending S into boreal habitats along US mountain chains. The Cascadian range extends from the N Cascades, Okanogan Highlands, and Selkirks of WA-BC S to about Lake Wenatchee in WA; then absent until the Blue-Wallowa Mtns of WA-OR, and the C OR Cascades S to Crater Lake.

Female, ventral

The dramatically pink wing fringes are sometimes visible in flight. Certain other *Colias* species have pink fringes, but none is edged with such a rich rose. "[It] is not given to large open spaces [and] should be sought in the pine forests near the larval hostplants" (Dornfeld). The butterfly exhibits an odd disjuncture in the Northwest, apparently skipping from southern Chelan County to south of Mt. Hood, omitting the southern half of the Washington Cascades. Like most other sulphurs, these cover a lot of ground in search of host plants and, for the males, females, rather than sticking to one area. Their flight, however, is noted by many to be slower, more "relaxed" and deliberate than that of others, such as the Clouded or Western Sulphurs.

Pair, ventral

Becker's White, male

Subfamily Pierinae: Marbles and Whites

Whites are familiar to almost everyone in the form of the ubiquitous Cabbage White. Many may not realize that Cascadia is also graced by a number of indigenous pierines. They are distinguished by having wings largely clothed in white scales, often with gray or green (=yellow + black scales) veining or marbling, and the forelegs of the males being reduced almost like those of nymphalids. Of the 700 or so species worldwide, about 20 occur in North America. The only other butterflies likely to be mistaken for whites on the wing are small parnassians, form "alba" female sulphurs, male Northern White Skippers, and certain moths. With practice, you can learn to distinguish one white from another on the wing through subtle differences in brightness, flight, and behavior, much of the time. As with the related sulphurs, such determinations should not be admitted for occurrence records, as even the most experienced watchers make mistakes except with Sara's Orangetips.

The great majority of whites and marbles feed as larvae upon mustards (Brassicaceae) and a few related families that produce mustard oils. The Pine White is a dramatic departure. The related Chiricahua Pine White ranges through S AZ and Mexico, and its females are brick-red to orange and mimic Monarchs. Another Mexican species not distantly related, *Euchaeris socialis*, has the remarkable habit of feeding and pupating communally in a big silken bag, in which the adults emerge before spring. Collectors love to find a whole bagful of the perfect adult butterflies. The larvae consume a species of tree *Arbutus*, causing Northwest butterfly folk to imagine it moving north to feed on our own Puget Sound madronas, even as European Cabbage Whites have occupied our broccoli beds.

Sara's Orangetip   *Anthocharis sara* LUCAS 1852

N Fk Feather R., Plumas Co., CA
Aka Sara Orange-tip (NABA), Pacific Orangetip, Western Orange Tip, Stella's Orangetip

RECOGNITION
< 1.5 in. Unmistakable. Small, white males, usually yellow females, with **red- to citrus-orange FW tips. Loose, granular green marbling and yellow veins on VHW.** Orange apical patches are larger and brighter on the males; framed in variable black bars, lines, and checks; and capped outwardly with yellow in females. **VARIATION** Subtle differences among regional races—brighter yellow in females, broader black borders to the orange tip, and so on—have led to several names and perhaps future splits. **HOST PLANTS** Crucifers incl. several rockcresses (*Arabis*) on the dry side and bittercress/toothwort (*Cardamine*)

Female, ventral

Female, dorsal

Male, dorsal

Male, ventral

on the wetter side of the mtns. I observed oviposition in the pedicel of a floret of *C. penduliflora*. Nectar favorites incl. dandelion, daisies, strawberries, monkeyflower, collinsia, and its own host mustards. **ON THE WING** M March to M August, peak in April (low), July (high). One generation, pupae overwinter. **HABITAT AND RANGE** Nearly every open habitat in Cascadia except the wettest, deepest forests, rocks and ice, and cities and suburbs, sea level to peaks. Roadsides, rail lines, unsprayed rights-of-way, old fields, meadows, montane summits, slopes and seeps, island grasslands and bluffs, alpine tundra, forest clearings and edges, dappled glades, canyons, and steppe-desert. S Yukon S to Baja and E to WY. Common throughout Cascadia away from the outer coast strip and rainforest zone.

Pair, dorsal

Very few butterflies grace such a sweep of Northwest habitats. You are as likely to find it among the sage violets of the steppe in April as around a mossy seep with saxifrages high in the Olympics in July. Everyone is charmed by this demure yet bright and surprising beauty. Sometimes on the wing it projects the image of disembodied neon-orange patches flicking on their own.

But all its charm failed to keep developers from snuffing out the orange flickers in the Kent Valley and all around the immediate environs of Seattle. Nor does its beauty exempt it from taxonomic contest, and its nomenclature is likely to change soon.

Western subspecies—some of them perhaps full species—have such names as Flora, Stella, and Julia. Authors of yore seldom left clues to their dedications, so we may never know which wives, daughters, nieces, or sweethearts these pretties were named for. Todd Stout's awaited revision will likely change the ways we view and name their relationships.

Gray Marble *Anthocharis lanceolata* (LUCAS) 1852

N Fk Feather R., Plumas Co., CA
Aka Boisduval's Marble, Lanceolate Marble, California White Tip, *Falcapica*

RECOGNITION < 2 in. White above except for black-barred FW apex and cell-spot, fine black border-line. **FW tip bluntly hooked. Below, FW tip and entire HW smoked with fine gray or brown-gray marbling.** White dash runs

from costa toward body on VHW. Western, Margined Whites have gray along veins; Cabbage White yellowish below; none are hook-tipped. **VARIATION** Nothing that would confuse its identification. **HOST PLANTS** Rockcresses (*Arabis*) and other crucifers. **ON THE WING** E May to E July, peak in L May. Single-brooded, chrysalides overwinter. **HABITAT AND RANGE** S-facing slopes of wooded canyons, mountain clefts, walled ravines, gullies and washes, sunny clearings. Montane CA, dipping into OR, NV, and Baja. Siskiyous, S Cascades, and Warner Mtns of OR, Curry to Lake cos.

Male, dorsal

Actually an orange-less orangetip, this odd species' wingshape brings to mind the only eastern species in the genus, the Falcate Marble (*A. midea*); both *falcate* and *lanceolata* mean "hook-tipped," as does the subgenus (*Falcapica*) within which these two species reside. A distinctive insect of hot mountains, the Gray Marble has a frail, spectral presence. But that impression is deceiving, as Dornfeld knew: "An erratic flyer, it skillfully avoids netting." Comstock

Male, ventral

described it thus: "One of our mountain dwellers, occurring at suitable elevations. [I]t is something of a rarity, and must be sought in the late spring, when banks of snow still abound, and the ground is sodden with its melting." Students have been surprised by my inordinate excitement over a drab little insect that looked more like a stonefly than a butterfly on the wing, until they see its subtle, striated patterns up close.

Large Marble   *Euchloe ausonides* (LUCAS) 1852

San Francisco, CA
Aka Creamy Marble (NABA), Dappled Marble

E. A. INSULANUS EXTIRPATED IN BC, ENDANGERED IN WA, FEDERAL CANDIDATE

RECOGNITION < 1.75 in. **Creamy white**, black pattern on FW tip and **thin black rectangle in DFW cell lightly white-scaled in the middle. VHW and FW tip marked by roving yellow-green marbling** that crosses the yellow veins. Females may have a yellowish cast. Desert Marble smaller, bluer/grainier-marbled, cell-spot lacks white scales, has pearly cast. **VARIATION** The type, sometimes up to 2 in. in wingspan, inspired the common name. It has more extensive green marbling below and dusky females. Most Large Marbles in Cascadia are smaller, with narrower black apical markings and broader, deeper green, variable marbling. *E. a. insulanus* (Island Marble) is larger, with all dark markings expanded above and wing bases strongly shadowed, marbling below

Female, dorsal

broadened and yellower. **HOST PLANTS** Many crucifers, incl. tall tumblemustard (*Sisymbrium altissimum*), lending some usefulness to this rampant exotic. Pelham also lists several species of *Arabis* and *Descurainia*. On San Juan Is., introduced mustards and native Puget Sound peppergrass (*Lepidium virginicum* var. *menziesii*). Nectars on everything from garden rocket to fiddlenecks (*Amsinckia*). **ON THE WING** L March to L July, peak in May-June (earlier lower, later higher). Single-brooded, pupae overwinter. **HABITAT AND RANGE** Montane slopes, meadows, and canyons, sage-steppe, weedy flats, clearings in pine and aspen forests esp., and desert hillocks. Great Lakes to AK, S CA to NM. Most of our region E of Cascade Crest, W in Siskiyous. Island Marble formerly flew on Vancouver and Gabriola Is. but is now known only from San Juan Is., WA.

Though on average bigger than the next, this species is not very large except in California. The alternative name Creamy Marble is a reference to its ground color, which distinguishes it from the pearlier *E. lotta*. Males course slopes and ravines with a low flight, but zigzag, not straight back-and-forth like a swallowtail. In 1998 John Fleckenstein, who was surveying grassland butterflies for the Washington Natural Heritage Program, made the remarkable rediscovery of the Island Marble (*E. a. insulanus*) near American Camp in the San Juan Island National Historic Park; there it feeds largely on exotic mustards, putting the National Park Service in a pickle for its management.

Male, dorsal

Pair, ventral

California Marble *Euchloe hyantis* (W. H. EDWARDS) 1871

Ukiah, Mendocino Co., CA
Aka Pearly Marble, Pearly Marble Wing, Edwards' Marble, *creusa* (WWB)

RECOGNITION < 1.5 in. Off-white, smaller than previous species, with similar black tip marks but **thin black bar on DFW cell is closed, without any trace of white scales** in the middle. Differs from the Desert Marble by having a **yellowish wash to the green marbling, and lacking the pearlescence between the marbling**. **VARIATION** Two populations occur in Josephine Co., OR. Those in the Illinois Valley are smaller, with more and darker green marbling and black above; Rogue Valley individuals

are larger, lighter-marked above and below, with yellow-scaled veins below. **HOST PLANTS** Jewel-flower (*Streptanthus*). *Arabis* and *Draba* species are also possibilities. **ON THE WING** M March to E June. A single generation, pupae overwinter. **HABITAT AND RANGE** Open montane and foothill slopes, moraines, dry meadows, serpentine outcrops, clifftops and faces. Seaward ranges of CA, Baja N into the Siskiyous of SW OR in the Illinois and Rogue valleys.

Throughout its range, with few exceptions, this butterfly specializes on jewel-flower, which is often restricted to particular soil types; according to Opler, the eggs are laid under its clasping leaves, and the larvae

Male, dorsal

Male, ventral

must burrow tiny holes through the leaves to reach the flowers and developing pods upon which they feed. Populations are distinctly colonial, and the butterflies are often more sedentary than the Desert Marble, with which it used to be considered conspecific. *E. lotta* uses a wide array of mustards and lacks specialized larval behavior; nor does *Streptanthus* occur in that butterfly's range. The Cascade–Sierra Nevada crests essentially divide the two species: *E. hyantis* may occur up to the crest from the West, but *E. lotta* is usually found in low-lying deserts to the east, including the bases of these ranges. *E. lotta* flies earlier and lower where the two ranges approach each other. This lack of synchrony and other factors effectively prevent the two from hybridizing.

Desert Marble   *Euchloe lotta* (BEUTENMÜLLER) 1898

Kenab, UT
Aka Pearly Marble, Pearly Marble Wing, Southern Marble, *hyantis*

RECOGNITION < 1.5 in. **Shiny white**, smaller than previous species, with similar black tip marks but **thick black bar on FW cell is closed, without any trace of white** scales in the middle. **Green marbling dark, sometimes bluish, and grainy. Pearly sheen to** the white on both sides, in contrast to the flat creamy cast of the Large Marble. **VARIATION** Individual but no notable interpopulation variability. **HOST PLANTS** Of the cruciferous hosts, Pelham lists for WA the rockcress *Arabis furcata*, *Boechera atrorubens*, *B. pendulocarpa*, and *Halimolobos whitedii*; also uses tall tumblemustard (*Sisymbrium altissimum*) and tansy mustard (*Descurainia pinnata*). **ON THE WING** L March to L June, peak in April. **HABITAT AND RANGE** Desert flats, sagesteppe, bitterbrush plateaus, pinyon-juniper forest, dry gullies and aridland outcrops, 250

Male, dorsal

Female (left) and male (right), ventral

to 8,600 feet. S BC to Sonora, roughly between Cascade and Rocky Mtn crests. E lowlands of Cascadia, essentially absent from the mtns.

In Cascadia, the Desert Marble is largely true to its name, abjuring the moister mountains in favor of arid bottomlands and plateaus. Late in its flight period it overlaps with the Large Marble, which has a much broader range of habitat tolerance and begins emerging later than the hardy *E. lotta*. The small size, pearly sheen, and lack of

white scales in the cell-spot will normally distinguish Desert Marbles under these conditions. On the wing, it will usually be the smallest of the seven species of whites (Becker's, Spring, Western, Cabbage, Large and Desert Marbles, Sara's Orangetip) that may be flying together in the lively sage-steppe spring. Adults are the commonest steppe whites in April, sheltering from chilly winds among showy phlox in the lee of basin big sage.

Pine White   *Neophasia menapia* (C. & R. FELDER) 1859

Washoe Co., NV
Aka White Pine Butterfly

RECOGNITION < 2 in. Males milky white, females creamy; **heavy black markings on FW tips and leading edge,** black costal teardrop dripping into cell; black chain-like pattern around HW trailing edge, strongly on female. **VHW veins black, fine in male, heavy in female; orange-red edging** around female (seldom male) VHW margin. **Weak flight. VARIATION** Individuals vary greatly, but there is little or no consistent variation over the range except for red scaling on males' VHW common in CA, less so in OR and WA, and mostly absent in BC. **HOST PLANTS** Ponderosa, white, lodgepole, and other pines, Douglas-fir, and prob. true

Female, dorsal

Female, ventral

Male, dorsal

Male, ventral

firs. Scott lists mountain hemlock and Sitka spruce as well; I have found it on deodar cedars (*Cedrus deodara*) in Sedro-Woolley, WA, and suspect western hemlock in the Coast Ranges. Nectars on hawkbit, goldenrod, tansy ragwort, yarrow, daisies, tansy, Canada thistle, pearly everlasting, blue lobelia, tithonia, buddleia, and others. **ON THE WING** L June to M October, peak in August. One generation, eggs overwinter. **HABITAT AND RANGE** Coniferous forests, sea level to mid-montane; urban neighborhoods with ornamental pines and Douglas-firs, e.g., Seattle, Bellingham, Portland, and Ashland. Pinelands from Great Plains to W Coast, S BC to C AZ. Forested Cascadia except for deep rainforest, flying in the canopy.

One of declining summer's compensations is the graceful, floppy flight of Pine Whites, as they appear around the crowns of firs. Considered primitive, it is one of only three butterflies in Cascadia whose larvae feed on conifers. Often common throughout the ponderosa pine belt (the favored food), where its colonies flare and flicker unpredictably. In certain years the population erupts over localized areas, sending millions onto the wing at once, when roadside pines are slathered with larvae and pupae, every spider web, goldenrod, and pool is coated in pale wings, and the sky is filled with white gliders. Such outbreaks have taken place in recent years in Malheur and Spokane counties and the Blue Mountains. Pine Whites thrive among shore pines, yet show spottily in adjacent Coast Ranges. Common in the San Juan Islands, where I observed one flying onto a ferry at Shaw Island, only to disembark on Orcas Island.

Margined White   *Pieris marginalis* SCUDDER 1861

Gulf of Georgia, nr Port Townsend, WA
Aka Veined White, Sharp-veined White, Mustard White, Green-veined White, *Artogeia, napi*

RECOGNITION < 2 in. Bright white, sometimes lemony yellowish cast below or apricot tinge above. **Veins on ventrum more or less distinctly outlined in black scales (look gray-green), base of wings dusky esp. in spring; summer males** can be immaculate white. Often orange mark at VHW base. If dark-scaled at FW apex, not confined to charcoal wingtips as in Cabbage White but continues down the wing at the vein-ends, the "margin" of the name. If black spots in or

Male, dorsal

Female, dorsal

Male, ventral

Male, ventral

near FW cell, the lower one (in females) not discrete as in *P. rapae* but "leaks" down along trailing edge. FW tips more rounded than the Cabbage White's, and lacks Cabbage's discrete black dot on vFW. On Margined White, **black scales concentrated near the veins and relatively absent from cells between veins**;

on Cabbage, they are uniformly distributed throughout the cells. These scales form the darkened veins on *P. marginalis*, and the sprinkled-pepper look of *P. rapae*. **VARIATION** The type is the Pacific Coastal/Cascadian race, as just described. Varies from immaculate white males to buttery yellow females, and from prominent gray-green veins in spring to unscaled veins in summer. Emerging in January, a variety to the S in the redwoods and along the mid-California coast displays very strong black veins, even above. SW OR individuals are not so veined as these, but smaller, darker-veined and less yellow than those to the N. Variable overall. **HOST PLANTS** Many crucifers, chiefly species of bittercress/toothwort (*Cardamine*) and watercress (*Nasturtium officinale*). Nectars on salmonberry, spring beauty, dandelion, coltsfoot, plectritis, stream

Puddle party

violet, lawn daisy, and toothwort in spring, and wallflower, fireweed, hawkbit, and other composites in summer. **ON THE WING** E March to E October, peaks in April, June, August. One to four broods, as seasons allow; one N and higher up, three or even four in SW WA, weather permitting. Pupae overwinter. **HABITAT AND RANGE** Edges of deciduous and coniferous woods; roadsides, glens, glades, seeps, dappled and shady places. Rockies, Cascades, Sierra, and Coast ranges, Yukon to C CA and AZ in coastal and boreal sites. Nearly all moist, cooler, and wooded parts of Cascadia, incl. unsprayed second- and third-growth timberlands.

Long considered part of the Eurasian Green-veined White (*P. napi*), the West Coast Margined White has been separated out as full species. One of our simplest, loveliest butterflies, it is also the very best

adaptee to maritime Northwest forests. Following a long wet winter, the first bright individuals emerging in March always strike an encouraging note; and repeat this, after a lapse of weeks between broods, when the fresh white generation emerges after Midsummer Day. The amount of black scaling is controlled by day length and cold. Dusky-veined whites fly as trilliums, Indian plum, and bleeding heart bloom; rice-paper white ones come out with the brambles and foxglove. Introduced Cabbage Whites do not (as formerly thought) out-compete native Margined Whites; rather, Cabbages adapt to town, farm, and garden, the natives to forest and country. Margined Whites have dropped out of the cities of Cascadia, except perhaps in the woodsiest edges. They have adapted well to forestry, except where aerial herbicides are used.

Cabbage White   *Pieris rapae* (LINNAEUS) 1758

Sweden
Aka Cabbage Butterfly, Small White, European Cabbage Butterfly, Imported Cabbageworm, *Artogeia*

RECOGNITION < 2 in. White, pointed **DFW** discretely tipped with charcoal. Sharp black dots on the mid-outer **DFW**, one in males, two in females, and one black spot on leading edge of **DHW**. Prominent black spot on **VFW, with smaller satellite**, absent on Margined White even when it has dorsal spots. **Below, pale to bright mustard-yellow** VHW and DFW tip, speckled with black scales in cooler-season broods. Other whites lack charcoal wingtips, and most have green or gray veins or marbling below. See previous species. **VARIATION** Varies in size, black scaling, and yellowness with season, temperature, and moisture. In dry zones, spring individuals can be nearly pure white; in wet, cool areas, very dusky below. **HOST PLANTS** Caterpillars mine the leaves of brassicas, sometimes burrow into the caudex.

Cabbage (*Brassica oleracea*) and its variants favored, along with nasturtium and many but not all weedy and wild crucifers. Nectars at buddleia, red osier dogwood, mints, fireweed, birdsfoot trefoil, peas, plectritis, blackberry, hawkbit, geranium, host mustards, and many others. **ON THE WING** E March to E November, peaks in May, July, September (one January record). As many generations as the growing season will permit, usually three or four. Overwinters as pupae or feeding larvae in mild winters. **HABITAT AND RANGE** Croplands and vegetable gardens, and practically every open habitat all over the temperate, settled world. All Cascadia, more common in disturbed places than in natural habitats. On the open coast, thrives on sea-rocket (*Cakile*). Highly vagrant, also forms local colonies.

Female, dorsal

Male, ventral

Male, dorsal

Male, ventral

No butterfly is more familiar, less well liked, or more often misidentified. Even those who would never confuse a swallowtail with a Monarch commonly call this species "cabbage moth," because people want their pests to be moths, not butterflies. *P. rapae* can be a significant competitor for cabbage, kale, Brussels sprouts, cauliflower, broccoli, collard greens, radishes, and nasturtiums.

In England, repeated use of DDT against it led to greater losses, as the larvae gained resistance and their natural predators, carabid beetles, proved more susceptible. Gardeners are advised against using Btk products to combat *Pieris* larvae, as it is deadly to all larval Lepidoptera, turning a would-be butterfly garden into a barren. Better to pluck off the larvae, accept a little steamed protein in the broccoli, or simply grow more and share: after all, how much kale can you eat? I appreciate the species as often the only butterfly to be seen, flying on earlier, cloudier, colder days than most other butterflies. Introduced to Quebec ca. 1860, it is one of only two alien butterflies in the Pacific Northwest. I have found it, with the Margined White, on Cape Alava, the westernmost point in Washington; and going to roost in lichens 20 feet up in a subalpine fir at Windy Pass, high in the North Cascades. The Cabbage White is adaptable, pretty, interesting, and here to stay, so we might as well enjoy it.

Becker's White   *Pontia beckerii* (W. H. EDWARDS) 1871

Virginia City, Storey Co., NV
Aka Great Basin White, Sagebrush White, *Pieris, chloridice*

RECOGNITION < 2 in. Robust; black markings near tips of DFW and a **prominent open black rectangle at the end of the cell of the FW** above and below; **bright green borders to the veins of VHW and VFW tip**, broken midwing to show a white open area. Larger, much greener-veined than Western White. **VARIA-**

TION No recognized ssp. or regional variation. The green coloration can vary from teal-bluish in the spring generation to yellowy chartreuse in the fall generation. **HOST PLANTS** Flower buds and developing seeds of a wide array of aridland mustards, incl. in Cascadia *Descurainia pinnata, Sisymbrium altissimum, S. linifolium, Lepidium perfoliatum, Stanleya pinnata, Brassica nigra, Thelypodium sagittatum,* and *T. laciniatum.* Frequent nectarer on rabbitbrush, alfalfa, thistles, sweetclover, yellow star-thistle, asters, white borage, pink allium, yellow cleome, and

Male, ventral

Pair, dorsal

its host mustards. **ON THE WING** M March to M September, peaks in May and August. The chrysalis hangs head-down and spends the winter. Two to four generations, N to S and higher/lower, with fresh adults in both spring and fall. **HABITAT AND RANGE** Sage-steppe, dry coulees, and E foothill canyons throughout the arid interior, disturbed and non-. The Great Basin and adjacent drier parts of W N Am; all lower, drier E WA and E OR, with a few records W of the crest near the Columbia and in the Willamette Valley and adjacent Cascade foothills; from near sea level to 9,000+ feet.

Viewers are often struck by the beauty of this butterfly, expecting something like a Cabbage White, then beholding the bright moss- or copper-green pattern below and never suspecting such colors existed in butterflies. The "green" is really composed of black and yellow scales working like

Ben-Day dots in a comic strip to convey the impression of greenness to the retina. This may have been selected for on account of the camouflage it furnishes against color-sighted birds—a first line of defense, since the mustard oils ingested by whites may render them distasteful to birds. The insect has adapted to feed on Eurasian crucifers such as tall tumblemustard, showing that these invaders, for all the damage they cause to native and agricultural systems, give some service. Thousands of acres covered with the rampantly adventive yellow star-thistle (*Centaurea solstitialis*), if useless for cattle, supply a vast store of nectar that beekeepers and Becker's Whites have discovered. Henry Edwards (the first captor) and W. H. Edwards (the first describer) honored German naturalist Ludwig Becker, who died in frontier Australia, by naming the butterfly after him.

Spring White   *Pontia sisymbrii* (BOISDUVAL) 1852

N Fk Feather R., Plumas Co., CA
Aka California White, Colorado White, *Pieris*

RECOGNITION
< 1.5 in. Small, males usually milk-white, females cream to yellow, with black FW tip checks and a **closed bar at the end of the FW cell. Veins of the**

VHW are crisply lined with parallel brownish black bars, broken across the middle, lending a **railroad-track pattern** that sometimes shows through above. **VARIATION** Lots in the region; yellower toward BC, sometimes even in the males, and females duskier in the Cascades and C WA. Larger in the Siskiyous, more so and whiter into CA; and less dusky with fewer yellow females toward the SE, Basin, and Rockies. **HOST PLANTS** An array of herbaceous

Female, dorsal

rockcresses and mustards incl. *Sisymbrium altissimum, Arabis furcata, Boechera atrorubens, B. pendulocarpa, Turritis glabra*, and *Streptanthus.*

Male, dorsal

Pair, ventral

Nectars on sagebrush violet (*Viola trinervata*) and other flowers. **ON THE WING** L March to L August, peak in April-May, often following snowmelt by mere days. A single generation, pupae overwinter. **HABITAT AND RANGE** Rocky desert-steppe, sagelands, hills and their folds, subalpine ridges in the Cascades, alpine slopes in the Olympics. W of the Great Plains, N Yukon to N Mexico; most of Cascadia E of the crest; also the arctic-alpine of (at least) the NE Olympic Peninsula; and the Siskiyous.

Spring Whites often turn up as singletons on isolated summits or in dryland gullies, and you may forget what this little pale butterfly is until you view its distinctive underside. It is one of the earliest butterflies out in the eastern coulees, clinging to

bare earth on 45-degree April days while 30-mph winds howl through the black stones and blue sage. The males are strong hilltoppers, watching for females newly emerged. The notable disjuncture of the butterfly in Washington, skipping from the east side of the Cascades to the Olympics, is mirrored by only one other butterfly, the Lilac-bordered Copper. This may tell of separate incursions from either the North or the South in the past, or of a glacial refugium in the Olympics. Shapiro found that certain of its hosts produce orange egg-mimic bumps that may induce females to oviposit elsewhere; this "false egg" phenomenon is also known to occur between passionflowers and longwing butterflies in the American tropics.

Checkered White   *Pontia protodice* (BOISDUVAL & LECONTE) 1830

New York
Aka *occidentalis* (WWB), *Pieris*

RECOGNITION < 2 in. White above, more or less **marked with black, charcoal, or brown checks, bars, and chevrons; VHW may be yellow-veined with brown or olive chevron-marks**. Female much more heavily marked, esp. in spring, with pinkish brown (Western White females more sharply marked with gray-black); summer males may be nearly immaculate

except for black cell check-mark above and tan tracery below, while summer Western Whites are strongly veined below as in the spring. Best told from Western White by the latter's blacker, more continuous pattern on the DFW, greener, broader markings below esp. along veins, longer FW, and by habitat. **VARIATION** Extreme, but no ssp. recognized. Short day length or

Female, dorsal

Female, ventral

Male, dorsal

Male, ventral

cold produce a generation with VHW veins traced in greenish gray, so early spring individuals much darker than summer ones. **HOST PLANTS** A wide array of weedy and indigenous crucifers. **ON THE WING** E June to L September, no obvious peak. Two or three broods in SE OR. Pupae overwinter, giving adults in spring farther S. **HABITAT AND RANGE** Waste ground and other disturbed, weedy sites, old farmland, canals and streams, foothills; seldom high in elevation, but almost anywhere

during expansion. Resident in S US and Mexico, migrating here, expanding N in summer to C-W Canada. Records few over much of OR, commoner in SE deserts, more so E into ID; very rarely seen in NE, SE WA and SE BC.

Because Checkered Whites come from the south in leapfrogging summer generations (like some sulphurs), there are more records for Oregon, especially in the eastern basinlands. Only four specimens have been verified for Washington, all from the Blue Mtns and Pend Oreille. Nowhere can you expect to find the Checkered White in the Northwest, but it could turn up almost anywhere. Collectors and watchers constantly try to turn Western Whites into Checkered Whites. Any potentially serious specimen or photograph should be examined by an expert. A classically unmarked summer male would be easy to distinguish, or a very brown-checked female. But many individuals, especially in spring (by which time Checkereds would be unlikely to be here),

can be highly ambiguous. Where common, usually present in the hundreds compared to the thousands of Cabbage Whites. The species' migratory fortunes have as much to do with the changing agricultural landscape as they do with the weather. With climate change, localized colonies may begin to persist in the North.

Western White *Pontia occidentalis* (REAKIRT) 1866

Empire Creek, Clear Creek Co., CO
Aka Peak White, Checkered White (wwʙ), *Pieris, callidice*

RECOGNITION < 2 in. Milky white with joined black "V" markings on the outer third and cell of the FW, much heavier on females. **VHW veins lined by gray-green, more strongly in the spring brood**; never as bright green or heavy as in Becker's White, and unbroken in middle of wing. See previous species (and sidebar) for differences between the two. **VARIATION** Highly variable, though not as much as the Checkered White, mostly

with season. Spring and fall individuals average darker and smaller than those of the summer generation. **HOST PLANTS** Seems to prefer native crucifers to weedy alien mustards. Pelham lists daggerpod (*Anelsonia eurycarpa*), several peppergrasses (incl. *Lepidium perfoliatum, L. campestre, L. densiflorum,* and *L. virginicum*), and *Thelypodium sagittatum.* Nectars on alfalfa, clovers, hosts, alpine wildflowers. **ON THE WING** M March to M September, peaks in June, July, August. Resident year-round. Two or three generations, spring, midsummer, late summer, in lowlands, with one or two following snowmelt at high elevation. Pupae overwinter. **HABITAT AND**

Male, dorsal

Male, ventral

Checkered and Western Whites, Compared

Telling these two native whites apart is seldom simple and sometimes futile. Study the photographs and field marks on these pages, and study the butterflies in the field. The two insects' gestalt (or jizz, to birders), together with their habitat and behavior, may enable you to acquire a reliable search image. As F. M. Brown pointed out, "When frighted, *occidentalis* usually will streak for the shelter of the forest while *protodice* will dodge about over the open meadows." Any records of the Checkered White in the Northwest should be accompanied by voucher specimens or by good photographs, both dorsal and ventral.

RANGE Open mountain habitats, esp. sub- and arctic-alpine; rimrock heights; lowland clearings, fields, roadsides, and disturbed sites such as railroad yards, where it may expand its range (Shapiro). N Alaska across Canada to Hudson Bay, S to mid-SW. All cos in Cascadia except for the maritime strip, though much commoner in E and in montane zones, present from sea level to 10,000+ feet.

Western Whites can often be told on the wing from Cabbage and Margined Whites by the smudged impression they give. The Western White hilltops, rambles, and roams, and can turn up in virtually any locality. I have found it among Cabbage Whites in a Puget Island pasture, hilltopping solo on the highest point in the Willapa Hills, numerous on mountaintops in the Cascades and Olympics, and as a master of the fierce Gorge wind on basalt clifftops at Stonehenge, Maryhill. It will turn up in a parched, dusty, weedy roadside and cause you to think it must be a Checkered White, until its darker, crisper markings put you right. If you see no other butterfly on a summer climb in Higher Cascadia, you can at least expect a Western White or two ripping over the summit and around your head. Netting it is a different matter.

Male, ventral

Pair, dorsal

FAMILY LYCAENIDAE: GOSSAMER WINGS

The approximately 5,000 species worldwide (about 150 in North America, 55 in Cascadia) share egg, larval, and pupal shape—like spineless sea urchins, slugs or sowbugs/pillbugs, and smooth, hunkered pellets, respectively—and such traits as reduced forelegs in males and a predominance of structural scales and resultant shimmering colors. The caterpillars of many species live mutualistically with ants, exchanging honeydew for protection from invertebrate predators. Lycaenid larvae in general go through four instars instead of the usual five. The breakdown of subgroups remains tentative. There are blue coppers and hairstreaks, copper blues and hairstreaks, and tailed coppers and blues—somewhat confusing until you learn the individual genera and species, which are actually quite distinctive in most cases. All share the trait of glittering, silky wings that give the impression of near-nothingness: hence, gossamer.

Subfamily Lycaeninae: Coppers

Chiefly North Temperate in distribution, coppers make up only one per cent of the Lycaenidae. Some shine like molten ingots, others like an old penny, but still other coppers are not copper at all. Most have at least some orange zigzag patterning on the outer hindwing, and the sexes are dimorphic, the females usually orange to the males' brown, or gray to the males' blue, purplish, or bright copper. Males lack stigmata on the forewings, and the caterpillars do not have evident honey glands, though some are ant-attended. Some authors divide the coppers into several other genera, which may have a good basis in fact. These are given in the Aka section, while the (some say "garbage-pail") genus *Lycaena* is used overall for simplicity of association. Host herbs and shrubs belong chiefly to the Polygonaceae, Ericaceae, and Grossulariaceae.

Male (left) and female (right) Mariposa Coppers
(*Lycaena mariposa ximena*)

American Copper   *Lycaena phlaeas* (LINNAEUS) 1761

Westmanland, Sweden
Aka Little Copper, Small Copper, Flame Copper

RECOGNITION
< 1.25 in. Both sexes, **DFW bright coppery or brassy red** with prominent black-brown spots and border; **DHW dark gray-brown with thick, bright orange submarginal zigzag**, lined inwardly by small blue spots. Orangey, gray-tipped VFW, purplish gray VHW with black dots and **fat, striking orange submarginal zigzag**. **VARIATION** The isolated PNW population is nearest both in appearance and proximity to *L. p. arctodon* (Beartooth Copper), the N Rocky Mtn race named from Beartooth Pass, MT. The next closest is *L. p. alpestris* described from Mt. Dana, Mono Co., CA. Both W ssp. are quite brassy on the upperside, but the High Sierra ssp. is darker gray beneath. All colors are somewhat suppressed and duller in *L. p. arethusa* from nr Calgary, AB; it flies at lower elevations and comes no closer to Cascadia than Glacier NP, MT. **HOST PLANTS** Prob. alpine sorrel (*Oxyria digyna*) as in CA, though sorrel dock (*Rumex acetosa*) is reported for the Beartooths, and

Dorsal

Ventral

Polygonum phytolaccifolium is abundant in the Seven Devils. **ON THE WING** M August to E September. Overwinters as an egg, first-instar, or half-grown larva. One generation at high elevations, more in the lowlands. **HABITAT AND**

RANGE Circumpolar: Eurasia, arctic AK and Canada; High Sierra and N Rockies, NE OR; disturbed lowlands of NE-MW US and Canada. In Cascadia, the high arctic-alpine zone of the Wallowa Mtns in NE OR (Matterhorn Peak, Mt. Howard) and ID (S. Seven Devils).

The so-called American Copper occurs in widely differing conditions in the New World: as an arctic butterfly across the Far North and on high-elevation slopes in the Rockies and Sierra, along mountain streams in Alberta, and in weedy fields and vacant lots across the Northeast. Opler suspects that the eastern form may represent a very early (perhaps Colonial period) introduction of the European Small Copper, which would make sense given this disjunct distribution. Arctic-alpine *L. phlaeas* has been left behind in high outposts between Yosemite and Yellowstone, and in Oregon's Wallowa Mtns and Idaho's Seven Devils, where Kim Zumwalt recently found it on the trail to Purgatory Basin above Black Lake. Backpacking butterfliers may well find more.

Lustrous Copper   *Lycaena cupreus* (W. H. EDWARDS) 1870

"Oregon" (Crane Creek S of Lakeview, Lake Co., OR)
Aka Snow's Copper, *L. cuprea*

RECOGNITION < 1.25 in. Easily recognized by its **brilliant copper dorsum with black border and spots** (heavier in females), **light to dark gray VHW with black dots** and narrow orange zigzag, and (in WA) high rockslide habitat. American Coppers have dark DHW; Ruddy Coppers lack heavy black borders and spotting, are silvery white below. **VARIATION** The type dwells in C-S OR,

NW ID, and N CA. The N WA *L. c. henryae*, described from Caribou Pass, nr Pink Mtn, BC, tends to be oranger above and darker gray below, with smaller black spots, and lives in the arctic-alpine. CA and Great Basin forms are midmontane. **HOST PLANTS** Alpine sorrel (*Oxyria digyna*) in N WA (Pelham); mountain sorrel (*Rumex paucifolius*) and other docks in CA and OR. Nectars on yarrow and pussypaws (Dornfeld) and yellow groundsels (Comstock). **ON THE WING** L May to L August, peak in July-August, depending on altitude and snowmelt. June is best in the Ochocos, August on Slate Peak and Steens most years. Half-

Female, dorsal

Male, dorsal

grown larvae diapause. **HABITAT AND RANGE**
Mid-elevation slopes, high sagey meadows,
and roadsides; alpine ridges and rockslides (*L.
c. snowi*). Scattered in the mtns of W N Am in
N Cascades (WA), W Blues, Ochocos, Steens,
Warners, and S Cascades (OR), BC Coast Range,
Rockies, Basin and Range, and Sierra Nevada.

To find Lustrous Coppers in Washington, go
to Slate Peak, on the edge of the Pasayten
Wilderness in the N Cascades, between 7,000
and 7,500 feet. There, these bright cinders
haunt high ridges and rockslides along with
smoky Melissa's Arctics. A flash of brassy red
announces the butterfly's presence, but getting a good look is another matter; alighting
on a flower or stone it might be approached,
but seldom is pursuit across the talus successful. Habitats are more common and ne-
gotiable in Oregon, where Dornfeld called *L.
cupreus* "a jewel among Coppers." Comstock,
who gave it the name Lustrous Copper, said
that it "flashes its gaudy wings over the meadows of the high Sierras [and] delights the eye
of the beholder with its rich metallic lustre."

Male, ventral

Tailed Copper   *Lycaena arota* (BOISDUVAL) 1852
N Fk Feather R. Cyn, Plumas Co., CA
Aka Arota Copper, *Tharsalea*

RECOGNITION < 1.25 in. Males purplish brown above, females brown-spotted light orange; VFW orange and gray-brown, dark-spotted; **gray VHW has a complex design of white-rimmed black spots, bars, and swooshes,** and a prominent submarginal row of white crescents. **Both sexes, above and below, have orange zigzags running out onto a short but conspicuous tail.** Larger than most hairstreaks, with fancier pattern below. **VARIATION** The three populations of this species in W OR differ in pallor and size. Those from the Siskiyous/ SW Cascades are larger and darker as in Sierra Nevada, and those from the Warner Mtns smaller and paler, as in NV, while those in the Willamette Valley are small and bright with reduced spotting, similar to SF Bay Area coppers (Warren). **HOST PLANTS** Currants incl. *Ribes aureum, R. velutinum, R. divaricatum,* and *R. californicum.* Nectars prolifically on yellow and mauve composites incl. goldenrod, buckwheats incl. *Eriogonum nudum,* pearly everlasting, and clovers. **ON THE WING** M June to L September, peak in July-August. One brood, eggs overwinter. **HABITAT AND RANGE** Moist meadows and clearings, riparian, shrubby hillsides, mountain canyons. A band across the C West, most of CA, Baja N to W OR. S-C and SW OR sparingly; N into Willamette Valley.

Female, dorsal

Tailed Coppers tend to be sedentary and, though sometimes common in the Warners, tend toward rarity elsewhere. We have one 1897 record for Benton County, Oregon, and one from 1929 in Yamhill County, about which Kenny Fender in his 1931 list for the McMinnville, Oregon, area wrote, "A small local habitat of this species has thus far been the only colony found in this region." Dana Ross rediscovered it in the Luckiamute watershed in Benton County in 2003, and Andy Warren in Polk County the following year. It may have narrowly avoided extinction in the Willamette Valley, along with the Great Copper, Fender's Blue, and several other holdouts. The one Washington record (Yakima County, 1959) is considered erroneous. Tailed Coppers increase along the southern reaches between the Siskiyous and the Warners. Dornfeld wrote, "The butterflies do not stray from these colonies and seldom move more than a few hundred feet. [T]he males spend the morning hours pursuing mates

and passing intruders from perches on shrubs and trees." The tail at first suggests a hairstreak, but the crazy pattern below sorts it out from anything else.

Ventral

Male, dorsal

Gray Copper   *Lycaena dione* (SCUDDER) 1868

Denison and New Jefferson, IA
Aka Dione Copper, Great Gray Copper, *Gaeides*

IMPERILED IN BC

RECOGNITION < 1.75 in. **Large and bulky. Upperside rich slate to mole gray to brownish gray with orange zigzag on DHW, thicker and invading FW margin in female.** Underside with gray or black spots and orange marginal zigzag on VHW. **Male with two black DFW cellspots,** female with little orange on gray dorsum except for margin, more prominent red-orange zigzag on the **silvery gray, inky black-spotted underside.** Similar to *L. xanthoides,* but their exclusive ranges tell them apart. **VARIATION** No ssp. Great, Blue, and Lilac-bordered Coppers all show enlarged black spots in N CA and SW OR. **HOST PLANTS** Various larger docks (*Rumex*), incl. the tall, rose-going-to-rufous curly dock (*R. crispus*) and introduced sheep sorrel (*R. acetosella*). Nectars on yellow sweetclover (*Melilotus officinalis*) and milkweeds. **ON THE WING** M June to E September, peak in August. A single generation, eggs overwinter. **HABITAT AND RANGE** Open habitats with docks, incl. abandoned and fallow fields and meadows along streams and canals, sandy riverbeds, flowery banks, marshy lakeshores, occasionally cattail marshes. E MW and S-C Canada, extending NW across MT to ID panhandle and SE BC.

Female, dorsal

Female, dorsal

Gray and Great Coppers are close in relationship and appearance, yet do not overlap in occurrence. For most of the time since their description, they have been considered eastern and western subspecies of the same species. Scott lumped them with the intervening species, *L. editha*. The most convincing evidence now favors an interpretation of three different species. The Gray Copper barely qualifies for inclusion here, based on a record in the Idaho panhandle, and some 20 records around Cranbrook in southeastern British Columbia, where it is more common than formerly thought. It is a fairly adventitious species and should be sought along ditches and in wet fields in Spokane and Pend Oreille counties, Washington. Farther east, Gray Coppers visit milkweed flowers together with Viceroys in hot August. Dione, who bore Aphrodite from Zeus, was a Titan—a suitable namesake for a giant copper.

Female, ventral

Edith's Copper   *Lycaena editha* (MEAD) 1878

Lake Tahoe, Placer Co., CA
Aka *Gaeides*

RECOGNITION
< 1.25 in. Male **dorsum dark mole-gray to brown**, with small dark spots esp. on FW cell, sometimes a vague orange HW zigzag; female browner with much creamy suffusion and larger spots, prominent light orange zigzag. vFW orangey. **vHW striking, with large ovoid, round, and kidney-shaped brown spots set against a tan to gray ground**, white crescent-bands, and orange-and-brown crescents along the edge. No other butterflies have such a pattern; Mariposa Copper has black spots on gray. Related Great and Gray Coppers are much larger. **VARIATION** Highly

Female, dorsal

Male, ventral

variable within and between populations. Shape and degree of confluence of the vHW spots, the ground color, and the amount of orange all vary considerably throughout the range, with several names applied. Though Edith's grows larger and less spotted in the Shasta-Siskiyou region and some adults may be confused with those of the Great Copper, Gordon Pratt and his colleagues showed that their larvae are readily distinguishable, and suggested this race may be of recent origin, having followed weedy docks along the railroads. **HOST PLANTS** Annual or perennial docks (*Rumex*), such as *R. paucifolius* in SW OR. Nectars on yarrow, spreading dogbane, and other mountain flowers. In a meadow near Little Payette Lake, ID, they nectared preferentially on a small mariposa lily (*Calochortus* sp.). **ON THE WING** M June to E September, peak in July (earlier or later as per elevation). A single generation, eggs overwinter. **HABITAT AND RANGE** Comstock called Edith "a child of the uplands." Flowery meadows, streambanks, roadsides, clearings. NW US. Selkirk and Blue Mtns in WA, S in ID and Wallowas, Ochocos, S Cascades, Siskiyous, and Warners in OR. Expanding in Spokane Co.

Female, ventral

Male, dorsal

Theodore Mead ranged over the West collecting butterflies for the great lepidopterist W. H. Edwards of West Virginia, hoping for his daughter's hand. Most of the species Mead discovered were named by Edwards, some after him. But Mead described this species himself, naming it in honor of his intended, whom he did eventually marry. From above, Edith's resembles a diminutive Gray or Great Copper, and their ventral patterns sometimes converge, but they remain separate where Edith's Copper meets the other two species. In Washington, it was long known only from the Blue Mountains, until I found it southeast of Mt. Spokane in 2000. In 2004, Chris Schmidt first found the species in British Columbia south of Cranbrook. Subsequent records in both areas suggest it may be expanding its range in our direction from the south and east.

Great Copper *Lycaena xanthoides* (BOISDUVAL) 1852

Sacramento Co., CA
Aka Great Gray Copper, Gray Copper, *Gaeides*

RECOGNITION < 1.75 in. **Large and bulky** for a copper. Upperside brownish gray with orange zigzag on DHW, thicker and invading FW margin in female. Underside with gray or black spots and orange marginal zigzag on VHW. **Male with one black DFW cell-spot**, female with pale orange infused over brownish dorsum, **light tan underside with large gray-black spots**, white band basal to VHW zigzag, suggestion of a short tail on HW. **VARIATION** Highly variable in SW (Jackson Co.) OR, some resembling Edith's Coppers in the vicinity; on the whole they have larger, blacker

Female, dorsal

Female, ventral

spots and a grayer ground color below than the type, and less orange on both sides. **HOST PLANTS** In CA, various larger docks (*Rumex*) used, incl. curly dock (*R. crispus*). In OR, caterpillars feed on willow dock (*R. salicifolius*), and adults nectar exclusively on Willamette Valley gumweed (*Grindelia integrifolia × nana*). **ON THE WING** L May to L August, peak in July. A single generation; eggs overwinter, can survive inundation but do better when not flooded. **HABITAT AND RANGE** Grassy hillsides, gulches, and clearings farther S in its range; in the Willamette Valley, seasonally flooded wetland prairie areas dominated by tufted hairgrass (*Deschampsia cespitosa*). Essentially CA, from Baja to OR, where it occurs chiefly in the Siskiyous, Medford to Siskiyou Summit; and sparingly N in the Willamette Valley.

Kenny Fender found it on Ralph Macy's farm in Yamhill County, along with many other butterflies now rare or absent, in 1928. Corvallis-area records stretch sparsely from 1896 to 1970, but it hasn't been seen there since; and a 1954 record from Coburg in Lane County came from a site later destroyed by construction of I-5. Happily, Paul Severns rediscovered it in several Lane County wetland prairie remnants in the summer of 2004, showing that Dornfeld was correct when he wrote: "Very likely small colonies are hidden in unexpected places elsewhere in western Oregon." Its numbers are very low, but Severns' research has determined the butterfly's specific management needs, and also that adults may fly more than a kilometer from their birthplace, so we can hope that they will be able to colonize newly restored habitats.

Male, dorsal

Male, ventral

Gorgon Copper   *Lycaena gorgon* (BOISDUVAL) 1852

N Fk Feather R. Cyn, Butte Co., CA
Aka Buckwheat Copper, *Gaeides*

RECOGNITION
> 1.5 in. **Large** for a copper. **Males bright brown with rich purple iridescence, females dull brown or straw-yellow with black and fawn patches**, orange

submarginal zigzag pronounced. Whitish or creamy gray below with the modest orange marginal zigzag reduced to small lunules, and black spots many and pronounced. Checked white fringe. Bigger and grayer below than Purplish; when the Great Copper occurs nearby, it is grayer above, has larger, browner spots below. **VARIATION** Three ssp. occupy the Warner Mtns and the Rogue and Klamath drainages. Warner Mtns coppers have larger black spots on the yellowish underside, the females tawny above. Rogue coppers have smaller spots on a whitish ground, the females dusky, some nearly melanic. Klamath individuals are intermediate between the two. **HOST PLANTS** In OR, *Eriogonum nudum*. Nectars esp. on the buckwheat host and yellow composite remnants near it, and spreading dogbane. Shapiro notes "an extreme preference" for woolly sunflower (*Eriophyllum lanatum*) in some places. **ON THE WING** L May to L August, peak in July. Eggs overwinter. **HABITAT AND RANGE** Mountain slopes, canyons, roadsides, seepages, oak-pine woodlands, and chaparral, where *E. nudum* grows. N Baja through montane CA to SW OR (Lake, Douglas, Josephine, Jackson, Klamath cos). Apparently absent N of Canyonville, Douglas Co., despite host presence.

Essentially a California endemic, the Gorgon looks overgrown for a copper. The chalky, ink-spotted, orange-lunuled

Female, ventral

Male, ventral

Male (left) and female (right), dorsal

underside (usually what's showing when the butterfly is at rest) suggests a big blue more than a copper, to my eyes. I have encountered it nectaring and mudpuddling along the Illinois River Canyon road, not far from the type locality, just when the mountain azalea and Siskiyou iris were fully in bloom, in company with Leanira Checkerspots, Moss's Elfins, and Cedar Hairstreaks. It has a powerful flight but seldom strays far from the host buckwheats, according to Andy Warren. Since this butterfly is a beautiful thing, it must have been its size that put Boisduval in mind of the three horrible, island-dwelling monsters called the Gorgons. The worst of them was Medusa, whom Perseus slayed. Perseus' guide and helper in this task, Hermes, gave his name to another handsome copper: yellow-tailed *L. hermes*, restricted to the California/Baja border district, is about half the size of a large Gorgon.

Ruddy Copper   *Lycaena rubidus* (BEHR) 1866

Horse Prairie, E of Lakeview, Lake Co., OR
Aka *Chalceria, rubida*

RECOGNITION < 1.25 in. **Male brilliant fiery copper above** with purple shades, narrow black border and white fringe. **Female dull gold to brown with black spots and dull orange zigzag**. Underside buffy to silvery white with spots small, if any, and no orange zigzag. Female similar to Blue Copper, but latter may have biggish black spots below, lacks any orange zigzag above, and sometimes has some blue scaling. To be sure, associate with males or host plants. Lustrous Copper males are much more spotted, with broad black border. American Copper brassy, with dark HW. **VARIATION** The ssp. in WA and along the Columbia in OR has dark females and olive-buff undersides with small but distinct rows of black spots and white crescents on the VHW. From the Ochocos and

Wallowas of OR S through the Malheur Basin and W ID, dark females occur, and individuals have a near-absence of spots below on a creamy to pale tangerine background. S Cascades and the Sierra Nevada have much orange on females and VHW light and immaculate. But there is much variation, and these averages don't always hold, with all phenotypes flying together in some sites. **HOST PLANTS** Species of dock (*Rumex*) incl. *R. salicifolius* (Newcomer), *R. venosus* (Pelham), and alpine sorrel (*Oxyria digyna*). Adults, esp. males,

Female, dorsal

Male, dorsal

nectar on alfalfa, buckwheats, rabbitbrush, yarrow, sweetclover, shrubby cinquefoil, and thistles. **ON THE WING** M May to L August, peak in June-July (later higher). One brood, eggs overwinter. **HABITAT AND RANGE** Hot, dry areas, edges of meadow, banks of watercourses, sagebrush/juniper flats, pine forest glades, sandy canals, washes, and dry creekbeds. Lower elevations in WA, low and high in OR. W except SW. E WA S of the Spokane R. (except N into Okanogan Valley); E OR, all ID; absent from OR Cascades N of Crater Lake.

When I hear "copper," this is the butterfly that comes to mind. The shimmering male is one of the most brilliant butterflies in North America, the hot-ingot glow even shot with the deep purple flames of the forge when fresh. I got to know it in the sandy bottoms of prairie creeks, where it streaked over hot sand to investigate potential mates and settled to nectar at watercress alongside Gray and Purplish Coppers. The Blue Copper is closely related, and the females of the two can be hard to tell apart away from their host plants. The larvae may be symbiotically involved with ants, like those of many

Male, ventral

lycaenids; Jon Pelham has found it in association with *Formica subpolita*. A rewarding and demanding place to seek Ruddy Coppers is the Juniper Dunes Wilderness in Franklin County, Washington. It may also be found along old railway sidings, and high in the Oregon Ochocos at Big Summit Prairie.

Blue Copper   *Lycaena heteronea* BOISDUVAL 1852

Nr Sausalito, Marin Co., CA
Aka Varied Blue, Bluish Copper, *Chalceria*

RECOGNITION
< 1.5 in. **Large** for a lycaenid. Male brilliant to purplish blue above, often basally greenish, with narrow black border and **veins standing out against nearly transparent blue. Female soft gray-brown with black spots**, sometimes slightly yellowish and/or blue-shot. Ventrum clear, silvery white, whitish, or sordid yellow-tan with sharp black dots on VFW, **VHW usually unspotted** in our region, or spots blurred, without white rings. **No orange marginal zigzag** above or below. Male resembles Boisduval's and Silvery Blues above, but these are slower, smaller, less intense blue, and more distinctly spotted below, white or black with white rings. Female Boisduval's Blues less spotted above; female Ruddy Coppers very similar, but usually have more yellowish infusion and some orange zigzagging on DHW.
VARIATION The spots on the underside vary dramatically throughout the species, from virtually unspotted in coastal CA to heavily spotted with gray blobs in CO, generally becoming more unspotted toward the W; but a single population can contain both immaculate and very spotty butterflies. The ventral color of females varies also, tanner below near Mt. Lassen, pale gray in the Ruby Mtns of NV, and silvery or yellowish to the N. Various ssp. names have been applied across the range. **HOST PLANTS** Many buckwheats incl., in WA, *Eriogonum sphaerocephalum, E. douglasii, E. compositum, E. nudum, E. elatum,* and *E. microthecum*; and in OR, *E. heracleoides* and *E. umbellatum*. Nectars on the

Female, dorsal

Female, ventral

Male, dorsal

Male, ventral

hosts as well as on sunflowers, asters, rabbit-brush, yarrow, gaillardia, fiddleneck, and milk-weeds. **ON THE WING** E May to E September, peak in July. One generation, eggs overwinter. **HABITAT AND RANGE** Sage-steppe, grassland, pinewood openings, montane and subalpine slopes and ridges, canyons, alluvial plains, and open plateaus. W N Am, mid-BC to mid-AZ and coastal CA, E to Great Plains. SE BC, ID, E WA, E OR, and W into Klamath-Siskiyous.

Anyone only generally acquainted with butterflies would instantly take this bright sky-blue creature for a blue, as did Boisdu-val. In fact, the nature of its blue (some-times reflecting green, sometimes lilac), and its size and rapid flight, enable prac-ticed lepidopterists to quickly recognize the Blue Copper even on the wing; and its wing venation and other structures ally it with the coppers. Structure tends to be conser-vative, while color is evolutionarily plastic. The genetic difference causing the Ruddy Copper to flash red and the Blue Copper to shimmer azure may be very minor. How-ever, its haploid chromosome number is 68, compared to the standard copper quotient of 24 and the Ruddy Copper's 38. Blue Cop-pers are among the commonest coppers and strongest in flight but are not particu-larly skittish. Males patrol the landscape for females instead of perching and flying out like most coppers. Warren writes that they "frantically patrol between flowerheads" and defend perches on their buckwheat hosts, where females hang out; and fre-quently visit mud. Once along the Minam River, he found a mud-puddle club of hundreds.

Purplish Copper   *Lycaena helloides* (BOISDUVAL) 1852

San Francisco, CA
Aka *Epidemia*

RECOGNITION < 1.25 in. Males dark brown above refracting **amethyst-purple**; females orange with heavy black spotting and brown borders on dorsum, orange and black-spotted on the VFW; both **warm cocoa-brown to pinkish tan with fine black dots on VHW. Marginal

orange zigzag on D/VHW usually well developed on both sexes; other coppers have white or gray undersides or copper on top. **VARIATION** Aside from strong sexual dimorphism, variation is largely in size and brightness of the orange zigzag, amount of dark spotting, and depth and extent of orange in females, some so bright as to resemble Lustrous Coppers, others smudgy and almost melanic. **HOST PLANTS** Many herbaceous docks and knotweed/smartweeds incl. *Rumex acetosella*, *R. obtusifolius*, Polygo-

Female, dorsal

Male, dorsal

Male, ventral

Two More Coppers to Watch For

Dorcas Copper / *Lycaena dorcas* W. Kirby 1837 / The Pas, MB. The Dorcas Copper occurs to the N and NE of our territory, across AK and Canada. A univoltine bog and fen specialist, it occupies a much narrower niche than the Purplish, eating shrubby cinquefoil (*Potentilla fruticosa*) and marsh cinquefoil (*P. palustris*) to the W. Its males' purple is bluer, females darker and less orange above, wings rounder, and marginal orange HW zigzag is thin, basal, and fragmentary. Much alike and possibly hybridizing, *L. dorcas* and *L. helloides* can be difficult to distinguish in the N Rockies. Guppy and Shepard show *L. dorcas* only to Lillooet, BC, but Ferris records it in ID and WA as *L. d. florus*. However, it has also been suggested that *L. florus* may be a species distinct from both *L. helloides* and *L. dorcas*, feeding on blueberries (*Vaccinium*) instead of cinquefoils or docks. Kondla has found what he considers *L. (d.?) florus* in BC "within spitting distance" of the US border above NE WA. Field workers should watch for purplish coppers in habitats with huckleberries, and see if they can make a connection.

Bronze Copper / *Lycaena hyllus* (Guerin-Meneville) 1831 / "Amerique du Nord" / Aka *Hyllolycaena, thoe*. The Bronze is quite large and bright above, rounded in outline, two-toned orange and dove-gray below, with a fat, prominent orange HW zigzag. Chiefly eastern and marshy habitat–limited, it is especially subject to fragmentation; the first local extinction I observed befell a colony when a church parking lot replaced a marshy "vacant" lot (Pyle 2011). In BC it has been found in the NE corner and the Flathead River valley in the SE; Norbert Kondla encountered it beside sewage lagoons nr Prince George, possibly an introduction. NW MT and C ID records suggest that the Bronze Copper might also occur in our area. Flight peaks L July to E August.

num amphibium, P. punctatum, P. hydropiper, and *P. persicaria*; strongly associated with silverweed (*Argentina egedii* at the coast, *A. anserina* in the Columbia Basin). Nectars on garden thyme, white heather, catnip, Douglas aster, white clover, creeping buttercup, birds-foot trefoil, blue and purple mints, gumweeds, tansy ragwort, hawkbit, white fleabane, Canada thistle, glasswort, and knotweeds. **ON THE WING** L April to M October, peaks in May and August. Two, perhaps three generations, depending on growing season, elevation, and moisture. There may be single-brooded populations in higher mtns (but see sidebar).

Eggs overwinter. **HABITAT AND RANGE** Almost every habitat from vacant lot to wildland, except deep forest and the arctic-alpine: field corners with knotweed and fleabane, streambanks with docks, back-beach swales, high-country meadows, gardens and parks. Across the NW of the continent, and throughout Cascadia.

A multivoltine generalist with the broadest niche of any Cascadian butterfly but the Cabbage White, the Purplish Copper can be extraordinarily abundant. I saw thousands on the wing, basking, and nectaring in an extensive knotweed marsh alongside

Flathead Lake in northwest Montana, and courting in the evening on Nisqually National Wildlife Refuge in Washington. The butterfly is one of the great survivors in the urban landscape yet turns up in many habitats, often as a member of a tough gang of Mylitta Crescents, Woodland Skippers, and other highly adaptive species. Together, they help keep western Washington from being completely butterfly-free. In courtship, the male hovers just over the perched female while they both flutter their wings in a blur. The eponymous purple glints are often obvious on fresher males, but when the sun strikes a new emergent just right, the ultra-violet flash can be almost blinding. The epithet means "like helle," likening this species to *L. helle* of central and northern Europe. That species' common name, Violet Copper, clearly explains why.

Lilac-bordered Copper *Lycaena nivalis* (BOISDUVAL) 1869

Gold Lake, Sierra Co., CA
Aka Nivalis Copper, Lilac-edged Copper, Snowy Copper, *Epidemia*

SPECIAL CONCERN IN BC

RECOGNITION < 1.5 in. Above much like Purplish Copper in both sexes: male copper-brown with purple sheen in the right light, female light orange or yellow with dark spots and border and brown in-filling (OR, dusky brown in C Cascades), both with orange marginal zigzag on DHW. Underside **bright yellow to pale buff with black spots, lilac-purple band across outer third or more of VHW with embedded orange zigzag**, or pale grayish mauve over all or most of VHW. **VARIATION** Great and confusing, from non-contrasty, light

Female, dorsal

Male, dorsal

Male, ventral

Male, ventral

Male (left) and female (right), dorsal

pinkish beige covering much of the VHW, to strikingly two-toned, bright yellow and lilac below. At the extremes, these look like different species. Worse, both types often appear in the same populations. Those in the Siskiyous are more uniform, big and very brightly colored with yellow and pink-purple bands. The pallid one-tones predominate E of the Cascades, becoming even paler to the NE. Several names have been given where degrees of difference seem to warrant them, but for most of us the trick is to determine the monotone coppers, esp. worn ones, as *L. nivalis* at all. **HOST PLANTS** Douglas knotweed (*Polygonum* *douglasii*) is known, others likely. Nectars on herbaceous spiraeas, yarrow, woolly sunflower, and many others. **ON THE WING** M May to L August, peak in July. A single generation, eggs overwinter. **HABITAT AND RANGE** Chiefly montane, from 1,000 to 7,000 feet. Flowery hillsides, meadows, and streambanks, canyons, gravelly roadsides, forest edge, and high sage-steppe. W ranges, BC through CO and CA. WA mtns E of Cascade Crest plus Olympics; OR mtns except Coast Range; ID, S BC.

A fresh Lilac-bordered Copper, banded Easter yellow-and-mauve below and flashing violet above when it opens, provides one of the loveliest sights of all our butterflies. What fluke of glacial history causes it (like the Spring White) to occupy the high Olympics, yet to skip the western Cascades of Washington but not those of Oregon? And how is its multiplicity of forms to be interpreted evolutionarily and taxonomically? Several named races are mapped as occurring together in the Blues and Siskiyous; while subspecies often meet and blend, they should not fly in the same locality and remain distinct. This may be a case of polymorphism (a genetic predisposition for more than one form), or even separate species, as some suspect.

Mariposa Copper   *Lycaena mariposa* (REAKIRT) 1866

Gold Lake, Sierra Co., CA
Aka Reakirt's Copper, Forest Copper, Makah Copper, *Epidemia*

MAKAH COPPER CANDIDATE IN WA

RECOGNITION
< 1.25 in. Males coffee-brown above with mild purple iridescence, females pale to yellow-or-ange to almost black with heavy black spots and borders, both with **black-and-white checked fringes**. Orange DHW zigzag vague on male, prominent on female. VFW bright yellow or orange with black spots; **VHW brown-gray to frosty-gray jotted with black dots and dashes in a sort of Morse code–like pattern**; sometimes strongly two-toned with inner half charcoal, outer half pale ashen, divided by a prominent row of black arches. Marginal macules often form crescents or chevrons. **VARIATION** Significant geographical variation across the region. Heretofore, those in the NE have been referred to *L. m. penrosae*, of the Rockies; those of the Cascades, Olympics, and SE OR to the Sierra Nevada type; and those of the NW coast

Female, dorsal (ssp. *thea*)

to *L. m. charlottensis*, described from Haida Gwaii (Queen Charlotte Is.), but see remarks. **HOST PLANTS** Various heaths (Ericaceae) incl. dwarf bilberry (*Vaccinium cespitosum*) in N CA, bog cranberry (*V. oxycoccos*) in WA, and bog bilberry (*V. uliginosum*) in BC. Nectars on aster, pearly everlasting, yarrow, oxeye daisy, yellow sedum, and spiraea. A major nectar source in WA is swamp gentian (*Gentiana douglasi-*

Female, ventral (ssp. *thea*)

Male, dorsal (ssp. *thea*)

Male, ventral (ssp. *marya*)

ana), whose small white blooms peak with the butterfly's flight period; and in the OR Coast Range great burnet (*Sanguisorba officinalis*). **ON THE WING** L May to L September, peak in July-August. Single-brooded, eggs overwinter. **HABITAT AND RANGE** Mountain and coastal bogs and meadows, sunlit clearings in the lodgepole-pine belt, roadsides, moist meadows, and sphagnum bogs, but also dry slopes and summits, sea level to high elevations. NW N Am, WY to Yukon, S to C CA. All mtn ranges in BC, ID, WA, OR, and N CA, as well as lowlands in maritime outposts on Haida Gwaii and Vancouver Is., and on intermittent coastal, Coast Range, and inshore bogs toward the S.

W. J. Holland noticed the strikingly different appearance of Mariposa Coppers from Queen Charlotte Island, and named them accordingly in 1930. Eighty-seven years later, Paul Hammond and I (Pyle and Hammond 2018) described nine new subspecies to compass the distinctive variation and evolutionary history of Mariposa Coppers throughout their range. One of these, which Sally Hughes and I found in 1975 on boggy Ahlstrom's Prairie, between Lake Ozette and the Pacific Ocean in Olympic National Park, adjacent to the Makah Indian Reservation, is the Makah Copper. Probably an ancient post-glacial entity, it spread down the coast on peatlands during a time of lowered sea levels, giving rise to other populations in Washington coastal bogs as well as in Coast Range and Clatsop County bogs in Oregon, found by Candace Fallon and Mike Patterson. Mary Paetzel discovered the sole Siskiyou bog colonies. Much of the potential coastal and montane habitat has been logged or converted to commercial cranberry bogs. The much more widespread mountain Mariposas can be found in abundance on roadside flowers throughout our late summer ranges. Brightly checkered fringes and dot-dash-dot underside quickly give them away. *Mariposa* means "butterfly" in Spanish, so this is the "Butterfly Copper."

Subfamily Theclinae: Hairstreaks

Like the blues, hairstreaks are an artificial assemblage of genera that might have their origin in more than one ancestral line. In fact, what we call "blues" and "hairstreaks" run together at several points in the tropics. In North America, however, hairstreaks make up a more or less recognizable and related cluster of butterflies. Many of these, though not all, have hairlike tails projecting from the outer angle of the hindwing. There may be one, two, or rarely three tails per hindwing, and even the tailless species tend to have a drawn-out stub that looks as if it is about to grow a tail. The tails often have bright orange and/or blue "hairstreak

spots" near them, further exaggerating the "false-head" mechanism by drawing birds' attention to the rear wing rather than the body. Thus, hairstreaks often bear bird-strikes near the tails, ending up safe, but tailless. Swallowtails and other tailed butterflies have all converged on this effective trait.

The term "hairstreak" is an old one, with alternative explanations of its origin. The "hair" part almost certainly refers to the tails. The "streak" may have come from the streaky patterns of the undersides of many species, or from the rapid, streaking manner of flight. They tend to hang about particular branches, darting fleetly out at passersby before resuming their posts, and may often be told by this behavior even before you see their colors and patterns. Green hairstreaks and elfins, on the other hand, fly close to the ground where their herbaceous or low-shrubby hosts grow. Hairstreaks have especially proliferated in the tropics, where brilliant metallic colors and unbelievably long, elaborate tails make them some of the showiest butterflies anywhere. Of the 2,000 or so species worldwide, fewer than 100 occur in North America, 22 in Cascadia. Their immature stages are similar to those of coppers and blues, with grublike larvae and unadorned, streamlined and blunt chrysalides. The caterpillars feed on leaves and flower parts of a variety of herbs, shrubs, trees, and parasites of trees.

Comparison of Hairstreaks (Subfamily Theclinae)
Specimens are shown approximately at life size

Great Blue Hairstreak
Atlides halesus

Golden Hairstreak
Habrodais grunus

Sooty Hairstreak
Satyrium fuliginosa

Halfmoon Hairstreak
Satyrium semiluna

Behr's Hairstreak
Satyrium behrii

California Hairstreak
Satyrium californica

Coral Hairstreak
Satyrium titus

Coral Hairstreak
Satyrium titus

Sylvan Hairstreak
Satyrium sylvinus

Gold-hunter's Hairstreak
Satyrium auretorum

Mountain Mahogany Hairstreak
Satyrium tetra

Hedgerow Hairstreak
Satyrium saepium

Comparison of Hairstreaks (Subfamily Theclinae)
Specimens are shown approximately at life size

Western Green Hairstreak
Callophrys affinis

Bramble Green Hairstreak
Callophrys dumetorum

Sheridan's Green Hairstreak
Callophrys sheridanii

Thicket Hairstreak
Callophrys spinetorum

Johnson's Hairstreak
Callophrys johnsoni

Brown Elfin
Callophrys augustinus

Moss's Elfin
Callophrys mossii

Cedar Hairstreak
Callophrys gryneus

Hoary Elfin
Callophrys polios

Western Pine Elfin
Callophrys eryphon

Gray Hairstreak
Strymon melinus

Golden Hairstreak   *Habrodais grunus* (BOISDUVAL) 1852

Mt. Diablo, Contra Costa Co., CA
Aka Chinquapin Hairstreak, Live Oak Hairstreak, Boisduval's
Hairstreak, Yellow Hairstreak, Canyon Oak Hairstreak

CANDIDATE IN WA

RECOGNITION
< 1.25 in. **Large** for
a hairstreak. **Toasty
brown above, golden
tan below**. Deeper
brown-shaded
on males, brown-
tipped and -bordered on tanner females.
Ventrum faintly striated with brown and white,
submarginally rimmed with metallic silver
crescents and flecks; VHW blue-scaled near
the **short, sharp tails**. **VARIATION** Cascades
and Coast Range individuals are ochre-yellow
or golden, with much lighter markings than
those occurring from the Siskiyous down into
CA, which are darker brown above and more
heavily marked below. **HOST PLANTS** Golden
chinquapin (*Chrysolepis chrysophylla*). In SW OR

and CA, canyon live oak (*Quercus chrysolepis*),
huckleberry oak (*Q. vacciniifolia*), and tanoak
(*Notholithocarpus densiflorus*) may also be
used. Nectars on pearly everlasting, goldenrod,
thistles, and other late-summer composites,
and on catkins of golden chinquapin (Neill).
ON THE WING E July to L September, peak in
August. Single generation. Adults said to be
somewhat crepuscular; Warren writes that they
rest and fly among the shade of the hosts for
most of the day, becoming more active from 3
to 6:30 p.m. **HABITAT AND RANGE** Groves of
golden chinquapin (and oaks in CA), roadsides
and edges from Baja (and AZ relict stands) to
Skamania Co., WA. OR Cascades, sparingly
in OR Coast Range (Mary's Peak, Benton Co.;
Chinquapin Point, Lincoln Co.), and Siskiyous.
Should be further sought among disjunct,
dispersed, and isolated chinquapins growing
along Hood Canal in Jefferson Co., WA.

Male, dorsal

Ventral

Golden Hairstreaks are strictly linked to their host plant, their chalky eggs, like tiny squashed golfballs, conspicuous on the downy undersides of its leaves in fall, winter, and early spring. The species follows the tree's occurrence north, sometimes abundant but thinning from California up to and just over the Columbia. After years of searching for the plant and the hairstreak in Washington, Sarah Anne Hughes, John Hinchliff, and I finally found both in the southern Big Lava Bed in Gifford Pinchot National Forest in early September

1980. The host trees are liable to damage from nearby logging and herbicide use but spread with moderate disturbance. GPNF biologists have since sought to survey for additional populations and to accommodate the species. The future of this big, beautiful hairstreak in Cascadia will depend upon foresters managing *for* a tree once routinely eliminated as a "weed species." While adults spend most of their time among the foliage of the trees, which they match very well, they are conspicuous when they come down to nectar early or late in the day.

Great Blue Hairstreak   *Atlides halesus* (CRAMER) 1777

"Virginien"
Aka Great Purple Hairstreak

RECOGNITION > 1.5 in. **Big** for a lycaenid, "tropical-looking" with a **long tail on each HW** (two on females). Male **brilliant iridescent blue above** with black borders and double stigmata, female's blue duller, more localized near base. Uniform black to purplish gray beneath (VFW blue-streaked) with metallic blue, green, or gold patches near tails. **Bright coral-red spots at base of VHW/ VFW; abdomen red below**, shiny blue above. **VARIATION** Little among the W population, which has only one tail in the male, and no red bar at the outer angle of the VHW, unlike the E US ssp. **HOST PLANTS** Oak mistletoe (*Phoradendron leucarpum*), which parasitizes Garry oaks in the Willamette Valley, other oaks in S OR; and additional mistletoes on other trees farther S. Nectars prolifically on composites (beggarticks or fleabane) and on spreading dogbane (*Apocynum androsaemifolium*). **ON THE WING** E April to E October; OR records chiefly in July-August. Number of broods varies

N to S, with two or three overlapping flights in OR. **HABITAT AND RANGE** Breeds only among oak mistletoe in the region, so mostly found on oak savannah, but can stray into any habitat and to higher elevations and latitudes. Breeding from Mexico into S US, N along W Coast. Jackson to Lake cos in S OR, Yamhill, Marion, and Benton cos in Willamette Valley.

Anyone who encounters this spectacular animal as it nectars singly and single-mindedly is likely to exclaim aloud. Such is its size, color, and overall appearance, flashing scarlet spots and iridescent tails waving in the breeze, that it definitely transports the imagination to the tropics. While there are many dramatic hairstreaks in Central and South America, most of our species are more subtle; this one gives just a glimpse of neotropical wonders to the south. It barely enters our area of concern as a wanderer and a marginal breeding species among remnant oak communities in Oregon. The larvae are like little green slugs with red and yellow highlights and orange down; pupae, black-mottled brown, look like the bark they are often formed against.

Male, ventral

It is doubtful that this species survives the winter where hard frosts occur with any frequency, but it reestablishes itself from spring migrants. This may account for the small number of spring records in the Willamette Valley and relatively more in the summer. Pioneer collectors Kenny Fender and Ralph Macy knew it in Yamhill County in the '30s; recent records include Corvallis (Warren), Lane County (Paul Severns), and Polk County (G. and A. Peters). The absence of mistletoe from Garry oak in Washington means that strays might be found there, but no summer breeders, at least not until mistletoe jumps the Columbia with climate change. The alternate name Great Purple Hairstreak has surprising currency in spite of the butterfly's striking blue color.

Sooty Hairstreak   *Satyrium fuliginosa* (W. H. EDWARDS) 1861

Norden, El Dorado Co., CA
Aka Sooty Gossamer Wing, *fuliginosum*

RECOGNITION
< 1.25 in. **Small, rounded, tailless, and dull; gray above and below. Males lack FW stigmata**. Female fuller-winged and warmer colored. Dorsum varies from taupe or mouse-brown to slate or blackish gray; ventrum cool ashy gray or gray-brown. Unmarked above. Below, a small sub-basal cluster of more or less pronounced or smudgy, white-ringed black dots, repeated in a submedian row; submarginal row of vague crescents—reminiscent of the pattern of blues. Gray-brown fringes. Boisduval's Blue females may look similar but differ in having some blue

Female, ventral

Warren reports that males perch on manzanita near the lupine hosts. **ON THE WING** M June to M August. A single generation, eggs over-winter. **HABITAT AND RANGE** In Jackson Co., OR, frequents rocky outcroppings, subalpine slopes, peaks and ridges, from 5,800 to 6,800 feet. NE, N-C, and NW CA, and SW OR.

It was long thought that we had only one species, occupying much of the West. But now two are recognized, and the original name, *S. fuliginosa*, refers only to those Sooty Hairstreaks in northern California and southwestern Oregon. All the rest are considered to belong to the next species, *S. semiluna*. As Andy Warren points out, it is amazing that one type of Sooty Hairstreak (that has sex brands) flies at low elevations in May, while quite a different-looking sort (with rudimentary male stigmata) flies from late July into late August, just to the west and at high altitude. These populations are probably separated by only 20 air miles but may not have come into contact for a very long time. Inexperienced—and sometimes veteran—butterfly folk easily take these un-conventional hairstreaks for female blues. I certainly have. When worn, there is little to distinguish a Sooty from a similarly tatty fe-male Boisduval's Blue. When fresh it is more distinctive but glimmers with blue-green iri-descence that may further confuse the issue.

scaling at bases of wings above (Sooty has **no blue scales**), white fringes, and a dark bar in the D/VFW cell. **VARIATION** Large, dark, and angular Sooties occur from Mt. Ashland W to Dutchman Peak in Jackson Co., OR. A smaller, narrower-winged, grayer type was discovered by Erik Runquist on the Cascade-Siskiyou National Monument in E Jackson Co. All these *lack* stigmata on the male FW. **HOST PLANTS** Lupines, incl. *Lupinus albicaulis* and *L. croceus* in N CA. Little nectaring has been observed. Andy

Halfmoon Hairstreak   *Satyrium semiluna* KLOTS 1930

Moose, WY
Aka Sooty Hairstreak, Sagebrush Sooty Hairstreak, *S. fuliginosa/-um*

CRITICALLY IMPERILED IN BC

RECOGNITION < 1.25 in. **Small, rounded, tailless, and dull; gray above and below. Males have FW stigmata,** but may be small. Female fuller-winged and warmer colored. Dorsum varies from taupe or mouse-brown to slate

or blackish gray; ventrum cool ashy gray or gray-brown. Unmarked above. Below, a small sub-basal cluster of more or less pronounced or smudgy, white-ringed black dots, repeated in a submedian row; submarginal row of vague crescents, reminiscent of the pattern of blues. Gray-brown fringes. Boisduval's Blue females may look similar but differ in having some blue scaling at bases of wings above (Halfmoon has **no blue scales**), white fringes, a dark cell bar on the DFW, and usually one to three basal black spots on VHW. **VARIATION** Individuals vary a lot anyway, but a dizzying array of regional forms also occur. These differ primarily in size, color, and maculation, with very small, dark, immaculate ones on and around Mt. Hood, and bigger, paler, more spotty types to the S and E; also in development of stigmata, from prominent to nearly vestigial; and in habitat, altitude, and behavior. **HOST PLANTS** Lupines, incl. silky lupine (*Lupinus sericeus*) and prairie lupine (*L. lepidus*). Nectars prolifically on groundsels and other mountain wildflowers. Males perch on rabbitbrush, basin big sage, and other shrubs near lupines where females fly. **ON THE WING** M May to E September, peak in June-July, depending on location. A single generation, eggs overwinter. **HABITAT AND RANGE** Subalpine, high meadows, windy ridges, knolls and summits, sage-steppe plateaus, open slopes, pine forest openings, basin hillsides and mounds, and mountain roadsides, 1,000 to 8,500 feet. The upper W, N CO to N CA, W WY, SW MT, S to C ID, E OR, WA E slope Cascades; BC in S-most Okanagan.

See previous species, in which this one was formerly included. Halfmoon's range is very similar to that of Behr's Hairstreak, riding a lobe of suitable conditions northward up the Washington Cascades. But its habitat, host plant lupines, and flight period largely overlap with those of the Boisduval's Blue, so its likeness to that butterfly is all the more striking. Even still, the butterfly does have its own look. Perch awhile

Female, ventral

Male, ventral

Ventral

by a patch of woolly sunflowers with both species nectaring, and you will soon detect the distinctive traits of each. The Halfmoon can look much like a female Boisduval's Blue that has been rubbed below, and they both frequent lupines, but practice will give you the eye for it. Less ubiquitous than that blue and not often as numerous, the subtly lovely Halfmoon Hairstreak is always a special find.

Behr's Hairstreak   *Satyrium behrii* (W. H. EDWARDS) 1870

Mono Lake, Mono Co., CA
Aka Buckwheat Hairstreak, Orange Hairstreak, *Callipsyche*

CRITICALLY IMPERILED IN BC

RECOGNITION < 1 in. **Stub-tailed, female brassy or toasty golden, male oranger above with dark brown borders**, broadest along the leading edge, which contains a gray stigma on the male FW. Below, **agouti gray-brown dashed with white-edged black bars on the disc and margin**. Submarginal row of lumpy black chevrons encloses a blue patch below the lowest spot, an orange-red aurora in the second spot. Hedgerow Hairstreak is coppery, not brassy, above, and tailed; Golden is larger; both lack the complex pattern below. **VARIATION** Little across Cascadia, aside from those north of Chelan Co., WA, which average a little larger, darker orange above, and maybe more heavily spotted below. **HOST PLANTS** *Purshia tridentata* (antelope bitterbrush). Nectars on the host and wild buckwheats (*Eriogonum nudum, E. umbellatum, E. compositum*, others), "in which it delights" (Comstock). **ON THE WING** E May to E September, peak in June-July. A single generation, eggs overwinter, chrysalides hatch in summer. **HABITAT AND RANGE** Oak-pine forest, canyons, riparian areas, and shrub-steppe through much of the inner-W US, C CO to E CA; OR mostly E of the Cascade Crest, more narrowly up the range in WA, with records E along the Spokane River; barely into BC's Okanagan Valley; S ID.

Unlike the previous species, Behr's Hairstreak often occurs abundantly. Tapping bitterbrush clumps in midsummer is a good way to see it, since the females spend much of their time among the host plants and the males seek them there by perching and flying out at passing objects. If you can find a patch of sulphur-flower buckwheat in full bloom in a clearing among bitterbrush thickets, you may find these bright hairstreaks teeming among Lupine Blues, hoverflies, and other pollinators. Behr's is easier to approach than most hairstreaks. The flight is rapid among the bitterbrush scrub, but according to Comstock, "It is a docile insect [when nectaring] so preoccupied that it may be picked by hand." Hans

Male, ventral

Hermann Behr was the first to comment on the decline of the Xerces Blue, in 1875. His collections were destroyed in the 1906 San Francisco earthquake and fire.

California Hairstreak *Satyrium californica* W. H. EDWARDS 1862

Capell Creek, Napa Co., CA
Aka *S. californicum*

SPECIAL CONCERN IN BC

RECOGNITION < 1.25 in. Dark grayish brown above with **marked rufous patches near the HW margins**, sometimes also on the FW, more so in females. **Beneath, putty gray** with postmedian rows of prominent, oval or arched, white-ringed black spots, and a series of **submarginal red-orange spots all around the HW**, often extending halfway up FW. Blue tornal (="thecla") spot near HW tails is red-capped and has orange on both sides. Similar to *S. sylvinus nootka*, which is browner below and has VHW orange more restricted to tornus. In *S. californica* the **black spot basal from the blue "thecla" spot is a full-V chevron**, while on *S. sylvinus* it forms a check-mark or swoosh. **VARIATION** Within

Male, ventral

populations but not markedly between them, except Cascades and Siskiyou material may be lighter than that in the E ranges; and the reddish spotting on the DHW is often fused into a patch, esp. on females, in the Sierra and Cascades, and smaller and broken up above and brighter below in the Great Basin. HOST PLANTS Antelope bitterbrush (*Purshia tridentata*) is primary in Cascadia, with snowbrush ceanothus (*Ceanothus velutinus*) secondary, and perhaps *Quercus garryana* in SW OR. Elsewhere oaks and rosaceous shrubs and trees such as serviceberry and cherry are reported. Nectars profusely on spreading dogbane, chokecherry, oceanspray, willows, thistles, buckwheats, bitterbrush, and yarrow. ON THE WING E May to E September, peak in June-July. A single generation, eggs overwinter. HABITAT AND RANGE Chaparral, buckbrush scrub, oak woodlands, and shrubby canyons, throughout intermountain W from Baja to BC. Much of OR E of Cascade Crest and Siskiyous, most of ID, WA-BC chiefly up E flank of Cascades, with a few E outliers along upper Columbia R., Dishman Hills of Spokane (possibly misidentified), and Blue Mtns, 1,000 to 8,000 feet in Cascadia.

Though associated with oaks in the southern part of its range, the California Hairstreak apparently has nothing to do with our Garry oak but subsists here on shrubs instead. It may be difficult at first to tell apart the dark forms of the less common Sylvan Hairstreak, but the darker ventrum and more extensive orange spotting should do it in most cases; a good look at the butterfly while at nectar or in the hand will show the fine differences. Males are extremely flighty, posting themselves on prominences to fly out at possible females, especially in the afternoons. Though hard to keep your eye on, these frenetic insects have the virtue of returning to the same bush after being disturbed, so patience with net or binoculars is often rewarded with a second and third chance. And, unlike the Coral Hairstreak, where there is one California, there are usually more.

Sylvan Hairstreak   *Satyrium sylvinus* (BOISDUVAL) 1852

N Fk Feather R. Cyn, Plumas Co., CA
Aka Western Willow Hairstreak, *S. sylvinum*

RECOGNITION < 1.25 in. Triangular hairstreak shape, tailed in our area. **Gray-brown above, modestly spotted dull orange on the edge**, not suffused sharply reddish as in *S. californica*. **Underside gray-brown or silvery white** crossed by rows of **small, rounded, white-ringed black dots. vHw orange restricted to smallish patches**, much less prominent than on *S. californica*, on either side of **tornal blue patch**, which **is seldom orange-capped**; no orange on vFw margin. On *S. sylvinus* the **black spot basal from the blue "thecla" spot forms a check-mark or swoosh**, while on *S. californica* it is a full-V chevron.

VARIATION Quite variable overall but also geographically dimorphic. The type, of NE CA, is pale gray below. "Columbia Basin segregate" applies to disjunct white-underside populations in Yakima, Kittitas, and Douglas cos and the NE Blue Mtns in WA. Large, pale Sylvans in S Harney Co., OR, orangish above, are usually tailless. In between and around these colonies lives *S. s. nootka*, which is tailed and putty to gray-brown beneath; it ranges around Cascadia in most mountainous and some lowland districts. Of course, intergrades occur between the light- and dark-bottomed forms. **HOST PLANTS**

Male, ventral

Ventral

Willows: *Salix prolixa* on Vancouver Is.; white form exclusively on *S. exigua* (coyote willow) in E WA; prob. *S. sitchensis* and *S. scouleriana* in mtns. Favorite nectar plants incl. spreading dogbane, milkweeds, pearly everlasting, and horehound. Warren reports significant travel from willows to nectar sources. **ON THE WING** E May to M September, peak in July. Single-brooded, eggs overwinter. **HABITAT AND RANGE** Willow-bearing streamsides, lakeshores, wetlands, and nearby meadows and canyonsides, from sea level to mid- and occasionally high altitudes. The white-underside segregate occurs in lower, hotter canyons. Much of the W, Baja to BC to E CO. In Cascadia, mostly from W slope of the Cascades E, but present on E Vancouver Is., sparsely in Olympics, Salish Lowlands, NW OR Coast Range; and Siskiyous. Warren expects it to be found in all OR cos.

To see the beautiful, silvery white Sylvans you need to visit hot coyote willow canyons northeast of the Yakama Indian Nation in summer. You might encounter the browner form practically anywhere there are willows, though it is much less frequent as you approach the coast. It is useful to have the ssp. *nootka* (described from Vancouver Island) to cover this insect, which has gone by various names heretofore. Unfortunately, its type locality does not lie in the realm of the Nootka people; but the taxon's range does correspond fairly well with that of Nootka rose. I've found the butterfly numerous about willows at the head of a lake in the Sinlahekin Valley and elsewhere, flicking around my head like smaller, speeded-up versions of the Common Wood Nymphs that were drunk on the same willows' fermented sap.

A Puzzlement

The Sylvan and closely related hairstreaks have brought deep confusion to Northwest lepidopterists over the years. We have Jon Pelham and others to thank for the picture given here; however, the odd interposition of apparent "subspecies" and other factors suggest that there may be more good taxa here than we presently recognize. A similar species sometimes listed for the Northwest is the Acadian Hairstreak / *Satyrium acadica* (W. H. Edwards) 1862 / London, ON. It is larger and grayer than *S. sylvinus nootka*, with prominent round spots; the biggest orange spots, either side of the tail, surround a large blue "thecla" spot. Closer to home, in 1920, large, pale *S. a. coolinensis* was described from Coolin, Bonner County, in the Idaho panhandle, but Kondla and Scott showed that the locality given for it was almost certainly in error (either that, or the butterfly was on the edge of extinction there). *Satyrium acadica* hasn't since been found west of south-central Montana or southwestern Alberta and must now be considered absent from Cascadia. Still, it's something to keep an eye out for in the extreme northeast.

Coral Hairstreak   *Satyrium titus* (FABRICIUS) 1793

Millhaven Plantation, Screven Co., GA
Aka *Harkenclenus*

IMPERILED IN BC

RECOGNITION < 1.25 in. Warm mole-brown above and below; female can be quite fulvous. FW, HW triangular on male, rounded on female; **prominent submarginal band of coral-red spots on VHW** and just the stub of a tail. Reddish spots on dorsum and black-and-white dots on ventrum vary between individuals and populations; ventral black spots usually understated in Cascadia. Males have distinct pale sex patches on DFW. No other hairstreak has the row of coral spots; orange-spotted blues are whitish below. **VARIATION** Obvious sexual dimorphism in wing shape. N NV and S-C OR populations tend to be paler than those farther N, with few if any submarginal orange spots on the DHW, tanner below, with bolder black submarginal spots. WA corals are larger, grayer on top (lacking fulvous areas common on those in OR), with still better defined ventral markings. **HOST PLANTS** Chiefly chokecherry (*Prunus virginiana*). Pelham has also confirmed Woods' rose (*Rosa woodsii*) in WA. Nectars on *Peritoma serrulata*, yellow composites, milkweeds, and spreading dogbane. **ON THE WING** L May to E September, peak in July. Single-brooded, eggs overwinter. **HABITAT AND RANGE** Flies in chokecherry places: canyons, edges of meadows and

Male, ventral

Female, ventral

clearings, trailsides and creek shores, hedgerows and clumps of brush. N Am except the Deep South and Far North. Sparingly throughout Cascadia E of the crest, more common in WA than OR; widespread in ID.

Many hairstreaks occur in numbers when you find them, but this is seldom the case with Corals; nor can you predict where and when you will come upon one, because their host cherries and roses are vastly more common and widespread than they are. Colorado collector Raymond Jae used to hunt this butterfly on *Peritoma serrulata* in Front Range canyons, where they were reliable and social. Why so sparing here is anyone's guess: Corals turn up in a wide variety of locales, such as mid-altitude trailsides in Oregon's Wallowas, and a cherry copse in an arid Adams County coulee. Certainly one of the most attractive and sought-after hairstreaks, classically photographed with its beautiful coral spots against orange *Asclepias tuberosa* in the East.

Gold-hunter's Hairstreak *Satyrium auretorum* (BOISDUVAL) 1852

N Fk Feather R. Cyn, Plumas Co., CA
Aka Golden Hairstreak

RECOGNITION <
1.25 in. Tailed (short on male, longer on female) with subtle patterns below. **Tan to toasty brown above, warm brown below with concentric, smeared dark spotbands** and a very small, pupilled orange spot by the small blue "thecla" patch on the tornus. Blue "thecla" patch flanked by heavy black spots; white fringe outside row of brown border chevrons. Suggests the Hedgerow Hairstreak but lacks the continuous line below. **VARIATION** OR individuals vary somewhat but resemble those of the type locality. **HOST PLANTS** Oaks (*Quercus*), prob. *Q. garryana* in SW OR. Adults visit California buckeye and spreading dogbane, abundantly so in the occasional outbreak year. **ON THE WING** E June to M July. A single generation, eggs overwinter. **HABITAT AND RANGE** Oak-pine edges and chaparral. Essentially a CA endemic, just breaching the border into Lake, Klamath, and Jackson cos, OR.

Male, ventral

Boisduval named *S. auretorum* ("belonging to gold") after the gold hunters who were rife in California in those days, including his primary collector, Pierre Lorquin. Lorquin never hit paydirt, but he struck the mother-lode of new butterflies, many of which he sent to Paris for Boisduval to name. Watch for this and the next species among other hairstreaks when visiting southernmost Cascadia. Comstock called the Gold-hunter's Hairstreak "a decided rarity"; Tilden found it "common but very local," sometimes

around "lone oak trees in fields"; and War-ren reports dozens on dogbane east of Ash-land. Dornfeld was unaware of it in Oregon. Ray Albright found the state record near Lakeview in June 1981. Since then it has been found in Klamath County, and regularly since 2001 in Jackson County east of Ash-land. Erik Runquist's butterfly studies in the area led both to this discovery and to signif-icant support for the Cascade-Siskiyou Na-tional Monument, designated by Bill Clinton in 2000 and enlarged by Barack Obama.

Mountain Mahogany Hairstreak *Satyrium tetra* (W. H. EDWARDS) 1870

Arroyo Bayo, Santa Clara Co., CA
Aka Chaparral Hairstreak, Gray Hairstreak, *adenostomatus*

RECOGNITION < 1.25 in. Tailed (short on male, longer on female) with subtle patterns below. **Dark gray cast above, plain mouse-gray below with median stripe vague, irregular, and lined with white that fogs onto the outer half.** Small blue "thecla" patch flanked by heavy black spots; white fringe outside row of brown border chevrons. Suggests the Hedgerow Hairstreak, but *S. tetra* is gray above, not russet. **VARIATION** S OR individuals "average larger and darker, above and below" than those in C CA (Warren). **HOST PLANTS** Mountain mahogany (*Cercocarpus montanus, C. ledifolius*). Nectars on dogbane, rabbitbrush, and buckwheats, among others. **ON THE WING** E July to L August, peak in L July. Single-brooded, eggs overwinter. **HABITAT AND RANGE** Oak-pine edges and chaparral. Just misses being a CA endemic, poking into OR from the E Siskiyous across the S Cascades to Klamath Falls and the lakes of Lake Co.

Male, ventral

The species' common name comes from its host plant, whose exserted styles curl into downy white swirls about the time its flight period ends. Watch for it among other hairstreaks when visiting southernmost Cascadia. The Mountain Mahogany Hairstreak can be quite common in the Warner Mountains, less so in the Siskiyous. Of it, Comstock wrote, "Wherever the Chamiso [*Atriplex canescens*] occurs, and the summer sun beats fiercely down on the 'elfin forest,' there will be found this vigorous little butterfly." Kojiro Shiraiwa and I found 31 eggs on the underside of mountain mahogany leaves, arrayed between the veins, in the Laguna Mountains in December 2008; Koji notes that its robust thorax, like a skipper's, distinguishes it from other hairstreaks.

Hedgerow Hairstreak   *Satyrium saepium* (BOISDUVAL) 1852

N Fk Feather R. Cyn, Plumas Co., CA
Aka Bronzed Hairstreak, Russet Hairstreak, Buckthorn Hairstreak

RECOGNITION < 1.25 in. **Bright russet or shiny copper-brown above**. Tan to chestnut below, with a **continuous, crooked, postmedian line of white-edged black**, sharp or understated; and a vaguer submarginal row. **Blue "thecla" spot with little or no orange**. Tails short and fat on males, longer on females. Gray-black stigma on costal DFW of male. See the previous two species for differences; neither occur N of S OR. **VARIATION** Nothing appreciable or consistent among NW populations. **HOST PLANTS** *Ceanothus* species—at least *C. velutinus* (snowbrush ceanothus) and *C. integerrimus* (deerbrush) are used in WA, and in SW OR, *C. cuneatus* (buckbrush). Nectars preferentially on plants that offer good platforms of small flowers in bunches, such as dogbane, buckwheats, goldenrods, pussytoes, pearly everlasting, yarrow, daisy, and western clematis. **ON THE WING** M May to L September, peak in July (earlier lower, later higher). Single-brooded, eggs overwinter. **HABITAT AND RANGE** Shrubby canyons, hillsides, chaparral, oak scrub, and pineylands where buckthorn, deerbrush, and snowbrush ceanothus grow, < 1,000 to > 7,000 feet. Most of the intermountain W. S BC, mtn ranges E of Cascade Crest in WA and ID, but in OR also on W side in the Coast Range, W Cascades, and Siskiyous.

A russet butterfly with tails on canyon flowers is likely to be this species. Its bright rusty top and duller underside are both iridescent when fresh, metallic copper on one side, copper-green on the other, but this soon wears off. It is approachable and often

Female, ventral

abundant—Dornfeld wrote of it "swarming" in the chaparral along Century Drive near Bend, the males guarding *Ceanothus* "summits." This is one of several butterflies that shift westward south of the Columbia River. Virtually all Washington records are for east of the Cascade Crest, but McCorkle repeatedly found individuals on Rickreall Ridge north of Monmouth in the Willamette Valley. These and Sylvan Hairstreaks roughhouse together where willows and buckbrush grow near one another. It is a long way from the rough scrub of the West to a neat European hedgerow, but Boisduval knew that many hairstreaks haunt shrubby habitats when he chose the epithet *saepium* ("of the hedge"), and Holland knew his Latin when he coined the English name.

Male, ventral

Genus *Callophrys*: Green Hairstreaks, Cedar and Mistletoe Hairstreaks, and Elfins

Recent revisions suggest that the green hairstreaks (subgenus *Callophrys*), cedar and mistletoe hairstreaks (subgenus *Mitoura*), and elfins (subgenus *Incisalia*) are so closely related as to warrant only a single inclusive genus among them. Certainly, they are close: *C. (C.) sheridanii* and *C. (I.) augustinus* have even hybridized. *Callophrys* (Billberg 1820) is the oldest of the three classical generic names, the other two having been described by Scudder in 1871.

Subgenus *Callophrys*: Green Hairstreaks

Green hairstreaks have the richest and most beautiful green coloration anywhere in the realm of butterflies displayed on their ventral surfaces. These much-loved "greenies" are damnably variable. The confusion and frustration they have caused among lepidopterists trying to pin down their relationships is hinted at by some of the names applied to them: *perplexa*, *neoperplexa*, *homoperplexa*, and *superperplexa*. All the North American green hairstreaks have been both lumped into three species and split into seven. As Jon Pelham puts it, "We must figure out who's who based on unreliable appearances and any behavioral or other characters that can be found." As you'll see, some such behavioral clues can be quite reliable and very helpful. One of the best places to study green hairstreaks is Satus Pass in Washington, where *Callophrys affinis*, *C. dumetorum*, and *C. sheridanii* all occur in near proximity through the season. Green hairstreaks eat mostly flower parts as caterpillars.

Western Green Hairstreak   *Callophrys affinis* (W. H. EDWARDS) 1862

Vic. Fort Bridger, WY
Aka Immaculate Green Hairstreak, Green-winged Hairstreak, Green Hairstreak,
Washington Hairstreak, Immaculate Bramble Hairstreak, C. *dumetorum*

SPECIAL CONCERN IN BC

RECOGNITION < 1.25 in. Males and females
both **entirely gray above**, occasionally with
a "cold tawny glow" (Warren). **VHW grainy,
yellowish or bluish green**; paler than C.
dumetorum, **with little black scaling; most of
VFW is green** (C. *dumetorum* has half-brown
VFW). **VHW white line usually present, often
complete but faint, and straight**. Fringes tend
toward white. **Adults perch on and fly out from
the tops of shrubs, usually basin big sage**. C.
sheridanii perches on the ground. **VARIATION**
C. a. *washingtonia*, described from Alta Lake,
Okanogan Co., WA, by Harry Clench in 1944,
applies to all NW populations. It is darker
green below and less tawny above than the
type. **HOST PLANTS** Buckwheats *Eriogonum
umbellatum* and E. *heracleoides* (BC); E. *sphaerocephalum* and E. *elatum* (WA); E. *heracleoides*
(OR). **ON THE WING** E April to M July, peak
in May (sometimes later at higher elevations
or colder sites). Single-brooded, chrysalides
overwinter. **HABITAT AND RANGE** Lithosols in
sage-steppe, arid hills and ridges, mountain
peaks. Often defends summits of rock mounds.
Interior W US, esp. Great Basin and surrounding aridlands. In Cascadia, NE OR, E Cascades,
Okanogan Highlands, Blue Mtns, and Columbia
Basin of WA, W ID, and S interior of BC.

Male, ventral

You'll find this spe-
cies lumped with
the Bramble Green
Hairstreak in some
books, but they are
clearly different
butterflies in the
Northwest. Look
for this one in sage

Ventral

country when the spring phloxes are blooming, along with its frequent companion the Desert Marble. Not that it is restricted to the lowlands; it flies on and near Manastash and Umtanum ridges (Kittitas County, Washington) with the very local Nevada Skipper, and on the summit of Steens Mountain at 9,600 feet. We find it among the early lupines in May at Sun Mountain above the Methow Valley, and on the 5,800-foot summit of

Chumstick Mountain in Chelan County, on subalpine heath, primrose pink with *Douglasia nivalis*, weeks later. Sheridan's Green Hairstreak may be found on the same mountaintop, usually earlier and higher, but overlapping; for further tips on telling the two apart, see Warren (2005). *C. a. washingtonia* (Washington Green Hairstreak) is one of only two kinds of butterflies that commemorate the Evergreen State in their names.

Bramble Green Hairstreak   *Callophrys dumetorum* (BOISDUVAL) 1852

Brannan Is., Sacramento Co., CA
Aka Bramble Hairstreak, Perplexing Hairstreak, *C. perplexa*

RECOGNITION < 1.25 in. Both sexes brown dorsally, **females often with orangish suffusion.** VHW dark grass-green to lighter spring-green or bluish; **VFW green restricted to leading third, trailing a little around the tip, the rest of wing gray or brown**; other species green on VFW. Ventral postmedian **white line black-edged, variable and curved parallel to convex wing margin**, usually incomplete, often mostly absent; more complete in E-side colonies. Fringes of HW tinged with gray-brown. **Adults perch and fly out from low shrubs, such as salal, seldom on highest point.** Males tend to perch on prominent points, on or near the ground. **VARIATION** Much among individuals, esp. in female dorsal color, from gray to brown to tawny orange. The population E of the Cascades, Yakima Co., tends smaller and tawnier. **HOST PLANTS** Sole larval host in W WA and most of W OR is *Hosackia crassifolia*; in Yakima Co., WA, and Polk Co., OR, *Acmispon nevadensis* is used. Nectars on the host plants, buckwheats, desert parsley, and other spring bloomers. **ON THE WING** L March to M July, peak in May (early at sea level, later higher). One generation, pupae overwinter. **HABITAT AND RANGE** Open sites in forest biomes, clearings in Douglas-fir and ponderosa pine forest, undulating heathlands, road-cuts,

Ventral

powerline rights-of-way; never far from patches of the host plants. W Coast, Baja to WA. Two populations in Cascadia: sparingly E of the Cascade Crest in S Yakima

Ventral

ICZN. This is good, because the Latin epithet means "of the brambles." Its habitat is often brambly, and its biology a perplexing briar patch. By no means does the Bramble Green Hairstreak occur everywhere its host plants are found; I have checked many stands of *Hosackia crassifolia* along the Olympic coastal strip without success. Louis LaPierre finally found it in the southwest Willapa Hills near Longview. One interesting population abounds in the Hoodsport Heaths, unsprayed Christmas tree farms in the Olympic foothills of Mason County, Washington; this artifical, ericoid-rich habitat may approximate an earlier successional biome now eliminated from the industrial forestscape. The Bramble is the only green hairstreak in northwestern Cascadia and is much more limited on the east side. It was to such eastern Washington specimens that Gorelick gave the curious subspecific name *oregonensis*, though it does occur across the Columbia in Oregon as well. It flies within a mile of the Western Green at Status Pass but in very different habitat.

and Klickitat cos, and S, halfway down OR Cascades; Salish Lowlands from Kitsap Co., S to the Columbia in WA, Coast Range, S Cascades, Siskiyous and Warners in OR.

This butterfly, long called *C. dumetorum*, was changed to *perplexa* and now has returned to *dumetorum* by an action of the

Sheridan's Green Hairstreak   *Callophrys sheridanii*
(W. H. EDWARDS) 1877

Nr Sheridan, WY
Aka Sheridan's Hairstreak, White-lined Green Hairstreak, Little Green Hairstreak, *viridis*

RECOGNITION < 1 in. **Small. Both sexes slate gray or mole brown above**, but females may have tawny suffusion. Below, dark green with much black scaling; **most of VFW is green** (*C. dumetorum* VFW only partly green). Ventral postmedian **white line variable, often prominent, broad,** black-edged, and straight esp. in Columbia Basin; elsewhere diminishes, sometimes to obsolescence. **Adults perch on and fly up from the ground, and fly low. VARIATION** Andy Warren has studied this "ecologically and morphologically variable species" in OR in detail. In general, populations vary in size, bluer or yellower green below, grayer or tawnier above, wing fringe color, and white ventral line bolder or weaker, as well as in host plant use; and there is some correlation between host and phenotype. See Warren (2005) for

Pair, ventral

Pair, ventral

details of all the segregates. **HOST PLANTS** Buckwheats known to be or possibly used in PNW incl. *Eriogonum heracleoides, E. strictum, E. douglasii, E. umbellatum, E. compositum, E. nudum, E. marifolium, E. sphaerocephalum,* and *E. ovalifolium.* Nectars on earliest flowers in the desert, such as Gray's lomatium, and on many others later at higher elevations. **ON THE WING** E March to E August, peak in April-May, depending on elevation. One generation, pupae diapause. **HABITAT AND RANGE** Coulees, washes, and canyons, draws in sage-steppe, rocky chutes at high elevations, and alpine swales. Montane W US and SW Canada; Cascadia mostly E of the crest, to the Siskiyous through Crater Lake, as well as spotty sites in W OR Cascades, such as H. J. Andrews Experimental Forest, Lane Co., and a relict colony found by Dave McCorkle at Rickreall Ridge in Polk Co. in far W OR; these were formerly called *C.* nr. *dumetorum* (Coastal Green Hairstreak) and later *C. viridis,* a name described from San Francisco.

If you brave sharp March and April winds to search the coulees in thin early sun, the scrap of green you see clinging to desert parsley or the gully floor will be Sheridan's.

The first spring "hatcher" to emerge, it will soon overlap with Silvery Blues and Sagebrush Checkerspots. Later in its flight period, Sheridan's small size, gray females, and white line may get you through, but a less-than-fresh male with a partial white line will still be challenging. With green hairstreaks, it is always best to see a series of individuals before coming to a conclusion. Sheridan's and Western Greens sometimes co-occur, at which times the perching behavior will help set them apart: Sheridan's on the ground, Westerns on shrubs. Where it flies together with *C. dumetorum* on Rickreall Ridge, the Sheridan's uses buckwheat, the Bramble lotus. Like all green hairstreaks, these are beautifully camouflaged against fresh vegetation while at rest but fly up at the merest provocation, flickering brown-and-green, then perch invisibly again. Edwards named this butterfly for Lt. Gen. Philip Sheridan at the request of his subordinate, Lt. Carpenter. F. M. Brown later fixed Sheridan, Wyoming, as the type locality, since Carpenter's specimens came from the Bighorn Mountains near there. So the name doubly commemorates the cavalryman infamous for his definition of a good Indian.

Subgenus *Mitoura*: Cedar and Mistletoe Hairstreaks

Some authorities separate these from the genus *Callophrys*, and others split them up still further. Several *Mitoura* have co-evolved with cupressaceous conifers, while others made the adaptive leap to feeding on parasites of evergreens. Our two mistletoe feeders are straightforward, but the cedar-feeding types are complicated and far from settled. The *Thuja/Calocedrus*-feeding members fly from urban neighborhoods to high mountain wilderness and flatland second-growth. The *Juniperus*-feeding hairstreaks proliferate across the juniper scrub of the Basin and Range and thin out to the north.

Cedar Hairstreak   *Callophrys gryneus* (HÜBNER) 1819

"Virginien"
Aka Olive Hairstreak, Nelson's Hairstreak, Conifer Hairstreak, Juniper Hairstreak (NABA), Incense Cedar Hairstreak, *Mitoura grynea, nelsoni, siva, rosneri, barryi*

COLUMBIA BASIN SEGREGATE (NR. *CHALCOSIVA*) CANDIDATE IN WA

RECOGNITION < 1.25 in. **Near cedars or junipers. Gray, buckskin, rust-brown, or light mahogany above, redder near tails; below, yellowish, greenish, russet, or vinous brown,** sometimes with a strong **violet tint**, esp. when fresh; green farther E. **Variable white postmedian band below**, black-, rust-, or unlined, crooked but **not strongly zigzagged**. Tornal blue and black HW "thecla" spots vary from modest to expansive, seldom accompanied by any appreciable orange. Smaller, less chestnut, with subtler line below than *C. johnsoni*.
VARIATION This is a big mess, but interesting ecologically, evolutionarily, and historically. See Warren (2005) for details. The great variation among Cedar Hairstreaks (CH) around the region may be crudely summarized as follows. In N CA extending N into the Siskiyous and SW Cascades of OR, feeding on incense cedar, CH is characterized by a light reddish underside with a much-reduced submarginal band. From the interior ranges of BC, into the E Okanogan and Selkirk Mtns of NE WA and N ID, feeding on western redcedar, CH stands out for its burgundy undersides and strong, dark-edged white

Male, ventral

Male, ventral

Female, ventral (nr. *chalcosiva*)

band. Across N ID and W MT, feeding on western redcedar, CH goes larger, with highly grizzled, blackish brown undersides. Occupying SW BC, most of W WA, and NW OR and feeding mostly on western redcedar (but sometimes isolated junipers, as on Vancouver and San Juan Is.), CH is more chocolatey, less brightly burgundy beneath. Juniper-feeding CH flies in SE BC, SE WA, and E OR. Its underside tends toward grizzled yellowish browns (hazel to tawny or greenish but never bright green) farther S; toward violet from the Great Basin and farther N, and can be quite purple in E WA. **HOST PLANTS** Western redcedar (*Thuja plicata*), incense cedar (*Calocedrus decurrens*), fresh growth of western juniper (*Juniperus occidentalis*) and prob. Rocky Mountain juniper (*J. scopulorum*). Nectars on such flowers as clovers, pussypaws, oxeye daisy, yarrow, dandelion, sunflowers, fleabane, rabbitbrush, goldenrod, vine maple (flowers and honeydew), Oregon grape, white currant, buckwheats, lomatiums, goatsbeard, spring beauty, buttercup, and camas lily.

ON THE WING L March to E August, peak in May-June. Single-brooded in WA, double- farther S, chrysalides overwinter. **HABITAT AND RANGE** Forest edges and clearings, roadsides, shorelines, meadows, city gardens, almost anywhere (but not everywhere) the host cedars abound. Juniper groves and forests, pinyon-juniper savannah, and rain-shadow grassland. Most of the US to the extent of Cupressaceae. In Cascadia, cedar types chiefly in SW BC, Vancouver Is., Salish Lowlands, Olympics, Willapas, W Cascades, Okanogan Highlands, Selkirks, OR Coast Range, and Siskiyous. Juniper types in S-C BC, S-C WA and Blue Mtns, most of E OR and S ID. Widespread on *J. occidentalis*; segregated on dispersed stands of *J. scopulorum*.

Few butterflies have been more taxonomically juggled in recent years. Some treatments separate each variety as a distinct species, but widespread hybridization where they meet suggests a single species. As Scott put it, "Wherever two *gryneus* ssp. range near each other, they intergrade." And while host plant specialization is notable, sometimes they "go over" to a different host, a cedar type feeding on a city juniper. Adults descend from their treetops to find nectar and mates in May, when they may be seen thronging goatsbeard and nectaring on Oregon grape with Johnson's Hairstreak at the head of Lake Cushman in the southern Olympics. Unlike the rare Johnson's, the Cedar can be truly abundant at times; or merely appear as singletons. The purplish juniper segregate (nr. *chalcosiva*) may be sought across much of eastern Oregon and in Washington in the Juniper Dunes of Franklin County. Since junipers are frequently known locally as "cedars," but the reverse is seldom true, Cedar Hairstreak is a better common name than NABA's Juniper Hairstreak.

Thicket Hairstreak   *Callophrys spinetorum* (HEWITSON) 1867

Gold Lake, Sierra Co., CA
Aka Blue Mistletoe Hairstreak, *Mitoura, Loranthomitoura, Cisincisalia*

RECOGNITION < 1.25 in. **Tailed, bright steel-blue above**, with broad black borders. Male has narrower, diffuse border and gray-black stigmata; female more black, blue restricted basally. Chestnut-brown below, **prominent black-edged white line across wings** with zigzag W near well-developed,

double tornal tails (one longer, one shorter, white-tipped). Variable row of fat black chevrons with orange caps and blue bottoms. White marginal lines and fringe. Johnson's similar below, without strong W, brown (not blue) above. **Brown submarginal spotband runs all around VHW** of Thicket, only partial on Johnson's. **VARIATION** None significant in our region. **HOST PLANTS** Mistletoes (*Arceuthobium campylopodum, A. vaginatum, A. americanum*) on a variety of conifers, esp. pines (*Pinus ponderosa, P. contorta*) over most of the range; in SW OR, *A. tsugense* on western hemlock (*Tsuga heterophylla*) and *A. abietinum* on grand fir (*Abies grandis*) (McCorkle). Nectars on yellow composites, chokecherry, pearly everlasting, lomatium, buckwheats, *Arctostaphylos*, and willow catkins. Males visit mud, occasionally in numbers. **ON THE WING** L April to M August, peak in May-June. One or sometimes two generations, chrysalides overwinter. **HABITAT AND RANGE** Low- to high-altitude clearings among conifer forests, esp. mature ponderosa pine, but also lodgepole, true fir, Douglas-fir, and western larch. Mid-BC into Mexico, Rockies to the Pacific. Generally E of the Cascades in our region, in coniferous zones, with a handful of records W of the crest in the Chuckanut Mtns, W Cascades, and Siskiyous, but none in the Coast Range of WA or OR.

Ventral

Thicket Hairstreaks spend most of their time in the coniferous canopy, but males in particular come down to nectar and puddle. Collectors consider them uncommon, but Nabokov wrote of the good luck he had going out early in the morning on foot, finding numbers along mountain roadsides before most activity began. In June 1917, J. F. G. Clarke found Thicket Hairstreaks on Chuckanut Drive in Whatcom County, Washington, the only near-coastal occurrence. This rain-shadow record may represent a relict of a wider distribution in warmer, drier times. "Spinet" is an old word for thicket or spinney, from the Latin *spinetum*, hence *spinetorum* ("belonging to the thicket"). The butterfly is more of the forest than of the thicket, but males do possess and defend shrubby vegetation beneath the conifers. Yellow pine logging and mistletoe suppression by the U.S. Forest Service and timber companies no doubt suppress the species' numbers.

Johnson's Hairstreak   *Callophrys johnsoni* (SKINNER) 1904

"British Columbia"
Aka Mistletoe Hairstreak, Brown Mistletoe Hairstreak, *Loranthomitoura*, *Cisincisalia*

SPECIES OF CONCERN IN OR, CANDIDATE IN WA, ENDANGERED IN BC

RECOGNITION < 1.5 in. **Biggish**. **Male chocolate above, female oxblood. Ventral surface rich chestnut**, white postmedian line less zigzagged than on previous species, and **submarginal dark brown spotband runs only halfway around VHW**, all the way on the Thicket. **Double tails, the inner ones longer**. White tail-tips, marginal line, and fringe. Bigger than Cedar Hairstreak, less rufous above, darker brown below. **VARIATION** No variants described or named. **HOST PLANTS** Dwarf mistletoe (*Arceuthobium campylopodum*) on old-growth western hemlock and perhaps Douglas-fir in NW Cascadia, *A. tsugense* on western hemlock, and *A. abietinum* on grand fir in SW OR, possibly mature pines and true firs in CA. Nectars on Oregon grape in the foothills of the Olympics; Andy Warren found more than a hundred nectaring on dewberry (*Rubus ursinus*) in Multnomah Co. in a spectacularly good year. Males visit

mud. **ON THE WING** M May to E September, peaks in May and August. Long flight period may indicate progressive emergence, variable conditions, or two generations farther S. **HABITAT AND RANGE** A Cascadian/Sierran endemic, and our only old-growth obligate butterfly (in WA). Mature coniferous forests, sea level to 5,000 feet. C CA to SW BC. In BC, SE Vancouver

Male, ventral

Is., Lower Fraser Valley E to Hope; Olympic and Mt. Rainier NPs and a very few other W WA locales; sparingly in Cascades, Coast Range, Siskiyous, Blue-Wallowa Mtns in OR.

The species was named for Orson Bennett ("Bug") Johnson, the celebrated (and only) professor of zoology at the University of Washington in the institution's early years. Also the namesake of Johnson Hall on the UW campus, Johnson took students collecting in the vicinity of the city, was mentor of the Young Naturalists' Society, and built an important early collection, still extant at UW's Burke Museum of Natural History. Johnson's localities for his eponymous butterfly are long gone. King County records date from 1891, 1941, and 1969—with

nothing since. One of the few recent records in the WA Cascades was by David Droppers, surveying for the species along the Monte Cristo trail, Snohomish County, under old-growth hemlock ca. 270 to 300 years old. A colony persists in Vancouver's Stanley Park. The insect's apparent rarity stems partly from its existence as a creature of the canopy but largely from the fact that most of its preferred habitat has been logged. Examining the treetops from the old-growth canopy crane near Carson, Washington, in 2008, Thea Pyle found eggs some 300 feet high in the late-successional forest, later reared. Individuals do come down, however. A few miles north of Carson beside the Big Lava Bed, I found a male visiting mud beside a culvert.

Subgenus *Incisalia*: Elfins

The elfins are an essentially boreal group of tiny, frenetic hairstreaks, with subtle hues in pleasing patterns. These too, along with *Mitoura* and green hairstreaks, have been lumped into the generic catch-all *Callophrys*. There is a good structural argument for this, but an equally good reason to think of the elfins as a separate group based on traditional usage and the ready recognizability of this cluster of charming species. They can quickly be told from

cedar and mistletoe hairstreaks by their tail-stumps without tails, and from the greens by their various brown tones on the undersurfaces of the wings. Our four elfins have co-evolved with different groups of plants, three as specialists, one as a great generalist. On the whole they are creatures of the spring. The subgenus name means "cut-wing," referring to the apparent notch out of the hindwing just inside and above the tail-stump.

Brown Elfin   *Callophrys augustinus* (WESTWOOD) 1852

N end Lake Winnipeg, SK
Aka Western Elfin, *Incisalia*, *augustus/-a*, *iroides*

RECOGNITION < 1.25 in. **Warm brown to grayish brown above, females more or less infused with orange. VHW two-toned**: outer half violet to cinnamon or milk chocolate, crossed by dots; inner half mahogany to dark chocolate; **arcuate border between has no white line. VFW**

tan to mink-brown. Tail-stumps pronounced, but have no hair-tails. **VARIATION** Lots between individuals, between populations not so much. Cooler-country elfins often darker. **HOST PLANTS** Wide range in Cascadia incl. heaths (salal, madrona, manzanita, kinnikinnick,

Male, ventral

Male, ventral

rhododendron, huckleberry), rosaceous shrubs (bitterbrush, serviceberry), basin big sage, Labrador tea, dodder, buckwheats, buckthorns, and Oregon grape. Nectars on hosts, clover, chokecherry, bitter cherry, showy phlox, strawberry, blood currant, willow catkins, and others. **ON THE WING** M February to L July, peak in May. One generation, pupae overwinter. **HABITAT AND RANGE** Pine-oak woodland, hemlock-fir forest, salal thickets, roadside seeps, sage-steppe, tree farms, yards, gardens, parks, bogs, and many other clearings and glades across N and higher-elevation N Am to C BC; Cascadia except wettest and driest parts, prob. all cos.

The Brown Elfin flies when the wild rhodo-dendrons bloom along Hood Canal and the Mt. Hood Highway. It is the generalist of the genus—few of our butterflies accept such a wide array of host plants in the wild. This makes it an excellent, though little noticed, candidate for butterfly gardens. Fresh adults appear surprisingly early, when few other species are on the wing. In April, you may find them abundant among the sagebrush flats and along streambanks and paths where their host shrubs will later flower, and among thickets of bitterbrush and snowbrush ceanothus. Males fly out with vigor at passing objects. Hanging around a host heath on some of the earliest warm days in March, he holds to a leaf promi-nently in the sun, awaiting females that will later oviposit on the flowerbuds. A few holey purple blossoms later give away their pres-ence. Augustus was a Canadian Inuit on Sir John Franklin's arctic expedition of 1826. Zoologist John Richardson, grateful for his assistance, chose to honor him, and the epi-thet *augustus* was bestowed by Kirby in 1837; that name was preoccupied by another hair-streak, so the replacement *augustinus* was provided by Westwood in 1852.

Moss's Elfin   *Callophrys mossii* (HY. EDWARDS) 1881

Esquimalt, Vancouver Is., BC
Aka Stonecrop Elfin, Early Elfin, Schryver's Elfin, *Incisalia*

SPECIAL CONCERN IN BC

RECOGNITION < 1.25 in. **Dorsum cool ashy brown** on male with blackish stigma on DFW, sometimes rusty near tail-stump; redder on females. **Ventrum pruinose brown or reddish or golden brown, two-toned, divided by a white postmedian line**, darker within and lighter without. Other markings vague; may have some whitish frosting outside the white line, but lacks prominent marginal frosting of the Hoary Elfin. Fringe checked by dark scales running out beyond the vein into the white fringe. **VARIATION** Much individual variation (according to Warren, those in the Rogue River Valley are "so variable that no two look just alike") as well as variation among regional populations. In brief, W of the Cascade crest the type is grayer above, less contrasting below. The Rocky Mtn expression, E of the Cascade crest, is warmer brown above with more light scaling outside the white line below. Those of the Siskiyous tend to be paler above and tanner, sometimes almost golden brown, below, while the ones in the W OR Cascades out to the S coast have much to some brick-red below. Seaside elfins to

Female, ventral   Ventral

the N are smaller, frostier below. **HOST PLANTS** Species of stonecrop (*Sedum*), incl. *S. divergens*, *S. spathulifolium*, *S. lanceolatum*, *S. laxum*, *S. oreganum*, and possibly *S. stenopetalum*. Nectars on the hosts, *Lomatium columbianum*, marsh marigold, others; males mudpuddle. **ON THE WING** M February to M July, peak in April, depending on elevation. One brood, chrysalides overwinter. **HABITAT AND RANGE** Canyonsides, rocky slopes and ridges, balds, outcrops among forest, stony flats, buttes and brushy ravines, marine and riverine cliffs, roadsides, sea level to 7,000+ feet. NW US, SW Canada. S BC incl. Vancouver Is.; E WA and NE OR (Okanogan, Blues, Wallowas, Ochocos); Olympics, Orcas Is., and Lower Columbia in W WA; Cascades, Coast Range, Siskiyous in W OR.

Moss's Elfin commemorates a Vancouver Island doctor of Henry Edwards'

acquaintance. The name fits nicely, as it also refers to one of the butterfly's frequent habitats: mossy balds on rocky slopes where stonecrop grows. The distribution is broad but very patchy, and some localities are tiny, like a single rock face or isolated bald. More colonies will be discovered when difficult-to-reach stonecrop slopes are sampled, perhaps even on seastacks at the coast. The butterfly appears earlier in the year than most collectors and watchers go out, and is closely wedded to patches of *Sedum*. I've watched females ovipositing on the spectacularly tall roseflower stonecrop (*S. laxum*) in the Illinois River Valley in southwestern Oregon. Males congregate in canyons, females too when virginal, then retire to foodplants once mated. Mobs of Moss's Elfins sometimes charge Mourning Cloaks and anglewings like jays mobbing a bird of prey.

Hoary Elfin *Callophrys polios* COOK & F. WATSON 1907

Lakewood, Ocean Co., NJ
Aka Obscure Elfin, *Incisalia*, *polia*

C. P. MARITIMA IMPERILED IN OR; PUGET TROUGH SEGREGATE SGCN IN WA

RECOGNITION < 1 in. Dusky gray-brown on the dorsal surface, females a little warmer, sometimes with submarginal tan HW patches. Ventrum two-toned with vague, dark-edged dividing line with little white; inner half of VHW dark sienna, **outer third heavily frosted with silvery white scales as is outer edge of VFW**, and ringed with brown dots. Fringe checkered. Moss's Elfin larger, has different habitat, white line, unfrosted HW. **VARIATION** Our inland animal, *C. p. obscura*, is much grayer below and cooler brown above compared

Ventral

Ventral

AND RANGE Open, rocky areas in the mtns, coastal bluffs and dunes, forest roadsides, post-glacial prairie remnants, heaths and barrens, always closely around kinnikinnick. Boreal N Am, AK to NM, ME to WA. In Cascadia, ID panhandle; SE BC; Okanogan Highlands, and S and W Puget Sound lowlands in WA; NE mtns and C-S coast in OR.

This widespread butterfly was not discovered until the 20th century, and then in New Jersey. In Cascadia, Hoary Elfins have an odd distribution, skipping from the Okanogan to Kitsap, Mason, and Thurston counties around the Salish Lowlands; and from the Blue Mountains to Waldport and Pistol River on the Oregon coast. This extremely spotty range demonstrates classic relictualism: the species formerly occurred much more continuously during the cool post-glacial period, then retracted as the climate warmed. It could drop out altogether as our carbon-fest continues. The Oregon coastal colonies have already been drastically reduced by development. One of the most abundant colonies occupies the Glacial Heritage Preserve, near Mima Mounds, on the Puget Prairies. There you will see Hoaries fluttering low over extensive mats of kinnikinnick, darting and crazed, but always returning to the same or a nearby perch atop mound or mat. Don't be fooled by Brown Elfins, which also feed on kinnikinnick, or by Western Pine Elfins, dropping down to drink at its rich nectar.

to the more rufous eastern type, and has less bright frosting below. It applies to E Cascadia. The isolated OR coast population, *C. p. maritima*, which lacks tan above, is darker below with more gray frosting in a reduced band, diminished brown spots below, smudged fringe-checkers, and more rounded wings. An unnamed Puget Trough/ Salish Sea segregate is toastier above and quite reddish on the basal half below, bright chestnut on the VFW. **HOST PLANTS** The obligate host is kinnikinnick (*Arctostaphylos uva-ursi*). Most nectaring takes place on the host plant flowers, as does larval feeding. **ON THE WING** L March to E June, peak in May. One brood, chrysalides overwinter. **HABITAT**

Western Pine Elfin   *Callophrys eryphon* (BOISDUVAL) 1852

N Fk Feather R. Cyn, Plumas Co., CA
Aka Western Banded Elfin, *Incisalia*

RECOGNITION < 1.25 in. The easiest elfin to identify: **bigger, faster, and heavily zigzagged below.** Chocolate-brown above, male dark, female oranger, lighter. VFW warm brown; VHW

purplish brown, darker inner half, lighter outer, split by jagged white-and-black line. Basal half with dark brown bars and bands, outer half circled by **submarginal row of dark brown**

Male, ventral

Male, ventral

chevrons, and a single bar across the VFW cell. **Checked fringes**. Almost always **near pines**. **VARIATION** Nothing that would hamper identification. The type applies in and E of the OR Cascades; it tends plainer brown beneath than the more reddish or vinous, gray-edged, near-coastal Shelton Elfin (see sidebar), which Pelham applies to all WA. Those on the S OR coast tend toward the purpler race from Humboldt Co., CA, described as deeper mauve on VHW. **HOST PLANTS** Ponderosa pine (*Pinus ponderosa*) (inland) and lodgepole pine (*P. contorta*) (montane and coastal) recorded here, with western white pine (*P. monticola*) and other species likely. Nectars on yarrow, white currant, mustard, dandelion, spring gold, spiraea, lupine, chokecherry, buckwheat, buckthorn, pussypaws, and pussy willow catkins; males visit mud. **ON THE WING** L February to L August, peak in April-May. A single generation, pupae overwinter. **HABITAT AND RANGE** Mostly ponderosa pine forest clearings, edges, roadsides, streams, and meadows, but also lodgepole pinewoods, shore pine thickets. All across W N Am and E around the Great Lakes. Cascades E of the crest, Siskiyous N to OR/SW WA coast, uncommon on W slope Cascades and Coast Range, Vancouver and San Juan Is., and S Puget Sound, unrecorded from Olympics.

One of our two butterflies that utililze pine foliage for food, *C. eryphon*, a spring butterfly, very rarely flies with the Pine White, a denizen of high summer and fall. Some wandering or accidental introduction apparently occurs, since small colonies turn up in isolated stands of pines or even individual trees. For example, I found one near ponderosas at a farmhouse on Magnuson Butte in lonely Grant County, Washington, surrounded by wheat fields and far from the nearest forest—did it come in on firewood, or was it blown in from distant pineywood breaks? Even so, the butterfly does not occur everywhere there are pines, especially on the west side of the Cascades, where it is seldom abundant. In Washington, most records west of the Cascade crest have been in acid lodgepole lowlands of lower Hood

Ben Leighton and the Shelton Elfin

Ben Leighton was born on 13 September 1918, in Charleston, just outside Bremerton, Washington. From an early age he was a naturalist, an avid angler, and an artist, keeping detailed field notebooks. In 1938, after recovering from polio and graduating from Franklin High School in Seattle, he entered the University of Washington to study zoology, botany, and geography. With his bachelor's degree and a special wartime certificate he taught science and coached football at the high school in Shelton from 1943 to 1945. Returning to the UW, he completed a master's degree under Melville Hatch, half-century faculty member and founder of the Scarabs, which thrives to this day. Snapshots from this period show Ben (shirtless) in a meadow with a butterfly net and (suited) at a party to honor pioneer zoologist Trevor Kincaid.

Leighton's master's thesis, *The Butterflies of Washington* (BOW), was published in November 1946. Built on existing records from collections, the published literature, and much additional field work of his own, his annotated checklist became the fundamental basis for all subsequent studies of Washington butterflies and served as the immediate inspiration for *WWB* (Pyle 1974).

Ben earned his living as a color photographic specialist for Rayonier Laboratories and continued his butterfly work, often in collaboration with Don Frechin and the Chermock brothers. They described the Shelton Elfin (now *Callophrys eryphon sheltonensis*) from material he collected in the forest near his home.

Canal, where Hoary and Brown Elfins also fly. Recent Vancouver Island records exist, but there are none from the San Juan Islands in the past half-century. It flies among shore pines in Pacific and Clatsop counties at the mouth of the Columbia River, months before Pine Whites emerge in the same places, far from any other records. Western Pine Elfins are among the fleetest fliers I know.

Gray Hairstreak   *Strymon melinus* HÜBNER 1818

"Georgien in Florida"
Aka Common Hairstreak, Hop Vine Hairstreak, Cotton Square Borer

RECOGNITION < 1.5 in. **Deep slate, almost blue-gray above,** fading to battleship-gray with a **bright, discrete red-orange patch near the prominent tail,** and variable black and blue spots around it. Underside silvery to pearl-gray to gray flannel, crossed by strong, jagged, nearly articulated **bands of black bars lined outwardly with white,** sometimes inwardly with orange; **two orange spots cap blue-black "thecla" spots or spread around tornus. Tip of summer**

However, a chronic illness cut short his work, and Ben Leighton was long lost to Northwest lepidopterists; Jon Pelham and I sought his whereabouts for years. We found him in time to convey our respect for his early contributions (via social worker Barbara Soltess) but just missed meeting him before he died in January 1989, a deep disappointment.

Meanwhile, local journalist Carolyn Maddux discovered that Ben's butterfly collection resided at Shelton High School. An inventory of the collection revealed much historically valuable material, such as the state record for the Checkered White (*Pontia protodice*), and butterflies now extirpated from his collecting localities. Arrangements were made with teachers Emily Garlich, Pete Janda, and Sheryal Balding to exchange a synoptic collection and teaching guide, class lectures, and copies of BOW and WWB for Leighton's collection, so that it might be properly cared for at the Burke Museum. The important Ben V. Leighton Collection of Washington Butterflies is now safely curated and available for scientific study.

Now, when the biology teachers take their students out to watch the courtship of Shelton Elfins in the pinewoods across from the high school, I picture the shade of Ben Leighton among the shadows of the pines, net cradled in his long, graceful fingers, elfin grin on his face, glad to be afield once again in the company of butterflies.

male's abdomen peachy orange. Two sets of tails, the lower ones longer. FW triangular with straight outer edge, white fringe. Other grayish hairstreaks have ventral lines in spots, not a connected band, and smaller red spots. Female tailed blues are smaller, with rounded FW, not straight-edged. **VARIATION** Significant seasonal variation, with spring-generation individuals darker gray above and below than summer ones, and males darker than females. Otherwise, we have three poorly differentiated ssp., two of them described from Cascadia. The N CA

Female, dorsal

Female, ventral

Male, dorsal

sort with narrow submedian bands below, often with red edging to them, is reflected in some but not all Siskiyou grays. A variety described from Seton Lake, Lillooet, BC, flying E of the Cascade Crest in drier habitats, is generally lighter below with broader black edging. Another BC form, named from Wellington, is found in moister, W slope Cascadian locales and is generally smaller and darker, the bands still more broadly blacked. A blend zone occurs in the lower Columbia Gorge, where the Cascade Crest breaks down; or you could say the whole region is a blend zone for this highly mobile, hugely variable species. **HOST PLANTS** Highly polyphagous. Scott lists dozens of hosts in numerous families ranging from oranges to oaks, cactus to corn, pines to palms. Common Cascadian choices incl. many legumes, roses, and mallows. Occasionally considered pestiferous on hops and beans. Pelham has recorded it on Russian thistle, and I wouldn't be surprised if it used it on the roll, except that the larvae usually consume the flowers and forming fruits of these tumbleweeds. Nectars on a great array of flowers: wild onion, spreading dogbane, rabbitbrush, alfalfa, purple loosestrife, blue and white mints, white sweetclover, goldenrods, and so on. **ON THE WING** L March to M October, peaks in May and July. Multi-brooded: spring emergence continues through summer, overlapping with second (and third? fourth?) generation into fall. Chrysalides overwinter. **HABITAT AND RANGE** Virtually all habitats, though seldom in deeper forests or in the arctic-alpine: sagelands, hilltops, ditches, seeps, roadsides, weedy fields, montane meadows, clearcuts, shorelines, parks. Warren calls it the only lycaenid "regularly seen in yards and town gardens in the central and southern Willamette Valley." They usually breed at lower altitudes, though individuals sometimes ascend to summits. All the Americas from mid-Canada to Venezuela. Recorded from most cos of ID, OR, and WA, and all across S BC.

The Gray Hairstreak is surely one of the most successful generalists of all North American butterflies. No other species can so accurately be described as an omnivore. So, more than any other Cascadian butterfly—including the Cabbage White—you should not be surprised anytime, or anywhere, you find it. Neither should you expect it anywhere. The most reliable habitats might be sagebrush and bitterbrush steppe in spring, where it also reaches its highest abundance. Certain years favor huge hatches, but most often it is found in ones and twos. Far less common in western Washington than on the drier side of the mountains. Along with Brown Elfins, the Gray is one of the few butterflies you can find flying around in relatively recent clearcuts, where they both utilize red huckleberry

flowers. Grays are extraordinarily alert and flighty, even compared to other lycaenids. Often, a rapid, dark, mysterious darter will prove to be a Gray Hairstreak when finally netted or spotted at rest or nectar. The deep gray wings can look quite bluish in flight, causing butterfliers to mistake the butterfly for a smaller, rounder, female tailed blue. Males are great defenders of prominences of all kinds. I watched their jousting matches on a Mojave promontory all afternoon and right up to sunset, indefatigable.

Subfamily Polyommatinae: Blues

The blues comprise a group of small butterflies closely related to the hairstreaks and coppers in the family Lycaenidae. Many of them possess structural coloration that refracts various shades of brilliant blue, especially in the males. Females tend to be gray or brown with bluish highlights. Certain species display shiny turquoise

scintillae and orange lunules (aurorae) along the edge of the ventral hindwing, and two of our species even possess hairstreak-like tails adjacent to these spots. The status of this subfamily, and the genera, subgenera, and in some cases even species within it, is subject to evolving judgment and understanding. The immature stages

Boisduval's Blue (ssp. *pembina*) puddle party

Comparison of Blues (Subfamily Polyommatinae)

Specimens are illustrated at 200% of life size

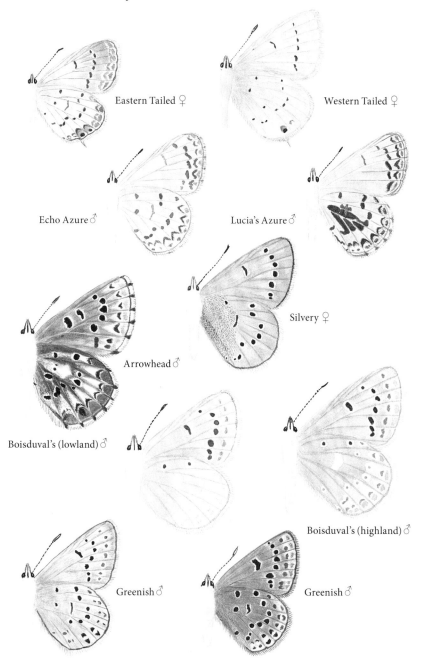

Eastern Tailed ♀

Western Tailed ♀

Echo Azure ♂

Lucia's Azure ♂

Silvery ♀

Arrowhead ♂

Boisduval's (lowland) ♂

Boisduval's (highland) ♂

Greenish ♂

Greenish ♂

Comparison of Blues (Subfamily Polyommatinae)

Specimens are illustrated at 200% of life size

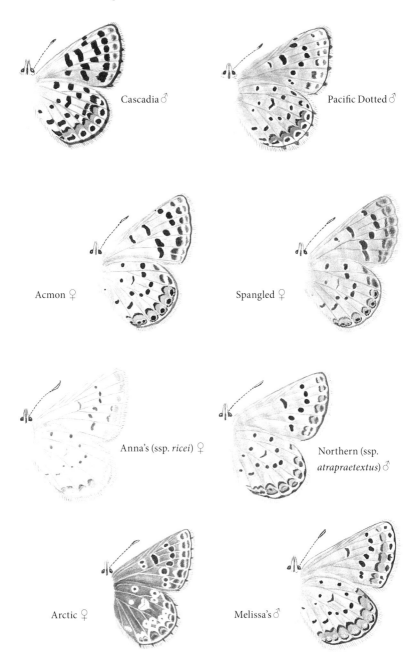

Cascadia ♂

Pacific Dotted ♂

Acmon ♀

Spangled ♀

Anna's (ssp. *ricei*) ♀

Northern (ssp. *atrapraetextus*) ♂

Arctic ♀

Melissa's ♂

Comparison of Azure Blues (*Celastrina* spp.)

Specimens are shown approximately at life size

Lucia's Azure
Celastrina lucia

Northwestern Azure
Celastrina echo nigrescens

Comparison of Buckwheat Blues (*Euphilotes* spp.)

Specimens are shown approximately at life size
Not pictured: Pumice Blue (*E.* "on *Eriogonum marifolium*")
& Rocky Mountain Dotted Blue (*E. ancilla*)

Cascadia Blue
Euphilotes "on *Eriogonum heracleoides*"

Summit Blue
Euphilotes glaucon

Bauer's Blue
Euphilotes baueri

Pacific Dotted Blue
Euphilotes enoptes

Columbia Dotted Blue
Euphilotes columbiae (C-N WA)

Columbia Dotted Blue
Euphilotes columbiae (SE WA/OR)

of blues are similar to other lycaenids, with eggs shaped like mushed spheres, larvae something like sowbugs/pillbugs, and pupae rounded like bullets. The caterpillars often feed on flower parts, and many secrete a sweet substance from glands on the tenth and eleventh segments. Ants attending these exchange protection from invertebrate predators for the secreted honeydew. Adults cling to the vicinity of the host plant, nectar in nearby meadows, and gather—males mostly—in great numbers at mud-puddle clubs. A few species are great wanderers: besides the resident species, our summer fauna is boosted by several migrants that cannot overwinter here but expand northward each year. Unlike hairstreaks, blues achieve higher diversity in temperate latitudes than the tropics. They are represented in Cascadia by two-thirds of all the species occurring in North America. Few habitats in season are without their blues.

Lucia's Azure   *Celastrina lucia* (W. KIRBY) 1837

Cumberland House, SK, Lat. 54°N
Aka Spring Azure, Boreal Spring Azure, Northern Spring Azure, *ladon*, *argiolus*

RECOGNITION < 1.25 in. **Flies high in shrubs and trees**. Males pale clear lucent blue above with distinct **overscaling of whitish scales** above. Both pale Echo Azures and the darker *C. echo nigrescens* lack such scales. Females light blue with black borders covering up to half the DFW. **Underside markings expanded** into variable broad charcoal blotches in the gray disc and/or along the margin. **VARIATION** Extent and shapes of sooty sections on VHW vary greatly, but never light as in *C. echo*. **HOST PLANTS** In the NE uses blueberries (*Vaccinium*). Red osier dogwood (*Cornus sericea*) in WA, prob. also other flowering shrubs in its limited

Male, dorsal

Pair, ventral

habitat in Cascadia, incl. redstem ceanothus (*Ceanothus sanguineus*), oceanspray (*Holodiscus discolor*), and *Prunus*. **ON THE WING** E April to L May. One brood, pupae overwinter. **HABITAT AND RANGE** Riparian canyons and shrubby glades. Occurs across boreal Canada and N US, S to WV, disjunct in CO and WA where it has been found in just a few sites, incl. Bear and Cowiche cyns in Yakima Co. Distribution muddy due to confusion with *C. echo nigrescens*. Records for *C. lucia* in Hinchliff (1996) referred to *C. e. nigrescens*.

Male, dorsal

That Lucia's Azure is so limited in the Pacific Northwest may have to do with post-glacial relictualism. Where *C. echo nigrescens* also occurs, which may also be heavily marked below, great care must be taken to distinguish the two by paying close attention to the ground color of the upperside. All the dark-marked azures used to be considered seasonal forms or melanic variants of *C. lucia* or *C. echo*. Now they are thought to represent at least two species. In *Mariposa Road*,

I described meeting *C. lucia* in Bear Canyon, rising from a fresh horse apple, where "a shrubby smorgasbord of cherry, ceanothus, oceanspray, and creek dogwood lined the trail, the buds and flowers of any of them suitable larval medium for the male and female Lucias dancing through the sunbeams and raindrops" (Pyle 2013). Aesthetics aside, *C. lucia* raises many questions and invites further study.

Echo Azure *Celastrina echo* (W. H. EDWARDS) 1864

San Francisco, CA
Aka Spring Azure, Echo Blue, Western Spring Azure, *ladon, argiolus, pseudargiolus*

RECOGNITION < 1.25 in. **Flies high in shrubs and trees**. Males clear silvery to **lilac-blue** (W WA/OR) above with no markings, females light to purplish blue with variable black borders covering up to half the DFW. E WA males may be plummy blue above, females positively purple with heavy dark margins, some almost black. Fringes are clear white. Underside frosty or bluish white, with **submarginal row of light**

Male, dorsal

Male, ventral

Female, dorsal (ssp. *nigrescens*)

gray, zigzag chevrons running around the VHW and **prominent ventral discal bars**; or darker above, markings below expanded into smaller or larger dark areas against a gray ground. **VARIATION** Our Pacific type is distinguished from C. *lucia* by lacking the white overscaling; males more delicately lavender than E-side C. *e. nigrescens*, with vaguer, lighter spotting below, commonly to the point of near-obsolescence; and a more stable appearance from place to place and brood to brood. C. *e. nigrescens* (Northwestern Azure) of E WA and NE OR is darker, plummy purplish above with dark gray margins on the female, dark fringes, and brownish gray beneath, and may have melanized markings below, ranging from heavily branded with sooty sections, through light spotting, to almost immaculate like C. *echo*. **HOST PLANTS** In Cascadia, chiefly red osier dogwood, elderberry, madrona, snowbrush ceanothus, oceanspray, huckleberries, cherries, spiraea, bitterbrush, buddleia, and numerous others, many of which serve as both

Males, ventral (ssp. *nigrescens*)

larval and nectar plants. Frequent visitors of puddles, ash-and-dung heaps, and flowers incl. coltsfoot, heather, garden currants, daphne, bluebell, hawkbit, goldfields, stream violet, willow catkins, and prob. many others. **ON THE WING** L February to E October, peaks in April and August. Two broods at least in W Cascadia, spring more common; one brood in cooler and N areas. Chrysalides overwinter. **HABITAT AND RANGE** Woodsy, shrubby, and riparian areas from sea level to high elevations, esp. red osier–lined streams and mixed habitats with many flowering shrubs. W US from SE WY to S AZ and S BC; throughout Cascadia (gaps in map are from poor sampling or reporting).

Extraordinarily adaptable, *C. echo* is ubiquitous except for driest desertlands, and our earliest fresh emerger on the wing. The Echo Azure was long considered part of Lucia's Azure (*C. lucia*), which was further conflated with the Holly Blue (*C. argiolus*) of Europe. Several species of American azures have now been split from the trunk. Azures and one of their chief host plants, red osier dogwood, spread widely together along watercourses throughout the Pleistocene interglacials, and later speciated here and there. No other butterfly, with the possible exception of its frequent companion the Margined White, is as well adapted to the moldering forests of the Maritime Northwest. Only the Gray Hairstreak utilizes a wider range of hosts. By exploiting so many food plants, Echo Azures can take advantage of whatever has a good bud-set in a given year, shift around easily and quickly, and occupy almost every habitat. I've watched females laying eggs in the unopened buds of ninebark (*Physocarpus capitatus*), slipping one egg per flowerhead sideways in between the carpels; ant-tended larvae eventually consume developing fruits.

Individuals resembling *C. lucia* below, with dark blotches, appear fairly commonly east of the Washington Cascades in spring but virtually never on the west side, and these belong to ssp. *nigrescens*. A sample of 93, collected just before a spray truck was about to destroy them, exhibited a perfect bell curve from *echo*-like immaculate to heaviest *lucia*-like fill-in. This may be a seasonal/temperature/moisture-controlled melanic form, or a result of hybrid introgression from contact with Lucia's Azures. It may also be a distinct species. *C. e. nigrescens* is recognizable over most of its range in Washington but trickier between Klickitat and Okanogan counties and central Oregon, where it seems to blend into the type, as one would expect from adjacent subspecies.

Arrowhead Blue *Glaucopsyche piasus* (BOISDUVAL) 1852

N Fk Feather R. Cyn, Plumas Co., CA
Aka *Phaedrotes, Scolitantides*

RECOGNITION < 1.25 in. **Large** for a blue. **Cool, dark to violet-blue** above with a dark brown, nebulous border on males, broader and darker on females with blue near the base and variable rusty edges. Tannish gray below, crossed by prominent arcing bands of white-ringed black dots. Inside **black-checked white fringe** runs a band of gray, and inside that **a row of orange-faced, black chevrons topped with a row of sharp white arrowheads, pointing toward one outstanding, isolated white arrowhead on the disc. VARIATION** Regional differences are subtle and inconsistent. Those from N CA into the Siskiyous and S OR Cascades are paler than Arrowheads occupying SE BC, E WA, and E OR to the mid-Cascades, which average larger, darker blue above with broader margins, and grayer beneath, but not as dark as the Rocky Mtn ssp. to the E. The amount of orangey brown on the females is highly variable. **HOST PLANTS** *Lupinus arbustus*, *L. sericeus*, *L. wyethii*, and prob. other lupines. Drinks from stonecrop, Canada thistle, other composites, mustards, mints, reeds, and mud. **ON THE WING** E April to L August, peak in May. A single generation, pupae overwinter. **HABITAT AND RANGE** Large lupine patches in desert, sage-steppe, ponderosa pine forest, canyons, dry gulches, wet meadows, and various montane situations, from basin level to high mountaintops. All the W states and provinces, S Canada to Baja. In Cascadia, E OR and E WA (W of the crest only at Mt. Rainier NP and Mt. St. Helens NVM), E Cascades to E Siskiyous, ID, and SE BC.

Female, dorsal

Female, ventral

Male, dorsal

Male, ventral

Of our regularly occurring blues, the Arrowhead is the most distinctive, the largest, and the least common. As Dornfeld writes, finding one is always something of a surprise. It seems to be absent from many seemingly suitable patches of lupine, and while a good colony can be fairly numerous, we more often find one or a very few. Once, on the south shore of Sprague Lake in Adams County, Washington, many individuals were sucking moisture from the ends of broken, rotting reeds. Only Lucia's Azure has such a boldly contrasting underside pattern, and it is smaller, frequents shrubs instead of lupines, and has a dark discal spot rather than a white wedge. Arrowhead Blues give the overall impression of lunkers. Sometimes Arrowheads can be picked out on the wing from among Boisduval's and Silveries, even before you see the diagnostic arrowhead.

Silvery Blue *Glaucopsyche lygdamus* (BOISDUVAL) 1841

Prob. Burke Co., GA

RECOGNITION < 1.2 in. Clear, brilliant blue above with pronounced black border on the males, females mole-brown with variable blue from base and diffuse black borders, both with white fringe. Pearl to battleship to brownish gray below **with a single postmedian arc of prominent, white-ringed black spots** enclosing discal bar and spots. **No marginal or** submarginal markings at all on VHW outside spotband. Boisduval's Blue less brilliant blue, always has *some* marginal/submarginal markings on VHW. Silvery often has greenish iridescent flush at base of VHW. **VARIATION** A good deal among individuals, but only subtly varied between populations. In general, they average darker, with broader borders, coastward; lighter and larger, inland; and brightest of all in the SE deserts. **HOST PLANTS** Many lupines (incl. *L. sericeus, L. lepidus, L. latifolius, L. sellulus, L. oreganus*) and vetches (*Vicia sativa, V. villosa, V. cracca*), and several other

Female, dorsal

Male, dorsal

genera of wild legumes incl. *Lotus, Medicago, Oxytropis, Lathyrus,* and *Astragalus.* Nectars on host plants, cherry blossom, dandelions, and many other flowers, and visits puddles and scat. **ON THE WING** M March to E September, peak in May (the higher the later, with the local spring). A single generation, pupae overwinter, sometimes up to ten months (James and Nunnallee). **HABITAT AND RANGE** Moist spots in all sorts of biotopes incl. grasslands, swales, banks of watercourses, canyons, clearings, oak openings, pinyon-juniper forest, meadows and pastures, alpine seeps, and tundra, from sea level to 10,000+ feet. N N Am, in cooler regions. Throughout Cascadia, except cities, coast, rainforest, and driest deserts; present in all cos.

As the Echo Azure is the early harbinger in the woods, the stunningly luminescent Silvery Blue brings on spring in open country. And like Sara's Orangetip, its frequent companion, the Silvery comes out progressively later from sea-level meadows, up through mountain runnels and lupine fields, to arctic-alpine slopes when the first glacier lilies are blooming. This vernal duo might be found in April at Tenino and August at Paradise, in a year of late snowmelt, both in springtime. Often you will find it the only butterfly on the scene in a habitat only recently freed from winter. Though it appreciates moisture, it is a good dowser in drylands, showing up with the least green in desert steppe. The Silvery is the closest living relative of the extinct Xerces Blue, but happily, it is much more adaptable. It is spreading along Washington highways on weedy pink and purple vetches. Downey showed that when Boisduval's Blues are also present, Silveries may specialize on a different lupine. A fresh male nectaring on a camas lily in a broad meadow full of the bright blue blossoms makes a most pleasing picture.

Male, ventral

Pair, ventral

Genus *Euphilotes*: Buckwheat Blues or Dotted Blues

The dotted blues are bright tiny elements of the east-side canyons and plateaus, but they are challenging to identify, or even understand, with certainty. There are two main species groups in the Northwest, the *Euphilotes battoides* complex and the *E. enoptes* complex. Males of the two groups have striking differences in their genitalia, and member species of one never use the same host plant as members of the other, when they occur in the same area. Recent work has shown that the genus includes a number of full "host plant species," coevolved with species of buckwheats (*Eriogonum*) on which their larvae largely specialize. Other *Euphilotes* species use a spectrum of buckwheats. All records and observation of dotted blues should be checked against local occurrence of buckwheat, and watched to determine their connections. Andy Warren, Dave Nunnallee, David James, Jon Pelham, and others are working to illuminate the Northwest *Euphilotes*, and new species will be described before they are finished. Molecular (DNA) work may be necessary to fully fill in the picture. Meanwhile, it's a real challenge to settle on just what species of *Euphilotes* you have before you in the net or the glass. The taxa can be nearly indistinguishable unless you know your buckwheats and can spot the associations. Sometimes it is best to be content with calling your insect a "buckwheat blue sp." They also resemble and often co-occur with Acmon and Lupine Blues but are usually smaller and lack the metallic spots (scintillae) on the hindwing edge below that both Acmon and Lupine possess. See James and Nunnallee (2011) and Warren (2005) for more details.

Cascadia Blue   *Euphilotes* "on *Eriogonum heracleoides*" (UNDESCRIBED)

Aka Square-spotted Blue, Bat Blue, Buckwheat Blue, Western Square-dotted Blue, Battoides Blue, *battoides*

RECOGNITION < 1 in. Males bright blue, females warm brown above, sometimes bluish at base; **fairly heavy black spotting below, against a nearly white ground**. Orange lunules on VHW banded or separate, more pronounced on females **with no scintillae** such as Acmon and Lupine Blues have. Checkered fringes, wings rounded. Other species usually more yellowish below with finer spots. Usually **associated with parsnipflower buckwheat**. **VARIATION** Lighter and brighter in the Cascades and Columbia Basin, less so toward the NE. **HOST PLANTS** *Eriogonum heracleoides* (parsnipflower buckwheat) and occasionally *E. douglasii*. **ON**

Female, dorsal

Male, dorsal

Pair, ventral

Pair, ventral

THE WING L April to L June in most of range; E July to E August in Warner Mtns. A single generation, chrysalides overwinter. **HABITAT AND RANGE** Buckwheat flats and slopes, pine forest clearings, desert steppe, canyons, alpine passes. NE and spotty SE OR, WA E of Cascade crest, most of ID to MT, S interior valleys in BC.

The Cascadia Blue, a member of the *E. battoides* complex, has recently been recognized as distinct and will soon be elevated to species status. It is often sympatric with the Pacific Dotted Blue, which it closely resembles, and the two tend to vary in parallel from region to region. On average, the Cascadia Blue carries heavier, more angular spotting on a paler background, and flies earlier. Certain populations feed on *Eriogonum sphaerocephalum* in the western Columbia Basin, and others on *E. thymoides* from Kittitas to Klickitat counties. These may be distinct, undescribed species of their own, or they might belong to *Euphilotes battoides* or some other already described taxon.

Pumice Blue   *Euphilotes* "on *Eriogonum marifolium*" (UNDESCRIBED)

Aka Square-spotted Blue, Bat Blue, Buckwheat Blue, Western Square-dotted Blue, Battoides Blue, *battoides*

RECOGNITION < 1 in. Males deep blue above, females brown; ventral spots not usually squarish, may be fused into irregular dark blotches (Warren). **Associated with marumleaf buckwheat**. **VARIATION** Highly variable in size, in amount of black, and degree of fusion of black spots below. **HOST PLANTS** *Eriogonum marifolium* (marumleaf buckwheat). **ON THE WING** June in valleys, July and August in higher mtns. A single generation, pupae overwinter. **HABITAT AND RANGE** Pumice flats and volcanic slopes on the E flank of OR Cascades, perhaps wider.

Female, dorsal

Andy Warren first found this butterfly among *E. marifolium*, which was growing on extensive pumice deposits at Dutchman Flat (6,450 feet), north of Mt. Bachelor in Deschutes County. He subsequently found it elsewhere in the central Cascades wildlands and recognized its distinctness from other buckwheat blues. It is a prime example of speciation through specialization on a specific resource.

Female, ventral

Male, dorsal

Male, ventral

Summit Blue *Euphilotes glaucon* (W. H. EDWARDS) 1871

Nr Virginia City, Storey Co., NV
Aka Square-spotted Blue, Glaucon Blue, *battoides*

RECOGNITION <1 in. Little orange on blue males, broader, connected orange bands on brown females; checkered fringes, black marginal line thick, as in other members of  the *E. battoides* complex. **VARIATION** Extensive throughout OR; see Warren (2005) for details. **HOST PLANTS** *Eriogonum umbellatum* (sulphur-flower buckwheat), esp. var. *hausknechtii* (Hausknecht's buckwheat); *E. ovalifolium* (cushion buckwheat) suspected in WA. **ON THE WING** E May to M August, depending on locality and elevation. A single generation, chrysalides overwinter. **HABITAT AND RANGE** Many habitats where sulphur-flowers grow, low elevations to high, with a fondness for high flat summits and plateaus. At least from Kern Co., CA, perhaps to Yakima Co., WA; much of S and E OR; E extent uncertain. The WA populations are tentatively assigned here but could represent something else.

Pair, ventral

Female, ventral

Pair, dorsal

The type and *E. g. oregonensis*, first described from Crater Lake, were long considered subspecies of *E. battoides*. These are the *E. battoides*-complex *Eriogonum umbellatum* feeders. They might at first be taken for Lupine Blues, which also hang around sulphur-flower buckwheats, but the checkered fringe and absence of metallic scintillae will settle the question quickly. What appears to be this taxon abounds on Bethel Ridge, Yakima County.

Bauer's Blue   *Euphilotes baueri* SHIELDS 1975

W side Gilbert Pass, 6,200 feet, Inyo Co., CA

RECOGNITION < .85 in. Similar to others in the *E. battoides* complex, female often quite blue above, black spotting heavy below. **Associated with cushion buckwheat. VARIATION** Smaller with lighter markings in the Alvord Desert. **HOST PLANTS** *Eriogonum ovalifolium* (cushion buckwheat). **ON THE WING** E May to E June in the SE deserts; E June in the Ochoco Divide. Single-brooded,

Male, ventral

pupae overwinter. **HABITAT AND RANGE** Desert and aridlands with cushion buckwheat. E CA to W NV, known in Cascadia from the Alvord Desert in Malheur Co. and the Ochoco Gap in Deschutes and Crook cos E of Redmond, OR.

Andy Warren has confirmed this species in eastern Oregon, and it may prove to be more widespread in the region when more stands of the sole host plant have been investigated. One of several butterflies able to subsist in the apparently forbidding rigors of the hot, dry Alvord Desert abutting the eastern wall of Steens Mountain.

Pacific Dotted Blue *Euphilotes enoptes* (BOISDUVAL) 1852

N Fk Feather R. Cyn, Plumas Co., CA
Aka Dotted Blue

Female, dorsal

Male, dorsal

RECOGNITION < .85 in. Males bright blue with broad black borders above, females warm brown above, sometimes bluish at base; orange **aurora narrow, often separated into separate lunules, black marginal line thin**; VHW orange on females rudimentary. **VARIATION** Extensive throughout the region; see Warren (2005) for details. **HOST PLANTS** *Eriogonum nudum* (barestem buckwheat); rarely *E. elatum* and *E. compositum*. **ON THE WING** M April to E August, based on latitude and altitude. One brood, pupae overwinter. **HABITAT AND RANGE** Canyons, mtns, subalpine passes; often on roadsides and the angle of repose below rimrock, and isolated rocky outcrops. S CA to S-C WA, much of SW OR and N in W Cascades and Coast Range.

Once the Columbia Dotted Blue was recognized as separate from *E. enoptes,*

Pair, ventral

lepidopterists began looking for the actual *E. enoptes* in Washington by exploring the few known historic stations for *Eriogonum nudum*; a highly disjunct and quite distinctive population exists on Rickreall Ridge, Polk County, in the Willamette Valley, also on *E. nudum*. Once we found the plant, in the South Fork Tieton Canyon, Yakima County, Thea Pyle collected the first Washington *E. enoptes* on it. It has since been recorded from a few other localities in the southern Cascades of Washington, including White Pass by Dave Nunnallee. Very large stands of barestem buckwheat, apparently pre-adapted for disturbance, have erupted in the eastern blast zone at Mt. St. Helens. So far I have found two other buckwheat-feeding lycaenids on it, but the Pacific Dotted Blue remains elusive in the National Volcanic Monument.

Columbia Dotted Blue *Euphilotes columbiae* (MATTONI) 1954

Brewster, Okanogan Co., WA
Aka Dotted Blue, *E. enoptes*

Female, dorsal

RECOGNITION < .85 in. Smaller than *E. battoides*-complex species and usually lighter-dotted below. Male bright blue above, female mouse-brown; **black margin usually broken into spots on DHW, female (and** sometimes male) with orange submarginal spots as well. **Yellowish gray below with dusky scaling and small clear black dots usually larger on VFW than VHW.** Orange submarginal aurora on VHW either separate lunules or confluent into a band; and heavy black terminal line, no scintillae. White fringe checkered black. **VARIATION** None significant in our region (Warren calls it "remarkably

Male, dorsal

Male, ventral

consistent"). **HOST PLANTS** *Eriogonum compositum, E. elatum, E. strictum.* **ON THE WING** M April to L June (*E. compositum* users); L June to M August (*E. elatum* users). Single-brooded, pupae overwinter. **HABITAT AND RANGE** Essentially all the Columbia Basin in N OR and E WA (Warren), Snake R. Basin, surrounding mtns, into ID.

This recently elevated species (formerly designated a subspecies of *E. enoptes*) has two foodplant "races." One of them feeds on *Eriogonum compositum* (arrowleaf buckwheat) and its varieties *lancifolium* and *leianthum*. The second utilizes *E. elatum* (tall woolly buckwheat). The two buckwheats are used even in the same vicinities, the butterflies using them flying in proximity over significant portions of their ranges but differing in flight times. With this adaptation, the species exploits two very capable plants, themselves adapted to rather different biotopes. In several areas *E. columbiae* larvae have been recovered from *Eriogonum strictum* (Blue Mountain buckwheat), which blooms between the other two in time.

Rocky Mountain Dotted Blue *Euphilotes ancilla*
(BARNES & MCDUNNOUGH) 1918

Eureka, Juab Co., UT
Aka Ancilla Dotted Blue, Barnes' Blue, *E. enoptes*

RECOGNITION < .85 in. Males violet-blue above, females brown with bluish tinge. More like members of the *E. battoides* complex than other members of the *E. enoptes* complex, with **large, bold spots beneath and prominent, well-developed orange aurorae** on females. **VARIATION** No ssp. **HOST PLANTS** *Eriogonum sphaerocephalum* (rock buckwheat). **ON THE WING** L May to E July. Single-brooded, pupae

Female, dorsal

Female, ventral

overwinter. **HABITAT AND RANGE** C Rocky Mtns to W Great Basin; Harney Co. in SE OR.

Known from Oregon previously from only a handful of specimens, this dotted blue was found by Andy Warren right in the towns of Hines and Burns by the hundreds, on extensive stands of the host buckwheat. They ignored the nearby Blue Mountain buckwheat. It will likely be found more widely.

Male, ventral

Leona's Little Blue   *Philotiella leona* HAMMOND & MCCORKLE 2000

MP 226, US 97, Klamath Co., OR

RECOGNITION < .75 in. **Tiny.** Male black-and-blue above, black outward, dusky blue basally. Female black with brownish overtones. **White below, crisply dotted with black**; dots large on vFW, smaller on vHW, in a single curved band enclosing some in the center; **no submarginal spots or orange aurorae.** Wings proportionately longish and narrow. **VARIATION** Only the type is known. **HOST PLANTS** *Eriogonum sperguli-*

Female, dorsal

Female, ventral; male, dorsal

Ventral

Leona's Little Blue came to light in July 1995, when Harold and Leona Rice investigated the Mazama ash fields east of Crater Lake. They were surprised to find examples of what seemed to be the Small Blue (*P. speciosa*), which had never been known in the Northwest. The new species was named for Harold's wife, and I dubbed it Leona's Little Blue. It is routinely larger than the Californian *P. speciosa*, darker, and less blue. In 1963, J. W. Tilden described the ash and pumice fields of the Sand Creek Basin and its fritillaries, and speculated on the effects that Mt. Mazama's eruption (6000 BP) may have had on subsequent butterfly evolution and distribution. *P. leona* is the second butterfly described from this extensive ancient formation. Its miniature size, dark color, sedentary habits, and rapid, low flight make it difficult to spot, and its range has not yet been extended far beyond the original area of its discovery. Detailed studies on the biology and ecology of *P. leona* were performed by David James (2012), and recent monitoring and surveying by Dana Ross. It may require conservation and management, as it seems surprisingly absent from much apparently suitable habitat.

num (spurry buckwheat). Males and females both nectar on a minutely pink-flowered fireweed relative, a small *Epilobium* sp., which resembles the larval host plant. **ON THE WING** M June to L July. **HABITAT AND RANGE** Volcanic ash and pumice fields. Currently known only from the type locality and vicinity in the Antelope Desert. Hammond and McCorkle predict that the ultimate range may extend to incl. volcanic landscapes from Newberry Crater (OR) in the N to Mts Shasta and Lassen (CA) in the S.

Western Pygmy Blue *Brephidium exilis* (BOISDUVAL) 1852

Sacramento, CA
Aka Pygmy Blue, Pigmy Blue, *exile*

RECOGNITION < .75 in. **Tiny**. Narrow wings **bronzy brown above with aquamarine flush near the base**, more in males. Inner VHW/VFW silvery, outer part coppery, VHW with **marginal row of bright, blue-green centered black spots edged with metallic gold**. White fringe, white striations across ventrum. **VARIATION** The amount of blue varies from little to nearly half the wings above, and the smallest individuals are half the size of the largest. Ours are not appreciably different from those in S CA or HI. **HOST PLANTS** An array of native and exotic chenopods, incl. saltbush (*Atriplex*), pigweed (*Chenopodium*), and Russian thistle (*Salsola tragus*). Mark Smith observed a female hovering over seablite (*Suaeda*) in Harney Co. Nectars in large numbers on rabbitbrush. **ON THE WING** M July to L September in SE OR, no noticeable peaks; common in Imnaha Cyn ca. 4–5 August. Several broods in the S, fewer N. Pupae over-

Female, dorsal

Female, ventral

winter in the permanent colonies in the S and SW. **HABITAT AND RANGE** Desert flats, gullies, and roadsides, incl. disturbed range. Resident around CA, Baja, Mexico, and TX coasts; expands N to Great Plains and Great Basin. In Cascadia, known from SE ID and E OR in Basin and Range, Ochocos, SE edge of Blues/Wallowas in Hells/Imnaha cyns, and three records by Umatilla NWR in Morrow Co., OR, and Benton Co., WA.

Western Pygmy Blues are among the smallest butterflies in the world. Watch one of these mites side by side with a massive Monarch on a rabbitbrush: it is remarkable to realize that they possess much the same complexity, organization, and skill. Western Pygmy Blues even migrate like Monarchs—at least, they migrate from areas of abundance, establishing temporary colonies in weedy habitats far beyond their northernmost wintering grounds, to die off in autumn. Seldom if ever year-round residents this far north, the ones we see are the summer- and autumn-generation descendants of the spring pioneers, and numbers vary from none to abundant in a given year. Records in the North will increase as climate change progresses. I found it in Washington by searching Russian thistle and rabbitbrush right across the Columbia River from where Neil Bjorkland had recorded the northernmost Oregon record the previous week.

Marine Blue   *Leptotes marina* (REAKIRT) 1868

Orizaba, Mexico, "near Vera Cruz"
Aka Striped Blue

RECOGNITION < 1 in. Males pale, transparent violet-blue above, females sky-blue or brown with broad dark borders and HW bands and spots. **Below, both sexes chalky white between a series of heavy, concentric gray-brown bands** like waves, and submarginal chevrons. Pair of black-and-blue spots at the HW tornus, sometimes orange-ringed. **VARIATION** The depth of blue and the amount of brown on the females vary considerably, along with their size and the brilliancy of the glittering tornal spots below. **HOST PLANTS** Legumes of

Female, dorsal

Ventral

many kinds, incl. native vetches, peas, clovers, alfalfa, and ornamentals like plumbagos, sweet pea, and wisteria. **ON THE WING** L May to E August. Continual broods in the S but, with no winter diapause, it cannot survive in the N. **HABITAT AND RANGE** Resident in Mexico and along the SW US border, migrating N throughout the SW and lower MW. Casual in Cascadia, recorded only four times from OR Cascades.

The only Northwest records for the Marine Blue are for Deschutes County, Diamond Lake north of Crater Lake, and the Metolius River. It is one of several species of essentially subtropical blues that regularly expand their summer ranges northward, only to die back in fall. But unlike the previous species, it doesn't seem to breed this far north. When favorable conditions promote a larger than usual migration from the southern lands in early spring, Marine Blues become quite common in the Rockies and Great Basin by midsummer, appearing overnight. "This dainty little blue fairly swarms in southern California during favorable seasons," wrote Comstock. In such years, additional sightings might well occur in Cascadia. The species' zebra-striped pattern is very distinctive as it pauses to nectar on weedy annuals along the watercourses it follows.

Eastern Tailed Blue *Cupido comyntas* (GODART) 1824

"l'Amérique septentrionale"
Aka Tailed Blue, *Everes*

SPECIAL CONCERN IN BC

RECOGNITION < 1 in. Male dorsum is solid, brilliant deep blue, female mole-gray shot with blue (more so in spring brood); both have **hairstreak-like tails near orange-and-black tail-spots. Ventrum pale gray with distinct rows of black spots, often at least two capped with orange above tail**, with small scintillae. Usually has a **discernible cell-end black bar on DFW**, usually lacking in *C. amyntula*. Smaller, wings much more rounded than Gray Hairstreak. **VARIATION** The ground color and heaviness of spotting below vary but are seldom as light as on the next species. **HOST PLANTS** A great array of legumes, incl. lupines, peas, locoweeds, vetches, alfalfa, and clovers. Nectars on marigolds, daisy fleabane, clovers, many other low flowers. **ON THE WING** E April to E August, peaks in May and July. Last-instar larvae overwinter. Multiple broods occur where climate permits; records suggest two generations here. **HABITAT AND RANGE** Generally, disturbed and weedy habitats where adventitious species of peas grow, such as vacant lots, parks, canals and creeks, riverbanks and beds, and fallow fields; but also undisturbed riparian sites in BC, OR. E US, SE Canada, and disjunct in SW and W incl. much of W Coast. In Cascadia, most of W OR, sparsely in E OR; NE and N-C WA; ID panhandle; SE BC.

Female, dorsal

Female, ventral

Male, dorsal

Male, ventral

Pair, ventral

Eastern Tailed Blue records compare oddly between the two states: common in western Oregon, rare in eastern; no records at all in western Washington, but several along rivers in the northeast corner. (I have found colonies along the flooded Columbia near Daisy in Stevens County, and at the flooded mouth of the Sanpoil River on the Colville Indian Reservation.) It is odd that the species is frequent in Clatsop County, Oregon, and utterly absent right across the Columbia in Washington. It has been thought a possible agricultural introduction in the West (Warren doubts this based on subtle differences from eastern types); if so, it has been here for most of a century: Stanley G. Jewett Jr. found it in several Oregon locations in the 1930s, and we have one anonymous 1906 record. John Downey (in Howe) states there is no way to tell the two tailed blues apart for sure by their looks alone, but they have regular genitalic differences. Some individuals, especially if worn, may indeed prove difficult; but the heavier spotting, more prominent orange lunules, and cell-end bar often stand out on *C. comyntas*. Warren has often found both species flying together in western Oregon, and readily discriminable. Habitat also helps. The Eastern tends to be found in drier, weedier places (in boyhood I collected it regularly on white clover in the lawn of a raw suburban park); while the Western prefers more natural settings (though Guppy and Shepard say this is not the case in the three known British Columbian colonies).

Western Tailed Blue   *Cupido amyntula* (BOISDUVAL) 1852

White Creek, Quincy, Plumas Co., CA

RECOGNITION

< 1.25 in. Bright purplish blue males, warm slaty females; Westerns less often have tail-spots dorsally, females usually have less blue, than Easterns. Unlike *C. comyntas*, the **ventrum is chalky white with understated spotting**, often virtually immaculate, esp. W of Cascades. **Usually only one orange lunule**, D and V, if present at all, with very slight scintilla. **Usually no cell-end bar on DFW**; commonly larger than *C. comyntas*. **VARIATION** Individuals vary greatly, from nearly immaculate to fairly spotted below. Duskier with larger spots and a grayish leading edge on the VFW through Canada and AK. In N Cascades, Okanogan, and BC, the ventral markings can be almost heavy enough to confuse with *C. comyntas*, when the absence of a dark cell-end bar on the upper FW

Male, dorsal

may help. **HOST PLANTS** Legumes incl. locoweeds (*Oxytropis*), vetches, milkvetches, and
peas. Pelham notes *Vicia sativa, Astragalus obscurus, Lathyrus lanszwertii,* and *L. pauciflorus; V.
americana, L. nevadensis* in BC. I find *V. gigantea*
much used in SW WA, *L. japonicus* (beach pea)
in San Juan Is. Nectars incl. hosts, composites,
knapweed, and rabbitbrush. Males mudpuddle frequently and abundantly, and visit scat
of coyotes and other animals. **ON THE WING**
L March to M September, peaks in May and
August. Larvae overwinter, producing a spring
flight that can engender a second, if conditions
allow (though Warren says it is univoltine in
OR). **HABITAT AND RANGE** Chiefly undisturbed
or largely natural moist habitats—streambanks,
meadows, trailsides, subalpine seeps and turf,
beaches, forest borders—from sea level to
high mtns. Boreal W N Am from Baja to Arctic
Ocean, E in Canada. Almost all Cascadia except
wettest parts of coast and driest basinlands.

Sometimes (as in w w B) combined with Eastern Tailed Blue. Most of the tailed blues you
find in Cascadia, especially in Washington,
will be Westerns. If the habitat leaves you in
doubt, the whiter, little-marked undersides
should come to the rescue. The two tailed
blues live close together in western Oregon, but it is a mystery why no easterns have
been found in western Washington—the

Male, ventral

Female, dorsal

Columbia River seems a complete barrier. Numbers vacillate from year to year: some summers a packed puddle will produce mostly Boisduval's Blues and a handful of Western Taileds, another season the same damp spot disturbed might send up hundreds of *Cupido*. As you watch them puddle or nectar, notice the way they rub their hindwings back and forth against one another, drawing attention away from the body and toward the bright tornal spots and tails. Birds commonly strike these false heads, allowing the butterfly to escape without mortal harm. These two blues elegantly demonstrate the principle of convergent evolution with the hairstreaks; and though their tails are tiny and the scintillae and aurorae may be no more than a few scales, they work: often you will see the tail-bits nipped away. Adults roost by the dozens at dusk atop beach peas on San Juan Island shorelines.

Reakirt's Blue *Echinargus isola* (REAKIRT) 1867

Mexico, "near Vera Cruz"
Aka Solitary Blue, Mexican Blue, *Hemiargus, isolus*

RECOGNITION < 1 in. Very small. Male thin lilac-blue above, female dusky, bluish basally. **VFW** arced with postmedian row of five prominent black, white-ringed spots, VHW with smaller, gray and white spots, bars, and chevrons. **DHW and VHW** have black and silver spots, two small and one large, in anal angle. Lower FW margin looks "clipped." **VARIATION** The size, amount of blue, and heaviness of spotting vary substantially, but the chain of black VFW spots remains constant. **HOST PLANTS** Many legumes, incl. *Melilotus* (sweetclover), lotus, alfalfa, wild licorice, and white clover. Both larvae and adults favor sweetclover for forage or nectar, respectively. **ON THE WING** Sole record E June. Continual broods occur in its S range, sending spring and summer flights N. No winter diapause, cannot survive in the N. **HABITAT AND RANGE** Waste ground, vacant lots, watercourses, old fields, clearings; Nabokov wrote of its "very isolated small summer colonies on hot hillsides." Resident in the extreme SW, TX, and Mexico, migrating

Male, dorsal

into much of W and MW to ID and MB. One
WA record to date, in Kittitas Co., none in
OR, and a couple in SW ID and NW Nevada.

Joe Albright found a pair along a small
stream near Ellensburg in June 1993. The
mother of these may somehow have been
introduced; but since *E. isola* does invade
northward annually, expanding its range
hundreds of miles in the process, it seems
likely that she (or they) arrived under their
own steam. This mass movement, like those
of the Marine Blue and Dainty Sulphur,
mainly fills the middle of the country, and
northwestern/northeastern arrivals are rare.
Reakirt's Blue is so small, fast, and inconspicuous that it is easily missed altogether,
or passed over for a fly or a small diurnal
moth. They can appear in any habitat including the high alpine, and usually as singletons, as the epithet suggests (*isola* is Italian
for "island," hence "isolated"). Namesake
Tryon Reakirt of Philadelphia published the

Male, ventral

first summary of Colorado butterflies in
1866. Some recent texts place *isola* in *Hemiargus*, but Nabokov's genus *Echinargus* has
been shown to be fully valid and the butterfly's correct home.

Greenish Blue   *Icaricia saepiolus* (BOISDUVAL) 1852

Mackenzie R., Fort Smith, NWT
Aka Greenish Clover Blue, Glossy Blue, *Plebejus*

**I. S. *INSULANUS* EXTIRPATED IN BC; I. S.
LITTORALIS FEDERAL SPECIES OF CON-
CERN, CRITICALLY IMPERILED IN OR**

RECOGNITION < 1.25 in. Extreme sexual
dimorphism. Male a **cool, grainy blue above
with greenish overtones** in the right light, black
border, and a **distinct black bar in the FW cell.**
Female blue-brown
to copper above,
often shot with
orange. Male below
light gray with tur-
quoise scaling at the
base, female warm
tan to brownish gray,
sometimes with

Female, dorsal

blue at base. Ventral black spotting varies, but **nearly always one or more pairs of pronounced, opposing spots near the anal angle of the HW: marginal dashes faced by submarginal chevrons, capping a subtle orange or rusty patch between** **them**. Other blues lack these. Coppery females lack submarginal orange zigzag of coppers. **VARIATION** Individuals, and to some extent populations, vary in terms of size, intensity of blue on males and reddishness of females,

Male, dorsal

Male, ventral

Pair, ventral

and ventral maculation. Cascadian mtn types average smaller than the Sierran, with reduced spotting below and seldom any basal blue on the reddish females. Larger, paler, spottier blues occur on and around Steens Mtn. Vancouver Is. Greenish Blues (*I. s. insulanus*), now thought gone, showed obsolescence of spots beneath and narrower borders in the males. Mainland BC blues run grayer beneath, bluer above on females, narrow-bordered, and stronger spotted. *I. s. insulanus* traits carry through in rare C coastal colonies in OR (Lincoln and Lane cos), whose small spots show with unique white haloes, and Warren considers them to be *I. s. nr. insulanus*. Other coastal colonies from Curry and Coos cos are a little larger, darker blue, and more heavily spotted, and relate to *I. s. littoralis*, from Del Norte Co., CA. **HOST PLANTS** Various clovers incl. *Trifolium repens*, *T. wormskioldii*, *T. thompsonii*, and *T. hybridum*. Nectars on meadow and naturalized flowers incl. the host clovers, bistort, chickweed, purple thyme, and various composites. **ON THE WING** L April to L August, peak in June-July. One generation, second- or third-instar larvae overwinter. **HABITAT AND RANGE** Lush wet meadows. Drier sites where clovers bloom, incl. roadsides, but chiefly found where feet get wet. Throughout W and N US and transborder Canada, AK to Maritimes, S CA, S Rockies. Much of BC, montane WA and OR from high Cascades E. Only Olympics in W WA, sparingly and very local along OR coast.

The Greenish Blue abounds in summertime in almost any moist, clovery meadow in its range. Both a generalist and a specialist, it can be found colonizing European white clover along roadsides, by which its range has certainly spread; or in a discrete colony in the lower reaches of Swakane Canyon, north of Wenatchee, where the caterpillars feed and adults nectar on the big rose flowerheads of the extreme endemic, Thompson's clover. The few maritime Oregon sites hint at an old distribution now confined to sparse remnants on central and south coast. Corvallis records from 1898 to 1912 probably bespeak early extinction in the Willamette Valley.

Boisduval's Blue   *Icaricia icarioides* (BOISDUVAL) 1869

E Br. N Fk Feather R. Cyn, Plumas Co., CA
Aka Common Blue, Icarioides Blue, Lupine Blue, *Plebejus*, *Aricia*

I. I. FENDERI FEDERALLY ENDANGERED, CRITICALLY IMPERILED IN OR; I. I. BLACKMOREI SPECIAL CONCERN IN BC, CANDIDATE IN WA

RECOGNITION < 1.5 in. Male bright azure to cerulean blue above. Female blue-shot gray-brown to warm brown with variable blue at base. Black border inside white fringe; FW cell bar usually present. Below, pearly gray wearing to dirty chalk. **VFW postmedian spots large, mostly black with white rings. VHW spots smaller, all-white to mostly white with small black pupils, never mostly black with white ring** as in Silvery Blue. Also unlike Silvery, **always has at least some submarginal marks,** even if rudimentary. **Mostly white bar in VHW cell.** Rarely a touch of rust in the submarginal spots, but no real aurorae, nor the prominent spot-pairs present in Greenish Blue.

Female resembles Sooty Hairstreak, which lacks FW cell bar and has no blue scaling. **VARIATION** Great and complex, both within and between populations, with several ssp. in the region, incl. ssp. *fulla* and ssp. *pembina*. Of the ssp. of strong conservation concern,

Female, dorsal (ssp. *fenderi*)

Male, dorsal (ssp. *fenderi*)

Female, dorsal (ssp. *blackmorei*)

Male, dorsal (ssp. *blackmorei*)

Male, ventral (ssp. *blackmorei*)

Female, ventral (ssp. *fulla*)

Males, dorsal (left), ventral (right) (ssp. *pembina*)

Fender's Blue (*I. i. fenderi*) of the Willamette Valley has prominent black pupils in the VHW spotband, with little white around them; while the Puget Blue (*I. i. blackmorei*) of the Salish Lowlands has these spots almost all white, with almost no black pupils. Other types vary in these and separate traits, such as brilliance and depth of male blue, amount of blue or reddish on female D and V, average wingspan, and so on. **HOST PLANTS** Strictly lupines, using some 40 species around the West—where more than one species occurs, usually the hairiest one. Cascadian records for *Lupinus latifolius*, *L. lepidus*, *L. sericeus*, *L. sellulus*, *L. argenteus*, *L. arbustus*, and *L. oreganus* var. *kincaidii* (Fender's Blue). Nectar records incl. lupines, Olympic onion (*Allium crenulatum*), yellow, white, and mauve composites, buckwheats, cinquefoil, clovers, selfheal, and many others. Males are major cast members at many butterfly mud-puddle clubs. **ON THE WING** E April to E September, peak in May–July, depending on elevation and moisture. A single brood, second-instar larvae overwinter. **HABITAT AND RANGE** John Downey found that *I. icarioides* virtually never

occurs farther than 50 yards from lupines. Flies in forest glades, roadsides, meadows, fields, and grasslands to shrub-steppe, canyons, and subalpine slopes. Great Plains to W Coast, Baja to BC. Most of Cascadia E of W Cascades, but also Vancouver Is., Salish Lowlands-Willamette Valley, Olympics, a few sites in the WA/OR Coast Range (N Willapa Hills, Mt. Hebo, Mary's Peak), and Siskiyous.

This is the most frequently encountered blue in the meadows and muddy trails of Cascadia, and it can be very numerous. Any sunny lupine patch in May is likely to be hopping with them. The species' old vernacular name, Common Blue, still applies in the Cascades; but it is no longer suitable overall, with three of its subspecies threatened or endangered, and another one extinct. Fender's Blue, discovered around 1930 by Kenny Fender on Ralph Macy's farm and described by Macy, was considered extinct due to intensive agriculture in the Willamette Valley. Rediscovered in 1989, it now receives intensive management and conservation efforts. The Puget Blue is being surveyed on post-glacial prairies south of Olympia, where development has eliminated much of its habitat; while on Vancouver Island (where it is called Blackmore's Blue), fire suppression and Scotch broom have choked out its lupines. The species really ought to be called the Lupine Blue, but unfortunately this name is preoccupied by *I. lupini*, a blue that has nothing to do with lupines. So we use the surname of the Parisian entomologist who described it and many other western butterflies: Jean Baptiste Boisduval chose the epithet *icarioides* because the butterfly reminded him of the European Common Blue, *Plebejus icarus*, now introduced in Ontario. Icarus was the mythic Greek with the faulty wax-and-feather ultralight; the suffix *-oides* means "like." Nabokov erected the genus name from elements of Icarus and *Aricia*, a closely related genus.

Shasta Blue   *Icaricia shasta* (W. H. EDWARDS) 1862

Slope above Donner Pass, Placer Co., CA
Aka Cushion-plant Blue, Yosemite Blue, Alpine Blue, *Plebejus*

RECOGNITION
< 1 in. **A dusky little blue**. Male dark purplish blue above, female bluish brown, both with FW cell bars. Black borders expanding into marginal dots

on DHW, orange-capped in females and some males. **Smudgy gray below** with whitish veins and overscaling. Dark brown discal dots on VHW; **subtle submarginal row of blue-green scintillae capped in turn by pale orange aurorae, black chevrons, and white arrows pointing basally.** Acmon Blue not dusky below except in Olympics; Anna's Blue larger and much lighter; dotted blues lighter, lack metallic scintillae. **VARIATION** Shastas from the E Cascades in OR are larger, paler, and have stronger spots than those in the Warners, Steens, and SE OR, which are smaller and darker, with bigger, muddier spots. **HOST PLANTS** Herbaceous peas incl. lupines, locoweeds, milkvetches, and clovers. Nectars on host legumes, pussypaws (*Cistanthe*), alpine buckwheats, and other alpine flora. **ON THE WING** M June to M August. Biennial, first winter spent as eggs, second as nearly grown larvae. **HABITAT AND RANGE** Alpine and montane in much of its range, on rocky ridges and fellfields, pumice flats, windy summits; high prairie elsewhere. Dornfeld describes OR habitat as near small streams in sunny forest openings (Cascades, down to 3,000 feet) or near melting snowfields on the high slopes and meadows of Steens Mtn (up to 9,500 feet). Scott calls it a resident of cushion-plant communities, regardless of elevation. Rockies and High

Female, dorsal

Female, ventral

Male, dorsal

Male, ventral

Plains W across Basin and Range to CA and OR. E slope of C Cascades and Ochocos, high Warner, Steens, and Pueblo Mtns.

"Delicate and very local," as Dornfeld called it, Shasta indeed flies on Mt. Shasta, and is one of only two butterflies named for a Cascade volcano. Its flight is famously feeble, and you have to look hard to spot this tiny shred of blue-gray against the stony backdrop, as the wind may take it away as soon as you see it. Small high-country moths come to mind at a glimpse, but as Comstock wrote, "The mouse-gray under surfaces, with a marginal row of metallic bluish green circlets on the secondaries, will serve to differentiate this distinctive little butterfly." The Spangled Blue (*I. acmon spangelatus*) of the Olympics resembles *I. shasta*, but Shasta's northern limit comes at about Camp Sherman, Jefferson County, Oregon. The favorite place to see it is the summit of Steens Mountain, where Shasta abounds in a spectacular setting. It is amusing to watch onlookers' reactions to grown men with nets, seemingly oblivious to Little Blitzen Canyon and Kiger Gorge, in full pursuit of next to nothing over the bare rocks.

Acmon Blue   *Icaricia acmon* (WESTWOOD) 1851

San Francisco, CA
Aka Silver-studded Blue, Emerald-studded Blue, *Plebejus*, *lupini* (in WWB, species combined)

FUCA BLUE (=STRAITS SEGREGATE) SGCN IN WA

RECOGNITION < 1 in. Males bright blue above, females mouse-brown shot with more or less blue, underside whitish or grayish; **orange aurorae on DHW and VHW, but not on VFW; blue-green metallic scintillae present outside the VHW aurorae.** Very difficult to tell apart from Lupine Blue without examining the genitalia. Typically, *I. acmon* is narrow-bordered if at all, its dorsal orange aurora is pale pinkish orange and meets the blue directly, while *I. lupini* males have broader black borders above and black edges to the big, bright red-orange lunules on the DHW. Lupines tend to be larger and deeper, purpler blue, Acmons smaller and powdery-pale blue; all these traits vary. Melissa's Blues have orange on VFW; dotted blues have no scintillae. **VARIATION** Varies in size, prominence of orange lunules above and below, and seasonally; females sometimes blue in spring. Our lowland shrub-steppe and W-side forms resemble the small lavender type, though another, larger, montane form may have the brighter lilac of a ssp. described from ID. *I. a. spangelatus* (Spangled Blue), endemic to the high Olympics, has bright scintillae as the name suggests but is duskier gray beneath with reduced orange aurorae. **HOST PLANTS** *I. acmon* uses *Eriogonum*, esp. snow buckwheat (*E. niveum*) in the Columbia Basin (a dozen species recorded or associated in WA by Pelham), as well as *Lotus*, *Lupinus*, *Melilotus*, and other legumes. A population SW of Mt. St. Helens is strongly associated with weedy roadside birdsfoot trefoil (*Lotus corniculatus*), on which it may spread. Along the Strait of Juan de Fuca the Fuca Blue feeds on beach knotweed (*Polygonum paronychia*). In the high Olympics the

Female, dorsal

Male, dorsal

Spangled Blue feeds on cushion buckwheat (*E. ovalifolium*). Nectars on the host plants, western clematis, goldenrod, rabbitbrush, milkweed, aster, marigold, blue mints, alpine cushion plants. **ON THE WING** E April to E October, peaks in May-June, August-September; one brood (two in lower and hotter areas such as E Columbia Gorge). Larvae diapause in second instar. **HABITAT AND RANGE** Open lowland and montane habitats from desert, steppe, and forest glades to roadsides, weedy disturbed areas, gullies and streambanks, alpine and subalpine slopes, and gravel strands. Formerly thought to occupy most of W N Am but now considered a W Coast species, with variable penetration inland. Widespread in OR and WA E of the Cascade Crest, W side in Siskiyous, sparingly in OR Coast Range, W Cascades, Willapa Hills. Two remarkably disjunct populations occur on the Olympic Peninsula: one in the high Olympics, the other a mile below, along the Straits of Juan de Fuca discovered by Ann Potter of WDFW. The former, *I. a. spangelatus*, was originally described as a ssp. of *I. lupini*, but genitalic dissections by Dave Nunnallee show that it belongs to *I. acmon*. The latter segregate, the Fuca Blue, a beach dweller, differs little from Acmon Blues far down the coast in California.

Male, ventral

Male, dorsal, ventral

Casual butterfliers are best advised to settle for discriminating *I. acmon/I. lupini* as a unit from the other orange-bordered blues, which is easy enough to do. Even experienced lepidopterists sometimes have difficulty doing better; it takes lots of practice and seeing many individuals to readily determine them to species. Acmons and Lupines can be sympatric, even in the same puddle-club, and neither elevation nor habitat type always distinguish them. It is possible to identify some by date; any low-elevation sample from late July to September is generally *I. acmon*. Also, any using legumes instead of buckwheats are Acmon, which employs both, whereas Lupines (perversely) feed strictly on buckwheats. Acmon's name, if not the Lupine's, is particularly appropriate: Acmon was one of the gnomes who bedeviled Hercules by stealing his weapons—fitting, for this small cause of large confusion, which has reigned since the two species were discovered.

Lupine Blue *Icaricia lupini* (BOISDUVAL) 1869

Gold Lake, Sierra Co., CA
Aka Buckwheat Blue, Large Silver-studded Blue, *Plebejus, lupinus*

RECOGNITION < 1.25 in. Males bright lilac-blue above, females mouse-brown shot with more or less blue, underside whitish to yellow-gray; **orange aurorae on DHW and VHW, but not on VFW; blue-green metallic scintillae present outside the VHW aurorae**. Can be difficult to tell reliably from Acmon Blue without genitalic dissection. Typically, *I. lupini* males have broader black borders above and black edges to the big, bright, red-orange lunules on the DHW, while *I. acmon* is narrow-bordered if at all, and its dorsal orange aurora is pinkish orange and meets the blue directly. Lupines tend to be larger and deeper, purpler blue, Acmons smaller and powdery-pale blue; all these traits vary. Melissa's Blues have orange on VFW; dotted blues have no scintillae. **VARIATION** Much, in shade of blue, prominence and color of orange lunules, size, hosts, and voltinism, and it is unclear how much of this is genetic vs. environmental. See Warren (2005) for a detailed discussion, incl. the possibility of new species. **HOST PLANTS** Solely buckwheats (*Eriogonum*), with a dozen species recorded or associated in WA by Pelham. Many populations specialize on particular buckwheats; for example, N Coast Range colonies employ *E. compositum*; Blue Mtn Lupines use *E. heracleoides*; a population near Burns feeds strictly on *E. sphaerocephalum*; and those in the Cascade-Siskiyou are found on *E. umbellatum*. Co-evolution is rife in these pairings, maximizing survival. Nectaring takes place mostly on the host plants, plus composites, onions, and other low wildflowers found on buckwheat mounds. **ON THE WING** L May to E August, the higher the later. Commonly a single generation, diapausing in the second instar, but James and Nunnallee suggest it may be univoltine, bivoltine, or even biennial. **HABITAT**

Female, dorsal

Male, dorsal

Male, ventral

AND RANGE Canyons, washes, montane slopes, avalanche chutes, damp roadsides, arid hills, and arctic-alpine fellfields. Dornfeld places *L. lupini* "in dry, brushy openings of the ponderosa forests" in the middle altitudes of the S OR Cascades. Most of the W, Sonora to BC, except NW OR and W WA. Cascades and most other ranges in OR plus SE deserts, and in WA from Okanogan to Klickitat and Skamania cos with peripheral Columbia Basin colonies and a few in the high Cascades, such as Mts. Hood and Adams. Disjunct in OR Coast Range.

The identities of the Lupine and Acmon Blues have gone back and forth, and many records for each are doubtless conflated. *I. acmon* lives among lupines sometimes, but never does *I. lupini*. Boisduval stated that Lorquin found the larvae on lupine in southern California, when it only feeds on buckwheats, and those specimens were actually northern Sierran. Lorquin may be forgiven for getting mixed up over these insects, as we are still doing today. At least the name conveys the butterfly's bright blue color, if not its associations. *I. lupini*'s relations with its real floral associates, the many wild buckwheats, are intricate and adapted under local selection.

Volcano Blue   *Icaricia* "on *Eriogonum pyrolifolium* var. *coryphaeum*"
(UNDESCRIBED)

RECOGNITION Dark blue males, brown females sometimes largely blue, prominent orange aurorae, **heavily spotted below**, esp. on VFW. **Occurs strictly with Shasta buckwheat in the high Cascades. VARIATION** Fairly consistent in size, color, and maculation, within and between sites. **HOST PLANTS** *Eriogonum pyrolifolium* var. *coryphaeum* (Shasta buckwheat). Warren writes, "Males visit mud at the base of melting snowbanks, and both sexes visit the flowers of their [host]." **ON THE WING** E July to E September, depending on snowmelt and other conditions. One brood, larvae overwinter. **HABITAT AND RANGE** "While its universal distribution, on high peaks along the spine of the Cascades is apparently rather restricted, this is often the most abundant butterfly species in subalpine habitats in the high Cascades of Oregon" (Warren). Near the Three Sisters, Warren found it more abundant than any butterfly he has seen, excepting overwintering Monarchs or migrating Painted Ladies. Known from Mt. Thielsen in the S to Mt. Bachelor in OR, and it prob. represents similar blues on Mt. Adams and Mt. St. Helens in WA.

Female, dorsal, ventral

Female, ventral

Male, dorsal

Paul Opler discerned this taxon and plans to describe it as a new species. While it is obviously related to Lupine and Acmon Blues, and occurs together with the latter and a little bit adjacent to the former, several physical traits and its habitat and host plant distinguish it. While several high Cascadean and Sierran butterflies are absent from the younger Oregon volcanic country, others have specialized there, including at least two butterflies on the Mazama ash fields. This seems to be another species that has evolved in close concert with this turbulent landscape; its vernacular name draws from this tight association.

Male, ventral

Northern Blue   *Plebejus idas* (LINNAEUS) 1761

"Ericetis, Svecica"
Aka Idas Blue, Dark-edged Blue, *Lycaeides, argyrognomon*

RECOGNITION < 1.25 in. **Males shiny violaceous blue with broader black border** than *P. anna* and *P. melissa* have. **No orange above.** Female mole-brown, entirely or largely lacking blue, with light to heavy **submarginal rows of orange chevrons around both DFW and DHW**. Light gray ground below (*P. anna* is whiter), with rows of concentric black spots ranging from pronounced to light; and **separate, black-capped orange lunules** around both VHW (esp.) and VFW, enclosing **row of iridescent turquoise scintillae. Mostly in higher elevation, moister habitats**, unlike *P. melissa*, which also has brighter orange borders and scintillae. *Icaricia acmon* and *I. lupini* males have orange on DHW and females have no orange on FW, top or bottom. **VARIATION** The N Rocky Mtn *P. i. atrapraetextus*, taking in the Selkirks of NE WA, SE BC, and N ID, Okanogan Highlands, Blue-Wallowa Mtns in WA and OR, may resemble *P. melissa* with its distinct dark spotting and orange lunules below in both sexes and above

in females, but it tends darker and purpler above and lives in higher, moister habitats. Its counterpart in NE OR Steens Mtn has narrower black borders on the male above. **HOST PLANTS** Heaths (Ericaceae) elsewhere: dwarf bilberry (*Vaccinium cespitosum*), *Empetrum*, and *Kalmia*; however, Pelham considers it very unlikely to use heaths in WA and has recorded *P. i. atrapraetextus* on *Astragalus canadensis* var. *mortonii* (Morton's Canadian milkvetch) and associated it with clover and lupine. James and Nunnallee found it with and reared it on *Lupinus sericeus* and *L. lepidus*. Nectars on yarrow, clover, aster, pearly everlasting, and others. **ON THE WING** E June to L August, peak in July. One generation, eggs overwinter. **HABITAT AND RANGE** Moist, cool montane meadows, trailsides, roadcuts, passes, alpine slopes and tundra, coniferous forest breaks, 3,000 to 8,000+ feet; dry meadows among conifers in OR. Eurasia, AK, Canada, northern states, S in Rockies. In Cascadia:

ID and WA Selkirks, Okanogan Highlands (E of Okanogan R) and Blues; in OR, Blue, Wallowa, Ochoco, Aldrich, and Steens mtns.

North American representatives of this circumboreal butterfly used to be confused with a different Old World species, Reverdin's Blue (*P. argyrognomon*); and with *P. anna*, until that was split off as a Far West species. *P. idas* can converge toward Melissa's Blue, but fortunately for listers, they

Female, dorsal

Male, dorsal, ventral

don't overlap much on the landscape. Twice, as he descended from Moses Meadows north toward Aeneas Valley, Jon Pelham encountered *P. idas* and *P. melissa* together—the Northerns old and worn, the Melissas bright. Norbert Kondla has also found Northern and Melissa's Blues in sympatry, in S BC. But normally, the two species occur several contour intervals apart. The Northern occurs mostly east of the Okanogan and John Day rivers, while Anna's flies almost exclusively west of them, both of them at higher, moister elevations than Melissa's, which frequents the hot, arid lowlands all over the east side. That's why Anna's and Northerns are the hikers' blues, prolific puddlers at streamsides and horse pee along mountain trails. *Idas* comes from the Greek *idanos*, "fair" or "comely," which in this case is an understatement.

Anna's Blue   *Plebejus anna* (W. H. EDWARDS) 1861

Truckee, Nevada Co., CA
Aka Northern Blue, Anna Blue, *Lycaeides*, *idas*, *argyrognomon*

RECOGNITION < 1.25 in. **Males shiny violaceous blue** with narrow black border (sometimes expanding into spots along D/VFW edge). **No orange above**. Female mole-brown, blued variably from base out, with light to heavy **submarginal rows of orange chevrons around both DFW and DHW**. White ground below (*P. idas* is grayer), with rows of concentric black spots ranging from heavy to obsolete; and **separate, black-capped orange lunules** around both VHW (esp.) and VFW, enclosing **row of iridescent turquoise scintillae. Cool, upper-elevation boreal habitats,** unlike *P. melissa*, which also has brighter orange borders and scintillae. *Icaricia acmon* and *I. lupini* males have orange on DHW and females have no orange on FW, top or bottom. **VARIATION** The Cascadian *P. a. ricei*, which occupies all our area, is extremely variable below, any one locality likely to produce individuals both boldly marked or nearly immaculate below. Few, however, have the orange aurorae well developed as happens in CA and in *P. melissa* and *P. idas*. Some in the Siskiyous approach this pattern. Warner Mtns individuals are even more variable. In *P. a.* ricei, the female dorsum has little to no orange, varies from "dead leaf" (Edwards) to clean white below, and most dramatically shows the loss of maculation (light to immaculate) that Nabokov called the "fade out aspect." *P. a. vancouverense*, named from Strathcona Park, Vancouver Is., has more of a basal blue blush on the VHW, large and strongly expressed black spots, blue scintillae, and orange aurorae below, and well-developed, linked orange lunules on the female upperside. I have seen similar expressions in the E Okanogan, near Loup Loup Pass. **HOST PLANTS** Legumes incl. lupines

Female, dorsal

Male, dorsal

Male, ventral

Female, ventral

and lotuses. Associated with *Lathyrus torreyi* (Torrey's pea) and *Vicia ludoviciana* in OR (Warren); and *Lupinus latifolius* ssp. *subalpinus* (subalpine lupine), *L. latifolius*, *Astragalus* (milkvetch, locoweed), *Lotus* (trefoil), and *Trifolium* (clover) in WA (James and Nunnallee). Nectars on wide array of mountain flowers incl. the hosts. **ON THE WING** E June to M October, peak in July. One generation, eggs overwinter. **HABITAT AND RANGE** Moist, cool montane meadows, roadsides and trailsides, forest openings, subalpine ridges and arctic-alpine turf, from around 3,000 feet up to rock and ice. Dry hillsides in the Warners. A near-Cascadian endemic: BC Cascades, Coast Range, Vancouver Is. S through Olympics; Cascades, Siskiyous, Warners, Sierra Nevada S to Sequoia.

See previous species. Anna's flies into fall, nectaring on pearly everlasting along with Hydaspe and Mormon Fritillaries along high mountain roadsides until frost. Vladimir Nabokov specialized in what he knew as *Lycaeides* when he was curator of butterflies at Harvard's Museum of Comparative

Zoology, and published extensively on their forms. In a long 1949 paper analyzing the genus, he wrote of Anna's Blue in a landscape worthy of his fiction: "[T]he first Mt. Rainier specimens [were collected] in the summer of 1910, above Paradise Valley at an elevation of about 7,000 ft. on an isolated stone ridge jutting over a snowfield." And he spoke of the "beautiful and very curious Vancouver Island race," which haunts that island's highlands (sea level populations are now extinct) and the Olympic Mountains. Anna, like Melissa, was another of W. H. Edwards' mysterious female dedicatees.

Melissa's Blue   *Plebejus melissa* (W. H. EDWARDS) 1873

Lower Twin Lake, Lake Co., CO
Aka Melissa Blue (NABA), Orange-bordered Blue, Orange-margined Blue, Orange-banded Blue, Edwards' Blue, *Lycaeides*

RECOGNITION < 1.25 in. Brilliant, watery lilac-blue **male has no orange lunules above**; mole-brown **female has strong orange lunules all along both DFW and DHW**; both sexes light gray below with large submarginal orange aurorae capping bright turquoise scintillae, the **orange spots continuing onto VFW**. Usually **hot lowland habitats**. Northern, Anna's Blues usually have weaker orange bits, fly in higher,

cooler habitats. Acmon, Lupine Blues males have orange on DHW; females lack orange on DFW, and both lack orange on VFW. **VARIATION** The amount of dorsal blue in females varies from none to some, with more in BC and in spring-flying generations farther S. Higher elevation, univoltine populations average smaller. **HOST PLANTS** Lotuses, locoweeds, lupines, licorice, milkvetches, vetches, and many other legumes; Pelham's WA records incl. *Astragalus inflexus, A. lentiginosus, A. canadensis*. Adapted to nonnatives such as *Sphaerophysa salsula* (swainson-pea) and esp. alfalfa (*Medicago sativa*). Wild licorice (*Glycyrrhiza lepidota*) likely

Female, dorsal

Male, dorsal, ventral

in Columbia Basin. Nectars on host legumes (esp. alfalfa), goldstar, daisies, mustards, milkweeds, and yellow star-thistle. **ON THE WING** L April to L September, peaks in May and August. Two or three broods in lowlands, one in higher locales (e.g., Lake Co., OR; Klickitat Co., WA). Eggs overwinter. **HABITAT AND RANGE** Low- to mid-elevation prairie, steppe, agricultural, and disturbed habitats such as roadsides and ditches. Often present in marginal waste ground and unsprayed alfalfa fields. W N Am from Great Plains to Cascades-Sierra. Throughout E Cascadia and E Siskiyous, usually below 3,000 to 4,000 feet, but up to 7,500 feet on Steens Mtn.

Pair, ventral

Lucky for us, the beautiful Melissa's Blue is abundant across the warmer, drier, lower portions of Cascadia, throughout most of the flight season. You may see it under extreme conditions when little else is flying. By adapting to use available materials, the species has become highly successful. For example, Melissas are pleased to nectar on yellow star-thistle and knapweed, and they, along with Orange and Clouded Sulphurs, find alfalfa fields peachy for breeding. There you will see them in courtship, the pairs flying in tight circles or figure 8s just inches above the ground. Late in the day, successfully mated couples stud the meadow, perching back-to-back on flower heads or grass blades, their scintillant scales shining blue-green, in Nabokov's words, "as seapools are left by the sea at low tide." Warren suggests that Friday's Blue (*P. fridayi*), a California species with even greener scintillae but reduced and yellower aurorae, might occur in Lake County, Oregon, and possibly in the Warner Mountains.

Arctic Blue   *Agriades glandon* (DE PRUNNER) 1798

Col du Glandon, Dauphiné Alps, France
Aka High Mountain Blue, Labrador Blue, Primrose Blue, Franklin's Blue, *Plebejus, aquilo, franklinii, rusticus, megalo*

RECOGNITION < 1.2 in. Males cool, light, grainy blue above, bordered with black; females slate-gray to brown with blue and sometimes orange highlights and often ghosty white spots across wings above. Both sexes have prominent **DFW and DHW cell bars** and often submarginal black rings on DHW. Beneath, **VHW spots fused and occluded by heavy white blotches** against dark brown or olive-gray background, esp. in HW cell. Anal angle of VHW may have a hint of orange and blue spotting. **VARIATION** Our *A. g. megalo*, described from Mt. McLean, Lillooet, BC, occupies BC, the Olympics, and the WA

Cascades. It is larger than other ssp., the males steelier blue and the females browner with more white spots above than populations E into the Rockies. The amount of white spotting above is highly variable in the females. *A. g.*

cassiope (Heather Blue), described by Emmel et al. as a full species, has not been found in OR, though the host plant (red heather, *Cassiope mertensiana*) grows in at least Deschutes and Wallowa cos. **HOST PLANTS** N hemisphere

Female, dorsal

Male, dorsal

Male, dorsal, ventral

Male, ventral

reports incl. woody Ericaceae and herbaceous Primulaceae, Diapensiaceae, Saxifragaceae, and Fabaceae. *A. g. megalo* uses *Douglasia laevigata* and *Saxifraga*. Pelham has associated it with *S. tolmiea* and/or *S. bronchialis* (Slate Peak and Olympics). Nectars on many alpine flowers. **ON THE WING** July and August, rarely June and September. Single-brooded, early instar larvae overwinter. **HABITAT AND RANGE** High arctic-alpine and subalpine meadows, ridges, trails, summits, and slopes, seldom below 5,000 and often above 8,000 feet. Arctic and arctic-alpine Europe, Asia, and N Am, AK to Lapland, S in Rockies to S NM, S BC incl. Vancouver Is.; Olympics and WA Cascades S to Skamania Co.

Over the past half-century the name *aquilo* (among others) has been used at the species level for some or all populations of this complex in North America. It is possible that that name should be applied to our fauna, so the current assignment is tentative. *Agriades* blues of any sort seem to be absent from the northern Oregon Cascades as well as the Blues, Wallowas, and Selkirks. Until recently, this species was not known south of Clallam and Yakima counties in Washington. Then Sharon Colman found it on Colonel Bob Lookout in the southwestern Olympics, and I came across it in Skamania County, at the very summits of Sunrise and Jumbo peaks in the Dark Divide. Arctic Blues are nordic creatures, well at home in stark conditions and often flying in foul weather, mothlike on the wing, when all the other alpine butterflies are tucked deep in tussock or cranny. The males project an uncanny coolness in the blue of their wings, and the females can look almost checkered in their gray and white spotting.

Sierra Nevada Blue   *Agriades podarce* (C. & R. FELDER) 1865

Donner Pass, Placer Co., CA
Aka Gray Blue, Arctic Blue, High Mountain Blue, *Plebejus, glandon, aquilo, franklinii*

RECOGNITION < 1.2 in. Males cool, light, grainy blue above, with black border; females brown shot with blue and often ghosty white spots across wings. Both sexes have prominent **DFW and DHW cell bars** and often submarginal black rings on DHW. VFW **tannish with prominent black pupils in the white spots**, except in the cell; VHW spots fused and occluded by **heavy white blotches** against brown or olive-gray ground, **esp. in cell**. VHW tornus may have hint of orange and blue spotting. **VARIATION** *A. p. klamathensis*, named from Water Dog Lakes, N Trinity Mtn., CA, covers populations in the S OR Cascades,

Pair, ventral

Klamath-Siskiyou, and the N Sierra Nevada. It differs from the type by being larger, narrower-margined, and darker below. **HOST PLANTS** Shootingstars (*Dodecatheon alpinum* and *D. jeffreyi*) reported in the Trinities and Sierra Nevada. Nectars on many alpine flowers. Single-brooded, young larvae overwinter. **ON THE WING** L June to E August, rarely September. **HABITAT AND RANGE** For CA, "marshy slopes and meadows that are lushly overgrown with deep grasses and dense stands of false hellebore" (Emmel et al.). In OR, moist meadows above 5,000 feet. *A. podarce* is a Sierra Nevada/ Siskiyou-Klamath endemic, S OR to NW CA and W-C NV. OR from N of Crater Lake S to Mt. Ashland, Douglas, Klamath, and Jackson cos, may be found in SE Josephine.

This species used to be lumped with the Arctic Blue, but it was elevated to the species level by Emmel et al. These striking blues abound near the top of Mt. Ashland, teeming in the harsh sun of the alpine summer. As with many blues, males come to mud given the chance. The type localities of the various subspecies of *Agriades* blues comprise a virtual gazetteer of famous and colorful place names: Pikes Peak, Tioga Pass, Donner Pass, Trinity Alps, Water Dog Lakes.

Male, dorsal

Female, dorsal

FAMILY RIODINIDAE: METALMARKS

The metalmarks are so called because many species possess metallic-looking ornamentation on the upper or lower surfaces of the wings. While some books list them as a subfamily of the gossamer wings, most current authorities consider them to be a discrete family. Almost all the 1,500 or so species of riodinids dwell in the Neotropics, with about 30 genera invading North America, a few genera in tropical Asia and Africa, and a single species each in Europe and Cascadia. Their caterpillars share traits of the gossamer wings (sluggy shape) and brushfoots (clumped hairs). Male forelegs are reduced like those of lycaenids (though in a different way—lost vs. fused segments); but, unlike brushfoots, their females' forelegs are fully developed. They are small butterflies, with short, stocky wings and disproportionately long antennae with slender, flattened clubs. The tropical metalmark fauna includes insects of extraordinary brilliance. While some American species are strikingly blue or painted in primary colors, most come in shades of brown and rust, or orange with black and white spots. The size and colors of some remind one of coppers, others suggest checkers or crescents, but their open-winged, flat or cocked manner of perching is entirely their own. Southwestern types can be confusingly similar, but we have just one unmistakable metalmark. The Mormon reaches Cascadia via the Great Basin, where it picked up its name.

Mormon Metalmark *Apodemia mormo* (C. & R. FELDER) 1859

W of Washoe Lake, Washoe Co., NV

CRITICALLY ENDANGERED IN BC

RECOGNITION < 1.25 in. **Short, broad wings, usually spread at 45 to 75 degrees.** Dark **brown-black above,** crossed by white bands of angular shards, spots, and checks, with **variable rusty highlights** on the disc, costa, and basal FW and HW. VFW russet basally, brown marginally with gray pointers; VHW tan to wood to ash, **mottled with large puffy white spots. Strongly and irregularly white-checkered fringes**; no metallic marks. Males smaller, more narrow-winged, with FW

Female, dorsal

Female, ventral

Male, dorsal

costa slightly convex. Thorax furry, resembling a puppy's head. **VARIATION** Cascadian populations fall under the type, which has an almost entirely dark DHW and much white mottling below. Dornfeld, and Powell (in Howe) recognized *A. m. mormonia* (Boisduval) 1869, type locality "Oregon." But Emmel et al. showed that both names refer to the same batch of specimens, collected by Lorquin and sent to Boisduval in Paris. Some of his duplicates ended up with the Felders in Vienna, who called them "*mormo*" (type locality "vom Salzsee"), while Boisduval named his lot "*mormonia*" ("Habite l'Oregon"). The first type locality was long conflated with Great Salt Lake, UT, and the latter with OR. Yet both refer to an alkaline lake on the eastern Sierra rim, then considered the frontiers of both OR and UT. Emmel et al.,

correcting both type localities, synonymized the names. **HOST PLANTS** Many buckwheats incl. *Eriogonum elatum, E. microthecum, E. sphaerocephalum, E. heracleoides, E. compositum, E. niveum* (esp. in Columbia R. cyns); *E. umbellatum* in W Gorge. Nectars on host buckwheats, western clematis, monardella, pearly everlasting, asters, Canada thistle, rabbitbrush, and goldenrods. **ON THE WING** L July to E October, peak in E September. A single generation, young larvae overwinter. **HABITAT AND RANGE** Canyons, arid flats, banks and roadsides. Sinaloa, Mexico, to the Similkameen River valley in BC, east from CA coast through Great Basin to Black Hills, S Rockies, and desert SW. In Cascadia, BC's Okanagan Valley N to Keremeos; patchily throughout E WA and OR, E of Cascade Crest except in Skamania Co., WA, and SW OR. Strongly aligned with Columbia, Okanogan, Spokane, Pend Oreille, Snake, John Day, and Deschutes rivers.

The metalmarks reach their northernmost New World extent in Cascadia, hence the Mormon is our link to an entire branch of butterfly development. It is among the few species in our fauna that appears wholly in the waning days of the season, spreading its wings as it nectars unalarmed among Juba Skippers on rabbitbrush. On hot, dry September afternoons it haunts basalt canyons along with Acmon Blues arisen from the same buckwheats. Colonies of Mormons are relatively few, small, and scattered. Good places to see them are Klickitat Canyon, Sun Lakes–Dry Falls State Park, and Bear Canyon near Naches in Washington; Sherars Bridge on the Deschutes River in Oregon. The name is appropriate, though based on a misunderstanding. When Austrian father and son Cajetan and Rudolf Felder described the butterfly, they thought it hailed from the "Mormonenlande" of Utah. Even though their specimens had really come from Nevada, the butterfly occurs across the Great Basin all the way to Utah, so their dedicatory moniker was not a misnomer.

FAMILY NYMPHALIDAE: BRUSHFOOTS

Carolus Linnaeus placed all butterflies in the catch-all genus *Papilio* in his 1758 *Systemae Naturae* but organized many of the modern-day brushfoots in a loose group he called "Nymphales." When Kluk split off *Nymphalis* in 1780, he established the type genus that would later give the family its root name. This big family of colorful butterflies is often compared to the passerines among the birds, both for their evolutionary sophistication and for the diversity of species and form. The near-loss of the forelegs, considered an advanced trait, gives the group its familiar name: the front pair of legs is reduced to tiny, brush-like appendages with fused tarsi that are held tightly beneath the thorax like an importuning kitten's paws. While vestigial and useless for support, these "T-rex arms" are not wholly without function; at least some nymphalids

still use their brush-feet to palpate host plants and other substrates.

Approximately 5,000 species of nymphalids occur worldwide, something under 200 in North America, and 60+ in Cascadia. Several groups formerly thought to constitute separate families, such as the longwings, satyrs, and milkweed butterflies, are better considered subfamilies of the Nymphalidae. Many of our biggest and brightest butterflies are nymphalids, though crescents are no bigger than blues. Oranges, reds, browns, and blacks are common among the brushfoots, whose protective devices include quicksilver spots and disruptive stripes as well as crypsis (camouflage), eyespots, tails, aposematism (distasteful coloration), and mimicry. We have representatives of all the North American subfamilies except the snouts (Libytheinae).

Subfamily Danaiinae: Milkweed Butterflies

Monarchs and milkweed go together like animals and oxygen—they can't do without it—and that goes for all the Monarch's relatives in this brushfoot subfamily. Tropical butterflies all, none are hardy beyond generally frost-free zones. This fact has led to the remarkable migration of the best-known danaiine, but most of the other 300 or so members simply remain resident in hot climes. Most of these live in tropical Australasia, with just four species in North America. Cascadia is marginal territory for the group, encompassing the northwesternmost edge of its New World existence. But since two species of milkweed host plants are widespread here (more in the Siskiyous), we do have Monarchs

All milkweed butterflies lack scales on their antennae. Most are fairly large, with orange and black markings, or else black with blue and green iridescence. By feeding on members of the plant family Asclepiadaceae, milkweed butterflies acquire distasteful chemicals that confer protection from predators, especially birds; and many species are involved in mimicry complexes. They also visit plants containing chemicals that serve as precursors for making the pheromones necessary for sexual identification and attraction. Males store the pheromones in velvety pads of androconial scales on the hindwings called alar pouches; they also possess eversible brushes in the abdomen, so-called hair pencils, which they wipe on the sex brands, then open, to waft their perfume near the antennae of the females, rendering them receptive.

Monarch   *Danaus plexippus* (LINNAEUS) 1758

"America septentrionali"
Aka Milkweed Butterfly, Wanderer

THREATENED PHENOMENON, WWF/IUCN; PETITIONED FOR FEDERALLY THREATENED, SPECIAL CONCERN IN BC, SGCN IN WA

RECOGNITION > 3 in. **Very large**, FW long and drawn-out. Deep, rich **orange above with black veins and margin**. Border has two rows of white dots, large orange ovals in tip of FW. Apical spots pale below, otherwise vFw bright orange; vHw pale orange to grayish umber, black veins heavier below. Black head, thorax, polka-dotted with white. Male has sex patch on DHW, female darker colored with broader black vein-scaling; males average larger. **VARIATION** Remarkably consistent; most variation is either between sexes or seasonal, from fall (fresh) to spring (worn). **HOST PLANTS** Showy milkweed (*Asclepias speciosa*) and narrow-leaved milkweed (*A. fascicularis*) are sole hosts in most of Cascadia; *A. cordifolia* may be used in Siskiyous, *A. cryptoceras* in SE OR. Nectars on milkweeds, buddleia, red clover, purple vetch, blue salvia, yellow yarrow, rabbitbrush, goldenrods, common sunflower, asters, coreopsis, Canada and other thistles, knapweeds, purple loosestrife, many other natives, exotics, and ornamentals. **ON THE WING** E June to L October, peaks in E July and L August. Three+ generations, migratory for winter. **HABITAT AND RANGE** All sorts of habitats during migration. Breeding and trav-

Female, dorsal

Male, ventral

Male, dorsal

eling largely along rivers, roadsides, and other corridors with milkweeds and nectar, adults frequent meadows, weedy fields, streambanks, gardens. Migrants bivouac in dense clumps of trees, commonly roosting overnight in willow, Russian olive, and black locust. Winter habitat *Eucalyptus* and conifer groves in CA, *Abies religiosa* forest in Trans-Mexican volcanic belt.

N and S America, naturalized elsewhere. Summer range incl. virtually all N Am to limits of milkweed (S Canada) and beyond. Can turn up anywhere in Cascadia. In OR, breeds esp. in Siskiyous, S Willamette Valley, Klamath, Summer, and Malheur lakes and basins, John Day and Snake rivers; in WA, Columbia Basin esp. on Columbia (W to Skamania Co.), Okanogan, Snake, and Yakima rivers, and Lower Grand Coulee; in BC, S interior N to Kamloops and Similkameen R. Rarely, Vancouver Is., Seattle, Portland, on garden or railroad-introduced milkweeds. Wedding releases cause spurious locality records.

North America's most recognized and certainly most famous and best-beloved butterfly reaches Cascadia as an uncommon, breeding summer visitor. Some years there are many more than others, depending upon how things have gone in the wintering grounds, and what kind of weather the spring migrants have encountered. Tagging/recovery records show that most of our Monarchs migrate to the California coast for winter, but my field data suggest that some interior Monarchs may fly to and from Mexico; see Brower and Pyle (2004) and Pyle (2015a) for details. Monarch larvae store cardenolides in their tissues, which toxins give the adults protection from educated birds. Their Müllerian mimics, Viceroys, occur with Monarchs along the waterways of the Columbia Basin. Monarchs face many threats, including dams, cars, chemicals, and Roundup Ready GM soy and corn in the North, development in California, and logging and industrialization in Mexico. We can encourage Monarchs in Cascadia by protecting native milkweed stands and nectar sources from herbicides, agriculture, land clearing, and other jeopardy. More tagging in the future will help us to understand and conserve them (visit David James' research and public projects at facebook.com/MonarchButterfliesInThePacificNorthwest). The fad of releasing Monarchs at weddings and other events, far from their points of origin, is extremely unhelpful to our efforts to illumine their natural whereabouts and movements. Happily this activity is unpermitted in both Oregon and Washington at this writing. The best places to enjoy wild Monarchs in Cascadia include the southern Oregon "lakes district," the mouth of Crab Creek and wildlife refuges in the eastern Columbia Gorge, and the Hanford Reach of the Columbia above Tri-Cities.

Queen   *Danaus gilippus* (CRAMER) 1775

"Rio de Janeyro, Brazil"
Aka *berenice*

RECOGNITION < 3.5 in. Large. **Deep fox-brown** above and below with black margins. Veins lined with black, more thickly below. Two rows of small white dots speckle black borders, larger ones spatter the apical quarter of the FW. Black bar at end of FW cell, black androconial patch on male DHW. Lacks the black veins of the larger Monarch, and is browner. **VARIATION** W US individuals belong to *D. g. thersippus* rather than the eastern *D. g. berenice*, which is characterized by lighter reddish brown wings, gray-scaled along the DHW veins. **HOST PLANTS** Milkweeds (*Asclepias*). Nectars on beggarticks, mistflower, milkweeds, many others. Male Queens must visit heliotrope, dodder, or other plants possessing pyrrolizidine alkaloids in order to make their pheromone, danaidone. **ON THE WING** Just one record in OR (25 August 1999) and three in WA (18 August 2000; 27 July and 26 August 2002). Successive generations in the S. Possesses no winter diapause in the N but may have a generation or two there in sum-

Female, dorsal

Female, ventral

mer before heading S or dying out with frost. **HABITAT AND RANGE** Open territory with milkweed and abundant nectar sources. Neotropical, expanding N in summer as far as S Canada.

Dana Ross found the first Queen ever recognized in Cascadia, at Smith Flat on Steens Mountain, in Harney County, Oregon, at

6,800 feet. He wrote, "The individual was flying 15–20 feet above the ground in a southwesterly direction, taking the same path as a Monarch seen earlier that day. I was about to record it as a relatively rare Monarch sighting when it came to within 25 feet of me and I noticed the rich brown coloration and slightly smaller size. I chased it for nearly a quarter-mile in an attempt to net it, but it stayed just ahead of me (and I ran out of 'gas'). It seemed to be 'migrating' with the southward-flying Monarchs, having followed the west slope of Steens Mountain south, or come down the east side and crossed the escarpment at the lower end of Wildhorse Canyon." In 2002 two Queens turned up in Richland, Washington, a month apart, found by Dennis Strenge and Charles Rogers. These may have been releases from imported rearing stock, or arrivals under their own steam. (One other, found in Tacoma by R. McNair-Huff in 2000, was almost certainly a release.) Watchers should be attentive for more Queens when scanning for or tagging Monarchs in the fall. They may wander north increasingly with climate change.

Subfamily Heliconiinae: Longwings and Fritillaries

Prolific in the Neotropics, longwings are closely coevolved with passionflowers. Most species display bright bands of color on long, narrow black wings, and many belong to mimicry rings in which multiple species of various groups of insects resemble a common pattern or model, to the confusion of birds put off by the distastefulness of at least some of the members. Larry Gilbert's group at the University of Texas found that longwings feed on pollen as well as nectar, the only butterflies known to do so, developing traplines to productive pollen sources with accumulating foraging experience.

The related fritillaries are mostly tawny orange above and decorated with silver orbs below. In general they bear little resemblance to longwings, except for the Gulf Fritillary, a longwing with a striking similarity to true fritillaries. The two groups were traditionally placed in different families, or at least subfamilies. But DNA studies have confirmed the close relationship between longwings and fritillaries, a fact hinted at by the Gulf Fritillary's appearance and the biology of the Variegated Fritillary, both species serving to bridge the two seemingly disparate tribes.

Zerene Fritillary (ssp. *picta*), female

Tribe Heliconiini: Longwings

Zebra *Heliconius charithonius* (LINNAEUS) 1767

St. Thomas, USVI
Aka Zebra Longwing, Zebra Heliconian (NABA), *charithonia*

RECOGNITION < 3.5 in. Unmistakable. Wings long, narrow, and rounded, both surfaces **black with yellow to chartreuse bands**. Red patch at base of VHW. Flight weak, wafty, and ghosty in the dusk. **VARIATION** Individuals arriving in Cascadia unassisted by humans likely belong to the Mexican/Texan *H. c. vazquezae* (Leonila's Longwing), which has a wider yellow band on the HW than the Floridian *H. c. tuckeri*. **HOST PLANTS** Passionflower (*Passiflora*). Nectars on many flowers. **ON THE WING** Flies year-round in the American tropics. Can appear anytime farther N, esp. after tropical storms in the S. **HABITAT AND RANGE** Tropical forest margins and hammocks; anywhere as a stray. American tropics, breeding along Gulfs of Mexico and California and in FL, straying N, sometimes perhaps even to Cascadian latitudes.

If you really want to see these elegant butterflies, visit a wild hammock in the Everglades, where they flutter in slow motion and roost communally at dusk near the host plants; or any butterfly house, such as the one at Seattle's Pacific Science Center, where they are easily reared favorites. Sightings near the University of Washington Arboretum in the 1970s were no doubt laboratory escapes, but there is one bona fide Cascadia record: L. I. Hewes (1936) wrote, "In Washington one winter, from a careful collector I learned of . . . a Gulf of Mexico species once found on

Dorsal

the Columbia River." J. F. G. Clark, pioneer Washington collector and Smithsonian curator, showed me the specimen in the National Museum of Natural History, and it was a Zebra. It might have arrived on winds following a hurricane, or come from a hobo larva that pupated on a boxcar and rode the rails north. Unlike the other vagrant heliconian, the Gulf Fritillary, the Zebra is far from a strong flier, but it rides the wind well. Repeat sightings, if highly unlikely, are possible.

Gulf Fritillary   *Agraulis vanillae* (LINNAEUS) 1758
S America, prob. Surinam

RECOGNITION < 3.5 in. Wings relatively long, tips drawn out and rounded. **Brilliant fiery orange above** with fritillary-like black bars and dots (white-pupilled basally) and veins. Female has heavy black chainlike border on DHW. Large, long, **bright silver ovals dominate VHW** and apical VFW. **VARIATION** Very little overall, except the shade of orange can be

Dorsal

duller, and the black and silver spots vary somewhat in size and shape. **HOST PLANTS** Passionflower (*Passiflora*). Nectars on host, zinnia, lantana, and many others. **ON THE WING** Flies most of the year in the tropics, E spring to L fall elsewhere, in multiple broods. Cannot overwinter in the N; adults overwinter in frost-free portions of their range. **HABITAT AND RANGE** Throughout S US and S through Mexico, C America, and W Indies to S America. Breeds along Gulfs of Mexico and California and in S-C CA, straying to N CA. Range shifting N.

Butterfliers in southern Oregon should be on the lookout for the Gulf Fritillary, shocking orange with large silver orbs beneath.

First-time viewers often question their senses when confronting a bright, fresh Gulf Fritillary. I recently had the same sensation in a weedy corner of Havana: can a butterfly really be this brilliant? A breeder on passionflowers around the San Francisco Bay area, it has been found as far north as Redding, Shasta County, California, and is bound to cross the southern frontiers of Oregon and be spotted there before long, especially as some *Passiflora* species and cultivars are semi-hardy in that state. Warming may even lead to eventual colonization in Oregon. Easy to encourage in butterfly gardens, but not necessarily easy to keep on passionflower vines, which the ravenous larvae tend to defoliate.

Ventral

Tribe Argynnini: Fritillaries

Variegated Fritillary   *Euptoieta claudia* (CRAMER) 1775

"Jamaïque"
Aka Claudia

RECOGNITION < 2.5 in. Tawny to brownish orange above, checked with black spots, bars, and zigzags; mottled cream-and-cocoa below with **white patches and cobweb network**, bright orange base of VFW. Round submarginal spots black above, smaller and bluish on VHW. **Wings angular,** FW tips truncate, not smoothly rounded like other fritillaries. Duller than Gulf Fritillary. **VARIATION** Most is of size, underside pattern, and intensity of color, all of which vary widely. **HOST PLANTS** A wide variety, incl. stonecrop, flax, plantain, and both *Viola* and *Passiflora*—the respective foodplants for fritillaries and the related longwings.

ON THE WING E June to L September, peak in July-August, in BC. Sole OR (Deschutes Co.) and WA (Okanogan Co.) captures both 19 July. Multi-brooded in the S and in the N summer; no winter diapause in any stage.

HABITAT AND RANGE Virtually any habitat from disturbed or waste ground in lowlands to pristine montane meadows, S Canada to Colombia, S America. Resident range S of hard-frost line; summer vagrancy reaches most of the US *except* most of the PNW.

Male, dorsal

Male, ventral

As much as any butterfly, the Variegated Fritillary may be found anywhere and expected nowhere. It is one of many species that migrate out of the South in spring and fill in the northern states for a few months, until they die off with the autumn chill. In good years, it fills up the mid-continent and flows on up into the Canadian Rockies, but seldom ventures northwesterly. There are several records for southwestern British Columbia and the Idaho panhandle, three in Oregon, and one in Washington, plus two reliable sightings. Keep an eye out for an unsilvered frit with long wings and a color and pattern that is a little different from the usual. A year that produces many Painted Ladies and other migrants is likely to bring others as well, and instances of migration are increasing with climate change. Variegated Fritillaries can be extremely abundant under the right conditions, and more are sure to show up around Cascadia. You might even find the fancy caterpillar on a garden pansy.

Genus *Boloria*: Lesser Fritillaries

The small- to medium-sized lesser fritillaries bear typical fritillarian spot-and-bar patterns of black-on-orange above but have very different undersides from the greater fritillaries (*Speyeria*), featuring violets, rusts, and yellow or opalescent crescents. Just one is silver-spotted in our area. Like their larger relatives, most species feed on violets as larvae, though some northern species make a break with this habit in favor of heaths, saxifrages, bistort, or willow. While one of our species reaches sea level, most bolorians occupy high-country habitats and the Far North: of six species of butterflies known to inhabit Greenland, two belong to the genus *Boloria*. Aside from their obvious smaller size, lesser fritillaries have narrower wings and more delicate patterns than the greater fritillaries, and their citrus to tawny orange ground colors separate them in flight from the redder checkers. As with the greater fritillaries, many bolorians are named for goddesses of various mythic traditions; they are also known as bog fritillaries because of their penchant for peaty wetlands.

Key to the Lesser Fritillaries (*Boloria* spp.)

VHW markings & submedian band color	Habitat	Species	
Marginal row of silver spots. Scattered small silver spots on disc.	Bogs and marshes, usually mid-elevations.	Silver-bordered Fritillary *Boloria selene*	
Marginal row of small white spots. Sharp white tooth in center of disc. Thin, but usually distinct, median band of white crescents.	Willow bogs at mid- to high elevations.	Freija Fritillary *Boloria freija*	
Marginal row of smudged, small white or buff spots. Brown to tawny submedian band with buff or white blunt arrowheads. Median band of white crescents is indistinct or missing.	Bogs and moist meadows, usually at 3,000 to 8,000 feet.	Arctic Fritillary *Boloria chariclea*	
Outer half of wing is medium orange-purple. Submedian band is dirty gold or beige, distinctly lighter than surrounding disc color.	Most semi-moist areas, primarily in clearings and along roadsides in forested areas.	Western Meadow Fritillary *Boloria epithore*	
Outer half of wing is frosty brown-purple. Submedian band is nearly indistinguishable from surrounding disc color.	Moist meadows around 2,000 to 5,000 feet.	Meadow Fritillary *Boloria bellona*	
Marginal band is checkered white, tawny orange, and dark brown. Submedian band of large, irregular white blocks.	Arctic-alpine rockslopes and ridges, usually above 7,000 feet.	Astarte Fritillary *Boloria astarte*	

Silver-bordered Fritillary *Boloria selene* (DENIS & SCHIFFERMÜLLER) 1775

Vienna, Austria
Aka Silver-bordered Bog Fritillary, Small Pearl-bordered Fritillary (UK), *Clossiana, myrina*

B. S. ATROCOSTALIS CANDIDATE
IN WA, IMPERILED IN OR

RECOGNITION < 2 in. Bright orange above with fine pattern of spots outward and bars and squiggles inward; **strong marginal black chains**, submarginal spots sometimes white in female. Below, orange VFW, chestnut VHW with **four rows of metallic silver spots** radiating out from base to margin, pale beige patches and black dots in between; **central silver spot elongated**. **VARIATION** Across the transboreal N, the species has heavier black margins above, and in the S Rockies

a yellower aspect below. Warren found WA specimens (Yakima Co.) to be smaller and paler than those from Crook and Grant cos, OR, with those from Baker Co. being intermediate. **HOST PLANTS** Violets, mostly marsh violet (*Viola palustris*) and bog violet (*V. nephrophylla*) in our region. Nectars on various composites, mints, and swamp verbena (*Verbena hastata*); I observed predation by ambush bugs (*Phymata*) on rabbitbrush. **ON THE WING** M April to E September, peaks in May, June-July, August. Two or three distinct generations at Moxee Bog, Yakima Co., WA (1,200 feet); one brood above 4,000 feet in Crook and Grant cos, OR. Second- to fourth-instar larvae overwinter. **HABITAT AND RANGE** Bogs, marshes, and willowy riparian sites, sometimes tall wet grass. Holarctic: much of the upper latitude N hemisphere, S in Appalachians, MW, Rockies,

Female, dorsal

Ventral

and Cascades. Not uncommon in SE BC; perhaps 20 WA wetlands in the Pend Oreille, Okanogan, Columbia, and Yakima drainages; a few OR colonies in the high Ochocos, Strawberries, S Wallowas, and a few more in the ID panhandle. Many of these are small and under stress of drying or succession.

Selene is the moon, who made love to the shepherd Endymion in his sleep. *B. selene* is our only silver-bearing lesser fritillary, creating a conceptual if not evolutionary link between *Boloria* and *Speyeria*. This circumpolar butterfly's distribution in Cascadia is very spotty, probably reflecting a much broader and more uniform range in the late Pleistocene. The remaining colonies

cling to marshy borders of old lakes or ancient sphagnum bogs. A celebrated colony occurred at Moxee Bog, a Nature Conservancy preserve southeast of Yakima, likely the first butterfly preserve in the country thanks to the efforts of Dave McCorkle. In 1970, I found hundreds here, many engaged in pre-sundown mating in wetter portions of the bog. Courting consisted of a gentle, slow fluttering of the wings as the partners crawled around the grassblades to which they clung, orbiting one another. But management changes and plant succession have crowded out violets and fritillaries, numbers declined, and recent surveys by David James have found it absent.

Meadow Fritillary   *Boloria bellona* (FABRICIUS) 1775

"America boreali"
Aka *Clossiana, toddi*

**B. B. TODDI
CRITICALLY
IMPERILED IN
OR, SGCN IN WA**

RECOGNITION < 1.75 in. **FW tips truncate, as if clipped**; dark to pale orange, heavily black-spotted above, but not the margin; VFW orange, purplish-tipped, inner half of VHW orange/rust with purple overtones and **whitish costal patch at base, like a plow with a rusty hole**; violet-gray outer with row of bluish spots. **Submarginal brown triangles on DHW tend to point inward**, unlike in *B. epithore*. **VARIATION** *B. b. toddi*, named from QC, has been used for our populations but might not strictly apply. It is darkened basally above compared to other ssp., and our populations show this darkening to some degree. **HOST PLANTS** Canadian white violet (*Viola canadensis*) in BC and WA; uncertain in OR. Nectars on many meadow

flowers incl. fleabanes, asters, oxeye daisy. **ON THE WING** E May to L August, peaks in June and August. Generally two generations, third- or fourth-instar larvae overwinter. **HABITAT AND RANGE** Meadows, clearings in aspen and pinewoods, moist streamsides with willow, 2,000 to 5,000 feet, and in lower riparian sites at the steppe interface. Canada, NE/N-C US, disjunct in Rockies and Cascadia. Okanogan Highlands, Kettle River Range, Selkirks, and Blue Mtns of WA; NE ID, and one colony in Umatilla Co., OR (nr Lehman Springs).

The Meadow Fritillary is a common element of eastern habitats, having adapted to hayfields and other human settings. It is also the most temperate member of this Nearctic group, reaching North Carolina. In the West, however, it occurs very patchily in less disturbed forest habitats at fairly high elevations. Okanogan and Ferry county sites are often rather disturbed and cowpie-strewn. Recent records in

Male, dorsal

Male, ventral

Washington are all from between the northern Okanogan and Columbia rivers, except for a colony on the Loup Loup Road. Old records from Spokane and Whitman counties in the Palouse Hills and Blue Mountains in Washington have not been repeated in many decades, and it hasn't been seen in the single Oregon locality since 1984. It may be a bellwether for butterflies of moist habitats retreating northward with warming. Bellona was the Roman goddess of war, who walked in company with Discord, Strife, Terror, Trembling, and Panic—as if Fabricius forged a sword from the plowshare wing-mark of this gentle creature of peaceful meadow scenes.

Western Meadow Fritillary   *Boloria epithore* (W. H. EDWARDS) 1864

Saratoga, Santa Clara Co., CA
Aka Pacific Fritillary (NABA), *Clossiana*

RECOGNITION < 1.75 in. Bright citrus-orange, sharply ink-spotted above with **lots of open orange and no black border**; FW has rounded tips unlikev "clip-winged" *B. bellona*. **VHW mottled lavender and russet** with submedian band of dirty, orangey yellow spots ending in a pale yellow anvil-shaped mark on costa; broken row of rusty brown or **violet postmedian dots cross purple-frosted disc. Submarginal**

Male, dorsal

Female, dorsal

Male, ventral

dark triangles on DHW tend to point outward (point inward on *B. bellona*). *B. chariclea* and *B. selene* are busier above with heavy black border-chains, and also differ in having white or silver marks below, respectively. **VARIATION** Those of W WA and W OR are more heavily marked and scaled with black on the basal half of the upperside, paler outer, than those of NE OR, which are deeper orange and have reduced scaling and narrower black bars. **HOST PLANTS** Violets; associated with *Viola glabella* and *V. sempervirens* in SW WA (Pyle); *V. adunca* (Pelham), *V. ocellata* (X. McGlashan) in CA; and prob. *V. nephrophylla* (Scott). Nectars on strawberry, dewberry, blackberry, cinquefoil, various yellow composites, pearly everlasting, and others. **ON THE WING** L March to L September, peak June–August. Single flight in spring, later in higher elevations. Diapause occurs in third or fourth instar. **HABITAT AND RANGE** Clearings, dappled woods, streamsides, meadows, open slopes, logging roads, unsprayed Christmas tree farms, rural gardens, lush and open habitats in mtns and lowlands, sea level to

8,000 feet. Greater NW, from SW Yukon to S-C CA, E to mid-MT, S BC, ID, all W WA and OR, and E-side mtn ranges S to the Blues and Warners. The sole bolorian to reach CA.

Western Cascadians' rain-jaded eyes blink at this brilliant butterfly, surely one of the brightest objects in the Maritime Northwest woods. They are even more surprised by the lovely underside patterns of purple and russet. Fortunately, the Western Meadow Fritillary is common and well adapted to the managed forest, at least where slash burns and herbicides have not sterilized the forest floor and killed off the violets they require. One intersection of five logging roads in the Willapa Hills, with abundant edge habitat and sunshine, I call Boloria Junction for this species. *B. epithore* is our most regionally restricted boloria, and at the same time the most widespread of our lesser fritillaries. Named for its resemblance to Thor's Fritillary of the Austrian Tyrol, *B. epithore* flies from arctic-alpine climes to the shores of Puget Sound and the open Pacific.

Astarte Fritillary   *Boloria astarte* (DOUBLEDAY) 1847

Rock Lake, nr Jasper, AB
Aka Arctic Ridge Fritillary, Boeber's Fritillary, *Clossiana*, *tritonia*

RECOGNITION > 2 in. **Large and robust for the genus, wings broad and slightly squared off. Paler orange above** than other bolorians, except the smaller *B. freija*, with heavy, sometimes smudged black markings, esp. the black border. VHW marked with **alternating black-edged bands of light orange and white or cream**, submarginal and postmedian bands of opposing white crescents enclosing a row of black dots, with an apricot band in between. Nothing like it. **VARIATION** The type flies here. Its FW are more squared, and the middle VHW row is pearlier white than in more arctic specimens. **HOST PLANTS** Spotted saxifrage (*Saxifraga bronchialis*). Nectars on mountain avens and other alpine flowers in wind-sheltered spots. **ON THE WING** M June to M August, peak in July, *only in even years*. Biennial: larvae overwinter twice, in first and fourth instars. In AB the butterfly flies every year, but in BC Coast Range and WA the brood

Female, ventral

Male, dorsal

is synchronized such that adults appear only in even years. **HABITAT AND RANGE** Arctic-alpine and high arctic rockslides, ridges, and tundra, often on S slopes, sea level and up in AK, usually above 7,000 feet in WA. S from Arctic Sea in AK to disjunct locales in N Rockies (MT) and N Cascades. S-C BC, high Okanogan, Whatcom, and Chelan cos, WA.

This largest of the lesser fritillaries dips into Cascadia in a few high redoubts in Washington's North Cascades. Andy Anderson and John Hopfinger, pioneer collectors and orchardists, first found it at Cooney Lake in the Sawtooth Range east of Lake Chelan in 1936. Most subsequent records have come from the vicinity of Slate Peak near Hart's Pass (where the similarly rare Lustrous Copper and Melissa's Arctic may also be sought), and the Pasayten and Glacier Peak wilderness areas. Backpacking butterfliers will have the best chance of finding new colonies of this exciting Far North insect. The Phoenician goddess Astarte's special sign was the new moon, suggesting the bright lunar crescent of white spots on the hindwings below.

Freija Fritillary *Boloria freija* (THUNBERG) 1791

W Gulf of Bothnia and Lapland, Sweden
Aka Freya's Fritillary, Zigzag Fritillary, *Clossiana*

RECOGNITION < 1.5 in. Orange dorsum, paler than others except larger *B. astarte*, dusky scaling basally; heavy black pattern, incl. **black border-chains**, checkered fringe, and black submarginal rounded spots. The complex underside is purplish chocolate traversed by rows of white crescents marginally and submarginally and a prominent **dark zigzag band** between the darker inner and lighter outer halves; **three prominent white marks on VHW**: anvil on leading edge, **sharp curved fang pointing out in the middle**, and arrowhead pointing to the base. Arctic Fritillary's fang is yellow and blunt, indistinct from the adjacent, similarly colored

Dorsal

band. **VARIATION** Our ssp. seems not to differ from those in the land of the Sami, whence it was described. Arctic populations have more basal dusting than ours, Rocky Mtn ones less. **HOST PLANTS** Rosaceae and Ericaceae: blueberry, alpine bearberry (*Arctostaphylos alpina*), kinnikinnick (*A. uva-ursi*), crowberry (*Empetrum*), *Rhododendron aureum, R. lapponicum* (Lapland rosebay), *Vaccinium cespitosum.* Nectars on bog rosemary, buttercup, aster, and yarrow; visits mud. **ON THE WING** L April to L August, peak in July. One brood, fourth-instar larvae overwintered for James and Nunnallee. **HABITAT AND RANGE** Willow bogs at high elevations, arctic-alpine slopes and tundra, upper forest meadows and roadsides. Circumpolar, Canadian N, S into Great Lakes, N Rockies, and S-C BC/N-C WA. More numerous in BC, the only WA records from N Okanogan Co.

First discovered in Washington in 1964, Freija has since been found in only a handful of sites. This apparent rarity may be real, or it may reflect "collector bias" due to *B. freija*'s unusually early flight period in the

Ventral

high-mountain spring: males sometimes emerge while snowbanks still stand nearby. Yet Caitlin LaBar found a fresh male at Long Swamp, Okanogan County, on 3 July 2014. The variable time of snowmelt from year to year and the subsequent swarming mosquitoes don't help in locating this elusive butterfly, which abounds in Alaska but which few have seen in Cascadia. Freija was the Norse goddess of love and beauty.

Arctic Fritillary   *Boloria chariclea* (SCHNEIDER) 1794

"Lappland"

Aka Titan's Fritillary (*wwb*), Titania Fritillary, Queen Titania's Fritillary, Helena Fritillary, Purple Bog Fritillary, Tacoma Fritillary, *Clossiana, titania, helena, montinus, butleri, boisduvalii, grandis*

RECOGNITION < 2 in. Tawny to deep orange above with **heavy but sharp black markings, incl. border-chain**. Females may have extensive white among the black margins. VHW purplish to reddish brown, **angular submedian band brown to tawny crossed with blunt, buff arrowheads**, white crescents along margin capped with brown chevrons pointed inward. Central arrowhead is indistinct from submedian band compared to sharp white discal tooth of *B. freija*. *B. epithore* lacks black border above, VHW chevrons point outward. *B. astarte* is larger and lighter, *B. selene* is silvered below. Mormon Fritillary may have white spots on dorsum like female, but ventrum very different, wings broader. **VARIATION** Ours belong to *B. c. rainieri* (Mount Rainier Fritillary), described from Mt. Rainier. It and *B. c. helena*, the Rocky Mtn race, are the

Male, dorsal

brightest and reddest of the ssp. Some would lump them, but they are separated by a distinctively paler Yellowstone race and by a large gap with no populations at all. Those to the N in BC (*B. c. grandis*, described from ON) become larger, darker, and purpler below, sometimes partially silvery on the median band beneath. **HOST PLANTS** An unusually wide variety, incl. willows, huckleberries, mountain avens, and violets. Pelham reared it on American bistort (*Polygonum bistortoides*) in the Olympics, and I've watched it there, near the bistort, ovipositing on partridgefoot (*Luetkea pectinata*). James and Nunnallee saw eggs on *Vaccinium deliciosum* and reared it on *V. parvifolium*, *V. scoparium*, and violets. Nectars frequently on yellow and mauve composites. **ON THE WING** M June to L September, peak in July-August. Biennial in N areas, prob. annual here. **HABITAT AND RANGE** Scandinavia to Siberia, all the N Am Arctic and Canada; S in Rockies to NM, and in Olympics and Cascades of WA, 3,000 to 8,000 feet. Unknown in E WA ranges, W ID, or OR.

As with the previous species, the type locality is Lapland. What to call this butterfly is a riddle. Several *Boloria* species are Holarctic, or occur on both halves of the northern hemisphere. The Arctic Fritillary lives from Scandinavia all across Siberia, Kamchatka, Canada, and the narrow fringe of greenery rimming Greenland's ice sheet. Various names have been and continue to be applied to the North American representatives. Depending on where you look, you may find it by all the scientific names listed in the Aka section, some interpreted as circumpolar and some as strictly North American. Some workers believe two species are involved, one of the taiga and the other of the arctic and arctic-alpine. *B. chariclea*, as the oldest and most inclusive name for the whole array, is the best conservative taxon to take them all in until some future taxonomic Nirvana arrives. But by any other name, all ours in Cascadia are *Boloria* (something) *rainieri*: Mount Rainier Fritillaries.

Male, dorsal

Male, ventral

Genus *Speyeria*: Greater Fritillaries

These Nearctic butterflies proliferate in nearly all montane and many moist lowland habitats from early to late summer. Fleet of wing, they are hard to catch or photograph except at flowers, especially thistles and mints. All species of *Speyeria* (aka *Argynnis*) feed strictly on violets as larvae: if there are violets around, there are probably fritillaries, and if there are fritillaries, you can be sure that violets lurk not far away, even if not in evidence. The greater fritillaries, medium to quite large in size, are some shade of orange above with variably sized black spots, bars, and chains. The quicksilver orbs below, almost unbelievably metallic in appearance, give the group its alternative name, the silverspots. The ground color of the ventral hindwing disc is often diagnostic. *Speyeria* species vary tremendously both geographically and within populations, rendering their certain identification more than challenging, and sometimes all but impossible. Watchers should feel no shame to put down any greater fritillary encounter as "*Speyeria* sp." This problem is not as acute in the Northwest as it is farther south and east, but it is sufficient for many names to have been proposed to compass our fauna. Some 70 species were once thought to exist in North America, now refined to about 15, with many supposed subspecies. Common and scientific names often refer to goddesses from various traditions (two of them dedicated to Venus), owing more to the classical educations and fecund imaginations of early lepidopterists than to any traits of their own, other than their indisputable beauty.

Coronis Fritillary, male

Comparison of Greater Fritillaries (*Speyeria* spp.)
Specimens are shown approximately at 50% of life size

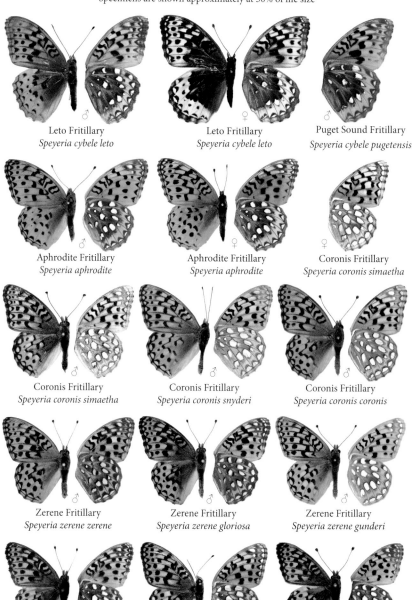

Leto Fritillary
Speyeria cybele leto

Leto Fritillary
Speyeria cybele leto

Puget Sound Fritillary
Speyeria cybele pugetensis

Aphrodite Fritillary
Speyeria aphrodite

Aphrodite Fritillary
Speyeria aphrodite

Coronis Fritillary
Speyeria coronis simaetha

Coronis Fritillary
Speyeria coronis simaetha

Coronis Fritillary
Speyeria coronis snyderi

Coronis Fritillary
Speyeria coronis coronis

Zerene Fritillary
Speyeria zerene zerene

Zerene Fritillary
Speyeria zerene gloriosa

Zerene Fritillary
Speyeria zerene gunderi

Valley Silverspot
Speyeria zerene bremnerii

Painted Fritillary
Speyeria zerene picta

Oregon Silverspot
Speyeria zerene hippolyta

Comparison of Greater Fritillaries (*Speyeria* spp.)

Specimens are shown approximately at 50% of life size

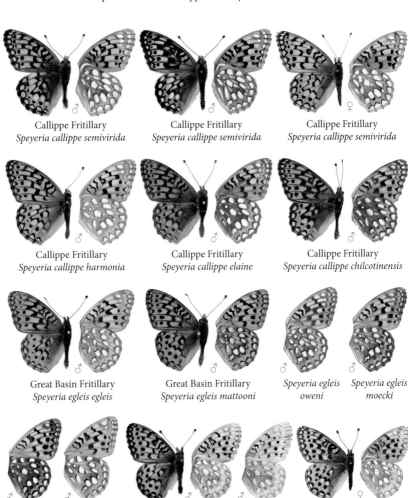

Callippe Fritillary
Speyeria callippe semivirida

Callippe Fritillary
Speyeria callippe semivirida

Callippe Fritillary
Speyeria callippe semivirida

Callippe Fritillary
Speyeria callippe harmonia

Callippe Fritillary
Speyeria callippe elaine

Callippe Fritillary
Speyeria callippe chilcotinensis

Great Basin Fritillary
Speyeria egleis egleis

Great Basin Fritillary
Speyeria egleis mattooni

*Speyeria egleis
oweni*

*Speyeria egleis
moecki*

Great Basin Fritillary
Speyeria egleis nr. *macdunnoughi*

Washington Fritillary
Speyeria mormonia washingtonia

Washington Fritillary
S. mormonia washingtonia

Mormon Fritillary
Speyeria mormonia erinna

Mormon Fritillary
Speyeria mormonia opis

Mormon Fritillary
Speyeria mormonia artonis

Comparison of Greater Fritillaries (*Speyeria* spp.)
Specimens are shown approximately at 50% of life size

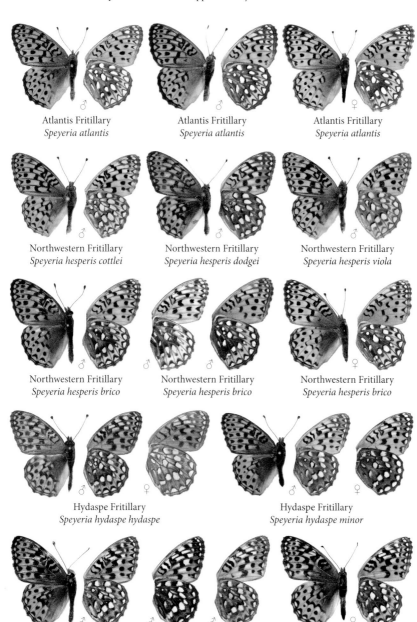

Atlantis Fritillary
Speyeria atlantis

Atlantis Fritillary
Speyeria atlantis

Atlantis Fritillary
Speyeria atlantis

Northwestern Fritillary
Speyeria hesperis cottlei

Northwestern Fritillary
Speyeria hesperis dodgei

Northwestern Fritillary
Speyeria hesperis viola

Northwestern Fritillary
Speyeria hesperis brico

Northwestern Fritillary
Speyeria hesperis brico

Northwestern Fritillary
Speyeria hesperis brico

Hydaspe Fritillary
Speyeria hydaspe hydaspe

Hydaspe Fritillary
Speyeria hydaspe minor

Hydaspe Fritillary
Speyeria hydaspe rhodope

Hydaspe Fritillary
Speyeria hydaspe rhodope

Hydaspe Fritillary
Speyeria hydaspe rhodope

Great Spangled Fritillary   *Speyeria cybele* (FABRICIUS) 1775

New York, NY
Aka *S. leto*

***S. C. PUGETENSIS* SGCN IN WA**

RECOGNITION < 3 in. Large. The most distinctive member of the genus. Male **fiery orange above, basally darker, with reduced black markings**, esp. on border. Below, VHW has **broad pale yellow submarginal band, cinnamon disc, with silver orbs reduced in size and number**. Female **ivory to yellowish above** with bold black markings, heavily suffused basally with black or dark brown scales, sometimes flecked with blue scales. Female below like male but with pale beige submarginal band and dark-**chocolate disc**. Neither has basal spot below cell on DFW, as somewhat similar Aphrodite Fritillary does. **VARIATION** *S. c. leto*, described from Carson City, NV,

occupies much of E Cascadia from CA into BC. Both sexes have much buffy overscaling, and are brighter and more lightly marked than those of *S. c. pugetensis*, described from nr Belfair, Mason Co., WA. The latter, flying W of the Cascade Crest (but not in BC), is more melanic and two-toned in both sexes. Females tend toward chestnut shades both in dorsal

basal suffusion and VHW disc, and the silver spots are still smaller than in *S. c. leto*. **HOST PLANTS** Chiefly stream violet (*Viola glabella*) in W OR (*fide* Hammond), also *V.*

Female, dorsal

adunca, V. bakeri, V. praemorsa, and *V. vallicola.* Nectars esp. on thistles. **ON THE WING** E June to E October, peak in July-August. One generation, newly hatched larvae overwinter. **HABITAT AND RANGE** Post-glacial grasslands, oak-pine glades, canyons, and roads at low to mid-elevation; lower mtns of the E side in draws, meadows, and forest margins. Coast to coast, halfway up Canada and halfway down US. Nearly all Cascadian mtn ranges; oddly absent from W BC (Vancouver Is., drier basins, outer coast, N Salish Lowlands, and Gulf Islands).

Female, ventral

Male, ventral

Female, dorsal

Male, dorsal

This spectacular insect is our largest, brightest, and most sexually dimorphic silverspot,

even though its silver spots are the smallest of any *Speyeria*. A fresh male burns incredibly brightly, and a big female is a stunning vision. Her cream-and-licorice two-tone mimics a Mourning Cloak, while the male consorts and confuses with the big Elegant Day Moth. Look for the more richly colored Puget Sound Fritillary (*S. c. pugetensis*) on Puget Prairie or Willamette Valley reserves such as Scatter Creek, Mima Mounds, or Finley National Wildlife Refuge; and the Leto Fritillary (*S. c. leto*) in many a mountain canyon east of the Pacific Crest. Sometimes at a good thistle-patch in full bloom, scores of fritillaries make a spectacle, and often this species dominates. Eastern Great Spangleds look quite different, much larger and duller. Cybele was the Romans' Great Mother, Leto was Apollo's mother, and Peter Puget was a naval comrade of George Vancouver, he of the sound for which the butterfly in turn was named.

Aphrodite Fritillary   *Speyeria aphrodite* (FABRICIUS) 1787

New York, NY
Aka Aphrodite

**S. A. WHITEHOUSEI
IMPERILED IN BC**

RECOGNITION < 3 in. Bright orange above with light border-chain on male, heavier on female; male veins lack sex-scales. Reddish

brown disc, darkening to auburn on female. **Prominent black dot at the base of the DFW** just below the black squiggly bars in the cell, which the Great Spangled lacks. VHW submarginal yellow band clear and narrow, silver orbs medium-sized. *S. cybele* has broader yellow band, smaller silver spots. Aphrodite Fritillary is the **only PNW *Speyeria* with yellow-green eyes;** all

Female, ventral

Female, dorsal

a. whitehousei, from Jaffray, in the East Kootenay district in SE BC, has a pale aspect. **HOST PLANTS** Many violets used elsewhere; *Viola bakeri*, *V. praemorsa*, and *V. vallicola* are likely hosts in NE Cascadia. Nectars esp. on mints (incl. beebalm) and thistles. **ON THE WING** L June to M September, peak in July-August, in BC. One brood, young larvae overwinter. **HABITAT AND RANGE** Transition zone mtns, pine and deciduous forest openings, canyons, and prairie. Much the same transcontinental, mid-latitude range as *S. cybele* but stops mostly at the Rockies; NW to the Selkirks in ID and S-C BC. In Cascadia, the only records are for the ID panhandle and E of the Okanagan R. in BC.

others have blue-green eyes. **VARIATION** Present in S-C BC and likely to be found in WA is *S. a. columbia* (Columbian Fritillary), described from Lac La Hache, BC; it is large and bright. *S.*

In much of the West, Aphrodite Fritillary lives in the woodland glades and sunny streamsides that the namesake goddess might find amenable. It should certainly turn up in the Okanogan Highlands or the Selkirks of northeastern Washington; its absence from the state list this long is something of a mystery. Beebalm (*Monarda*) and thistles attract the adults irresistibly. Females may aestivate during the hottest part of the summer, to emerge in early autumn and lay eggs where violets cannot be found by observant naturalists but are evident to small waking larvae in spring. Males sometimes disperse way beyond the breeding grounds after mating, appearing far from the nearest suitable habitat with violets. Aphrodite was the Greek goddess of love and beauty.

Coronis Fritillary   *Speyeria coronis* (BEHR) 1864

Gilroy, Santa Clara Co., CA
Aka Crown Fritillary

CRITICALLY IMPERILED IN OR

RECOGNITION < 3 in. Standard fritillary appearance above, with **bright yellow-orange ground color** rather than the fiery-orange of the preceding two species. Black chains along

margins light on males, heavy on females with pallor between links. VHW disc variable. **Silver discal orbs large and ovoid**, marginal silver spots **flattened, or large domes**.

VHW yellow submarginal band narrower than on *S. cybele*. Wings longer, larger than on *S. callippe*, and silver spots do not show through strongly from below. **VARIATION** "Subtle patterns of geographic variation in Oregon are largely obscured by great individual variability" (Warren). Disc color varies from olive-brown or warm brandy in WA (*S. c. simaetha*), often overlain with green, to yellow-brown in SE OR (*S. c. snyderi*), to light reddish brown in SW OR/N CA (the type). Those in the Siskiyous vary less than those farther N and E, and lack any green tint. **HOST PLANTS** *Viola trinervata* (sagebrush violet) and *V. douglasii* (Douglas' golden violet) in Columbia Basin; *V. beckwithii*

Female, dorsal

(Great Basin violet) is a major host in NE OR. Likely also *V. bakeri*, *V. vallicola*, *V. praemorsa* (canary violet), and *V. purpurea* (goosefoot violet). Nectars on composites (incl. bull thistle) and chokecherry. **ON THE WING** E May to M October, peaks in June, August (earlier lower, later higher), and in between. A single generation, first-instar larvae overwinter. **HABITAT AND RANGE** Lower-elevation canyons, lithosol balds, chaparral, sage-steppe, and forest glades, margins, and meadows; mid to higher mtns as summer progresses. Much of W US and CA to Baja. Mostly Cascades in WA, with a few Okanogan Highlands and Blue Mtns records. Much of OR E of the Cascade Crest, and the Siskiyous, with wanderers noted near Puget Sound and in scattered W-side locations. Not yet recorded in Canada or NE WA.

Coronis dominates in the basin steppe in spring, then in mid-montane meadows of the ponderosa zone in summer, where it can be abundant among the yellow daisies and first-blooming thistles alongside Boisduval's Blues and Purplish Coppers. Higher and later, other species of fritillaries such as Zerene and Hydaspe take over. As with other *Speyeria* species, the males come out a week or two before the peak female flight, so that a population will sometimes seem to be unisexual. Where you find the beautiful, two-toned sagebrush violets blooming under chilly spring winds, Coronis Fritillaries are likely to appear a fortnight later. They breed in the Columbia Basin, then wander uphill for the later-blooming nectar in a regular altitudinal migration (James and Pelham 2011). After weeks of reproductive delay, they return to the lowlands to lay their eggs where next year's violets will appear. Coronis should be viewed as a shrub-steppe endemic that leaves temporarily. This is an alternative strategy to the summer aestivation some species of greater fritillaries undergo.

Female, ventral

Male, dorsal

Zerene Fritillary   *Speyeria zerene* (BOISDUVAL) 1852

Chambers Creek, N Fk Feather R., Plumas Co., CA

S. Z. HIPPOLYTA ENDANGERED IN WA, CRITICALLY IMPERILED IN OR, FEDERALLY THREATENED; *S. Z. BREMNERII* EXTIRPATED IN OR, CANDIDATE IN WA, IMPERILED IN BC

RECOGNITION < 2.75 in. **Deep yellowish orange above**, darker and redder near coast and at higher elevations. VHW disc light orange-brown, vinous, or buckskin, **often shot with pale buff or olive highlights**. Silver spots rounded, medium in size. **VHW marginal spots triangular or domed, brown caps thicker in middle**; VHW submarginal yellow band bright, mid-width. *S. coronis* usually larger and paler, *S. callippe* has longer silver spots. **VARIATION** The type is large, deep orange-brown above, brick to purplish disc below with lavender band, spots small and silvered, slightly silvered, or unsil-

vered, flies in Warners, S Cascades, E Siskiyous; *S. z. gloriosa*, large, disc reddish brown with pinkish band in males, chocolate with buff band in females, usually bright silver spots, graces W Siskiyous and S OR coast N to Coos Bay; *S. z. hippolyta* (Oregon Silverspot), smaller, basally dark and yellowish orange above, rusty disc with sharp yellow band and small silver spots, occupies remnant habitats on C-N OR coast; an unnamed ssp. (Hinchliff's Fritillary), very similar, smallish, dark basally, sharply spotted and intensely silvered with dark rust disc, occurs on N-NE tier of subalpine Olympic Mtns.; *S. z. bremnerii* (Valley Silverspot), larger, red-brown disc, broad and bright yellow band, occupies BC Gulf and WA San Juan islands, Salish Lowlands, and WA Coast Range (larger, paler *bremnerii* from W-side Willamette Valley,

Male, dorsal (ssp. *gloriosa*)

Male, ventral

Ventral (ssp. *gloriosa*)

Female, ventral (ssp. *picta*)

Male, ventral (ssp. *picta*)

OR, are now apparently extinct); *S. z. picta* (Painted Fritillary), yellow-orange above, brick-red to tan below shot with paler streaks and well silvered, lives in the Cascades and E BC/WA/OR ranges to the N Rockies; *S. z. gunderi*, washed-out ochre above, yellow-brown disc below barely contrasting with yellow-buff band, silvered spots, flies in S Harney and Malheur cos, intergrades with the type in the Warners, and perhaps with *S. z. picta* N toward Ochocos and E. Several other *Speyeria* spp. vary almost this much across the region. For more details, see Pyle (2002), Warren (2005), and butterfliesofamerica.com. **HOST PLANTS** Blue violet (*Viola adunca*) used where available (coast, W valleys), perhaps stream violet (*V. glabella*), *V. bakeri*, *V. praemorsa*, and *V. vallicola* on the E side. I have observed females of both *S. z. bremnerii* and *S. z. picta* hunt over turf for violet scent in fall. Nectars on thistles, tansy ragwort, goldenrod, and dew. **ON THE WING** E June to L September, peak in July (August, coastal colonies). One brood, little larvae winter. **HABITAT AND RANGE** Coastal: salt-spray meadows, back-dune troughs, windy headlands and peaks, with nearby forest glades; glacial outwash prairies in the Puget Trough; canyons, meadows, roadsides, and clearings in the mtns; rabbitbrush flats in SE OR. NW US well into Canada; most of Cascadia, but rarer (or locally extinct) W of Cascade Crest except in Olympics and Siskiyous. Several remnant populations along C-N OR coast, extinct on Long Beach Peninsula, WA.

As Dornfeld wrote, "If one were to select an Oregon butterfly to illustrate the principles of geographic variability and subspeciation, none would serve this purpose better than the Zerene Fritillary." Of the six or more Cascadian subspecies, *S. z. hippolyta*, the famous Oregon Silverspot, has received most attention by far, as the first federally listed butterfly in the region. Dave McCorkle, Paul Hammond, and many others have worked with agencies to protect and manage its habitat and reinforce the population at Cascade Head and elsewhere on the Oregon coast. Found in coastal Washington in 1916 (Veazie), 1956 (McCorkle), and 1975 (Pyle), but poor summers and development since led to its extinction in the state. Habitat has been acquired by the state and the violet turf managed in hopes of eventual reintroduction. Meanwhile, the Valley Silverspot (*S. z. bremnerii*), extinct in the Willamette Valley, depends upon conservation efforts on behalf of native grasslands in the Puget Trough and the Gulf Islands. The mountain races are still common, with differing types in the Olympics, throughout the Cascades, on Steens Mountain, and in the Siskiyous. Hippolyta was the Amazonian queen wed by Theseus in *A Midsummer Night's Dream*. John T. W. Bremner was ship's surgeon on HMS *Zealous* at the Royal Navy's Pacific Station in Esquimalt, Vancouver Island; while stationed on San Juan Island (the type locality for *S. z. bremnerii*) in 1859, during the Pig War, he collected specimens that went first to Henry Edwards in San Franciso, then to Boisduval in Paris. The derivation of the name Zerene is a mystery.

Callippe Fritillary   *Speyeria callippe* (BOISDUVAL) 1852

San Francisco, CA

RECOGNITION < 2.5 in. Dorsum tawny to pale yellow-orange or washed-out brassy. **Stockier, squarer appearance than other *Speyeria* spp. Light spots on DHW stand out** as if the silver orbs are showing through from below. Males with bold black veins. Black border-chains prominent, much more so on females. **Silver spots big and elongated, almost tangent; submarginal silver spots triangular, thinly capped with green or brown triangles;** submarginal band only slightly paler than disc color. On average, smaller than *S. zerene*, larger than *S. egleis*. **VARIATION** VHW disc varies geographically from light brown to olive-beige or blue-green (WA, ID, OR; *S. c. semivirida*), dark brown (E Chilcotin, BC; *S. c. chilcotinensis*), reddish brown (SW OR/N CA; *S. c. elaine*) to pale yellow-buff (SE OR; *S. c. harmonia*), all usually with at least some green highlights. VFW can be quite pink basally, esp. in *S. c. semivirida*. Geographic variation around Oregon is complex; "in the shadow of Mt. Mazama's blast," Callippe is dwarfed, as are several other fritillaries in that same ashfield habitat; see Warren (2005) for more details. **HOST PLANTS** Likely *Viola bakeri, V. praemorsa,* and *V. vallicola* in much of our area. Nectar plants incl. mountain ash (*Sorbus*), dogbane, mints, blanketflower (*Gaillardia aristata*), western hawkweed (*Hieracium scouleri*), and Mt. Hood pussypaws (*Cistanthe umbellata*). **ON THE WING** E May to E September, peak in June-July. One brood, larvae diapause before feeding.

Female, ventral (ssp. *semivirida*)

Male, dorsal (ssp. *semivirida*)

Male, ventral (ssp. *semivirida*)

HABITAT AND RANGE Montane canyons, sage-steppe prairie, pine- and oakwood glades, grasslands. W provinces and states N of AZ, CA S to Baja. All Cascadia E of crest, and W into Siskiyous though limited in Columbia Basin.

In northern Cascadia, Callippe is the only fritillary likely to be green below, except for small Mormon Fritillaries in the alpine. A Washington record for the larger, green-disced Edwards' Fritillary (*S. edwardsii*, in Leighton 1946) actually referred to a big Callippe. Greater fritillaries are robust, living longer than many mid-sized butterflies, and wearing out in the process. As Callippe ages, it grows more and more bleached and pallid. You will see late-season individuals that actually look white, and wonder what they can possibly be until you get a good look; or you may come upon dozens of fresh, bright Callippes clambering over the blossoms of mountain ashes in July, as I did east of Mt. St. Helens. Inspired by this butterfly's prominent and rounded pale orbs, Boisduval

Pair, ventral (ssp. *elaine*)

named it in honor of the Aphrodite Kallipy-
gos, also known as the Callipygian Venus
("Venus of the beautiful buttocks"). The
Venus Callipyge is an ancient Roman marble statue, thought to be a copy of an older

Greek original. Boisduval saw a 17th-century
copy of it, sculpted by François Barois, in the
Jardin des Tuileries, a short walk from the
Muséum national d'histoire naturelle across
the Seine, where he toiled.

Great Basin Fritillary *Speyeria egleis* (BEHR) 1862

Vic. Gold Lake, Sierra Co., CA
Aka Egleis Fritillary, *montivaga*

RECOGNITION < 2.25 in. **Smaller** than other species of *Speyeria* except *S. mormonia*. Medium
yellowish to reddish orange above, commonly
with **heavy dark scaling on veins and basally,**
and slight pallor between the dark spots. Beneath, the silver spots are smallish and rounded
or oval, set in a variable disc that (in the NW)
is often **muddy yellow-brown broken by darker
shades of greenish olive or reddish or purplish
brown.** Caitlin LaBar noticed that, unlike other
Speyeria that have a dark ground color with
lighter highlights, *S. egleis* often **has a lighter**
ground color with darker shades forming shadows or halos around the silver spots. **VARIATION**
S. egleis varies considerably and complexly in
the PNW, from pale
and either silvered or
not in the Warners
(*S. e.* nr. *egleis*), to
darker and unsil-
vered in the SW Cas-
cades-Siskiyous (*S. e.
mattooni*), to small
and dark in Klamath

Pair, dorsal

Co. and points S (*S. e. moecki, S. e. oweni*), to silvered and quite greenish brown in NE OR/SE WA (*S. e.* nr. *macdunnoughi*). See Warren (2005) for details. **HOST PLANTS** Violets incl. *Viola bakeri, V. praemorsa, V. vallicola, V. purpurea,* and *V. adunca.* Nectars abundantly on rabbitbrush and spreading dogbane. **ON THE WING** M June to E September, peak in July. **HABITAT AND RANGE** Regional ssp. occupy specific habitats; usually clearings and ridges in the mtns, sunny meadows and hilltops, pumice flats and subalpine slopes. N Rockies, N Great Basin, N CA, much of ID, thinning to the NW; unknown in Canada. WA records in Okanogan Highlands, Palouse Hills, and S Cascades, more in Blue Mtns; Wallowa-Blues, Ochocos, C-S OR Cascades, common in the Warners and Siskiyous.

The species has long represented something of an enigma in Washington, with just a few disparate records here and there. In 1974 (wwb), I said of it, "Washington collectors prize it highly but often are not quite sure whether they have it or not." This still applies, especially if one adds butterfly listers and watchers. As Caitlyn puts it, "Egleis looks like everything but not exactly like anything." *S. egleis* occurs more regularly in the Blue Mountains, abounding on Diamond Peak, and increases still more as one travels south and east toward the Great Basin of its name. The small, dark population named for *Speyeria* authority Arthur Moeck is restricted to the young pumice fields around Mt. Mazama; Owen's Fritillary (*S. e. oweni*), occurring both to the north and south, seems to be an old taxon that was broken up as Moeck's Fritillary (*S. e. moecki*) arose on geologic deposits that violently interposed themselves. But reconstructing geologic histories and relationships they affect is always risky business.

Male, ventral (ssp. *mattooni*)

Male, ventral (ssp. *oweni*)

Atlantis Fritillary   *Speyeria atlantis* (W. H. EDWARDS) 1862

Hunter, Green Co., NY
Aka Northwestern Fritillary, Mountain Silverspot, *hesperis*

RECOGNITION < 2.5 in. Bright tawny to citrus or yellowish orange above with strong black spots and border-chains (heavier on females), darker at base, and veins lined with dark scales. **VHW disc medium to dark leaden chocolate-brown,**

variously shot with lighter streaks; **spots silvered, discal spots slightly narrowed, marginal spots sharply triangular.** Dark veins prominently cross buff submarginal band.

Aphrodite Fritillary has larger DFW basal spot, lacks dark dorsal margins, has yellow-green eyes to Atlantis' blue-gray. **VARIATION** NE WA/N ID populations resemble those of the NE type, and indeed they might both belong to one transboreal entity. **HOST PLANTS** Canadian white violet (*Viola canadensis*). Nectars on mints, thistles, goldenrod, and other composites. **ON THE WING** M June to M August, peak in July. A single generation, larvae overwinter. **HABITAT AND RANGE** Boreal forests and clearings, bogs, and fens. NE US, CO-NM, all subarctic Canada. PNW in SE BC and NE WA in Selkirk Mtns and Okanogan Highlands.

Female, dorsal

Female, ventral

This is sometimes lumped with the Northwestern Fritillary. Where it overlaps with *S. hesperis* and both are silvered, Pelham and Kondla find the Atlantis Fritillary distinctive in disc color. In certain high meadows in Washington's northeast corner, Atlantis Fritillaries look and behave very much like the common boreal butterfly that they are in the upper Appalachians or New England. There in high summer, they duck in and out of forest clearings around the edges of Bunchgrass Meadow, Pend Oreille County, and other large damp openings. Atlantis was the island paradise in the Atlantic Ocean where Poseidon fell in love with Cleito and they had ten children. All went well for a while, until Zeus got fed up and sent an earthquake that sank Atlantis in one day and one night. Atlantis reaches the very shores of the Atlantic in Maine and the Maritimes.

Northwestern Fritillary   *Speyeria hesperis* (W. H. EDWARDS) 1864

Turkey Creek Junction, Jefferson Co., CO
Aka Atlantis Fritillary, Mountain Silverspot, *atlantis*

Male, dorsal (ssp. *brico*)

RECOGNITION < 2.5 in. Deep yellowish orange above with bold black markings and border-chains (heavier on females), **thick, raised black scaling on veins and dark base of wings. VHW disc reddish to dark chocolate-brown, spots mostly silvered in the north, unsilvered south**. Buffy-yellow submarginal band narrow to medium, strikingly crossed by dark veins. The Hydaspe Fritillary resembles the unsilvered races somewhat but has a maroon hue below and a pinkish submarginal band, often vague. Note on *S. atlantis* compared to *S. aphrodite* applies here too. **VARIATION** Greatly varied over a broad and complex W range. *S. h. brico* was seen by its authors (Kondla, Scott & Spomer 1998) as applying to populations N and E from Okanogan Co., WA; it is usually silvered and can look very much like *S. atlantis*. *S. h. dodgei* is much redder below on the disc, less choco-

Male, ventral (ssp. *brico*)

Male, ventral (ssp. *dodgei*)

late, and it is usually unsilvered, its discal spots being a cheesy-buff instead. It flies southward through the Cascades, encompassing most of the OR populations from the Wallowas to the Siskiyous. Some individuals in NE OR veer toward ID's darker *S. h. viola*. From W Lake Co., OR, through the Warners occurs *S. h. cottlei*, larger and darker on both surfaces than the widespread *S. h. dodgei*. For more details, see butterfliesofamerica.com. **HOST PLANTS** Blue violet (*Viola adunca*), goosefoot violet (*V. purpurea*), evergreen violet (*V. sempervirens*), canary violet (*V. praemorsa*), and prob. others. Nectars on mints incl. beebalm, thistles, goldenrod, and other composites. **ON THE WING** M June to E September, peak in July. Eggs hatch in the fall, and the larvae overwinter. **HABITAT AND RANGE** *S. h. dodgei* is "strongly confined

Male, ventral (ssp. *cottlei*)

to the mountainous fir and pine forests and may be seen in canyons, along creeks, and in small clearings and meadows" (Dornfeld). This applies to much of the species' range, which takes in the intermountain W from AZ to AK and most of subarctic Canada. In Cascadia, most of S BC, ID, E Cascades, Okanogan Highlands, Selkirks, and Blues of WA, and all OR mtns except Coast Range and SE quarter.

Pelham interprets *S. h. brico* as appearing in boreal, spruce-fir-cedar forests of the interior wet belt, and *S. h. dodgei* as applying to populations in the S Cascades and the Blue Mtns.

In *The Butterflies of Cascadia* I lumped this species with *S. atlantis,* but Pelham's *Catalogue* treats them as two. Northwest *Speyeria* authority Paul Hammond rejects this split as it applies to Cascadia, as his field and rearing studies document what he sees as extensive intergrading of the types involved, and he has "found no evidence that two distinct species exist in the region." There

is a gap between the largely unsilvered *S. h. dodgei* and the largely silvered *S. h. brico,* essentially consisting of Chelan County, Washington, in which both subspecies barely appear. Silvered *S. hesperis* overlaps with true *S. atlantis* farther north, according to the school that separates them. I did not have a good sense of how the unsilvered *S. h. dodgei* differed from from nearby Hydaspes until I found it abounding in a wet meadow near Klamath Lake, where it finally struck me as entirely distinctive. I am still seeking similar enlightenment for silvered *S. hesperis* versus Atlantis Fritillaries.

Hydaspe Fritillary   *Speyeria hydaspe* (BOISDUVAL) 1869

Gold Lake, Sierra Co., CA
Aka Lavender Fritillary

RECOGNITION < 2.25 in. Rather rounded wings. Males deep reddish orange above, females more yellowish, heavily spotted and barred with black, often dusky near the base. VHW disc is rusty to maroon with purplish overtones, often giving a **burgundy tone.** Marginal and discal spots off-white, yellow, or cream, **unsilvered, partly silvered, or yellowish opalescent.** VHW submarginal band vague, dirty yellow invaded with pinkish, or absent. Unsilvered *S. hesperis dodgei* can look very similar but lacks purplish tones below, VHW submarginal band generally more pronounced. **VARIATION** The highly variable but often quite purplish *S. h. rhodope,* described from the Fraser R. lowlands, BC, occupies most of the region. The slightly smaller, paler *S. h. minor,* from Lillooet, BC, haunts the higher, E-side Cascades. Populations verging on the Sierran type, unusually pale below, appear throughout SW OR. **HOST PLANTS** Stream violet (*Viola glabella*), blue violet (*V. adunca*), and evergreen violet (*V. sempervirens*) on the W side, *V. bakeri, V. praemorsa,* and *V. vallicola* on the E. Nectars on hawkbit, blue penstemons, horsemint, spreading dogbane, yarrow, and bull

Ventral

Male, dorsal

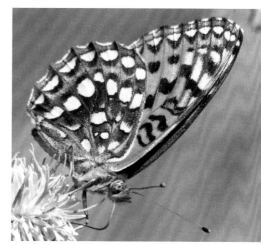

Ventral

thistle. Males visit mud. **ON THE WING** L May to L September, peak in July-August. One generation, newly hatched larvae overwinter. **HABITAT AND RANGE** Moist mtns, forest glades and edges, roadsides, streamsides, riverbreaks, hilltops, and meadows. Usually forested, absent from arid areas. NW US and Canada, with prongs reaching S into the Sierra, N to W-C BC, and SE to C CO; all mesic parts of Cascadia.

W. H. Howe wrote, "The center of distribution of the species is north of the Salmon River in Idaho, in southern British Columbia and in Washington," so this is a true Northwesterner. Few other fritillaries are found over such a wide range of conditions, and none so near the coast, except the rare Oregon Silverspot. Though it descends to sea level, it seeks higher elevations in the mountains, often hilltopping. Hydaspe haunts the sunnier fringes of wet Northwest woods, including managed forests if unsprayed. By far the most widespread greater fritillary in the region, it is often accompanied by the similarly adaptable Western Meadow Fritillary. On Boistfort Peak, at 3,114 feet the highest of the Willapa Hills, the fritillaries were zoned—Zerene lowest, Great Spangled next, and Hydaspe around the summit. I observed oviposition on a shale splinter at the base of blue violet in the northeastern Olympics and found Hydaspe abounding on yarrow in the Dark Divide of Skamania County, Washington, one of the few butterflies I have observed nectaring on that plant. According to the *Dionysiaca* of Nonnos, the oldest surviving epic Greek poem, Hydaspe was the brother of Iris, goddess of the rainbow. Boisduval's epithet was likely inspired by *S. hydaspe*'s opalescent spots.

Mormon Fritillary   *Speyeria mormonia* (BOISDUVAL) 1869

Little Valley, W of Washoe Lake, NV

**S. M. ERINNA,
S. M. EURYNOME
IMPERILED IN BC**

RECOGNITION
< 2 in. **Flies at high
altitudes, often
above timberline**.
**Smaller than all
other speyerias, larger than any bolorian**. Wings
short and rounded. Bright tawny ochre dorsum,
females darker with **heavy black marginal
chains**, often enclosing **white marginal spots**;
males less boldly bordered. VHW disc color
highly variable, spots silvered or not, long-
ovoid. High-altitude Hydaspe is larger, purplish
below. Arctic Fritillary females with white spots
above have narrower wings. **VARIATION** *S. m.*

washingtonia (Washington Fritillary), described
from Paradise Valley, Mt. Rainier, WA, is larger
with a greener disc and spots silvered or not,
darkly marked, and both dusky and hairy near
the body; it inhabits the whole of the WA and
BC Cascades, running into the predominant
BC ssp., *S. m. opis*, small with silvered spots
heavily outlined with brown-olive. *S. m. erinna*,
from Spokane Falls, holds forth in the Okanogan, W Kootenay, Selkirk, Blue, Wallowa, and
Ochoco mtns and the entirety of the higher OR
Cascades; it is lighter orange above, less hairy,
usually silvered, with disc ranging from reddish
brown to yellowish olive or light chocolate, with
or without greenish overscaling. From the Rockies, the very green *S. m. eurynome* just skirts
E BC. *S. m. artonis*, the striking Great Basin
race, haunts high meadows of Steens and Trout

Male, dorsal

Male, ventral

Creek mtns in Harney Co., OR, where Dornfield described it as "strangely pale and washed-out looking, almost concolorously yellow" below. Many Warner Mtn Mormons are intermediate between *S. m. artonis* and *S. m. erinna*. **HOST PLANTS** Violets incl. *Viola palustris*, *V. adunca*, *V. nephrophylla*, *V. bakeri*, *V. praemorsa*, *V. vallicola*, and *V. sempervirens* in WA. Nectars on asters, arnicas, pearly everlasting, other high-meadow flowers. **ON THE WING** E June to M October, peak in July-August. **HABITAT AND RANGE** From 3,500 feet to summits, subalpine meadows, arctic-alpine tundra, often where green false hellebore (*Veratrum viride*) grows. Most W mtns, AZ to AK, CO to CA. Absent from Olympics, Coast Ranges, and Siskiyous.

Visitors to Paradise at Mt. Rainier and other scenic alpine spots may spot numbers of these bright fritillaries flitting and nectaring over the montane meadows. Frosts permitting, they can fly very late in the year, sometimes surprising hikers even in the golden-larch days of October. In drier

Male, ventral (ssp. *artonis*)

Female, dorsal (ssp. *artonis*)

mountains, the species flies from sage-brush slopes to the arctic-alpine. I have twice found adults going to roost communally in marshes before sunset, in Colorado and Montana. Boisduval labeled the type locality "sur les frontières de l'Oregon" and also mentioned "Salt Lake," later mistaken for the one in Utah. Both terms actually referred to Washoe Lake in northwestern Nevada; but Boisduval clearly had Mormon country in mind when he named the insect. *S. m. washingtonia* is one of only two butterflies that commemorate the Evergreen State in their names, both of them suitably greenish.

Subfamily Limenitidinae: Admirals

In *Butterflies of British Columbia*, Guppy and Shepard give an elaborate etymology relating harbor-keeping deities to admirals of the harbor, and this may well be the correct origin of the common name. A simpler view has long been that the wing-bands resembled stripes of military rank. Biggish butterflies displaying dramatic color contrast, the admirals give their name to their own subfamily and tribe (Limenitidini) of nymphalids. The habit of admirals to claim and defend a sunny cove or haven in the forest might have inspired the limenitine scientific names—*limen* means "portal" in Latin or "refuge" in Greek. Young larvae hibernate in rolled leaves; older ones, and pupae, resemble birdlime with horns and humps. The admirals' famous genetic plasticity manifests in the high frequency of interspecies hybridization and elaborate mimicry of unrelated, distasteful butterflies.

White Admiral   *Limenitis arthemis* (DRURY) 1773

New York, prob. Catskill Mtns
Aka Banded Purple, Red-spotted Admiral (NABA), *Basilarchia*

RECOGNITION < 3.25 in. Large. **Coal-black, crossed above and below by narrow milk-white bands**.

Blue crescents line the scalloped margins above, and cap a submarginal row of brick-red spots on the DHW. White DFW apical spots, but the cell-spot obvious in Weidemeyer's Admiral is absent or very small. White-banded, reddish brown underside with submarginal red bands, blue marginal crescents, basal clusters of red and blue spots. Weidemeyer's has no red or blue spots above. **VARIATION** *L. a. rubrofasciata*, described from "Manitoba, Alberta, Saskatchewan," enters Cascadia in SE BC to the N Okanagan Valley. It has discrete red bands inside the ventral margins, whereas the type typically has nebulous red spots. **HOST PLANTS** Willows and aspens in BC; birch, alder, poplars, cherry, hawthorn, and serviceberry elsewhere. Adults visit flowers, sap, aphid honeydew, mud, carrion, and scat. **ON THE WING** M May to M September, peak in July. One or two generations, young larvae overwinter. **HABITAT AND RANGE** Occupies mixed and deciduous woods, glades, and willowy streambanks. Most of Canada, dipping down into northern US, up into AK. Most of BC, one WA record.

Artemis was the Greek Diana, lover of woods, deer, and the wild chase. This shows that the namers were not always arbitrary, for *L. arthemis* indeed loves wooded places, surveying sunny glades with a languorous flap-glide flight, shifting to a rapid flap-and-soar under chase. In southern British Columbia, it hybridizes with Lorquin's

Male, dorsal

Male, ventral

Admiral. Since it also hybridizes across the Northeast with the Red-spotted Purple (*L. astyanax*), most authors consider them conspecific. One White Admiral has turned up in Washington—not in the Pend Oreille, where we might expect it, but in Patti Ensor's backyard in Kennewick. As it more resembles the eastern race, it might have come from a chrysalis hitchhiking on a wide-ranging RV. An indigenous White Admiral may one day be found in Washington, perhaps in the Salmo-Priest Wilderness.

Viceroy   *Limenitis archippus* (CRAMER) 1875

Jamaica, but prob. NY (Jamaica Bay?)
Aka Mimic, *Basilarchia*

EXTIRPATED IN BC

RECOGNITION < 3.25 in. **Rich russet-orange above** with black veins, DHW a shade lighter than DFW; white dots punctuate black margin and subapical black triangle on FW. VHW and tip of VFW pale apricot, strongly contrasting with citrus of basal VFW. **Strong postmedian black line crossing DHW and VHW**, perpendicular to black veins, lacking in Monarchs. Smaller, wings shorter, less drawn out than Monarch's. Watch for partially banded, deep rust offspring of hybrid matings with *L. lorquini*. **VARIATION** Viceroys of the Columbia, Snake, and Bonneville basins are represented by *L. a. idaho*, the taxon to which all Cascadian Viceroys belong. It is not as deep and foxy as the typical E US look, with intermediate dark marks. **HOST PLANTS**

Dorsal

Chiefly willows, esp. peachleaf and sandbar (*Salix amygdaloides*, *S. exigua*), as well as apples, cherries, and poplars. Nectars on all sorts of sweet and rotting substances incl. willow sap and thistle, aster, goldenrod, and milkweed. I've watched adults visiting foamy maple sap, with Red Admirables and commas, where sapsuckers had loosed a late-summer maple syrup soda. **ON THE WING** E April to L September, peaks in May, July-August. Routinely two generations in our area, early instar larvae overwinter. **HABITAT AND RANGE** Willowy fringes and muddy banks of riversides and lakeshores, canyons, reservoir draw-down flats, parks. Most of E and C-W N Am from well into Canada to deep into Mexico, Rockies, and spotty to the W along watercourses and reservoirs. Yakima, Snake, and Columbia drainages and their tributaries in E OR, E WA, and N ID. Extirpated from S-C BC, formerly occurred N to Lillooet.

The Viceroy gains protection from predators as larvae and pupae by resembling bird droppings, and the adult is the most famous textbook mimic of a warningly colored model, the remarkably similar Monarch. Even lepidopterists can be fooled by the resemblance of a big female Viceroy to a medium Monarch, on the wing. Viceroys contain their own distasteful substances from the salicylic acid in willows, doubling the incentive for educated birds to leave both species alone. George Austin suggests that Viceroys colonized the West between the Missouri and Snake rivers, thence to the Columbia northward, and the Humboldt River and Great Basin southward. The butterfly used to occur farther north than it does today. John Hopfinger noted in letters to Charles Remington that Viceroys were common around Brewster on the Columbia prior to 1916, then dwindled until about 1960. Dams and agriculture took out many willows, even as the introduction of apples furnished an abundant new food source for Viceroys. But insecticides followed, and the Viceroy dropped out of the Okanogan and Upper Columbia basin. They are still common along the Yakima, Snake, and mid-Columbia rivers, especially where they meet at Tri-Cities and on the Hanford Reach. Oregon records are mostly in the Umatilla, Owyhee, and Malheur country. Find them in high summer, sailing out and back from head-high willow boughs; then go back in winter and try to spot half-eaten, rolled leaves with midveins protruding: the snug winter quarters for tiny larvae.

Female, ventral

Weidemeyer's Admiral   *Limenitis weidemeyerii* W. H. EDWARDS 1861

Boulder, CO
Aka Western Admiral, *Basilarchia*

RECOGNITION < 3.5 in. **Big, coal-black, with broad milk-white postmedian bands** top and bottom. White marginal dots; white spots in the DFW tip and cell. No blue on DFW, little red. Underside largely bluish gray crossed by basal black lines, black veins, postmedian white spotbands as above, marginal blue-gray crescents, and reddish spots in VHW submarginal band and VFW cell. Females larger, broader-winged, as in all admirals. White Admiral has bigger red spots and blue crescents on DHW. **VARIATION** *L. w. latifascia*, described from Bannock Co., ID, is our ssp. It differs from the type and other ssp. by having the widest white bands above and more white scaling below. Hybrids occur with other admirals. **HOST PLANTS** Salicaceae and Rosaceae: willows, aspens, cherries, serviceberry, oceanspray, ninebark. Adults are catholic feeders on flowers, fruit, honeydew, mud, scat, and carrion. **ON THE WING** E June to L September, peak in July. One or two broods, half-grown larvae overwinter. Males take and defend possession of sunny perches, gliding around them and darting out at passersby, stopping only to come down for mud or nectar. **HABITAT AND RANGE** Watercourses, parks, shrubby slopes, willowy places. Our ssp. "frequents streamsides, riverbeds or sage-covered flats that are continuous with alkaline lakes and a *Salix-Populus-Artemisia* association" (Perkins and Perkins 1967). Intermountain W, AZ to AB and E CA to mid-NE. In PNW, the three-corners area where SE OR, SW ID, and N NV meet.

Male, dorsal

Male, dorsal

This magnificent nymphalid is familiar to westerners who frequent watercourses lined with peachleaf and sandbar willows and plains cottonwoods, but it barely grazes Cascadia. Charles Remington first found it in Oregon, west of Jordan Valley, Malheur County, in 1964. Since then it has turned up in the Owyhee country, the Pueblo and Trout Creek mountains in Harney County, and elsewhere in the southeastern deserts and ranges of the state. Some (form "fridayi") show the reduced bands, increased red below, and partially orange forewing tips that indicate either the introgression of *L. lorquini* genes into the population or full-on *L. weidemeyerii* × *lorquini* hybrids. The epithet honors Edwards' close friend J. W. Weidemeyer (wHY-duh-myer). Together with neighbor Mourning Cloaks, male Weidemeyers make frenzied sallies at passing Monarchs, magpies, dragonflies, and one another. Such behavior serves both to protect good mating territory and to investigate potential females.

Male, ventral

Lorquin's Admiral   *Limenitis lorquini* BOISDUVAL 1852

E Br. N Fk Feather R. Cyn, Plumas Co., CA
Aka Orange-tip Admiral, *Basilarchia*

RECOGNITION < 3 in. Dark brown-black above, creamy white spotbands concave toward base, diffuse **rusty orange FW tips**. Bands cross middle of both wings, orange tips reach and run down margin. White cell-spot on DFW. Below, complex pattern of alternating brick-red and blue-gray bands and black lines

on either side of white bands, rusty wingtips expanded. Weidemeyer's bigger, blacker, lacks orange win-tips. California Sister bigger, with narrower bands, wingtips discrete and orange-juice-orange, white band convex toward base. **VARIATION** Individuals vary greatly throughout Cascadia, precluding geographic definition, though there's something of a lighter E, darker W trend. This is more pronounced in BC, where admirals E of the Cascades have smaller, darker orange wingtips and narrower bands, with medium-light red markings below and a cluster of basal white spots on the VHW (*L. l. burrisoni*); while those in SW BC have bands more broken by black veins, are much darker and richer below, and solid brick-red in the basal VHW, without the basal light spots on the VHW (*L. l. ilgae*). Some SW OR individuals are paler and resemble the N CA type. **HOST PLANTS** Often willows (*Salix lasiandra, S. amygdaloides, S. exigua, S. lasiolepis*) but also quaking aspen, black cottonwood, serviceberry, hardhack, oceanspray, apple, cherry, and snowbrush ceanothus. Nectars on dogbane,

Female, ventral

Dorsal

mustards, yarrow, tansy, thistle, ripe fruits incl. cascara berries. Both sexes visit mud. **ON THE WING** M February to E October, peaks in June, July, and August. Single- or double-brooded, perhaps three farther S; larvae overwinter. **HABITAT AND RANGE** Extremely general—rivers, roadsides, parks and gardens, canyons and gullies, ditches and lakesides, anywhere with host plants from sea level to mid-montane. W Coast, Baja to mid-BC, inland to W NV, C ID, and W MT. All Cascadia.

Few Northwest butterflies inhabit so many kinds of places; only the Cabbage White, Anise Swallowtail, Brown Elfin, Echo Azure, and Mylitta Crescent come close. Such a beautiful butterfly—abundant, ubiquitous over a long flight period, and territorial—is the perfect guest for the butterfly garden. In a Victoria rose garden, I watched a male Lorquin's launching again and again after a glaucous-winged gull. In the Blue Mountains, several males occupying a copse of bitter cherry paid little attention to one another, apparently having established parity. But each time a Two-tailed Tiger Swallowtail or a Great Spangled Fritillary happened past, it was vigorously pursued by the admirals' collective campaign. These generalized courtship-cum-territorial sorties are typical of the limenitines. When basking, they hold their wings from 180 to 45 degrees, or slowly pump them open and closed; then launch without warning into the standard flight that Comstock described as "a series of short twitching motions, with the wings held nearly flat, interspersed with leisurely volplaning." Often the same or a nearby perch will be retaken. Pierre Lorquin (1797–1873) was a collector and gold-hunter who sent much new and important material back to Boisduval in Paris. His name is commemorated not only by this handsome insect but also by the oldest bug club on the West Coast, the Lorquin Society of Los Angeles.

California Sister *Adelpha californica* (BUTLER) 1865

California
Aka Sister(s), *Limenitis, Heterochroa, bredowii*

RECOGNITION < 3.5 in. **Large, broad-winged**, brown-black with white bands and **discrete citrus-orange FW tips**. White bands narrow, convex toward base, break into spots on FW. Orange spots large, clear orange, not rusty; subapical and discrete, not reaching and running down margin as in Lorquin's Admiral. DHW has orange tornal spot. Ventrum repeats dorsal pattern but paler, basal third striped with orange and blue-mauve, outer brown, white-checked margin lined by creneled blue band. **VARIATION** Most is

Male, dorsal

Male, ventral

individual, having to do with size and intensity of orange patch and blue stripes. **HOST PLANTS** Oaks, incl. in CA and S OR evergreen species such as canyon live oak (*Quercus chrysolepis*) and California live oak (*Q. agrifolia*), and golden chinquapin (*Chrysolepis chrysophylla*). James and Nunnallee successfully reared the species on Garry oak (*Q. garryana*). Adults visit all manner of enticements from rabbitbrush, blackberry, California buckeye, and buddleia to honeydew, carrion, mud, scat, and the spilled ullage of wine barrels. **ON THE WING** L May to L October, peaks in June and July. Two or three broods in OR, depending on elevation and seasonal conditions (Warren). Larvae overwinter. **HABITAT AND RANGE** In breeding range, oak-lined watercourses, montane oak groves, parks; in dispersal, anywhere. Resident CA into Baja and S OR. In OR, common in Siskiyous to Willamette Valley, sparing in W

A handful of California Sisters

Cascades, Coast Range, and rare E and N. In WA, a dozen+ SW records, and one from Gig Harbor. Southward migration reported near Siskiyou Summit in September.

Many reports of this species actually refer to big female Lorquin's Admirals. The previous species, after all, is thought to mimic California Sister, which is more massive and more sedate in flight. Comstock wrote, "It spends much of its time in solitary flight about the upper branches of the live-oaks, or perched on high vantage points where it can survey the woodland life below." Once you see that orange-juice apex, you will no longer be in doubt. California Sisters disperse widely, accounting for far-flung sightings; warm summers of major movements of

Painted Ladies and other species produce them in the North. How far up they breed is unclear, but they happily use our only northern oak in Oregon, so Washington residency may become a reality with increased warming. The majority of Washington records come from my western Wahkiakum County butterfly garden. California Sister was recently split from the even larger Arizona Sister (*A. eulalia*), and the name that had been used for both (*A. bredowii*) was found to apply to still a third, related neotropical species. The common name came from the resemblance of its colors to a nun's habit in someone's fervid imagination, with a stray lock of bright red hair escaping the wimple's confinement.

Subfamily Apaturinae: Emperors

Hackberry Butterfly   *Asterocampa celtis* (BOISDUVAL & LECONTE) 1835

Vic. Savannah, GA
Aka Hackberry Emperor

RECOGNITION
< 2.25 in. Warm tawny, olive, or grayish brown above, complexly and variably marked above with brown, black, and white spots and bars. FW has **white spots over outer half, two white-pupiled eyespots on DFW, row of submarginal dark eyespots around DHW.** One dark bar and two dark spots in FW cell. **Pupiled eyespots all along ventral margin**, often with some blue, and light brown squiggles on lilac-gray ground of ventrum. Female larger, lighter, tawnier overall. Male's wings narrow and concave at tips, female's broader, rounder. Unmistakable.

Male, dorsal

Male, ventral

RANGE Various kinds of hackberry woods in the S half of the country, AZ to MN to ME, as far NW as UT, ID (Gem, Washington, Twin Falls, Cassia, and Oneida cos). Sight records reported from Asotin Co., SE WA, 2012, 2013.

It is not even certain that this distinctive butterfly occurs in the Pacific Northwest, but we think it may. I sought it among abundant hackberry thickets in extreme southeastern Washington for decades. Then in October 2012, Ray Stanford had one land on him during a pit stop on a Hells Canyon jet boat trip, about a mile north of the Oregon state line; and in September 2013, Charles Rogers reported sighting several individuals north of Heller Bar. Since then, my successive expeditions over several seasons to the confluence of the Snake and Grande Ronde rivers, involving extensive baiting, have produced only brief, possible sightings, and no immature stages, despite hours of searching. If the species is indeed shifting northward with warming, its numbers must yet be very small. And if they do occur in Washington and Oregon at all, it will be among the basalt canyons of the Snake River or tributaries in or near Hells Canyon, where tough stands of hackberry take root in the lava flows and rimrock above the shoreline, and run up side gullies and gorges. Someone may eventually catch or photograph it. Until then, it lies in the realm of probable cryptofauna, somewhere near Bigfoot.

VARIATION Highly variable overall; generally warmer brown in the W. **HOST PLANTS** Netleaf hackberry (*Celtis reticulata*), other hackberries toward the E. Adults in this mostly tropical subfamily seldom if ever nectar but visit scat, carrion, and particularly noxious baits such as rotting fruit, fish, fowl, and shrimp paste left out in the sun. **ON THE WING** E spring to L fall in one to three broods, to the S and E. Putative sightings in WA in September and October, indicating one or two generations here if correct. Eggs overwinter. Populations fluctuate dramatically from year to year. **HABITAT AND**

Subfamily Nymphalinae: Spiny Brushfoots

The brushfoots of subfamily Nymphalinae are considered "smart" butterflies—perceptive, highly responsive, agile, and adaptable. Individuals learn, responding quickly to altered circumstances such as nectar supply or availability of a formerly occupied territory. Their larvae have branched spines, rare in the Lepidoptera, and their chrysalides are thorny.

Tribe Nymphalini: True Nymphs

Scott characterizes the immatures of this tribe thus: "As much variety in shapes occurs among the Nymphalini as in all other butterflies and skippers combined." The adults, too, cover a wide gamut, from dark with bright bands to mottled with oranges, pinks, and reds, and from brilliant to cryptic, often in the same butterfly. The anglewings and tortoiseshells are superb leaf- and bark-mimics, while the ladies and buckeyes flash impressive eyespots. The chrysalides, frequently gilded or silvered, hang upside-down and often bear sharp horns. Spiny caterpillars feed on dicots including broadleaved trees and shrubs, mallows, thistles, and stinging nettles. These are called "true" nymphs because they are closest to *Nymphalis*, the type genus for the family Nymphalidae. Some true nymphs, mostly anglewings and tortoiseshells and sometimes ladies, overwinter as adults in cold climes. Hibernation

Green Anglewing, male

makes them superbly suited for the boreal zones, and the colder the winter, the better. As told in his classic 1951 Peterson field guide to eastern butterflies, A. B. Klots found six species on the wing in a New England dump one warm winter's day.

California Tortoiseshell (*Nymphalis californica*) outbreak

Genus *Vanessa*: Ladies

The butterflies with the pretty names are as colorful as you might expect. All four display strong flighty behavior and share certain characteristics of marking and life history; but they are quite easily distinguished if you see the right field marks. Each has a slightly different ground color of orange, and differing shapes, bars, and eyespots. In all ladies, the antennae are long and brown, leading to strikingly white-tipped black knobs. These ladies shift about a good deal over the landscape, and they exhibit population expansions and contractions, some of them sensational. One of only two indigenous butterflies in Hawaii is the largest lady, the lava-red Kamehameha, though the American and Painted Ladies and Red Admirable are now also established there.

American Lady *Vanessa virginiensis* (DRURY) 1773

"America balsamita"
Aka American Painted Lady, Hunter's Butterfly, Virginia Lady, *Cynthia*

RECOGNITION < 2.25 in. **Citrus-orange above, rose-pink on VFW.** FW falcate (clipped, concave below tip). HW elongated, **outer third of VHW has two very large eyespots.** Edge smooth, checked black above, lined by orange crescents. Black bars and blotches on DFW, white spots in black apex and one in orange, subapical bar pale orange (female) or white (male). DHW clear orange with little black, submarginal row of five eyespots smudged black with dark blue centers. VFW tips violet with small eyespots; submarginal sky-blue crescents on all four wings rimmed by lilac line. VHW complexly patterned in pink, black, olive, and cream patches and spider-webbing. Eyespots ringed in black, yellow, and olive, centers iridescent blue-capped black; VHW eyespots small on other ladies. Common Buckeye's big spots are on VFW, Common Wood Nymph lacks colors. **VARIATION** Most is in size and intensity of color. Males and females are similar in this and all vanessas, females often larger, paler. **HOST PLANTS** Pearly everlasting (*Anaphalis margaritacea*) and pussytoes (*Antennaria*) are preferred, also cudweed (*Gnaphalium*), sagebrush (*Artemisia*), burdock (*Arctium*), thistles (*Cirsium*), sometimes other composites, lupines, mallows, and nettles. Nectars on buddleia, cosmos, asters, tithonia, pearly everlasting, Canada thistle, dahlias, cat's ear (*Hypochaeris radicata*), and showy stonecrop (*Hylotelephium spectabile*). **ON THE WING** M April to E November, peak in August-September. Usually single-brooded here, prob. as an annual migrant; thought to survive winters as an adult elsewhere, but overwintering rare in the NW: one winter adult record (February, Wahkiakum Co., WA, Thea Pyle). **HABITAT AND RANGE** Fields, parks, gardens, canyons; many sunny, flowery kinds of places across most of the continent, incl. CA and anywhere in OR; sightings in WA rare, mostly in S cos, but records increasing in the N, to S BC and ID panhandle. Males hilltop and branch-perch—and will pursue rufous hummingbirds that pretend to the same territory.

Dorsal

Ventral

The American Lady, which we in (at least northern) Cascadia all too rarely see, is one of the loveliest American butterflies. The line of northern residency is obscure and undoubtedly plastic. It is not clear to me why it is common in New England and much of the rest of the country but quite rare in the Rockies and Cascadia. I have found it common only twice in the region, at Sherars Bridge on the Deschutes River in Oregon, and in the recovering blast zone at Johnston Ridge, Mt. St. Helens National Volcanic Monument, Washington, where pearly everlasting was thickly clothing the post-eruptive pumice barrens. Half the Washington records are from my butterfly garden in Wahkiakum County, all in late summer or fall. The dearth of spring records in Cascadia argues against them hibernating here, as they do elsewhere. The old name Hunter's Butterfly (*V. huntera*) honored John Hunter (1728–1793), the foremost physiologist and surgeon in Britain in his time, buried in Westminster Abbey near Charles Darwin. Hunter was also a great naturalist; his studies appropriately included animal hibernation, which adaptation *V. virginiensis* may be evolving.

Painted Lady   *Vanessa cardui* (LINNAEUS) 1758

Sweden
Aka Cosmopolite, Cosmopolitan Butterfly, Thistle Butterfly,
Painted Beauty, Cynthia of the Thistle, *Cynthia*

RECOGNITION < 3 in. **Salmon- to coral-orange above with black blotches forming a cat's-eye pattern.** FW drawn out, **not falcate,** tips white-spotted black. From DFW costa, **subapical bar always white,** not orange as in West Coast Lady. Basal brown, with silky hairs, invades much of DHW; submarginal row of five eyespots small, black, or with tiny blue centers, blue bar on tornus. VFW pinky orange, white dots at tip. **VHW olive-tan webbed with chalky veins and patches,** rimmed from outside in with scalloped yellow line, cream line, blue crescents, then **five small bright blue eyespots ringed black and yellow.**

VARIATION Individuals vary with generation, experience, and age. Spring migrants often small, pale, and beat, fresh summer brood large, bright, and richly painted. Any regional variation is swamped, as this butterfly mixes up its genes all over the world. **HOST PLANTS** Thistles (*Carduus, Cirsium*) preferred, though everything from mallows to lupines to potatoes

Dorsal

will do when thistles are unavailable. Nectars on buddleia, rabbitbrush, white and mauve Canada thistle, helianthella, Douglas aster, red clover, chokecherry, red osier dogwood, mints, and many others; common dandelion is a particular favorite in spring, zinnias in summer. **ON THE WING** E March to E November, peaks in May, July, and September. As many broods as it can fit in from spring arrival to autumn departure or death, usually two or three. Nabokov: "Despite statements to the contrary, does not hibernate anywhere in the Old World where there is frost," same likely true in New World: possesses no winter diapause. We have one mild January record in Clatsop

Co., OR (Mike Patterson), and its tolerable range may be extending N with warming. **HABITAT AND RANGE** All kinds, sea level to high peaks, deserts to forest gaps. Ranges throughout the vegetated world. Ubiquitous in PNW some years, absent in others.

Normally fast and flighty, Painted Ladies perch at length just after eclosing or in afternoon cloud, slowly fanning their wings for long, easy looks. They hilltop and consort around tall trees in the waning sun, basking in the last rays and then taking off like a bat to tussle mid-air, again and again, far into dusk. At home on every continent but Antarctica, *V. cardui* was, until recent, warming years, the only butterfly in Iceland. Hence, Cosmopolitan Butterfly: if it isn't there, it is bound to show up some day soon. Resident in southern latitudes, it builds up in springs of favorable rains and nectar, then bursts out. Given decent travel weather, additional quick broods flood the northern states, and few habitats are without their Painted Ladies all summer long. In a good year, highways may close from their sheer, greasy numbers (e.g., I-5 in southern California in 1992). Such outbreaks come only periodically; other years you might look in vain. The final brood of Painted Ladies largely dies off in the fall, but there is published support for a southward flight of some proportion. Mike Patterson observed them along with California Tortoiseshells coursing southward offshore, crossing the Columbia River mouth, in September 2000. We do not know whether many autumn Painted Ladies make it back to the resident populations in the Southwest. Commercial kits sold for classroom and wedding releases have obscured our picture of their natural movements. The tatty, vaguely orange scraps of early spring arrivals seem an entirely different species from the iridescent, Dayglo orange ones with Paul Newman–blue eyespots that appear in deer season, briefly, before dying off or departing.

Ventral

West Coast Lady   *Vanessa annabella* (FIELD) 1971

"1st val. W. Arroyo Verde Pk," Ventura, CA
Aka Western Painted Lady, *Cynthia, carye*

RECOGNITION
< 2 in. Smaller than other ladies. **Citrus-orange above with blue spots.** FW truncate, margins lightly scalloped, effect enhanced by checkered fringe. Black-mottled DFW, white spots in black tip; **subapical bar always orange**, not white as on Painted Lady. DHW clear orange with little black, **submarginal row of four bright blue eyespots** crisply black-ringed. VFW similar, paler, pinker; VHW **marbled crazily** with dark brown, tan, and cream, with white arrowhead in cell.

Ventral eyespots obscure, unlike *V. cardui*, two middle ones dark peacock-blue with thin rims. **VARIATION** Nothing consistent. This species produces numerous aberrations in which the usual pattern and colors are strongly altered. Several of these in CA were given form names but are of no current standing. **HOST PLANTS** Preferred are mallows, incl. streambank globe-mallow (*Iliamna rivularis*), cheeseweed (*Malva neglecta*), hollyhock (*Alcea rosea*), *Sida, Sidalcea*, and *Sphaeralcea*; nettles are also accepted. Nectars on composites (Douglas aster, gum-weed, marigold, mums, goldenrod), periwinkle, toothwort, and spreading dogbane. **ON THE WING** E March to M November, peaks in May, August, and October. One to three generations

Dorsal

Ventral

in WA and OR, increasing to S, continuous in sub-freezing CA. I have found active larvae in mid-winter at Cascade Head on the C OR coast; overwintering uncertain elsewhere in PNW. **HABITAT AND RANGE** Meadows, marshes, montane valleys, gardens, vacant lots, flower-beds in the city. Resident along W Coast, Baja, Mexico; disperses E through W states to KS, S Canada. May be encountered anywhere in Cascadia, expected nowhere. How far N adults are resident vs. recolonizing in spring is unknown, and no doubt varies with severity of season.

That this species shows up more consistently in spring than any other vanessid leads me to believe it is the hardiest and best candidate for regular resident status in our region. Wherever this lady normally keeps the winter, it is likely to expand as the climate ameliorates. Sightings increase inland as the season progresses; in eastern Colorado, I never saw it until fall. Though *V. annabella* doesn't engage in the impressive mass movements of *V. cardui*, nor become as numerous, it clearly moves about and is more consistently present year to year. This is one of those insects, like the Gray Hairstreak and the Western White, that always slightly surprises, no matter how well you know it shouldn't. I have seen it next to the coast in Neah Bay, in my front yard in the rainforest, in subalpine meadows, and on potted mums in Seattle's Pioneer Square. This species was long conflated with the South American Lady, *V. carye*; but William Field of the Smithsonian Institution, revising the group in 1971, concluded that this was indeed a different, and nameless, species. Leaving the Red Admirable in *Vanessa*, he elevated the old genus *Cynthia* for the other ladies, and renamed the present species for his young daughter, Annabella. Though sunk back into the synonymy, *Cynthia* contributes to the lovely sequence of names applied over time to this lady. The common name is certainly appropriate: it is found near the western seaside more than any other vanessid.

Red Admirable   *Vanessa atalanta* (LINNAEUS) 1758

Sweden
Aka Red Admiral, Alderman, Nettle Butterfly

RECOGNITION < 2.5 in. **Coal-black above with white apical "lady spots" and solid scarlet, vermilion, or orange bands** right across FW top to bottom, and rimming DHW to blue spots at inner angle. Hairy and browner near base. VHW mottled blackish brown, variegated with blue, green, violet, and chestnut; white spots near VFW tip and HW leading edge, bright blue marbling between red and white bars, on base and costa. **VARIATION** N Am admirables have a larger subapical white bar than European, but show no consistent geographic variation here. Later broods larger and more intensely colored. **HOST PLANTS** Stinging nettle (*Urtica dioica*) almost exclusively; also false nettle (*Boehmeria*) and pellitory (*Parietaria*), all Urticaceae. Despite published reports of hop (*Humulus lupulus*, Cannabaceae) being used, David James recorded no larvae on the plants in eight years of intensive monitoring and found that third-instar larvae refused hops and died. I've recorded nectaring on *Ageratum*, hyssop, bull thistle, oxeye daisy, garden chrysanthemums and dahlias, rabbitbrush, buddleia, fireweed, Puget Sound gumweed (*Grindelia integrifolia*), aphid honeydew, willow sap, and rotting pears and apples. **ON THE WING** Records in every month, mostly May to October, peaks in July

Dorsal

Ventral

and September. Number of broods and latitude of adult overwintering depend on severity of season. **HABITAT AND RANGE** Infiltrates N in summer throughout the N hemisphere to NWT, Hudson Bay, Scandinavia. May be found in any open habitat in country, city, field, forest edge, park, garden, or glade. Every Cascadian county, sea level to mountaintops, extending N with warming, but often absent or uncommon.

Though perhaps first and most widely known as the Red Admiral, *Vanessa atalanta* is actually a lady and has nothing to do with the admirals of the genus *Limenitis*. As E. B. Ford pointed out, the name Red Admirable goes back over 250 years. Nabokov strongly preferred it, considering Red Admiral an expression of "vulgar parlance." The species was conflated with the true admirals because they both have epaulette-like bands across black wings. Alderman, another traditional name, refers to ancient British ceremonial garb. Nettle Butterfly is an even older English title: Winston Churchill struggled with his estate gardeners to keep nettles for this butterfly, famous for landing on people in gardens, sometimes the same person day after day. In Greek mythology, Atalanta was a virgin huntress, beloved by Meleager, Melanion, and others whom she beat at footraces and other athletics. Our Atalanta dashes about wildly well into dusk, chasing other ladies and mounting the treetops before roosting for the night. It is, in Nabokov's words, "a most frolicsome fly . . . with an almost frightening imitation of conscious play." Or they will visit flowers and fruits

in the garden, sipping for hours. I once observed a dozen or so Admirables besotted all afternoon on rotten fallen pears behind an English pub; nor am I likely to forget the first ones I ever saw, in a country barnyard in Colorado. Like its relative, the Painted Lady, the Red Admirable migrates north in spring and, to a lesser degree, south in fall. Some years see many arrive and increase, other years next to nil. Occasionally, and increasingly, adults overwinter in England and here in the Pacific Northwest. Jon Pelham once found a winter adult among a cluster of Milbert's Tortoiseshells in a Seattle warehouse. Admirables are seen deep into fall each year; but the paucity of early spring sightings suggests that successful Cascadian overwintering is still an uncommon occurrence, a result of mild winters. Climate change will usher a concordant response in this and other summer-migrant butterflies.

Dorsal

Genera *Aglais* and *Nymphalis*: Tortoiseshells

The tortoiseshells are much like anglewings, and closely related, but more robust and much simpler to identify. Anglewings have concave trailing edges to the forewings; on tortoiseshells these are straight, and the wings are broader overall. Only the Compton Tortoiseshell has a silver comma below as all the anglewings have. Two of our species also occur in the Old World, one flies continent-wide, and the fourth is essentially a westerner. Two have the classic black-mottled orange pattern of polished sea-turtle shell, two look very different. Tortoiseshells are famous for highly fluctuating numbers from year to year and expansive migrations that are sometimes downright spectacular.

Milbert's Tortoiseshell *Aglais milberti* (GODART) 1819

Nr Philadelphia, PA
Aka Nettle Tortoiseshell, Fire-rim Tortoiseshell, *Nymphalis*

RECOGNITION < 2 in. Above and below, **inner half dark, outer light**. Dorsal base dark chocolate with two orange bars in FW cells like cats' eyes. **Dorsum rimmed by fiery yellow, then orange bands**, submarginal row of blue crescents, and brown border with scalloped edge. Two-tone below, umber inner/light brown outer, finely striated darker, blue border crescents all around wings. Nothing like it. **VARIATION** The E N Am type has a much broader orange band, almost subsuming the yellow. The W *A. m. subpallida*, described from Custer Co.,

Ventral

CO, averages broader yellow bands. Like most nymphs, these vary a lot within populations and between seasons in size and intensity of color. **HOST PLANTS** Nettles (*Urtica*) exclusively. Spring awakeners nectar on garden flowers, cuckooflower (*Cardamine pratensis*), coltsfoot, and sap flows; summer hatchers visit dandelion, pearly everlasting, Douglas and other asters, helianthella and other mountain sunflowers. **ON THE WING** M January to L October, peaks in April–June, July-August, but like any tortoiseshell or anglewing, it might be seen in flight any day of the year. Two or three broods, adults overwinter. **HABITAT AND RANGE** Wherever nettles grow in lowlands and mtns, esp. along watercourses, and later in the season up among alpine talus slopes and seeps. Thrives in parks and gardens where nettles are tolerated. Most of N Am (except S, lower MW, and far N) and everywhere in Cascadia with enough moisture and nitrogen for nettles.

This species shares its taste for nettles with another in the genus, the European Small Tortoiseshell. In 1898 Holland wrote of it, "This pretty little fly ranges from the mountains of West Virginia northward to Nova Scotia and Newfoundland, thence westward to the Pacific"—still about right. As the weather turns cooler, they bask beside the first nettle shoots, only marginally easier to approach than Mourning Cloaks that came out with them. Often the first butterfly spotted as winter thinks about trading places with spring, a February Milbert's might nectar on dooryard snowdrops before anything else opens; then probe fruitlessly at nectarless crocuses, before moving on to heathers. Gliding by, it shows its yellow bands to

Dorsal

be very pale already, from five or six months of life. *A. milberti* practices a noticeable altitudinal migration each year, breeding up in the lowlands before flying uphill and colonizing the high mountains by midsummer. The large, dazzling individuals one finds in a subalpine meadow on Mt. Hood or Mt. Rainier look very little like their small, drab parents emerging from a hollow tree in the lowlands in March to mate, find nettles, and lay eggs for the summer generation.

Compton Tortoiseshell   *Nymphalis l-album* (ESPER) 1781

Vienna, Austria
Aka Comma Tortoiseshell, Compton's Tortoiseshell, False Comma, *Roddia, vau-album, j-album*

RECOGNITION < 3 in. **Large.** Broad, irregular wings, basally **rich rusty** above with large yellow submarginal spots, white spot near FW tip, the whole **heavily blotched with big black spots.** Yellowish border and submarginal band above, with black rim in-between; longish blunt tails; **small silver V or J ("comma") in** VHW cell. **Conspicuous white bar drops from** DHW costa, between black spots, lacking in *N. californica*; below, bark shades of gray, tan, and brown, striated and dotted, darker on the inner half, white-frosted on the outer, blue-green submarginal band following V edge; pattern much bolder in males than females. **VARIATION** W Comptons are supposed to have the ventral gray of the E form replaced by warm brown and gray-brown mottling, more discretely patterned; but the two looks blend across boreal Canada. Defining ssp. in such a vagabond can be a fool's errand. **HOST PLANTS** Birches, willows, aspens. Nectars on rotting fruits and sap. **ON THE WING** E March to M October, peaks

Female, ventral

Male, ventral

in April and August. Single-brooded, adults overwinter. **HABITAT AND RANGE** Clearings in boreal woods; anywhere during dispersal, often along streams ("wooded rivercourses and sun-spangled canyons," wrote Dornfeld). Holarctic; in N Am, breeds along US-Canada border, disperses N into AK, S into MW, Rockies, PNW. Common in interior BC, irregular but not rare in NE WA/ID, thinning out in NE OR. N Cascades, Okanogan Highlands, Selkirks, Blue-Wallowa Mtns; not recorded in Olympics. Disjunct records on Vancouver Is. and in Klamath Co., OR.

The biggest of our true nymphs is also the rarest. The species possesses a vast circumpolar range, and spreads out unpredictably, sometimes for long distances. Numbers vacillate, with clusters of sightings some years. They never build up to the huge outbreaks of the next species, but Kondla twice in ten years witnessed "population blooms in the Pend-d'Oreille valley, as common as or more common than *N. californica*." We know they overwinter, but the hibernaculi are seldom seen; Noble Proctor found a cluster spending the winter in a mountaintop antenna shelter. Rapid and obvious on the wing, Compton Tortoiseshell will fold its wings and abruptly alight against bark

or dead leaves: an autumn-colored butterfly disappearing into an autumn landscape. Morton Elrod, in his 1906 *Butterflies of Montana*, wrote: "It was interesting to see them remain in the same quiet attitude on the top rail of a fence or the skinned log in the cabin, where they were very conspicuous, as on the trunk of a tree where they were invisible." Make sure you see the white spot on the hind wing, or the silver-white comma, as false records often come in from wishful watchers of big old California Tortoiseshells. The current and alternate Latin epithets, *vau-*, *j-*, or *l-album*, all refer to that whitish V, J, or L mark, which has led many to consider the species a link between anglewings and tortoiseshells—an idea supported by DNA research. The common name was bestowed by English naturalist Philip Henry Gosse (1810–1888). Clerking in a Newfoundland whaler's office, he "beguiled the tedium of his life by investigations into natural history" (*Brittanica*), such as finding this butterfly in Compton, Quebec.

Dorsal

California Tortoiseshell   *Nymphalis californica* (BOISDUVAL) 1852

N Fk Feather R. Cyn, Plumas Co., CA
Aka Western Tortoiseshell

RECOGNITION < 2.5 in. **Rich russet over most of upperside** with yellow highlights; hoary-edged, rough-lobed black border has short rounded tails. DFW has big black spots on leading edges and small ones in middle; DHW clear orange with black spot on leading edge yellow-edged, no prominent white bar as on Compton. **Underside striated brown bark tones with variable white marbling**, darker inner half, lighter outer. Teal-blue submarginal line parallels ragged edge. **VARIATION** Individually variable, but no consistent regional differences warranting ssp. Some individuals blackish beneath, some brown, some frosty. **HOST**

PLANTS Rhamnaceae: snowbrush ceanothus (*Ceanothus velutinus*) and deerbrush (*C. integerrimus*), redstem ceanothus (*C. sanguineus*) in BC. Occasionally uses ornamental ceanothus on the W side in migration. Nectars on fir needle exudate in spring, on fir sap and various fruits in fall. Summer adults nectar on the hosts and other plants, and puddle. **ON THE WING** L January to M December, peaks in April and August, any day of the year possible. One or two generations, adults overwinter. **HABITAT AND RANGE** May appear in any situation during migration, incl. parks and gardens. Mountain slopes, canyons, riversides,

Dorsal

passes and peaks, lanes and shorelines at lower elevations. Regular breeding range incl. Rockies, Cascades-Sierra axis, and related ranges. From there, moves out over most of W and E to Great Lakes and MO. Recorded from nearly every Cascadian county and district, but breeds mostly in the montane *Ceanothus* zone.

This enigmatic butterfly builds up its numbers for years until it bursts out in phenomenal mass movements. In such years California Tortoiseshells show up a long way from their points of nativity, defoliating deerbrush and snowbrush ceanothus over wide areas and becoming the most abundant butterfly along the mountain streams and roads: thousands on the wing, and more thousands of larvae on the ragged ceanothus. Then their numbers crash, and scarcely will this species be seen in the entire region for the next several years. Some

recent peaks have lasted for several summers, moving around the mountains. In such years, the species routinely masses around the Cascade passes and peaks, and we receive many reports of multitudes of migrating "monarchs" at high elevations. What happens after the mass migrations? California Torts don't die right away; many nectar and hibernate where they fetch up in the fall, so you can find winter individuals far from the breeding grounds. Others just keep moving. Mike Patterson has observed mass movements at the mouth of the Columbia River, one to three Cal Torts per minute passing the South Jetty with Painted Ladies and Red Admirables, destination unknown. Are these irruptions controlled by crowding, host plant degradation, climate, or a combination of factors? Is the collapse related to starvation or parasite buildup? We have much to learn.

Ventral

Dorsal, pre-hibernation

Dorsal, post-hibernation

Mourning Cloak   *Nymphalis antiopa* LINNAEUS 1758

Sweden
Aka Camberwell Beauty (UK), Grand Surprise, Antiopa, Spiny Elm Caterpillar, *Vanessa*

RECOGNITION > 3 in. Large. **Dark chocolate with maroon tones to reddish brown above, ragged edge bordered by yellow** (fading to cream), flecked with violet, lined inside by bright blue spots. **Cindery black beneath** with fine pattern of black and blue, blue-green chevrons inside pale border. Males and females alike, general for the genus. Admirals are banded with white mid-wing. Unmistakable. **VARIATION** Coarsely consistent throughout the N hemisphere, Cloaks everywhere are covered by Linnaeus' Swedish original in Pelham's *Catalogue*. However, names have been proposed to capture geographic variation; for example, "*N. a. hyperborea*" for those in extreme N AK, distinctly reddish above, smaller with broader yellow borders and bigger, more violet-blue spots. Some people who feel the type is restricted to the Old World employ "*N. a. lintnerii*" for bigger, blacker, more southerly N Am cloaks. **HOST PLANTS** Willows favored, but also alders, birches, maples, poplars, hackberries, elms, roses, apples, spiraea, and other broadleaved trees and shrubs. Nectars on currants and asters and visits sap and fallen fruits. Warren notes that adults often feed at flowers after hibernation but seldom before. I have watched them nectaring at pussy willows in Germany and cherry laurels in SW WA. **ON THE WING** E February to M October, peaks in April, June, August-September. One brood likely throughout N Cascadia, two possible farther S. Adults overwinter. **HABITAT AND RANGE** All sorts of riparian corridors, oases, glades, groves, and woodsy dells, as well as parks, yards, and city squares, AK to Venezuela, Lapland and Siberia to Spain and China. All Cascadia except wettest coastal rainforest, more abundant in drier regimes E of the Cascades.

From the great array of color descriptors in different books, variation is clearly in the eye of the beholder when it comes to this butterfly, which is anything but lugubrious in spite of its name. The Mourning Cloak was described in a poem by Nabokov as "velvety-black, with a warm tint of ripe plum" through which "gleams a row of cornflower-azure grains." I like to characterize it as dark chocolate, blueberries, and French vanilla. One of our most easily recognized animals, it catches the eye of many who wouldn't ordinarily notice butterflies. By using diverse host plants, it claims an immense range. Not that Cloaks are always

Ventral

common: if numerous in the Cascades, they are scarce and special near the coast; common in Anchorage and Mexico City; uncommon in Seattle and Portland. Like many other butterflies, it has a problem with cool and damp: dry cold is more hospitable for winter survival. The consummate hibernator (and aestivator through hot summers), the species also migrates to an uncertain degree. Following the Monarch migration in September, I watched many Mourning Cloaks heading south over Dixie Butte, out of Oregon's Blue Mountains. Few butterflies are so cryptic at rest yet so conspicuous in flight. It makes an audible "click" when taking wing, perhaps startling predators that come too close. Once in flight, it is extremely difficult to net, invariably veering over the rim at the last moment. Males fly out from perches vigorously at passing females, intruding males, or anything else. Charles Remington found that if a male in possession of a good sunny post is removed,

another will take its place, day after day. The Mourning Cloak is as intelligent and adept as butterflies get, as well as tough. When you try to reconcile that tatty, pallid survivor of bitter winter with the bright, fresh ones of fall, you might be seeing one of the oldest butterflies: with luck, a strong female could live a full year as an adult. Antiope, after all, was an Amazon. The shocking contrast between the drab underside and the gorgeous dorsum gave rise to an old name, the Grand Surprise. As for Mourning Cloak, it is said to come from the disparity between the many young widows and the few still able-bodied men after the Civil War. After a year of mourning, the bereaved young woman could wear purple as well as her black widow's weeds. It became fashionable to wear a purple cloak with a hem of yellow silk, perhaps intended to draw the eye toward the shapely and erotically charged ankle, and give the wearer a jump on the competition.

Genus *Polygonia*: Anglewings and Commas

These robust brushfoots share with *Nymphalis* their camouflaged underside, brightly colored upperside, and hibernation in the adult stage. They are classic startle-coloration strategists—blending into their background when perched, flashing bright bird-startling colors when flushed. *Polygonia* ("many-angled") refers to the ragged-looking, uneven edges of the wings, which led to the traditional common name for the group, the anglewings. The trailing edge of the forewings are concavely curved, unlike in tortoiseshells. They also possess a silvered mark on the ventral hindwing (one eastern species, *P. comma*, is called the Comma because of this; another, its comma opposed by a dot, is the Question Mark, *P.*

interrogationis). The names of this interesting and beautiful group of butterflies have varied as much as their appearance. Some have traditionally been called commas (Green, Gray, Hoary), some anglewings (Oreas, Silenus, Satyr), some neither (Question Mark, Hop Merchant). Others, named for rustic deities, can go with or without a second moniker (Satyr, Zephyr, Faun). Here, we go with two commas and two anglewings, both traditional. Anglewings are sexually dimorphic and highly variable, so the proper identification of individuals ranges from simple to challenging. Each has its own distinctive field marks, however, which, when carefully observed, should enable you to identify most individuals.

Satyr Anglewing   *Polygonia satyrus* (W. H. EDWARDS) 1869

Vic. Empire, Clear Creek Co., CO
Aka The Satyr, Satyr Comma (NABA), Hop Butterfly, Golden Anglewing

RECOGNITION < 2.25 in. Female's upperside bright golden orange or tawny, male's bright russet, both with black blotches across the inner half incl. a **prominent triangular black spot in the DHW cell** (as opposed to *P. gracilis*); rusty brown DHW margin vague to obsolete, eclipsed by diffuse yellow patches. Female light warm tan to purplish taupe below, male two-tone brown, warm chestnut and maple; **both sexes bearing fine dark striations parallel with the body, mixed with little black dots. Comma usually curved and barbed at both ends**, like a narrow letter C with serifs. Brighter orange above than Variegated Fritillary. **VARIATION** *P. s. neomarsyas*, described from Salmon Meadows, Okanogan Co., WA, is applied to all Cascadian populations. It is seen as being darker above and below than the Colorado type. But there is in-region variation, too: the species definitely trends darker near the coast, with chocolate highlights, and paler in the interior, a sandy willow-tan below, esp. in males. Sexual dimorphism marks this and all anglewings, with females often displaying a bland pattern

Male, dorsal

Male, ventral

the last one overwintering as adults. **HABITAT AND RANGE** Canyons, woodsy glades, streams and canals, edges and parks. Most of Canada, Great Lakes states, all the W, and all Cascadia.

In warmer, drier, hotter, and built-up environments, this is the commonest (and often the only) anglewing present. It persists in cities where nettles grow at the edges of woods in parks and vacant lots. People denigrate native nettles as noxious weeds due to their sharp sting. By eliminating them, they exclude three of our most attractive butterflies that might otherwise be common even in town: Satyr Anglewing, Red Admirable, and Milbert's Tortoiseshell. Male anglewings take up posts in sunny spots, from which they fly out at potential mates or intruding males; I watched one Satyr Anglewing pursue a Western Tiger Swallowtail from 5 to 50 feet in the air on the University of Washington campus. This species should not be confused with members of the subfamily Satyrinae, both named for the satyrs of Greek mythology, the Pan-like, randy goat-men of wild places. The 19th-century lepidopterists who gave these names were fond of comparing butterflies to rustic beings who shared their favored habitats, both on a permanent bacchanal.

and purplish monotone cast. **HOST PLANTS** Stinging nettle (*Urtica dioica*); in CO, hops are also used. Nectars in spring on sap from willow wounds, as well as lilacs, cherry laurels, cascara, and other early blossoms; in summer on thistle. In my experience, will visit apple-plum-nectarine fruit bait. **ON THE WING** L February to E November, peaks in April and July–September. One N or two S generations,

---

Oreas Anglewing   *Polygonia oreas* (W. H. EDWARDS) 1869

"mountains of northern California"
Aka Oreas Comma (NABA), Silenus Anglewing, Dark Gray Anglewing, *progne*

RECOGNITION < 2 in. **Most ragged and lobed margin** of all, effect enhanced by **broken yellow border-line**. Submarginal spots are discrete, bright orange chevrons.

Male HW notably hairy. **Underside cinder-black**, frosted outer third, esp. VFW tips; female not as black below. **Comma doubly-pointed**, oblique, like a seagull in flight or silver clock-hands at four o'clock. If gray below, lacks the blue-green or chartreuse submarginal spots of Hoary or Green Commas. **VARIATION** In the really black *P. o. silenus*, the chestnut-brown dorsal margin invades disc, runs into black spots, leaving

Female, dorsal

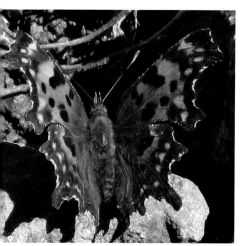

Male, dorsal

Female, ventral

orange DHW "islands." This ssp., described from Portland, occupies the W half of Cascadia except in SW OR, where smaller, paler adults resemble the CA type, grayer beneath, all the aforementioned traits understated, brighter orange with larger marginal gold spots on DFW. *P. o. threatfuli*, from Vernon, BC, is less lobed, similar to *P. o. silenus* above, much lighter and grayer below; somewhat blacker in the Blue-Wallowa Mtns. **HOST PLANTS** Currants, incl. *Ribes divaricatum* (straggly gooseberry), *R. lacustre* (swamp gooseberry), *R. rubrum* (cultivated red currant). Nectars on cherry laurel, Asian pear, pearly everlasting, and other early- and late-season flowers. **ON THE WING** L February to M September, peaks in May and July–September. Single-brooded, adults overwinter. **HABITAT AND RANGE** Deep forest fringe (esp. old growth), streams, clearings, subalpine meadows, ravines. W Coast: C CA to S BC; W OR and W WA, Cascades, mtns from SE BC S through WA and ID to NE OR; isolated in Great Basin and CO Rockies. *P. o. silenus* in Cascades and *P. o. threatfuli* in the Blue-Wallowa Mtns and NE WA/SE BC.

Some authors have lumped this species with *P. progne* (Gray Comma), but molecular work shows they are not conspecific. When you see an anglewing whose underside is nearly solid black, like charcoal-bark, you've got this butterfly. By far the rarest of our anglewings, it has fewer than 100 records for Washington, many of them very old. Oreas can turn up here and there from sea level to alpine heights, but it always comes as a surprise and almost always as a loner. I have seen perfectly black individuals from below Paradise on Mt. Rainier, the Long Beach Peninsula, and the head of Lake Chelan. Grayer Okanogan and Pend Oreille individuals approach *P. progne* (Gray Comma), a species of the East and the Canadian Shield, and some sources lump the two species. The Sileni were part men, part horses, and pursuers of nymphs; the Oreads were those lovely mountain nymphs. They meet up in this species. Progne (or Procne) was a Greek woman in the royal house of Athens who, after tragic doings, was changed into a nightingale, and her sister Philomela a swallow, by the gods. When you encounter these elusive and seductive creatures in the deepwood, their fanciful names and mythic connotations seem suddenly suitable.

Hoary Comma   *Polygonia gracilis* (GROTE & ROBINSON) 1867

Mt. Washington, NH
Aka Hoary Anglewing, *zephyrus*

RECOGNITION 2 in. Rich rusty gold above with black blotches, DHW lacks strong black triangle in cell; **submarginal yellow spots usually large, nebulous, overwhelming dark border and invading disc. Cool ashen gray or brownish gray below,** somewhat two-tone, contrast greater in male. Light part finely striated with black; submarginal **broken row of non-iridescent chartreuse-green spots** with black centers below (not blue-green). **Comma an unbarred curve,** like a sans-serif L. Shares Satyr Anglewing's flared yellow patches in the border but is gray below to the Satyr's warm tan. **VARIATION** *P. g. zephyrus* (Zephyr Anglewing), described from Virginia City, NV, occupies our whole area. To the N and E in Canada, perhaps blending into NE WA, may be found the type, which

Male, ventral

Dorsal

Male, ventral

is smaller and darker, more two-toned below, with smaller, more pronounced marginal spots. **HOST PLANTS** *Rhododendron menziesii* ssp. *glabellum*; white azalea (*R. albiflorum*) and various currants (*Ribes aureum*, *R. cereum*, *R. viscosissimum*, *R. lacustre*) in WA. Nectars on asters and rabbitbrush in summer and fall; visits willow sap at sapsucker holes, along with rufous hummingbirds, in spring. **ON THE WING** E February to M October, peaks in May and August. One or two generations, depending on altitude and latitude, prior to overwintering. Could be seen any day of the year. **HABITAT AND RANGE** The highest-altitude anglewing— usually mountainous habitats above 3,000 feet, along streams, roads, and trails; meadows among forest; occasionally at lower elevations along watercourses. Canada, AK, W states; all Cascadian mtns but spotty in Coast Ranges.

P. g. zephyrus, being one of the fleetest butterflies in the West, is properly named after Zephyrus, the Greek god of the west wind. It is usually very common in the mountains, while singletons make up the majority of lowland records, suggesting a degree of wandering. The Zephyr Anglewing appears as soon as the snow melts, and sometimes before; in the Salmo River country of Washington's northeast corner, I watched dozens settling and basking on sunstruck snowbanks. *P. g. zephyrus* was considered a full species until 1986, when James A. Scott folded it into the Hoary Comma, based on similar genitalia, ranges that fit together, and perceived intergrading. True genetic compatibility is hard to call in such cases. As Klots wrote in his classic 1951 Peterson field guide to eastern butterflies, intermediate specimens also occur between the Hoary Comma and the Gray Comma (*P. progne*). Authors often invoke "intergrading" to support their hunches, when what they actually see may simply be parallel variation with no evidence of interbreeding. But Scott based his lump largely on genitalia, where *progne/oreas* really do differ from *gracilis/zephyrus*. *Gracilis* means "graceful."

Green Comma   *Polygonia faunus* (W. H. EDWARDS) 1862

Catskill Mtns, NY
Aka Faun, Faun Anglewing, Faunus Anglewing, Green Anglewing

RECOGNITION < 2 in. Very ragged borders, esp. males. Upperside deep rich russet basally, tawny outward, and broad dark margin (black when fresh, fades brown) of DHW broken by **distinct, small yellow spots**. Thoracic hairs may refract green. Sexually dimorphic: female highly variable below, ashy gray to plain muddy brown, but markings almost always washed-out; male usually two-toned grayish brown and barklike, both with **two submarginal rows of blue-green iridescent spots below**. Blue reduced on females, as is the comma, which is curved, barbed or not, whitish and inconspicuous. **VARIATION** *P. f. rusticus*, named from Big Trees, Calaveras Co., CA, properly covers the species throughout the region. It is indeed rusty above, browner below and larger than *P. f. hylas* from Berthoud Pass, CO, which extends N through the Rockies and runs grayer. Presumably the two ssp. blend in ID. Larger individuals in the OR Coast Range may begin the long blend toward *P. f. fulvescens*, a tawnier insect of the CA redwoods. More closely related to European than other American anglewings, according to DNA studies. **HOST PLANTS** Usually Salicaceae (willows, birches, aspen, alders), incl. *Betula papyrifera* (paper birch) in BC

Males, dorsal

Male, dorsal

(Guppy); *Rhododendron albiflorum* (Pelham); *R. occidentale* in CA. Nectars heavily on Douglas asters and other fall flowers and fallen fruits, and sucks on scat of berry-eaters and aphid honeydew. In spring, emerging hibernants visit willow and other sap, then mountain ash blossom and mud. **ON THE WING** L February to L September, peaks in April-May, August. Single-brooded, adults overwinter. **HABITAT AND RANGE** Sun-dappled forest glades and corridors, particularly coniferous; woodsy gardens; groves of trees in grassland. A band across the provinces Atlantic to Pacific, S in Rockies and Cascades/Sierra. All Cascadia but drier basins, E deserts, and WA coastal strip.

Male, ventral

Faunus was a grandson of Saturn, a sort of Latin Pan, who spoke prophecy to men in their dreams; his namesakes, the fauns, were Roman satyrs. This faun, our Green Comma, hangs out mostly at low to middle elevations, often around clearings, paths, and edges of woodlands. Sometimes in company with other anglewings, especially Hoary Commas, it appears in great numbers about waterfalls, picnic grounds, or favorite glades in the autumn, prior to hibernation. A good place to see this kind of spectacle is Deception Falls above the Skykomish River on the Stevens Pass Highway in Washington. One October, hundreds sipped aphid honeydew at the trunks of noble fir saplings in Gifford Pinchot National Forest. Higher up, in the Indian Heaven Wilderness, they crowded purple patches of huckleberry scat left by coyotes, bears, and birds. Another summer, the Kettle River Range of northeastern Washington was positively crowded with bright Green Commas tanking up on mountain flowers before hibernation. Like all anglewings, these flit rapidly in and out of sight, often coming back to the same spot. Then you might see the same ones, a little worse for wear, on the earliest sunny days of the new year.

Tribe Junoniini: Buckeyes

Common Buckeye   *Junonia coenia* HÜBNER 1822
"United States"
Aka *Precis, lavinia*

RECOGNITION < 2.5 in. Warm light or dark brown above with two bright orange bars across FW cell above and below, cream patch basal from drawn-out FW tips, and **three or four small to massive eyespots along outer upperside**. FW eyespots yellow-ringed, black with blue pupils; HW eyespots yellow- and black-rimmed with black, blue, and orchid centers. VFW like DFW but duller, VHW rosy-brown or tan, crescent-marked. **VARIATION** As its epithet suggests, the W *J. c. grisea* is routinely grayer below than the E type, with broader orange bands on DHW. Seasonal polyphenism is great, varying from small and dull to large and bright, the former more migratory and the latter more sedentary (Scott). **HOST PLANTS** A wide variety of scrophs and plantains (penstemons, paintbrushes, veronicas, monkeyflowers), most of which possess the iridoid glycosides adults may require for courtship purposes. Nectars from many sources, incl. owl's-claws (*Hymenoxys hoopesii*) and, behind a Sonoma

Dorsal

Male, ventral

winery, the sweet spilled ullage of crushed grapes. **ON THE WING** L May to L October, peaks in June, August. Two broods likely in S OR, one in N, adults overwinter. **HABITAT AND RANGE** Disturbed, weedy habitats, "unkempt fields" (Dornfeld), roadsides, watercourses, gullies, washes, ditches, and other open areas. Resident along US coasts, throughout S and borderlands, and Mexico, summer visitor through much of US to S Canada. Warren considers it not a permanent breeding resident in OR. S, C, rarely N OR and ID. Photographed twice in WA in 2015, in Lincoln and Benton cos, apparently expanding N with warming.

Nothing else has this species' big bright eyespots, unless it be the American Lady or the female Common Wood Nymph; but the overall patterns, colors, and arrangements of their ocelli are very different. Eyespots this large and near the body are more likely to be fright-devices than targets for birds; once in Santa Barbara, I watched a Say's phoebe fly out repeatedly from its own post to catch and eat Common Buckeyes, wings and all. Like the ladies, this is a warm-weather butterfly that spends the winter far south of its usual summer range. While the spring's northward movement consists of a broad, dispersed wave with rapid, hop-scotching generations, autumn finds Common Buckeyes pouring southward in impressive streams along the East Coast. They are probably year-round residents along the southern Oregon coast, spring migrants and summer breeders in the northern counties. Sharp-eyed watchers—John Baumann and Jane Kabel—have recently confirmed the first two Washington records. The Common Buckeye loves to bask in muddy swales and dart back and forth over grassy flats—"an expert dodger," as Klots called it. Many attest to the species' wariness, nervous flight, and readiness to engage Carolina grasshoppers and other intruders. Such behavior, referred to as "pugnacious" (Dornfeld) and "quarrelsome" (Klots), may simply be courtship pursuit or males repelling other males from good perches.

Tribe Melitaeini: Checkers and Crescents

The checkers (or checkerspots) and crescents (or crescentspots) are surely among our comeliest and most confusing butterflies. To a beginner, they all tend to look alike, and not that different from the lesser fritillaries. In fact, the different groups and most species are quite distinctive; the problem is that they are extremely variable, and their variation overlaps. With practice and close attention, however, most individuals—especially considered in the context of their habitat, locality, flight time, behavior, and plant associations—can be pinned down reliably, so to speak. Some 200 melitaeines live in the northern hemisphere and the Neotropics, about 45 species in North America. Unlike most butterflies, they lay their eggs in clusters of a few (crescents) or many (checkers) on the host plant stems or leaves, and the larvae feed communally in a silken tent until going their own way after winter diapause. We have three genera. *Chlosyne* species have shorter, squarer wings than other checkers, often concavely curved. Checkers of *Euphydryas* are longer-winged, convexly curved, and really are frequently checkerboard-patterned. *Phyciodes* holds the smaller, orange crescents, so named for pearly lunar spots on their ventral margins.

Snowberry Checkerspots on coyote scat

Genus *Euphydryas*: Checkerspots

These "shapely dryads" (as the Latin genus translates), with their striking patterns of rich reds, blacks, yellows, and whites, are among our most numerous and attractive summer butterflies. The following accounts of the Northwest species owe much to Jon Pelham, who has studied them in depth for many years. In our region, these five species show dependable genitalic differences, though two of them tend to run together elsewhere; and while their many subspecies are distinctive on average, they vary greatly. To add to the puzzle, subspecies of different species often vary in parallel ways from place to place. Be resigned: some individuals cannot be assigned to species in the field with confidence and, rather than trying to torture out identifications with inadequate tools or knowledge, may honorably be listed simply as "checkerspot sp." Their bright checkered colors arose to advertise their distastefulness to birds—a quality acquired from chemicals in the plants their caterpillars consume, transferred to pupae and adults, which flaunt it with their slow and easy ("indolent") flight pattern.

Gillett's Checkerspot *Euphydryas gillettii* (BARNES) 1897

Yellowstone Park, WY
Aka Yellowstone Checkerspot, Gillette's Checker, *Hypodryas*

THREATENED IN BC

RECOGNITION < 2 in. Black above with red and white cell-spots and **broad red submarginal bands** lined on both sides by white spots. Beneath, alternating bands of cream and bright brick-red with black veins and borders of spotbands. Wings long, FW tips somewhat pointed. No other checker looks red-banded. Red Admirable larger, shaped differently, has no checkering. **VARIATION** No discriminable geographic variation over the small, narrowly endemic range. **HOST PLANTS** Chiefly the honeysuckle family (Caprifoliaceae), most commonly black twinberry (*Lonicera involucrata*) and red twinberry (*L. utahensis*). Other documented hosts incl. snowberry, veronica, valerian, ram's horn, paintbrush, and (in the lab) plantain. Important nectar sources incl. asters, wild geraniums, and groundsels (*Senecio*). **ON THE WING** L May to L July, peak in E July. One generation, young larvae overwinter. Males active above vegetation, females near the ground (and thus more often

Male, dorsal

Male, ventral

seen). **HABITAT AND RANGE** Damp meadows and glades among coniferous forest, subalpine meadows in WY; esp. on S-facing slopes. N Rockies from SW WY into AB, extreme SE BC, N and SW ID panhandle, NE OR (Wallowa Co.).

This most distinctive western checkerspot is barely known from Cascadia. Stan Jewett found it at Priest Lake in the Idaho panhandle, and it has also turned up in Nez Perce, Lewis, and Washington counties. In Oregon, longtime Northwest lepidopterist Harold Rice discovered it near Summit Ridge (Hat Point area of Wallowa County, above Hells Canyon) in 2003, and Andy Warren confirmed it in 2004, but not many

were present. It should be sought in the Salmo-Priest Wilderness of extreme northeastern Washington, near Mt. Spokane, and elsewhere in moister mountains along the Idaho-Washington-Oregon frontiers. Research by Ernest Williams suggests that colonies of this Northern Rockies endemic may be prone to extinction through plant succession in the absence of fire in the Greater Yellowstone Ecosystem. Barnes named this species for his wife, Charlotte Gillett, and her family, and Higgins grouped it with the similar Palearctic butterfly, *E. maturna*, in his subgenus *Hypodryas*. Birds avoid its red signal, but spiders and moose contribute to mortality rates, directly and indirectly.

Edith's Checkerspot   *Euphydryas editha* (BOISDUVAL) 1852

Twin Peaks, San Francisco Co., CA
Aka Whulge Checkerspot, Ridge Checkerspot, *Occidryas*

E. E. TAYLORI ENDANGERED IN BC, ENDANGERED IN WA, CRITICALLY IMPERILED IN OR, FEDERALLY ENDANGERED

RECOGNITION < 2.25 in. **Proportionate mix of black, orange, and white above**; *E. anicia* is often redder, *E. chalcedona* and *E. colon* usually blacker overall. Wings more rounded than *E. anicia*'s. Abdomen usually black, red-ringed, not white-dotted as on the other species. On VFW, second white spotband from margin runs down to the trailing edge, lowest spot inwardly rimmed in black. On VHW the **"editha line" runs through the red or orange postmedian**

Male, ventral

band, splitting off little orange sub-spots.
VARIATION Great over its W range, with 26 ssp.
Distinctive are *E. e. colonia*, described from
Mt. Hood, and *E. e. taylori*, described from
Victoria, BC. *E. e. colonia*, our largest ssp. and
a real moose of a checkerspot, is magnificently
colored with much broad red almost pushing
out the submarginal yellow bands. It frequents
the Olympics and the W Cascades from
the Wenatchee Mtns to the Siskiyous (*E.
e. edithana*, smaller and paler, takes over

in the E Cascades). Taylor's Checkerspot
(*E. e. taylori*), rather small and the darkest
of our ssp., has plenty of black separating
the spotbands, and the stubbiest, roundest
wings. Extirpated from most of its former
range incl. Vancouver Is., it occupies just a
few remaining sites in the Salish Lowlands,
the Willamette Valley, and on Denman Is., BC.
For more details, see Warren (2005), Pelham
(2008), and butterfliesofamerica.com. **HOST
PLANTS** Various, depending on what the
season and moisture have made available,
and often different before and after diapause.
Records here incl. paintbrushes (five species)
and few-flowered blue-eyed Mary (*Collinsia
sparsiflora*); exserted paintbrush (*Castilleja
exserta*) and other snapdragon-family plants
(penstemons, monkeyflowers) are reported
elsewhere. Individual populations specialize:
Taylor's Checkerspots now use mostly
introduced plantains (*Plantago lanceolata*
and *P. major*) as well as native plantain (*P.
maritima*), harsh paintbrush (*C. hispida*),
and the increasingly rare golden paintbrush
(*C. levisecta*). Nectars on camas, stonecrop,
phacelia, pussypaws, spring gold and other

Male, dorsal

Male, dorsal

composites, strawberry, and others. **ON THE WING** E April to L August, peak in E May (low), July (high), generally in vernal conditions. A single generation, larvae overwinter. **HABITAT AND RANGE** Post-glacial grassland/mounded prairie, coastal bluffs and islands on rain-shadow turf, alpine, subalpine, and arctic-alpine meadows, sage-steppe hills. E slope of Rockies to Pacific, N Baja to S BC, most of montane

Cascadia except the WA-OR Coast Range and Selkirks; rare in Salish, Willamette Lowlands.

While checkerspots can be vexingly similar and variable, we are lucky that our Northwest subspecies all share a reliable clue at least to their species identification in the "editha line." Edith's Checkerspot is arguably the most-studied, best-known non-economic

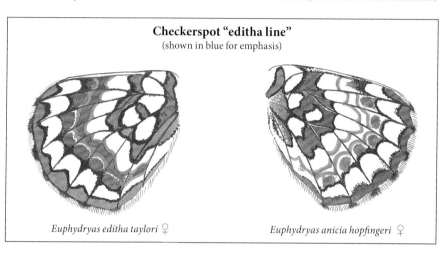

Checkerspot "editha line"
(shown in blue for emphasis)

Euphydryas editha taylori ♀   *Euphydryas anicia hopfingeri* ♀

Female, ventral (ssp. *taylori*)

Pair, dorsal (ssp. *taylori*)

insect in North America, thanks to 50 years of investigations out of Paul Ehrlich's lab at Stanford University. Among the findings, populations are prone to fluctuations and to flickering out in stressed and fragmented habitats, a trend exacerbated by global warming. Montane subspecies are robust, except where resource extraction is too intense. But *E. e. taylori* (Taylor's Checkerspot), narrowly restricted to the western Washington-Oregon lowlands, was nearly lost in British Columbia, the Willamette Valley, and Puget Trough. It went from "swarms" (Dornfeld 1980) to presumed extinct in the Willamette Valley until rediscovered by Andy Warren in 1999. Extensive habitat survey, followed by intensive management on Joint Base Lewis-McChord (Washington), Fitton Green Open Space (Oregon), Denman Island Provincial Park and Protected Area (British Columbia), and other remnant prairies, along with captive breeding and release, is turning things around. The largest colony I have ever seen remains to be revisited on a private island in the San Juans. Unlike for Edith's Copper, the identity of the Edith for whom Boisduval named this species is lost to us.

Chalcedona Checkerspot　*Euphydryas chalcedona* (DOUBLEDAY) 1847

Vic. San Francisco, CA
Aka Variable Checkerspot (NABA), Western Checkerspot, Snowberry Checkerspot, Colon Checkerspot, *Occidryas, colon*

RECOGNITION
< 2.75 in. Large in S part of range. Variable and similar to other checkers, but **blacker** than Anicia and Edith's, with **numerous white to cream-colored dots** inward and red-orange spots toward the margins. **Submarginal spots on DHW larger, paler** than *E. colon*'s dots. VHW with red and yellow alternating bands and red border. VHW **"editha line" runs through yellow,** not red. **Wings more rounded** than *E. anicia*, but not always obviously so. **VARIATION** The checkerspots of SW OR considered to be this species resemble the type, with increased pale markings below and narrower red bands on VHW. Other populations discussed in Warren (2005) are ascribed to *E. colon* by Pelham (2008). **HOST PLANTS** Penstemons, monkeyflowers, paintbrushes, and other figworts (Scrophulariaceae) in SW OR. Visits

Male, ventral

many mountain flowers and mud. **ON THE WING** L April to E August, depending on altitude. One generation, larvae diapause. **HABITAT AND RANGE** Chaparral, "along roadsides, small streams, and in clearings" (Dornfeld). Canyons and mtns through most of CA; into S OR in Coos, Curry, Jackson, Josephine, and SW Douglas cos.

The ancient Greek town of Chalcedon faced Byzantium across the Bosphorus. As well as this butterfly, it gave its name to the mineral chalcedony, and to Chalcedonian Christians, one of whom was Anicia Juliana, poet, princess, and granddaughter of Valentinian III. Now Chalcedon and Anicia are twin species of checkerspots that some authors lump and call the Variable Checkerspot (a redundancy if ever there was one!), while others treat them as two. Nor is it certain whether the split of *E. chalcedona* and *E. colon* is appropriate, and they are often considered conspecific. The two seem to meet and perform as different species in southern Oregon, though some have the genitalia of one but the wing pattern of the other. Both differ biologically from *E. anicia* wherever they meet in the Pacific Northwest. The arrangement here follows Pelham's *Catalogue*. Chalcedona is one of the most abundant butterflies in California, unlike Edith's Checkerspot, with several of its races at risk. Comstock wrote, "Its flight is indolent, with frequent stops for refreshment on a variety of flowers, hence it is easily captured." Those I watched cruising the brushy trails near the Purisima Mission were the largest checkerspots I've ever seen, nearly three inches across.

Male, dorsal

Snowberry Checkerspot   *Euphydryas colon* (W. H. EDWARDS) 1881

Kalama, Cowlitz Co., WA
Aka Colon Checkerspot, Chalcedona Checkerspot, Variable Checkerspot, *Occidryas, chalcedona*

RECOGNITION < 2.25 in. Variable and similar to other checkers, but usually **blacker** than Anicia and Edith's. Above, most populations **coal-black with numerous cream-colored dots** inward and often red-orange spots toward the margins. **DHW submarginal spotband of small dots,** larger in *E. chalcedona.* VFW reddish orange with buff or yellow spotbands, VHW with red and yellow alternating bands and red border. VHW **"editha line" runs through yellow,** not red. **Wings more rounded** than *E. anicia,* but not always obviously. Mormon Metalmark and Field Crescent smaller, no red below; Gillett's Checkerspot has broad red bands. **VARIATION** Particularly red in the C Cascades from Lewis Co. to King Co. on the W slope and from Yakima, Kittitas, and barely into Chelan cos on the E slope of the Cascades. Blacker N, S, and E of there, blackest in OR W of the Cascade crest and Skamania and Cowlitz cos

in SW WA (the type). East of the crest, smaller and paler, with more light spots on DHW and black spots on VHW, and narrower red bands below (*E. c. wallacensis*). The very dusky Olympic Mountain populations are referable to *E. c. svihlae.* Further variation shown at butterfliesofamerica.com and discussed by Warren (2005) under *E. chalcedona.* **HOST PLANTS** Largely snowberries (*Symphoricarpos albus, S. oreophilus, S. mollis*) and figworts (Scrophulariaceae), incl. *Penstemon fruticosus, P. rupicola, P. davidsonii,* and *P. procerus;* also *Castilleja, Plantago, Lonicera,* and a one-time, post-diapause record on common mullein (*Verbascum thapsus*). Larry Everson found it feeding on Oregon ash (*Fraxinus latifolia*) in Clackamas Co., OR. Nectars on bistort, pearly everlasting, yellow composites, and other flowers; males hilltop and visit mud with equal ardor. **ON THE WING** L April to L

Female, dorsal

Male, dorsal

August, peak in June (low), July-August (high). Larvae diapause in various instars and can aestivate for years if necessary. **HABITAT AND RANGE** Chaparral, open woods, mountain canyons and streamsides, roadsides, meadows, slopes, and snowberry thickets. Cascadia E to the Continental Divide, S through CA and moister parts of the intermountain W, N Mexico to S Canada, disjunct in YT and AK. Olympics, Selkirks, S Cascades and Blues in WA, S BC, W ID, and much of OR except driest basins and coastal fringe.

See previous species for discussion of its split from this one, the blackest checker-spot. The straight species, described from

Male, ventral

Male, dorsal

downstream of Mt. St. Helens, thrived on subalpine slopes of the volcano prior to its 1980 eruption and is now recolonizing the revegetating ashfields; you can find this black and buff type flying in the hundreds along with hundreds more of the big, red *E. editha colonia* on Silver Star Mountain in Clark County, Washington, an easy hike near Portland. Both taxa flock among the steep flowerfields there in July, and country roadsides around Medical Lake, west of Spokane, still abound in the subspecies named for (and from) Wallace, Idaho. Pelham named *E. c. svihlae* for a pioneering lepidopterist couple in the Olympics. This taxon has a different habitat and host plant from populations across Puget Sound, feeding on small-flowered penstemon (*Penstemon procerus*), the only scroph present, and skipping snowberries; it may share a common origin with an extinct lowland population on Vancouver Island.

Puddle party

Anicia Checkerspot   *Euphydryas anicia* (E. DOUBLEDAY) 1847

Rock Lake, nr Jasper, AB
Aka Paintbrush Checkerspot, Variable Checkerspot (NABA), *E. chalcedona*, *Occidryas*

RECOGNITION < 2.25 in. Highly variable. Where ssp. vary in parallel with those of *E. editha*, *E. anicia* tends to have **longer, more pointed wings** and **more red, incl. two cell bars top and bottom**. Above, checkered with some combination of brick-red, black, and white or cream. Below, red-orange VFW, VHW with alternating bands of red and white or cream, second white band on VFW not reaching the trailing edge. The black line between the median light band and the postmedian red band **("editha line") runs through the cream**, not through the red.

VARIATION Several of the 24 ssp. occur across Cascadia, varying within and between populations in ways both subtle and dramatic. Some are mostly red or orange above, others all white and black with almost no red. Small dark forms hilltop on high summits; pale, larger checkers occupy low, dry country; and richer-colored races fly in between. Their names—*hopfingeri*,

Female, dorsal

Male, ventral

Male, dorsal

veazieae, bakeri, macyi—amount to a who's who of pioneer NW collectors. For more details, see Warren (2005) and butterfliesofamerica.com. **HOST PLANTS** Largely figworts (Scrophulariaceae), incl. species of paintbrush (*Castilleja*) and various penstemons, esp. *Penstemon davidsonii*, *P. fruticosus*, *P. deustus*, *P. procerus*, *P. confertus*, *P. glandulosus*, *P. pruinosus*, *P. speciosus*, and *P. gairdneri*; Pelham records *E. a. veazieae* on *Castilleja thompsonii* and *Collinsia sparsiflora*. Nectars on a wide range of flowers incl. chokecherry, dogbane, penstemons, and stonecrop; visits mud. **ON THE WING** M March to M August, peak in May–July. A single generation, third-instar larvae diapause. In very cold or dry zones, they reportedly hibernate or aestivate through repeated seasons. **HABITAT AND RANGE** A great array of drier settings from sage-steppe and desert to high grasslands, lithosols to conifer forest edges and openings, gullies, canyons, alpine ridges, and mountain summits. Much of intermountain US and Canada W of the Great Plains, AK to Mexico. E Cascadia generally, W of crest only in Whatcom Co., WA, nr Mt. Baker; absent from Olympics and Mt. Rainier.

No other western butterfly is both more widespread and more geographically plastic in its appearance. Anicia Checkerspots can occur in great numbers in a favorable year, swarming the purple penstemons in June both for nectaring and egg-laying. High-country Anicia is one of our most abundant and reliable hilltoppers. Mountain peaks and ridgetop promontories, on sunny days from soon after snowmelt until the early frosts of autumn, flicker with the orangey forms of checkerspot males "jousting," basking, and fighting the wind as they seek females. These high-elevation individuals are darker and smaller than the Anicias of the lowlands. Some lists subsume Anicia within *E. chalcedona*. While they may indeed act like a single species in parts of California or Nevada, these taxa certainly behave as two separate and often sympatric species in the Pacific Northwest.

Male, dorsal

Leanira Checkerspot   *Chlosyne leanira* (C. & R. FELDER) 1860

N Fk Feather R. Cyn, Plumas Co., CA
Aka California Checkerspot, Paintbrush Checkerspot, *Thessalia*

RECOGNITION
< 2 in. Orange or black above with yellow spots. VFW orange with yellow spots, VHW pale yellow with black veins and basal network, **ventrum crossed ¾-out by a continuous large black chain with white spots inside the links**. **VARIATION**
The type enters Curry and W Josephine cos in extreme SW OR via Siskiyou Co., CA. C. *l. oregonensis*, described from Mt. Ashland, Jackson Co., OR, is black above with rows of small, pale yellow spots; the DFW may have red spots near the tip, more and larger in the

Male, ventral (ssp. *oregonensis*)

Male, dorsal (ssp. *oregonensis*)

female. It is found on the Siskiyou Plateau and SW OR in N Josephine, S Douglas, Jackson, and Klamath cos. *C. l. basinensis*, described from the Sweetwater Mtns, Lyon Co., NV, occupies roughly the basin of pluvial Lake Lahontan. Entering SE OR from Lake Co. to Malheur Co., it displays orange above traversed by pale yellow spots, black submarginal line, veins, and basal clouding; below, the black chain is lighter. **HOST PLANTS** Paintbrush (*Castilleja*), incl. *C. angustifolia* var. *dubia* for *C. l. basinensis*. Bird's-beak (*Cordylanthus*) reported elsewhere. Nectars on yellow daisies and others. **ON THE WING** E May to L July, peak in June. One generation, third-instar larvae diapause. **HABITAT AND RANGE** Isolated colonies of the type "lie in hidden canyons and on hillsides beside small streams in the Siskiyous and Cascadian foothills" (Dornfeld). The lowland sort flies on desert hills and flats, gullies, roads, and serpentine outcrops, often associated with limestone elsewhere. CA and Great Basin, Siskiyous, S Cascades, and SE OR.

Pretty Leanira presents several faces that intermix over a wide area of the arid West, and we see two or three of the well-differentiated outliers. As Dornfeld put it, "This elegant species can be recognized immediately by the unique color and pattern of the underside." The striking black circlets against an off-white background present a pattern like no other. I encountered the butterfly for the first time above the Illinois River at the edge of the Kalmiopsis Wilderness, where males basked and sipped at the road earth and nectared unperturbedly at yellow composites. This was when Siskiyou iris and azalea were blooming nearby, and Sternitsky's Parnassian and Gorgon Coppers were on the wing.

Male specimen (ssp. *basinensis*)

Gorgone Checkerspot *Chlosyne gorgone* (HÜBNER) 1810

"Burke Co., in southern GA"
Aka Gorgone Crescentspot, Hübner's Crescentspot, Great
Plains Checkerspot, *Microtia, Charidryas*

RECOGNITION
< 1.75 in. Crescent-like above, orange-banded and black in about equal amounts, with small pale orange crescents in the black border, prominent black dot-row on the DHW, and checkered fringes. VFW orange inner, mottled brown and white outer. VHW olive-brown crossed by white crescents, chevrons, and bars, **edged by a black line zigzagging across the disc before taking a final, long zag toward abdomen. VARIATION** ID individuals, like those from most of the species' range, are referable to *C. g. carlota*, described from Cedar Hill, Jefferson Co., MO, which is bigger and paler than the SE type. **HOST PLANTS** Composites, incl. common sunflower (*Helianthus annuus*). Nectars on goldenrod and other summer flowers. **ON THE WING** L April to M July, peak in May-June. Single brood in N, third-instar larvae overwinter. **HABITAT AND RANGE** Stream and canal banks, roadsides, meadows, old fields,

Male, dorsal

open forests. Chiefly C states and provinces, with outliers in SE, NE, and W MT/ID.

This is a long shot for inclusion in the Cascadian fauna, based on only a few records from southwestern Idaho that have not been repeated in recent years. Opler believes the Idaho and Utah colonies have disappeared. Occurrences outside the main central stronghold of the species might represent accidental agricultural introductions. However, this is a species whose numbers fluctuate dramatically. In eastern Colorado, it was one of the most abundant butterflies in the 1960s. As annual butterfly counts show, even where the habitat has not been noticeably altered and sunflowers remain abundant, it is now scarce there. Elsewhere, it has increased. We should be vigilant for the species all along the eastern edge of Oregon and Washington

Male, ventral

Hoffmann's Checkerspot *Chlosyne hoffmanni* (BEHR) 1863

Gold Lake, Sierra Co., CA
Aka Aster Checkerspot, Pacific Checkerspot, *Charidryas*

SPECIAL CONCERN IN BC

RECOGNITION
< 1.75 in. Upperside banded orange and yellow-orange with brown-black checkering. Median band yellower, contrasting

with bright orange postmedian row, running together with it on the DFW. **Basal third of DHW, and inner DFW below cell, black with little orange.** Underside similar to *C. palla*, spots in postmedian red band may be **longer, more rectangular, less crescentic**; wings squarer. Where it occurs with or near *C. palla* (OR) and *C. acastus* (WA, OR), field marks usually separate them; when they look alike, genitalic dissection will

Female, dorsal (ssp. *manchada*)

Female, dorsal (ssp. *manchada*)

Male, dorsal (ssp. *segregata*)

Female, ventral (ssp. *manchada*)

two-toned look. Both ssp. are variable: the type colony of *C. h. manchada* in the C Cascades is oranger than the more melanic population farther S around Mt. Adams. **HOST PLANTS** Western showy aster (*Eurybia conspicua*) is a known PNW host at lower elevations, Cascade aster (*Eucephalus ledophyllus*) higher up. Nectars on various daisies, pussytoes, and other flowers; males puddle. **ON THE WING** E May to E September, peak in July. One generation, half-grown larvae diapause. **HABITAT AND RANGE** Moist montane meadows, canyons, streamsides, and coniferous forest clearings, generally 1,000 to 7,000 feet. A tight distribution up and down the Cascades and Sierras, from Manning Provincial Park (BC) through Mt. Rainier NP (WA), Crater Lake NP and Cascade-Siskiyou National Monument (OR), on down to Yosemite and Sequoia NPs (CA).

This is a Cascadian butterfly in the narrowest sense, shared with California. It flies up and down the range, both sides of the crest, selected for traits that elegantly meet its needs of life exactly here. It splits up a broad range of area, habitats, and altitudes with the similar but ecologically distinct Northern and Sagebrush Checkerspots. *Chlosyne* checkers found in the high, damp Cascades north of the Columbia may safely be attributed to *C. hoffmanni*, while *C. palla* lives in the Okanogan Highlands, the Pend Oreille, and the Blue Mountains. Hoffmann's Checkerspot is one of the more numerous butterflies on the Chumstick Mountain (Chelan County, Washington) Fourth of July Butterfly Count, males gathering in the muddy road by the score along with Boisduval's Blues and Lorquin's Admirals.

do so. **VARIATION** Fairly straightforward, for once among the checkerspots. *C. h. segregata*, described from Crater Lake, Klamath Co., OR, occupies the OR Cascades and Siskiyous. In it, the inner spotband above is relatively wide, light, and contrasting. *C. h. manchada*, described from Tumwater Cyn, Chelan Co., WA, flies in the Cascades of WA and S BC. It differs in having a narrower, less distinct and very light inner spotband on the upperside, but more dark scaling basally, creating a more contrasty,

Sagebrush Checkerspot   *Chlosyne acastus* (W. H. EDWARDS) 1874

Provo Cyn, Utah Co., UT
Aka Acastus Checkerspot

RECOGNITION < 1.75 in. **Males pale orange above**, females yellowish, orange, or blackish, with variable black bars, crescents, and checks. Sometimes orange bands alternate with yellow or red rows, giving a two-toned effect. **Very light chalky white underside** (*C. palla* is pale yellow, basally infused with orange on VFW), banded red-orange alternating with **large oval spots, flat or pearly white, sharply crescent-edged in black.** Submarginal white band has five white-centered orange circles. **VARIATION** Desert populations paler and more washed-out than those farther N and uphill. Different populations also vary in wing shape and intensity of banding. Many females, esp. but not only in *C. a. sterope* (Palouse Checkerspot) of E WA and OR, are black-and-white checked with no orange above, and these are often

confused with dark females of *C. palla*. Studies to clarify the species' status and relationships are ongoing; for more details, see Warren (2005) and butterfliesofamerica.com. **HOST PLANTS** Incl. green rabbitbrush (*Chrysothamnus viscidiflorus*), gray rabbitbrush (*Ericameria nauseosa*), *Erigeron linearis* (desert yellow fleabane), and asters in the genus *Dieteria*. I observed the black-and-white females drinking from chokecherry flowers along a hot May roadside in the Methow Valley. **ON THE WING** L April to L June, peak in May. A single flight N of CA-AZ; a bivoltine population occurs in S AB, according to Norbert Kondla. **HABITAT AND RANGE** Sage desert, pinyon-juniper savannah, in washes, gulches, canyons, badlands, and brushy flats, mostly below 5,000 feet in SE deserts and below 3,000 feet in Columbia and Snake basins

Female, dorsal

Female, dorsal

Male, dorsal

(Warren). Palouse Checkerspots haunt wooded canyons, coulees, and drier foothills. Arid W, Sonora to AB, SK, Dakotas, NE. In Cascadia, E OR basinlands, E-C and SE WA, SW ID.

This species and the Northern Checkerspot have been a source of much confusion over the years; indeed, *C. a. sterope*, light-colored except for many females being black (not orange) on top, was considered a subspecies of *C. palla* until Jon Pelham recognized it as belonging to *C. acastus*. Sagebrush Checkerspots usually fly earlier and lower than Northerns, but they overlap in various locations. While a given specimen of the Sagebrush Checkerspot might fall within the range of variation of the Northern Checkerspot, a series of them will look distinctly paler overall and much whiter below. All

Male, ventral

our desert-country checkerspots need much additional attention. This one, as Dornfeld wrote, "is essentially a butterfly of the arid land overgrown with sage and rabbitbrush"—not a situation conducive to most butterflies, who prefer moist mountain meadows on the whole.

Northern Checkerspot   *Chlosyne palla* (BOISDUVAL) 1852

N Fk Feather R. Cyn, Plumas Co., CA
Aka Pale Checkerspot, Creamy Checkerspot, *Microtia, Charidryas*

RECOGNITION < 1.75 in. Upperside bright or pale red-orange, banded with lighter orange and lined and barred with black; or (females) blackish, banded with yellow-buff spots. **Orange forms usually have little black on the innermost upperside**, unlike Hoffmann's. Underside alternates bands of brick-red and yellow, cream, or milk, defined by fine black lines, the submarginal yellowish band enclosing orange, white-pupilled spots. Sagebrush Check-

Female, ventral

Female, dorsal

erspot pale, shiny below, Hoffmann's is darker basally. Some females are dimorphic, appearing black like *C. acastus sterope*. Where sympatric, *C. palla* has **pronounced orange flush on VFW**, reduced or absent on *C. a. sterope*. **VARIATION** *C. palla* displays a wide array of variation in Cascadia, with five phenotypically distinct

Male, dorsal

groups recognized in OR, and more in WA; they all intersect in BC. For details, see Warren (2005) and butterfliesofamerica.com. **HOST PLANTS** Pelham reared post-diapause larvae on western meadow aster (*Symphyotrichum campestre*). Nectars frequently on composites, umbels, buckwheats, waterleaf, yarrow, chokecherry, and thimbleberry. **ON THE WING** L March to E August, peak in June-July. One generation, larvae overwinter. **HABITAT AND RANGE** Occupies meadows, forest paths, roadsides, and edges, streambanks, aspen glades, gullies, serpentine outcrops, and clearings. Intermountain W, S BC to S CA and CO. NE, SE WA, most of montane OR and ID, unrecorded from basinland except E Columbia Gorge.

This highly variable butterfly with its broad range has attracted many names and interpretations. The pale orange checkers hunkering in the wind to nectar at Gray's

Male (left) and female (right), dorsal

lomatium in a chilly April coulee and the richly colored ones visiting asters in a high meadow of the Blue Mountains in July were all considered Northerns, but now we know that the former in the chilly coulees are *C. acastus*. It is a strange fact that the Rockies type flows north and west into Washington's eastern mountains, but not the Cascades, so that the main range is devoid of the species. This is a boon for identifying the similar, wholly montane Hoffmann's Checkerspot in the state, whereas in the Oregon Cascades, both occur together and must be carefully picked one from the other. The species reappears, heading south, in the Simcoe Hills and eastern Columbia Gorge.

Rockslide Checkerspot   *Chlosyne damoetas* (SKINNER) 1902

Flat Tops in Garfield Co., CO

Aka Whitney's Checkerspot, Damoetas Checkerspot, Pearly Checkerspot, Alpine Checkerspot, *Microtia, Charidryas, gabbii, whitneyi, malcolmi*

RECOGNITION
< 1.5 in. **Dull orange above with a greasy sheen (more so in Rockies)** checkered with blurred brown and black, dusky at base, females more contrasty. Below, alternating bands of dull orange and dirty white, black-veined and zigzagged. **Looks worn when it is fresh**. At high altitude. **VARIATION** *C. d. altalus*, described from Mt. McLean, nr Lillooet, BC, is paler and less greasy and rubbed-looking than the Rocky Mtn type. **HOST PLANTS** Fleabanes (*Erigeron*) are employed both for nectar and larval host. **ON THE WING** E July to L August, peak in E August, in the short arctic-alpine midsummer, the timing of which varies with the snowmelt. They hibernate half-grown and may spend one or more winters in diapause, depending upon weather cues. **HABITAT AND RANGE** Arctic-alpine talus slopes. Occurs patchily in the N Rockies, from S CO to Canada in C AB, BC.

I include the Rockslide Checkerspot because it occurs not far east of our territory in southwestern Montana and not far north at Mt. McLean in British Columbia. Perhaps it will turn up on some isolated alpine

Male, dorsal

Male, ventral

rockslide in Washington, Oregon, or Idaho. In Colorado, it flits among the boulders above timberline in company with the Lustrous Copper and the Magdalena Alpine, the three species forming a virtual guild of

rockslide specialist butterflies. Damoetas was a shepherd in the *Aeneid*; when Skinner named it, the butterfly shared the alpine with vast herds of sheep that have since mercifully diminished.

California Crescent   *Phyciodes orseis* W. H. EDWARDS 1871

Mt. St. Helena, Napa Co., CA
Aka Orseis Crescentspot, Long-wing Crescent

RECOGNITION < 1.5 in. In SW OR, upperside blackish brown with orange spotting, like the Field Crescent; underside tan-and-cream like the Mylitta Crescent with crescent in brown marginal patch. **Indented (concave) FW margin, black spots on trailing and outer edges of vFW, mostly orange antennal knobs.** Farther E, smaller and paler, other traits similar.

VARIATION According to Warren, two distinct populations exist in OR. Those in Josephine, Jackson, and SW Klamath cos are the type; they are "large and very dark, above and below." A second, poorly known form (Warren calls them *P. o.* nr. *herlani*) occurs in the Warner Mtns of Modoc Co., CA, and Lake Co., OR. "These adults are smaller and considerably paler above

Female, dorsal

Female (top) and male (bottom), dorsal

and below," and resemble both Mylitta and Field Crescents in different respects. **HOST PLANTS** Thistles such as *Cirsium cymosum* in Siskiyous, *C. andersonii* farther S. Since the California, Pale, and Mylitta Crescents all feed on thistles as larvae, it is intriguing that the first two should be rare, and the third extremely common. Clearly the larval host is not the only limiting factor. **ON THE WING** E April to E July, peak in May-June. One brood, larvae overwinter. **HABITAT AND RANGE** Very local. Roadsides, dry hillsides, montane canyons, streamsides in the Siskiyou Mtns and SW Cascades, Warners; CA Inner Coast Ranges, N and E Sierra Nevada.

The California Crescent is a narrow endemic globally, occurring only in southern Cascadia and two sections of the Sierra Nevada; a third population, from San Francisco north to Napa, apparently is extinct. Few butterfly enthusiasts have seen the species, which therefore has an air of mystery to it. This may result in part from its preference for undisturbed riparian banks—an increasingly rare feature in the West. Dornfeld recommended seeking it "in the Siskiyous of Jackson County . . . along small streams in the canyons of the Applegate River tributaries." A classic locality is Eight Dollar Mountain, Oregon. In California, I found it on a tributary of the Feather River in July, looking much like the Field Crescents with which it was flying above and like Mylitta below, as it is supposed to. Males of those species patrol the terrain in search of females, while the California perches along gullies and flies out at interlopers (Scott). This trait may aid in identification in some terrain, though it did not fit in that riparian locality.

Female (left) and male (right), ventral

Pale Crescent *Phyciodes pallida* (W. H. EDWARDS) 1864

Flagstaff Mt., Boulder, CO
Aka Pallid Crescentspot, Barnes' Crescent, *pallidus, barnesi*

RECOGNITION
< 2 in. **Largish; light both in ground color and density of markings.** Black bars, spots, and crescents delicate above. **Prominent, squarish black patch midway** along the trailing edge of FW, above and below, esp. on males. Males pale, washed-out orange and yellow; females more strongly marked on dorsum, sometimes with pale bands. **VHW spotbands below creamy or nacreous,** alternating with ochre or tan, separated by sharp brown lines; females may be entirely creamy

Male, ventral

Dorsal

on VHW, with no ochre. Pearly crescent on VHW margin large, **lightly haloed with brown**; spots in crescent-band may all be off-white in females. Mylitta lacks black patches and is smaller. **VARIATION** The main variation is the sexual dimorphism; our lone ssp., *P. p. barnesi*, described from Glenwood Springs, CO, is supposed to have stronger brown marking and greater prevalence of white below than SW individuals. **HOST PLANTS** Thistles, chiefly wavy-leaved thistle (*Cirsium undulatum*) in PNW. **ON THE WING** M April to E August, peak in May. Single-brooded. Late-instar larvae overwinter. **HABITAT AND RANGE** Dry foothill gullies, streambeds, hillsides, talus slopes. Arid interior W. Sparingly in E Cascadia, mostly at 100 to 2,000 feet along Columbia, Okanogan, Snake, John Day, and Deschutes rivers and tributaries.

This large crescent may first suggest a washed-out checker. It is tempting to try to make big female Mylittas into Pale

Crescents—I have done it many times. First, consider the habitat, range, and flight period; that will eliminate many apocryphal Pales. If you're still not sure, the aforementioned field marks are usually reliable, especially the chunky black patch. Pales are considerably larger and more

Male, ventral

Male, dorsal

distinctly marked below. This is one of the least-encountered Cascadian butterflies, partly because of the short flight period, the fact that few naturalists seek out dry canyons in hot weather, and because colonies genuinely seem to be few and far between. The Similkameen River canyon west of Oroville, Washington, Sherars Bridge on the Deschutes River in Oregon, and Hells Canyon, Idaho, are good places to look for this impressive crescent. Watch for it patrolling dry, rocky arroyos in search of nectar, thistles, mud, or mates.

Mylitta Crescent   *Phyciodes mylitta* W. H. EDWARDS 1861

Stanyan Hill, San Francisco, CA
Aka Mylitta Crescentspot, Thistle Crescent

RECOGNITION < 1.5 in. Bright orange above, males with very light, open pattern, females more strongly banded with black network. VHW banded with contrasting, crisp to muddy rows of white, tan, and brown spots. **Bright marginal crescent on VHW heavily haloed with brown, and the other spots in its row never form an off-white band** as in the Pale. FW outline indented (concave) as in *P. orseis* and *P. pallida*, unlike

Female, dorsal

Male, ventral

rounded margins of *P. cocyta* and *P. pulchella*. **Black spot on the trailing edge of VFW small, not prominent** as on the larger *P. pallida*. **VARIATION** Only the type occurs in Cascadia. Seasonally and sexually dimorphic: summer broods are yellower below with increased brown striation and reduced brown spotting, and females are larger with duller orange ground color and busier patterns. **HOST PLANTS** Thistles and relatives: commonly Canada thistle (*Cirsium arvense*), *C. vulgare*, *C. undulatum*, *C. remotifolium*, *C. edule*, and *C. hookerianum*; rarely ("in dire conditions," Pelham) diffuse knapweed (*Centaurea diffusa*) and star-thistle (*C. solstitialis*). Nectars prolifically on host thistles, goldenrods, tansy ragwort, Douglas aster, oxeye daisy, black-eyed Susan, hawkbit, pearly everlasting, rabbitbrush, red clover, dewberry,

Male, dorsal

Female, ventral

and creeping buttercup, among others. ON THE WING L February to M October, peaks in M May and July-August. Multi-brooded, one generation flying in spring, one or two more in summer and fall. Half-grown larvae overwinter. HABITAT AND RANGE Prairies, marshes, unmown city lots, weedy fields, forest glades, roadsides, meadows, industrial wasteland, and many other kinds of open space, from sea level to mid-montane. Throughout W N Am, all Cascadia, even in coastal WA.

Small orange butterflies cruising up and down a weedy lowland path will be Mylittas, one of the most ubiquitous butterflies in Cascadia. Fresh males present bright safety-orange streaks as they appear before you along a mown path through higher

vegetation. These fade, but continue to patrol marshy swales or bits of roadside, every 50 to 100 feet possessed by a different male seeking compliant females against all odds. They fly back and forth, momentarily alighting with slowly fanning wings, then launching again with few flaps and much gliding, low and erratic. The second generation is the more numerous: I see just a handful all spring, but one fall I observed 17 nectaring together on Douglas asters in my backyard, where new males patrol the same patches of territory year to year, thistles nearby or not. Mylitta is one of a small guild of butterflies reliably encountered on the west side, but it has diminished in Seattle and Portland with the infilling of vacant lots and the removal of thistles.

Northern Crescent *Phyciodes cocyta* (CRAMER) 1777

Black Rock, Cape Breton, NS
Aka Pearly Crescentspot, Northern Pearl Crescent, Orange Crescent, *tharos, selenis, pascoensis, morpheus*

RECOGNITION < 1 in. Males bright orange in the discs of the rounded (convex) wings above, with broad black borders. **Big open orange areas**, black-framed, distinguish males from other crescents, whose wing outlines are concave. Tan to golden below, with an **opalescent marginal crescent standing out in a more or less prominent chocolate patch**, less developed in females, which are strongly patterned with orange, white, brown, and black above. **Females usually lack a well-formed light bar across the cell of the vfw**, which female Field Crescents possess. **VARIATION** P. *c. pascoensis* (Pasco Crescent), described from Pasco, Benton Co., WA, may encompass all

our populations. Those of arid lowlands in the Columbia Basin lack strong seasonal dimorphism, and the brown apical patch on the vhw is understated. Those of montane and moister habitats, farther N, are more richly colored than those of the foothills and basins, with the chocolate patch more pronounced. **HOST PLANTS** According to Pelham various asters, incl. Cascade aster (*Eucephalus ledophyllus*), alpine leafybract aster (*Symphyotrichum foliaceum*), Geyer's aster (*S. laeve* var. *geyeri*), and for basin populations, alkali aster (*S. frondosum*). **ON THE WING** L April to L September, peaks in June-July, August. One generation in more northern, cooler, and higher areas, two farther S, warmer, and downhill. Partially grown larvae overwinter. **HABITAT AND RANGE** Wetlands, grasslands, meadows, forest glades, streambanks, springs, dry transition zone forest grassland, Palouse bunchgrass, disturbed lowlands. S Canada, N US extending S in the Appalachians, Rockies, and E Cascades. S BC; much of E WA E of the Okanogan R. in the Okanogan Highlands, Kettle River Range, and Selkirks; the Cascades S of Lake Chelan (N Kittitas, Chelan cos) and barely N (Okanogan Co.); and in the Blues; N ID; and OR along Columbia, Grande Ronde, Imnaha, and Snake rivers, Wallowa Lake.

This butterfly was long conflated with the Pearl Crescent (*P. tharos*), a beloved butterfly

over much of the country. It gives a Halloween jack-o-lantern impression on the wing: within its range, a small, orange flap-glider with black borders is likely to be a Northern Crescent. We have two ecotypes: a lowland, normally double-brooded insect, occuring around the edges and tributaries of the Columbia Basin; and one of higher elevations, in moister, less disturbed habitats, and single-brooded. I have found both types in early summer, abounding in wet Okanogan

Female, dorsal

Female, ventral

Male, dorsal

Male, ventral

meadows and arid Palouse prairie, respectively. For now, we call both *P. c. pascoensis,* but this may change. In naming the species after Cocytus, the river of lamentation in the underworld, Cramer seems to have anticipated the rending of flesh and tearing of hair in store for future students of crescent

taxonomy. The name *pascoensis,* once applied to whole species, came about because W. G. Wright, author of the monumental *Butterflies of the West Coast of the United States* (1905), stopped off at the Pasco train station and collected a few crescents next to a brothel.

Field Crescent *Phyciodes pulchella* (BOISDUVAL) 1852

San Francisco Co., CA
Aka Field Crescentspot, *campestris, pratensis, pulchellus, montana*

RECOGNITION < 1 in. **Males very dark above,** black and brown with small orange spots in bands; or brighter tawny with orange spots expanded. Ventrum orangey and lightly marked, with varying black spots on the trailing and outer edges of vfw. Females bigger and lighter, with stronger color-bands outside brown base; resemble female Northern Crescents, but **vfw has a strong pale bar at the end of the cell**, running perpendicular to the leading edge of the wing, absent or much reduced in

Northern. **FW margin rounded**, not squared like Mormon Metalmark or concave like California Crescent; **antennal knobs largely brown. VARIATION** *P. p. owimba,* described from Missoula Co., MT, occupies WA. James Scott, its author, characterizes it as having the scaleless underside of the antennal club (the nudum) orange, instead of black as in all other ssp. except one in AK. The male is less two-toned above than the CA type. Warren discusses the "enormous" range of variation in

Female, ventral

Male, ventral

OR, most of which has to do with size, pallor or darkness, and richness of color, and involves elevation, isolation, and influences from elsewhere, esp. CA. **HOST PLANTS** Asters incl. western showy aster (*Eurybia conspicua*) and Cascade aster (*Eucephalus ledophyllus*). Nectars on asters, pearly everlasting, other composites; adults visit coyote scat. **ON THE WING** M May to L September, peak in June-July. One brood, third-instar larvae overwinter, chrysalides eclose over an extended period. **HABITAT AND RANGE** Montane meadows, slopes, seeps, roadsides, forest edges, valley prairies, sea level to summits. W N Am E to NE, Mexico to AK. Common in most mtns of Cascadia, rare W of Cascade Crest in WA except in Olympics, very rare and local in Willamette Valley, OR.

This crescent too has undergone multiple name changes. The problem began when Hans Hermann Behr of the California Academy of Sciences mistook the males and females for different species and erected separate names on the same page of the same journal—*campestris* for the female, *pratensis* for the male, both from San Francisco—and *montana* for a Sierran form. Scott determined that the older Boisduval name *pulchella* also referred to this species, and took priority. It's a pity to lose two scientific names (*campestris* and *pratensis*) that both actually mean "field," but *pulchella* ("beautiful") isn't bad. In Oregon, the Field Crescent can be common in lowland sites, but in Washington it flies mostly at moist, mid- to high montane elevations. I watched an ant carry a chrysalis to its nest in the Olympics. On the McCloud River in northern California, this species outnumbered the very similar California Crescent about 20 to one.

Female (above) and male (below), dorsal

Subfamily Satyrinae: Satyrs, Browns, and Ringlets

Long regarded as a family of their own, the satyrs are distinguished by the base of the costal vein, at the leading edge of the forewing right by the thorax, which is swollen like an angioplasty balloon. They are now regarded by most as a subfamily of the Nymphalidae, brushfooted-ness being a more telling trait. Our members all belong to the tribe Satyrini, and the subtribes Coenonymphina (ringlets), Cercyonina (wood nymphs), Erebiina (alpines), and

Great Arctic, female

Satyrina (arctics and graylings). The antennal clubs are very slender. Most members of the tribe wear soft, earth-toned colors—grays, browns, tawny ochres—with fine striations, making them beautifully cryptic against lichens, soil, or bark.

Many satyrs also possess ocelli, or eyespots. Rather than mimicking big-eyed predators, as many think is the case with the buckeyes and the owl butterflies (*Caligo*) of the Neotropics, these smaller, marginal ocelli serve as bullseyes—attack-distractors. Birds frequently strike at the eyespots rather than the body of the insect, allowing it to fly free and unharmed except for a notch out of a wing or two. Of the approximately 2,500 satyrines in the world (some 50 in North America), the great majority possess such eyespots.

Larval satyrs graze on monocots, generally grasses, sedges, and canes, the exact species often poorly determined. They inhabit grasslands from subtropical canebrake to prairie, from steppe-desert to arctic-alpine tundra. Adapting to such habitats, satyrines have acquired a distinctive flight mode—flitting among the grass-blades and glades with quick half-flaps, almost skipping on the air more than flying. The English names of arctics and alpines denote their habitual mountain haunts. No doubt the sight of wood nymphs and satyrs drinking and mating in dappled sylvan settings put the classically educated namers in mind of the rustic deities of Greek Arcady: the companions of Pan and Dionysus, enjoying a summer-long bacchanal.

Ochre Ringlet *Coenonympha tullia* (MÜLLER) 1764

Zeeland, Denmark
Aka Ringlet, Common Ringlet (NABA), Northwest Ringlet,
Large Heath, *california, ampelos, ochracea*

C. T. INSULANA SPECIAL CONCERN IN BC

RECOGNITION < 1.5 in. Upperside clear, silky, **unmarked rich ochre**, light apricot, pale straw, creamy white, or muddy olive. VFW largely the same with light postmedian streak. VHW light to dark olive crossed by pale, broad "lightning-strike" zigzag, which may be nearly absent in ssp. *eunomia*. With or without small eyespot at apex of VFW and others around submargin of VHW. Nothing resembles it. **VARIATION** Ochre Ringlets show distinct patterns between regions and generations.

Pair, ventral (ssp. *ampelos*)

Geographic segregates are not really segregated, so they usually intergrade where they meet. *C. t. ampelos*, described from SE OR prob. nr Goose Lake, Lake Co., is apricot to pale yellowish ochre above, light olive below, with well-developed lightning-streak and often small eyespots on the vFW apex and vHW margin. It occupies most of OR and WA E of

Ventral (ssp. *insulana*)

the Cascades. *C. t. columbiana* (Columbian Ringlet), described from Aspen Grove, BC, larger, deeper orange-ochre above and greener olive below, sometimes with eyespots, flies in S BC and in the Okanogan Highlands and Pend Oreille of WA. *C. t. eunomia* (Eunomia Ringlet), described from Clackamas Co., OR, occurs in the Willamette Valley, the OR Coast Range, and SW WA from the Columbia to Hood Canal and Tacoma, and W Cascades. Its dorsum is darker and duller ochre than *C. t. ampelos*, and smaller, the ventrum "darkly ferruginous" (Dornfeld), or reddish gray-olive, with reduced lightning-streak and no ocelli. *C. t. insulana* (Vancouver Island Ringlet), named from Victoria, BC, is variably greeny olive below, tarnished brassy above; it flies on Vancouver–San Juan–Whidbey Is., the E-C Salish Lowlands in W King Co., and coastal Clatsop Co., OR. *C. t. ochracea*, described from Turkey Creek Cyn, Jefferson Co., CO, is the true Ochre Ringlet, bright rich apricot-ochre above, with pronounced eyespots below. It does not enter Cascadia but its genetic influence can be seen in the Selkirks and Blue Mtns, where color

Male, ventral (ssp. *california*)

Male, ventral (ssp. *eryngii*)

and ocellation both become more intense. *C. t. eryngii*, from "northern California," is the ringlet of the Siskiyous, blending E into the Warners and Klamath Basin. It is creamy white, sometimes with a faint ochre tint (Warren), above and below, or grayish below in the spring generation, and blends to the S into the straw to pure-white and more ocellated *C. t. california*, our oldest ssp., from 1851. Our youngest (1997), *C. t. yontocket*, from Del Norte Co., CA, is strictly coastal N into Coos and Curry cos along the immediate SW OR coast. It is pale like *C. t. eryngii* above but dark below like *C. t. insulana*, with the VHW design very distinct. All ssp. darker and richer in color in spring broods than in summer/fall; dark spring individuals have even been described as different taxa from lighter butterflies of the summer generation. **HOST PLANTS** Native and naturalized grasses and sedges; Scott lists needlegrass (*Achnatherum*), grama (*Bouteloua*), fescue (*Festuca*), brome (*Bromus*), and sedge (*Carex*). My nectar records incl. blue brodiaea, garden thyme, creeping buttercup, white clover, western clematis, alyssum, silverweed, Queen Anne's lace, starflower, blackberry, pussypaws, oxeye daisy, rabbitbrush, goldenrods, dandelion, asters, fleabanes, and yarrow. **ON THE WING** L March to L October, peaks in May, August-September. Two or three broods (one at higher elevations), larvae overwinter. **HABITAT AND RANGE** All sorts of grasslands: prairies, steppes, roadside verges, old fields, waste ground, marshes, forest glades, expansive lawns, subalpine meadows. Holarctic; Eurasia, NE N Am, upper MW, most of W, to S-C Canada and AK. Almost all Cascadia except Olympic Peninsula, high Cascades, Snohomish, Skagit, and Whatcom cos, WA, and adjacent mainland BC, central OR and WA coast.

Thomas Emmel organized all our varied ringlets into one giant superspecies. If its current designation as *C. tullia* is correct, the same butterfly may be found on Scottish moors (where it is called the Large Heath), looking very different, with large eyespots. But if North American ringlets prove to be a different species after all, the next oldest available name is *C. california*, an odd moniker for a coast-to-coast insect. No matter how distinctive the many varieties may be at their headquarters, they run into one another eventually: bone-white *C. t. california* grades through the faded straw *C. t. eryngii* in southwestern Oregon to the canteloupe *C. t. ampelos* on the east side and the olivaceous *C. t. eunomia* of the Willamette Valley. By whatever name, the Ochre Ringlet is one of the most ubiquitous butterflies in the temperate grassland realm. Not that it is everywhere, nor always abundant. On Vancouver Island it requires green grass as larvae but the absence of flood in winter—such places are rapidly gobbled by Scotch broom and developers, so the Ochre Ringlet has dwindled to a rarity in British Columbia. Until recently it survived in larger vacant lots in southwest Seattle. It is spreading along roadsides into new rural areas. But a great mystery attends the butterfly's evident absence between Seattle and Vancouver, British Columbia, when it occurs on three sides and suitable habitat seems extensive. The species is rainfall-limited, abounding on the Clatsop Plain on the drier Oregon side of the Columbia (where I found numerous adults stowed in spider webs beneath dried heads of *Achillea millefolium*), but with no modern records from the wet Washington coast.

Key to the Wood Nymphs (*Cercyonis* spp.)

Common (*C. pegala*) and Dark (*C. oetus*) wood nymphs are fairly easy to differentiate by their wing size and the relative size of the two FW eyespots. Great Basin Wood Nymphs (*C. sthenele*) are somewhat in between the other two species in appearance.

Common Wood Nymph
Cercyonis pegala

FW lower eyespot is same size or slightly larger than upper eyespot. VFW band behind eyespots is pale compared to the rest of the VFW. Slightly lighter outer band on VHW, not as distinct as Great Basin Wood Nymph.

Great Basin Wood Nymph
Cercyonis sthenele

FW lower eyespot is slightly smaller than upper eyespot, rarely missing compared to Dark Wood Nymph. VFW band behind eyespots is pale compared to the rest of the VFW. Slightly to distinctly lighter outer band on VHW, usually more obvious than Common Wood Nymph.

Dark Wood Nymph
Cercyonis oetus

FW lower eyespot is smaller than upper eyespot, often half the size or absent, especially on dorsal side. VFW band behind eyespots is same color as the rest of the VFW. VHW outer band may be slightly lighter but not as distinct as other two species.

Common Wood Nymph *Cercyonis pegala* (FABRICIUS) 1775

Vic. Charleston, SC
Aka Large Wood Nymph, Ox-eyed Wood Nymph, Blue-eyed Grayling, Goggle Eye, Hoary Satyr

C. P. INCANA
SPECIAL CONCERN
IN BC

RECOGNITION > 2 in. **Biggish**, some shade of brown from light cocoa (females) to dark chocolate (males). Twin eyespots on FW, white-pupilled, small and black on males, large and yellow-rimmed on females. Dark-velvet sex brands on cells of male DFW; DHW has one subtornal eyespot. Underside striated darker brown on lighter. VFW ocelli prominent, yellow-ringed, the lower one larger, females often blue-eyed. VHW more or less lighter on outer half with a **submarginal row of one to six eyespots**, more on males. Males and non-desert forms darker brown, females and desert nymphs larger and paler. Great Basin Wood

Nymph is smaller, shorter-winged, banded below. **VARIATION** A confusing jumble of names are associated with the highly variable individuals in our region, both the darker ones outside the Great Basin and the washed-out, big-eyed populations of the arid basinlands. Their relationships are not fully understood. Jon Pelham applies *C. p. incana*, described from Olympia, WA, more uniform brown below with well-developed ocelli, to most WA populations. Guppy and Shepard used it for the Vancouver Is. populations, and, for the rest of BC, *C. p. ariane* (Ariane Satyr), described from Plumas Co., CA, two-toned below, heavily striated, males often well-ocellated, females none or little. Warren considers W and NE OR populations also to be *C. p. ariane*. A number of larger, paler populations with large, often yellow-haloed eyespots occur in basinland oases and adjacent territories in E WA and SE OR. Several names have been applied to these

Female, dorsal

Female, ventral

Male, dorsal

Male, ventral

(*C. p. stephensi, C. p. gabbii, C. p. paucilineatus*). A distinctive, unusually small and dark version occurs along the Little Deschutes R. in N Klamath/S Deschutes cos; misdesignated as *C. sthenele silvestris* (Dornfeld 1980), it is actually undescribed (Warren 2005). **HOST PLANTS** Various fresh spring grasses. No specific host records in Cascadia; *Andropogon, Avena, Tridens, Stipa* elsewhere (Scott). Nectars on

spiraeas, brambles, alfalfa, western clematis, yellow mustards, penstemons, horsemint, bull thistle, Canada thistle, gaillardia, marigold, aphid honeydew, willow sap, and banana bait. **ON THE WING** M May to L September, peak in July-August. One generation, first-instar larvae overwinter. **HABITAT AND RANGE** Prairies, meadows, marshes, boggy seeps, old fields, irrigated pastures and hayfields, roadsides, unsprayed parks and lawns, cemeteries, overhung banks of canals and creeks, lakeshores, thickets, alderwood edges, oak and conifer forest glades. Sea level to 7,000 feet, usually below 3,000 feet. S Canada, most of the Lower 48 except Gulf Coast and far SW. Throughout Cascadia except for most of coast and Snohomish/Skagit/Whatcom cos, WA.

Ringlets fly twice in the summer, wood nymphs only once, but their broods often overlap in the late summer and early fall such that we find them flying together in old fields near woods: the Satyrs of September. Like the Ochre Ringlet, this species is highly variable, with many former names and subspecies. The different phenotypes all blend, showing regional averages that may or may not deserve subspecific recognition. I found individuals conforming to several named taxa, all from a small rural canal colony east of Denver, Colorado. This underscores Emmel's conclusion that a single plastic species is involved. I also found that a substantial number (>10%) of my sample (n. 300+) bore bird-strikes at the large ocelli on the wings, which illustrates the eyespots' highly adaptive role in diverting bird attack toward the expendable wing margins. As its "common" name implies, the species is usually abundant, displaying a dancing flight, cutting in and out of tall grass with half-flaps and drops (Ray Stanford dubbed them "Flip-Flops"). While polyculture farming may allow it to spread, intensive agriculture and high annual precipitation limit the occurrence of *C. pegala*. Formerly confined east of the 80-inch rain-line in the Lower

Columbia, it moved west into Wahkiakum County during a series of dry summers in the mid-1980s and has remained resident since, even withstanding occasional winter rainfall totals of 150+ inches. Warming will spread it further. North of Coos County, Oregon, it approaches the Pacific shore only around Grays Harbor. The Common Wood Nymph mirrors the Ochre Ringlet's apparent absence from northwestern Washington except immediately around Puget Sound: a double puzzle with no obvious answer.

Great Basin Wood Nymph *Cercyonis sthenele* (BOISDUVAL) 1852

San Francisco, CA
Aka Lesser Wood Nymph, Least Wood Nymph, Small Wood Nymph, Scrub Wood Nymph, Woodland Satyr, Little Satyr, Sylvan Satyr, *silvestris, paulus*

RECOGNITION < 2 in. Medium-sized. Shorter- and squarer-winged, more compact than Common Wood Nymph. Light to dark brown above, two black ocelli (upper larger) on FW, one on HW, with or without yellow rings and pupils, bigger on females; males with DFW sex brands. Light to silvery brown below, striated; VHW **strongly two-toned**: dark inner part, pale outer third often frosted with white overscaling. **Dark lines bounding VHW median band are lobed**, but not wildly zigzagged as in next species. Two prominent eyespots on VFW near-equidistant from margin; usually fewer than six ocelli on VHW. **VARIATION** C. *s. sineocellata*, described from Lake Co., OR, applies to populations in E OR, E WA, S BC, and ID. As the name implies, it lacks many eyespots around the VHW. It is light brown above, paler and often two-toned below with much whitish frosting. Populations in the Siskiyous are darker. Very dark, small ones in the W OR Cascades are readily confused with Dark Wood Nymphs. **HOST PLANTS** Undetermined grasses; recorded elsewhere: *Poa, Danthonia, Tridens, Avena,* and *Andropogon.* I have most often found adults among fescues. Nectars esp. on rabbitbrush (Warren), yarrow, goldenrods, and white sweetclover. **ON THE WING** L June to L September, peak in July-August. Single-brooded. Unfed first-instar larvae overwinter; four additional molts in summer. **HABITAT AND RANGE** Sage-steppe (to subalpine in BC), bunchgrass remnants, arid prairie, desert washes, oak-lined canyons, and pinyon-juniper, ponderosa pine, and Douglas-fir forests. Arid zones of W N Am, S BC to N AZ, E to mid-CO. Sparingly in S-C BC and W ID, more common in E WA and E OR beyond Cascades; S OR Cascades and Siskiyous, then coastal to Baja.

Male, ventral

Male, dorsal

Male, ventral

The type became extinct in San Francisco in the 1880s, well before the Xerces Blue, one of the first butterfly casualties to human progress. The whole species was thought extinct until Tom Emmel placed several other western nymphs under its taxonomic umbrella. Its range circumscribes the Great Basin and its arid outliers. Seldom as common as the other two wood nymphs, which have colonized secondary grasslands that *C. sthenele* seems to eschew. I found all three species on a bunchgrass natural area at the northern edge of the Blue Mountains, and David James found all three at Waterworks Canyon, Yakima County. Should you mistake larger female Dark Wood Nymphs or small male Commons for Great Basins, don't feel bad: it happens to the best of us.

Dark Wood Nymph   *Cercyonis oetus* (BOISDUVAL) 1869

Mt. Judah nr Donner Pass, Placer Co., CA
Aka Small Wood Nymph (NABA), Least Wood Nymph, Least Satyr

RECOGNITION < 1.75 in. **Small, blackish** or dark brown. Often two DFW ocelli, small and black, sometimes yellow-flushed and larger in females; males with prominent sex brands on DFW. **VHW median band bounded by wildly zigzagged dark lines.** VFW eyespots more prominent, pupilled, yellow-ringed; **lower ocellus displaced toward margin and much smaller.** Underside gravelly black, brown, or gray, sometimes whitish-frosted. VHW seldom strongly two-toned, but outer half sometimes lighter, with tiny eyespots. **VARIATION** Highly variable throughout the region. All females are larger and lighter with bigger eyespots. Pelham relegates the entire WA population to the CA type and writes that, in general, "populations from drier areas are lighter and populations from wetter areas are darker." Warren agrees for OR, adding that "on average, adults from montane, forested habitats [are] darker above and below than those from low-elevation basin habitats." Pelham further notes that "populations across the northeastern tier of counties [are] characterized by a poorly marked VHW with a 'smooth' (not 'frosty') pattern [and] median band often barely perceptible. Moses Meadows is one place where these are common." This matches the concept of *C. o. phocus*, described from Lake La Hache, BC. **HOST PLANTS** Various Poaceae, incl. bluegrass (*Poa*), reedgrass (*Calamagrostis*), and fescue (*Festuca*). The biggest nectarers of the genus, assiduously visiting mock orange, mints,

Male, ventral

Male, ventral

Male (left) and female (right), dorsal

C. incognita, described from Mendocino Co., CA, in 2012 (Emmel, Emmel & Matoon), may actually be a coastward expression of _C. oetus_.

The Dark Wood Nymph is the tonal counterpart of the Ochre Ringlet—the one small and bright, the other small and dusky, both flitting in uncounted numbers across the western grasslands; flipping in and out of old-growth basin big sage, going to rest invisibly against a hoary sagebrush trunk, a cow-pie, or the dark basaltic dust. Like many other satyrs, they commonly adjust their angle upon alighting, tipping their closed wings almost flat against the ground. This was long said to "mimimize their shadow," but it actually optimizes solar exposure for thermoregulation. On a hot day, the basking posture can be adjusted to dispel body heat rather than to collect it. We think of the Dark Wood Nymph mostly in lower country, but it also ascends drier heights. Thea Pyle and I found it visiting a campfire ring on an alpine saddle in the Kettle River Range, then patrolling the ridge trails north and south. "Small" Wood Nymph correctly places this species in relation to the "Large" (=Common) and "Medium" (=Great Basin) wood nymphs. But Dark Wood Nymph is the more descriptive, historical, and unambiguous name. Holland coined that English name for _C. oetus charon_, both for the butterfly's blackness and for Charon the boatman, who ferried the dead over the Rivers Styx and Acheron into the mythic underworld.

alfalfa, buckwheats, rabbitbrush, yarrow, pearly everlasting, oxeye daisy, and many others. **ON THE WING** L May to L September, peak in July. A single generation, young larvae overwinter. **HABITAT AND RANGE** Many grassy biomes incl. sage-steppe, E-side canyons, plateaus, montane meadows and marshes, small-town parks, dry hillsides, lake and reservoir shores. Low to middle elevations, reaching high altitudes in sagey sub-tundra. W states and provinces from Black Hills to E Cascades and Sierra, S Rockies to N BC. Almost everywhere E of the Cascade Crest in Cascadia, sparingly in W OR Cascades, E Siskiyous. Known nowhere near the coast, but

Genus _Erebia_: Alpines

Some 75 species of alpines occur around the northern hemisphere. The number of North American alpines has been increased from a dozen to 14 or 15 in recent years, as new species have been discerned in the Far North. Along with their near-relatives, the arctics, the lesser fritillaries, and the

sulphurs, alpines dwell in some of the highest altitudes and latitudes of any butterflies. Generally ocellated and colored in dark browns, blacks, and russets, they took their name from Erebus, the upper level of the underworld as Homer tells it. The blackest of all, completely unmarked, is the

Magdalena Alpine (*Erebia magdalena*) of the Rockies. In alpine regions south of the equator, species of satyrs have arisen with eyespots set in rusty patches similar to the common theme for this genus. These are seen as classic cases of convergent evolution: an effective pattern arising more than once under similar circumstances. But at an earlier time, unrelated but similar examples were placed in *Erebia*, even a New Zealand endemic since given its own genus: *Erebiola*. We have two species of alpines, one extremely widespread, the other one of the narrowest Northwest endemics.

Vidler's Alpine   *Erebia vidleri* ELWES 1898

Mtns above Seton Lake, nr Lillooet on the Fraser R., BC

Aka Northwest Alpine, Cascades Alpine

RECOGNITION < 2 in. Chocolate-brown with yellow-orange bands above and below. **FW band light orange above, yellow below**; broad, ragged, tapering down to trailing edge, with a pair of ocelli near the tip, one lower down. DHW orange band narrow, reaching halfway down from leading edge but **never to lower margin**. VHW crossed by postmedian ash-gray band enclosing tiny eyespots. **Frosty patches at leading edges of VHW** and VFW. **Checkered fringes** give margin a scalloped look. *E. epipsodea* lacks these and has rusty spots all across DHW. **VARIATION** No named geographic ssp., but the intensity and shape of the orange band, the size and number of eyespots, and the amount of gray frosting all vary considerably. **HOST PLANTS** Undescribed. Guppy and Shepard report a possible host association with pinegrass (*Calamagrostis rubescens*); sedges too are possible. Nectars freely on alpine arnica, yarrow, common dandelion, and other

Dorsal

Ventral

Ventral

subalpine composites. **ON THE WING** L June to L August, peak in July. James and Nunnallee found it to be biennial, overwintering first as an egg, secondly as a nearly mature larva. Flies both odd and even years. **HABITAT AND RANGE** Arctic-alpine and subalpine meadows, seeps, and swales, upper montane forest openings. Generally lush sites from 3,500 to 8,300 feet. PNW endemic, occurring solely in WA and BC, from S of Cle Elum, Kittitas Co., and S Olympics, Mason Co. to Mt. Hoadley in the mid-BC Coast Range. Its PNW range incl. all sides of the Olympic Mtns, the N Cascades, and the W Okanogan/Okanagan of WA/BC.

The epithet honors a Captain Vidler, who presumably discovered it. There is a Vidler Peak in the North Okanagan, British Columbia, due east of the type locality, but also east of any known records. In 1925 the first American specimens were taken by J. F. G. Clarke on Skyline Ridge, Mt. Baker, and since the species was not yet well known or pictured, he took it for *E. disa*, a Far Northern species. The next collections were made by Ruth Dowell Svihla at Sol Duc Hot Springs in the Olympics in 1931, and by John Hopfinger and Andy Anderson in the mid-1930s in several Okanogan County localities. Robert Kirk made the first collection south of Snoqualmie Pass, at Mt. Margaret, Kittitas County, in 1983. It remains to be seen whether Vidler's Alpine flies in the William O. Douglas and Goat Rocks wilderness areas. This exclusively Northwest butterfly flies long, low sorties up and down swales, perching occasionally in deep grass and mountain heather. Easily accessible places for watching the most striking of American alpines include Blue Mountain and Hurricane Ridge in Olympic National Park, Ptarmigan Ridge on Mt. Baker, Hart's Pass at the head of the Methow River, and Salmon Meadows above Conconully, Washington. The species' nearest look-alike, but apparently not its closest relative, is *E. niphonica* (Japanese Alpine).

Butler's Alpine   *Erebia epipsodea* (BUTLER) 1868

Rock Lake, nr Jasper, AB
Aka Common Alpine (NABA), *hopfingeri*

RECOGNITION < 2 in. Chocolate-brown with rusty red, eyespotted bands above and below. DFW/HW and VFW submarginal rust bands enclose white-pupilled black eyespots, top two largest; usually three or four on FW, three or four on HW. **DHW rusty band extends nearly to trailing edge.** Lighter below; VHW may have a vague median band between light scaling on inner and outer thirds (esp. on female) but lacks ash-gray postmedian band of *E. vidleri.* Wings rounded, looks black on the wing, with green and purple iridescence when very fresh. **VARIATION** Highly variable within populations, in terms of size, depth of color, and size of ocelli and their rusty halos. Females everywhere are lighter and yellower-banded. The type covers all the Butler's Alpines in our region, by consensus of the major authorities. **HOST PLANTS** Grasses; associated with *Setaria italica* (foxtail bristlegrass) in the Blue Mtns. Nectars on whitetop (*Lepidium*) and other crucifers, and composites. Adults visit mud and scat; bear scat in Okanogan. **ON THE WING** E May to E August, peak in May–July. A single generation, third- or fourth-instar larvae overwinter. **HABITAT AND RANGE** Moist montane meadows, bogs, fields, sage-flats, canyons, buckbrush chaparral, subalpine and lower arctic-alpine parkland. W half of Canada to YT-AK, Rockies to NM, PNW (ID-OR-WA). E Cascades, Okanogan, Selkirks, Blues in WA; Blues, Wallowas, Ochocos, and Aldrichs in OR.

Female, ventral

Male, dorsal

Male, ventral

Paul Ehrlich and others conducted many studies on this species at the Rocky Mountain Biological Laboratory in Colorado. Among other things disclosed is that, despite their apparently weak flight, a tenth of adults dispersed at least 500 meters, and some as far as 13 kilometers. They also showed that Butler's Alpine forms a huge, open population throughout much of the Mountain West, differing from most sub-arctic erebias, which are distinctly colonial in their highly fragmented, relictual, post-Pleistocene habitats. This may be the only *Erebia* species that global warming will treat kindly. "Common Alpine" is not unjustified for this abundant and widespread butterfly, but to prevent confusion with our other big dark satyr, the Common Wood Nymph, and for syntactic symmetry with its congener, Vidler's Alpine, the patronymic Butler's Alpine is preferable. Arthur Gardiner Butler was an English collaborator of W. H. Edwards. Designating the types from near Banff, Butler compared the new species to the similar European alpine *E. psodea*, hence *epi-* (Greek, "approaching") *psodea*. I first met it one June day in 1960 when my grandfather set me loose in a lush mountain meadow above Idaho Springs, teeming with Butler's Alpines after a cool Colorado rain, addicting me forever to erebias.

Genera *Oeneis* and *Neominois*: Arctics and Satyrs

From the subtle (almost non-) colors of most species of *Oeneis*, one might think that they would be unpopular among butterfly enthusiasts. The truth is quite the opposite. Some combination of their high, clean, wild haunts, challenging escape behavior, and softly handsome textures has attracted almost obsessive attention from loyal lepidopterists. These butterflies, along with *Erebia*, *Boloria*, and certain *Colias* species, embody the very mystique of the Arctic itself—and for those of us in more southern latitudes, the arctic-alpine of the high country wilderness.

Some 40 species of arctics haunt the mountain ranges, boreal forests, and cold steppes of the northern hemisphere. About a dozen of these have reached or arisen in North America. Their diversity drops quickly from north to south: BC revels in ten species, Washington enjoys four, and Oregon makes do with only one. California, making up for an utter absence of alpines, has two. The colors come in translucent, mica-like grays, tans, taupes, and tawnies, camouflaged at rest by striated and marbled undersides that evolved through eons of cohabitation with lichens, bark, and stone. Some have eyespots like their close relatives the alpines, but their flight is stronger, faster, and jerkier. They range from the highest, hardest landscapes to grassland

and forest, and all are biennial in development, taking two years to make a butterfly from an egg through the grace of grass. The

related but unique Ridings' Satyr precedes the arctics proper.

Ridings' Satyr *Neominois ridingsii* (W. H. EDWARDS) 1865

Loveland, Larimer Co., CO
Aka Grasshopper Satyr

RECOGNITION < 2 in. Above, **sandy brown-gray**, all wings crossed by **bands of oblong creamy white ovals**. Two pupilled black eyespots lie in FW bands, sometimes one small ocellus on HW. Below, similar pattern repeated less distinctly on FW; in place of the light spots, VHW has light and dark irregular bands against the heavily speckled and striated, grayish tan ground. Nothing similar exists, but in flight gives the impression of a large gray moth or a grasshopper. **VARIATION** The few OR populations are assigned to *N. r.*

stretchii (Stretch's Satyr), described from Mt. Jefferson, Nye Co., NV. It is a warmer, browner gray than the CO type, with a yellowish cast. Female larger, rounder, with DHW spot-bands more suffused. **HOST PLANTS** In CO, blue grama (*Bouteloua gracilis*) for the type and bluebunch wheatgrass (*Pseudoroegneria spicata*) for *N. r. wyomingo*; in NV, needle-and-thread (*Hesperostipa comata*) for *N. r. stretchii*. Nectars chiefly on composites. **ON THE WING** L June to M August, peak in July. One brood, third- or fourth-instar larvae overwinter. **HABITAT AND RANGE** Comstock called it "this strange waif [of] rocky summit and wind blown crag." Arid, sage-covered mtns, flats, and roadsides. Rockies, Great Basin, Black Hills, and W Plains from KS to CA, AZ into

Dorsal

Ventral

SD and AB; barely into N-C and SE ID; OR on Drake and Light peaks (Warner Mtns, Lake Co.), Pueblo Mtns (Harney Co.), Blue Mtn (Malheur Co.), Pine Mtn (Deschutes Co.).

James Ridings of Philadelphia collected around Pikes Peak in 1864. As his luggage never arrived, he stayed only a few weeks, but he managed to take this remarkable butterfly back to his friend W. H. Edwards. When you chase *N. ridingsii* in the afternoon, it constantly jumps up in front of you, flies a ways, then resettles invisibly with

its wings closed and flattened against the same-colored sand. In the morning, when it actively courts, it is more easily approached, flying out and back from perches that Warren describes as bare spots between sagebrush or clumps of bunchgrass: "During calm moments with little or no wind, males patrol hillside swales, at least from 11:00 hrs to 14:30 hrs." Many uncollected sage mountains remain to be sampled as possible satyr habitats in various southeastern Oregon ranges, such as Hart Mountain, Glass Buttes, and Wagontire Mountain.

Melissa's Arctic   *Oeneis melissa* (FABRICIUS) 1775

Chateau Bay, Labrador coast, Atlantic Canada
Aka Mottled Arctic

RECOGNITION < 1.75 in. Above and below, smoke-gray, thinly scaled to the point of near-transparency; sometimes dull brown or warmer tan, esp. females. **VHW** heavily peppered with black on whitish gray, granite-like; either uniformly or with a **vague, darker median band**, white-edged. Checkered fringes. Unusually, the rounded HW are larger in area than the more drawn-out FW. Nothing similar in Cascadia. **VARIATION** *O. m. beanii* (Bean's Arctic), described from Laggan (nr Lake Louise), AB, occurs in BC, WA, Rockies S to the Beartooth Plateau, MT. It is even grayer and more translucent than ssp. of the S Rockies, N BC, or the Labrador type and has little or no median band below. **HOST PLANTS** Both sedges and grasses are used, in the NW and in Asia. **ON THE WING** M July to M August, peak in July. Biennial, overwintering as larvae twice, but some flying every year. **HABITAT AND RANGE** Rarely below timberline (7,000 to 8,000+ feet in WA). "Most at home on exposed ridges that are covered with alpine grasses" (Brown et al.). Also high-elevation scree, talus, and fellfields. Holarctic: Siberia, Arctic America to Labrador, disjunctly S into NH, MT, WY, UT, CO, NM, and WA. In Cascadia, S Coast Range of BC, N Cascades of WA (Whatcom, Okanogan, Chelan cos.), and Strathcona Provincial Park, Vancouver Is. (one record).

Female, ventral

Female specimen

Male specimen

In 1974 (wwB) I described this butterfly (which I then knew only from Colorado) as "a wisp of wing a little darker than the wind." I stand by that, and it is even truer of Bean's Arctic of the Northwest. "When frightened, *melissa* flies downslope and is not pursuable. Later it returns, perching on gray rubble with its wings cocked, casting no shadow, invisible to the world." Most of our records come from Slate Peak on the Okanogan/ Whatcom county line, or fairly nearby. The southernmost locality is Cooney Mountain, barely into Chelan County; the eastern-most, Chopaka Mountain, which looms over the Okanogan Valley at the very rim of the

North Cascades. Every individual I put up there was within yards of the 7,887-foot sum-mit. The species is probably at risk of extinc-tion in the Lower 48 from global warming. We know nothing of Fabricius' Melissa, but Thomas E. Bean (1844–1931), an English te-legrapher for the Canadian Pacific Railway, used his position to collect extensively in the Canadian Rockies, where he found several new butterflies. This one he sent back to Henry J. Elwes (1846–1922), president of the Entomological Society of London and an *Oe-neis* specialist in Cheltenham, who forever linked the mysterious Melissa with him.

Chryxus Arctic   *Oeneis chryxus* (E. DOUBLEDAY) 1849

Rock Lake, nr Jasper, AB
Aka Brown Arctic

RECOGNITION < 2 in. Reddish to golden tawny, tan, or brown above with dark, pinked border. Male has prominent sex patch over cell, surround-ing gray-brown scaling over ⅔ of narrow DFW; female rounder, fuller-winged, clear yellow-brown. Both have **dark postmedian line forming a bird's head with the bill pointing out** between the first and second of three or four eyespots. VFW pale, VHW heavily striated with sienna and white, with **pronounced, dark-bordered median band**. Great Arctic bigger, lacks bird-bill mark, lighter brown below with weaker band. **VARIATION** The

Female (above) and male (below), dorsal   Male, dorsal

Female specimen   Male specimen

type applies to populations in the Rockies, BC, and N-C/NE WA. *O. c. valerata* (Valerata Arctic, Olympic Arctic), described from Hurricane Ridge, Clallam Co., WA, is endemic to the Olympic Mtns of WA; its ventral markings, both light and dark, are less distinct. Jon Pelham has discerned an unusually dark phenotype in the Okanogan Highlands, near Mt. Hull, lacking much of the namesake color (the epithet is from the Greek *chrysos*, "gold"); Norbert Kondla finds that same dark phenotype in the adjacent BC Okanagan. The strange, ghostly

white *O. c. ivallda* of the Sierra Nevada has
no NW counterpart. **HOST PLANTS** Roemer's
fescue (*Festuca roemeri*) in the high Olympics.
Scott lists oatgrass (*Danthonia*), ricegrass
(*Oryzopsis*), and canarygrass (*Phalaris*), as well
as several species of sedges (esp. *Carex rossii*)
in CO. I reared *O. c. valerata* to the final instar
on Kentucky bluegrass (*Poa pratensis*) and other
lawn grasses. Nectars on pearly everlasting,
showy phlox, puccoon, native geraniums,
paintbrushes, and alpine cushion flowers. **ON
THE WING** L May to L August, peak in June-July.
Biennial, flying every year in most locations.
First diapause passed in first instar, second
winter diapause as fourth-instar larva. **HABITAT
AND RANGE** Montane dry grasslands, pine forest roads and clearings, high sage/bunchgrass
slopes, shaley arctic-alpine hillsides, ridges, and
summits with sparse grasses. AK, Canada E to
Maritimes and Great Lakes states, Rockies to
NM, High Sierra; Olympics, N Cascades, Okan-
ogan, Selkirks; old records around Mt. Rainier.

It is strange that Chryxus skips the Oregon
Cascades, occurring on three sides—in the
Washington Cascades, the Idaho Rockies,
and the Sierra Nevada. Molecular studies
show that Californian *O. c. ivallda* dispersed
from the Rockies. Perhaps Oregon's more
recent volcanic past extirpated it, while it
survived in the older, colder North Cascades and High Sierra. Think of a water-spill
drying up in the sun, leaving drops and
pools here and there. That's not unlike
the way a widespread arctic-alpine species
shrinks when the glaciers withdraw, trailing

Male, ventral

relictual colonies behind them in this and
that range, with great gaps in between. Isolated records at Mt. Spokane, White Pass,
and Chinook Pass have not been duplicated;
these might represent small, flickering populations. Localized populations occur in
sites such as Mt. Hull and Moses Meadows
in the Okanogan Highlands. Most of our
records come from Okanogan and Clallam
counties, where the type and *O. c. valerata*
may be seen at Hart's Pass and Hurricane
Ridge, respectively. The latter thrives on the
high ridges of Olympic National Park, over-
looking the Strait of Juan de Fuca, where it
is one of the most geographically restricted
butterflies in the United States.

Great Arctic　*Oeneis nevadensis* (C. & R. FELDER) 1867

Sierra Nevada, Plumas Co., CA
Aka Nevada Arctic, Great Grayling, Felder's Arctic, Pacific Arctic

O. N. GIGAS **SPECIAL CONCERN
IN BC, CANDIDATE IN WA**

RECOGNITION < 2.5 in. Large. **Pale to bright
tawny above** with darker, white-dashed margins
that look scalloped. **Male has large brown discal
sex patch** on DFW from outer costa to base;
female has heavy dark scaling over the inner
DFW. Black, white-pupilled eyespots appear
on FW (one or two on male, two or three on
female) and HW (one near tornus). VFW similar
to DFW; lacks the bird-head median line of the
somewhat similar Chryxus. VHW striated bark-
brown and white, sometimes with irregular dark
median band. Macoun's similar but lacks sex
patch. **VARIATION** The type, as just described,
covers our Cascades population. According to
Warren, occasional insects arise that resemble
the pale, whitish Sierran *O. n. iduna*, but this
ssp. does not occur anywhere in the region.
O. n. gigas, described from Vancouver Is.,
resident in the islands and BC Coast Range,
is larger and darker with VHW median band
more pronounced. A similar but smaller form,

with shorter, rounder FW and reduced male
stigmata, occurs on a few mountaintops in the
OR Coast Range; Warren calls these *O. n.* nr.
gigas. **HOST PLANTS** Various grasses, maybe
sedges; reared larvae accept several species of
both in captivity. Nectars seldom, sometimes
visiting bistort and popcornflower. **ON THE
WING** L April to L September, peak in June-July.
Biennial, with larva diapausing twice over two
winters. Flies almost exclusively in even years
in most Cascadian locales; a few populations
(e.g.,Vancouver Is.) regularly produce adults
in both odd and even years, and the OR Coast
Range population has been found only in odd
years. **HABITAT AND RANGE** Forest clearings
and open pinewoods, dirt roads, wet and
dry meadows and slopes, canyon floors;
near the coast, often bare summits. Near
sea level to 7,000 feet. BC Coast Range and
Cascades S to N CA. Virtually a Cascadian
endemic, occurring on Vancouver and Orcas
Is., Cascades, Siskiyous, Warners, N Sierra
Nevada, outliers in OR Coast Range, and
one record in Blue Mtns, Umatilla Co., OR.

Female specimen

Male specimen

These big, floppy, puma-hued arctics, anything but arctic, haunt sunny forest gaps. Long known as the Nevada Arctic, this species has yet to be found in its namesake state. The epithet *nevadensis* was intended to designate the Sierra Nevada, rather than the state. Given this twisted history, the common name for the large Vancouver Island subspecies, Great Arctic, has been adopted for the entire species. Great Arctics are perceptive and aggressive. Richard Guppy

described them defending summits on Vancouver Island, and Barry Bidwell watched one interact with a bat on Mt. Rainier. Emily Hendrickson discovered the Great Arctic on Mt. Constitution, Orcas Island, where it has not been confirmed since 1950, despite searches with possible phantom sightings. Disjunct, odd-year colonies exist in the northern Oregon Coast Range, such as on Saddle Mountain, where they hilltop as they do on Vancouver Island, but not in the Cascades. None are known in between San Juan and Clatsop counties, the species giving the whole Olympic Peninsula a pass. Vern Covlin's single Blue Mountains record is remarkable, suggesting the species should be sought in all northeastern Oregon ranges. Striking in flight but cryptic against bark or

earth, they pop up and settle a little way ahead in the road, or disappear onto a tree trunk, deceptively difficult to follow, catch, or photograph.

Female, dorsal

Male, dorsal, ventral

Male, ventral

Macoun's Arctic   *Oeneis macounii* (W. H. EDWARDS) 1885

Lake Nipigon, ON
Aka Canada Arctic

RECOGNITION < 2.5 in. Large. Rich yellowish brown; much like Great Arctic, but **male has no androconial sex patch on DFW.** Veins and margins dark above, female peppered with dark scales basally. Two or three eyespots on the FW (rarely four), one on the HW. VHW striations less white but more diffuse than *O. nevadensis*, dark median band more pronounced, with gray fogging either side. **VARIATION** No named ssp. or described variation. **HOST PLANTS** Undetermined grasses. **ON THE WING** L May to L July, peak in June-July. Biennial, flying mostly in even years in BC. First winter spent as first- or second-instar larvae, second winter in fourth or fifth instar. **HABITAT AND RANGE** Open lodgepole pine and Douglas-fir forests, nearby glades and fields, sparsely wooded hilltops. Canada from QC through E BC, dipping into the Lake states. Barely Cascadian, east of the Okanagan R. in the S interior of BC, its habitat usually considered a butterfly barren.

Ventral

Male specimen

This boreal forest butterfly is very similar to the Great Arctic, but their ranges do not overlap by much, if at all. According to Norbert Kondla, *O. macounii* and *O. nevadensis* do get close in British Columbia, but they are separated by a narrow swath of habitat that is hostile to both species. He doubts that Macoun's Arctic will show up in Cascadia until the next episode of global cooling. Even so, any potential females found in northeast Washington or south-central Canada should be considered tentative unless consorting with the much more obvious males. John Macoun, serving as botanist for

the Geological and Natural History Survey of Canada, collected the type specimens in 1884. Canadian lepidopterists today speak of the butterfly's weak and labored flight compared to most arctics, and how it vanishes onto pine trunks or into the tangle of low branches. Males perch on stumps or limbs to fly out at the wandering females and whatever else comes along.

MOTHS: HONORARY BUTTERFLIES

Most of the Lepidoptera are what we call moths, rather than butterflies. As a group, they offer great beauty and mystique and much more challenge. Inevitably, we mistake certain colorful and diurnal species of moths for butterflies. Each year I receive queries from people who notice the abundant, early spring flight of the pretty black and white (and chestnut and blue) geometrid moth, the Western White-ribboned Carpet (*Mesoleuca gratulata*). They invariably want to know what kind of butterfly it is, and why it isn't in the field guide.

This happens in the summer with the big, wine-and-cheddar-colored Elegant Sheep Moth (*Hemileuca eglanterina*), and the eye-spotted giant silkmoths, Polyphemus and Ceanothus, hanging about people's porchlights in the morning. Even experienced collectors and watchers still have their heads turned by the beautiful orange and brown Infant (*Archiearis infans*) in early spring,

and by the Rusty Tussock Moth (*Orgyia antiqua*) in late summer, both day-flying, crazy speeders that make you think you've got some sort of checker or hairstreak, until you get it in the hand and see it's a moth. The most surprising moth to many is the stunning scarlet-and-graphite Cinnabar Moth (*Tyria jacobaeae*), introduced from Europe to battle tansy ragwort with its hungry caterpillars, known to children as "tansy tigers" for their orange and black bands. We consider all these moths honorary butterflies on our summer butterfly counts. In England, where moth-watching is almost as popular as butterflying, an annual National Moth Night is observed.

Very few people can claim a close acquaintance with Cascadian moths, and it is unlikely anyone will give you a hard time for collecting them. There are many more of them than butterflies (especially in western Washington and Oregon), and they are ever so much more poorly known. Moths offer their own particular fascination, charm, and beauty, and unbounded opportunity for natural history discovery and adventure. They also present their own special conservation needs. It is my hope that spotting these beautiful organisms will hook a few good naturalists into taking up the serious study of moths. For more information on the moths of our region, including distribution maps and digital guides to moth identification, visit pnwmoths. biol.wwu.edu and John Davis' collection of photographs at mothphotographersgroup. msstate.edu/JDIndex.shtml.

Elegant Sheep Moth (*Hemileuca eglanterina*)

CHECKLIST OF PACIFIC NORTHWEST BUTTERFLIES

These are all the butterflies recorded in Washington, Oregon, and adjacent British Columbia, Idaho, and California. "Accidental" records that may seldom (if ever) be repeated are included, in order to encourage watchfulness for such rarities. Names and order follow the March 2016 revision of Pelham's *Catalogue*. Order of appearance is intended to progress from primitive to advanced, as indicated by structure and best available molecular information. No linear arrangement can fully express parallel development of the different groups. Use this list to check off the butterflies you have encountered in the field and identified to your satisfaction. Remember, any checklist is provisional; names will surely be added, subtracted, and changed as our knowledge grows.

Great Arctics (*Oeneis nevadensis*), in flight with a greater fritillary (*Speyeria*)

Superfamily Hesperioidea, Family Hesperiidae: Skippers
Subfamily Eudaminae: Dicot or Spread-wing Skippers I

☐ 1. Silver-spotted Skipper	*Epargyreus clarus*
☐ 2. Northern Cloudywing	*Thorybes pylades*
☐ 3. Western Cloudywing	*Thorybes diversus*
☐ 4. Mexican Cloudywing	*Thorybes mexicana*

Subfamily Pyrginae: Dicot or Spread-wing Skippers II

☐ 5. Common Sootywing	*Pholisora catullus*
☐ 6. Mojave Sootywing	*Hesperopsis libya*
☐ 7. Dreamy Duskywing	*Erynnis icelus*
☐ 8. Propertius Duskywing	*Erynnis propertius*
☐ 9. Pacuvius Duskywing	*Erynnis pacuvius*
☐ 10. Persius Duskywing	*Erynnis persius*

☐ 11. Alpine Checkered Skipper *Pyrgus centaureae*
☐ 12. Two-banded Checkered Skipper *Pyrgus ruralis*
☐ 13. Common Checkered Skipper *Pyrgus communis*
☐ 14. Northern White Skipper *Heliopetes ericetorum*

Subfamily Heteropterinae: Different-winged Skippers

☐ 15. Arctic Skipper *Carterocephalus palaemon*

Subfamily Hesperiinae: Monocot or Folded-wing Skippers

☐ 16. Garita Skipperling *Oarisma garita*
☐ 17. European Skipperling *Thymelicus lineola*
☐ 18. Common Roadside Skipper *Amblyscirtes vialis*
☐ 19. Fiery Skipper *Hylephila phyleus*
☐ 20. Uncas Skipper *Hesperia uncas*
☐ 21. Juba Skipper *Hesperia juba*
☐ 22. Common Branded Skipper *Hesperia comma*
☐ 23. Western Branded Skipper *Hesperia colorado*
☐ 24. Columbian Skipper *Hesperia columbia*
☐ 25. Lindsey's Skipper *Hesperia lindseyi*
☐ 26. Nevada Skipper *Hesperia nevada*
☐ 27. Peck's Skipper *Polites peckius*
☐ 28. Sandhill Skipper *Polites sabuleti*
☐ 29. Draco Skipper *Polites draco*
☐ 30. Mardon Skipper *Polites mardon*
☐ 31. Tawny-edged Skipper *Polites themistocles*
☐ 32. Long Dash *Polites mystic*
☐ 33. Sonora Skipper *Polites sonora*
☐ 34. Sachem *Atalopedes campestris*
☐ 35. Woodland Skipper *Ochlodes sylvanoides*
☐ 36. Rural Skipper *Ochlodes agricola*
☐ 37. Yuma Skipper *Ochlodes yuma*
☐ 38. Dun Skipper *Euphyes vestris*

Superfamily Papilionoidea: Scudders
Family Papilionidae: Parnassians and Swallowtails
Subfamily Parnassiinae: Parnassians and Festoons

☐ 39. Clodius Parnassian *Parnassius clodius*
☐ 40. Mountain Parnassian *Parnassius smintheus*

Subfamily Papilioninae: Swallowtails, Kites, and Birdwings

☐ 41. Pipevine Swallowtail   *Battus philenor*
☐ 42. Oregon Swallowtail   *Papilio machaon*
☐ 43. Anise Swallowtail   *Papilio zelicaon*
☐ 44. Indra Swallowtail   *Papilio indra*
☐ 45. Canadian Tiger Swallowtail   *Papilio canadensis*
☐ 46. Western Tiger Swallowtail   *Papilio rutulus*
☐ 47. Pale Tiger Swallowtail   *Papilio eurymedon*
☐ 48. Two-tailed Tiger Swallowtail   *Papilio multicaudata*

Family Pieridae: Sulphurs, Marbles, and Whites
Subfamily Coliadinae: Sulphurs, Yellows, and Oranges

☐ 49. Dainty Sulphur   *Nathalis iole*
☐ 50. Cloudless Giant Sulphur   *Phoebis sennae*
☐ 51. Tailed Orange   *Pyrisitia proterpia*
☐ 52. Clouded Sulphur   *Colias philodice*
☐ 53. Orange Sulphur   *Colias eurytheme*
☐ 54. Western Sulphur   *Colias occidentalis*
☐ 55. Christina's Sulphur   *Colias christina*
☐ 56. Queen Alexandra's Sulphur   *Colias alexandra*
☐ 57. Labrador Sulphur   *Colias nastes*
☐ 58. Giant Sulphur   *Colias gigantea*
☐ 59. Skinner's Sulphur   *Colias skinneri*
☐ 60. Pink-edged Sulphur   *Colias interior*

Subfamily Pierinae: Marbles and Whites

☐ 61. Sara's Orangetip   *Anthocharis sara*
☐ 62. Gray Marble   *Anthocharis lanceolata*
☐ 63. Large Marble   *Euchloe ausonides*
☐ 64. California Marble   *Euchloe hyantis*
☐ 65. Desert Marble   *Euchloe lotta*
☐ 66. Pine White   *Neophasia menapia*
☐ 67. Margined White   *Pieris marginalis*
☐ 68. Cabbage White   *Pieris rapae*
☐ 69. Becker's White   *Pontia beckerii*
☐ 70. Spring White   *Pontia sisymbrii*
☐ 71. Checkered White   *Pontia protodice*
☐ 72. Western White   *Pontia occidentalis*

Family Lycaenidae: Gossamer Wings
Subfamily Lycaeninae: Coppers

☐	73. American Copper	*Lycaena phlaeas*
☐	74. Lustrous Copper	*Lycaena cupreus*
☐	75. Tailed Copper	*Lycaena arota*
☐	76. Gray Copper	*Lycaena dione*
☐	77. Edith's Copper	*Lycaena editha*
☐	78. Great Copper	*Lycaena xanthoides*
☐	79. Gorgon Copper	*Lycaena gorgon*
☐	80. Ruddy Copper	*Lycaena rubidus*
☐	81. Blue Copper	*Lycaena heteronea*
☐	82. Purplish Copper	*Lycaena helloides*
☐	83. Lilac-bordered Copper	*Lycaena nivalis*
☐	84. Mariposa Copper	*Lycaena mariposa*

Subfamily Theclinae: Hairstreaks

☐	85. Golden Hairstreak	*Habrodais grunus*
☐	86. Great Blue Hairstreak	*Atlides halesus*
☐	87. Sooty Hairstreak	*Satyrium fuliginosa*
☐	88. Halfmoon Hairstreak	*Satyrium semiluna*
☐	89. Behr's Hairstreak	*Satyrium behrii*
☐	90. California Hairstreak	*Satyrium californica*
☐	91. Sylvan Hairstreak	*Satyrium sylvinus*
☐	92. Coral Hairstreak	*Satyrium titus*
☐	93. Gold-hunter's Hairstreak	*Satyrium auretorum*
☐	94. Mountain Mahogany Hairstreak	*Satyrium tetra*
☐	95. Hedgerow Hairstreak	*Satyrium saepium*
☐	96. Western Green Hairstreak	*Callophrys affinis*
☐	97. Bramble Green Hairstreak	*Callophrys dumetorum*
☐	98. Sheridan's Green Hairstreak	*Callophrys sheridanii*
☐	99. Cedar Hairstreak	*Callophrys gryneus*
☐	100. Thicket Hairstreak	*Callophrys spinetorum*
☐	101. Johnson's Hairstreak	*Callophrys johnsoni*
☐	102. Brown Elfin	*Callophrys augustinus*
☐	103. Moss's Elfin	*Callophrys mossii*
☐	104. Hoary Elfin	*Callophrys polios*
☐	105. Western Pine Elfin	*Callophrys eryphon*
☐	106. Gray Hairstreak	*Strymon melinus*

Subfamily Polyommatinae: Blues

☐ 107. Lucia's Azure	*Celastrina lucia*
☐ 108. Echo Azure	*Celastrina echo*
☐ 109. Arrowhead Blue	*Glaucopsyche piasus*
☐ 110. Silvery Blue	*Glaucopsyche lygdamus*
☐ 111. Cascadia Blue	*Euphilotes "on Eriogonum heracleoides"*
☐ 112. Pumice Blue	*Euphilotes "on Eriogonum marifolium"*
☐ 113. Summit Blue	*Euphilotes glaucon*
☐ 114. Bauer's Blue	*Euphilotes baueri*
☐ 115. Pacific Dotted Blue	*Euphilotes enoptes*
☐ 116. Columbia Dotted Blue	*Euphilotes columbiae*
☐ 117. Rocky Mountain Dotted Blue	*Euphilotes ancilla*
☐ 118. Leona's Little Blue	*Philotiella leona*
☐ 119. Western Pygmy Blue	*Brephidium exilis*
☐ 120. Marine Blue	*Leptotes marina*
☐ 121. Eastern Tailed Blue	*Cupido comyntas*
☐ 122. Western Tailed Blue	*Cupido amyntula*
☐ 123. Reakirt's Blue	*Echinargus isola*
☐ 124. Greenish Blue	*Icaricia saepiolus*
☐ 125. Boisduval's Blue	*Icaricia icarioides*
☐ 126. Shasta Blue	*Icaricia shasta*
☐ 127. Acmon Blue	*Icaricia acmon*
☐ 128. Lupine Blue	*Icaricia lupini*
☐ 129. Volcano Blue	*Icaricia "on Eriogonum pyrolifolium"*
☐ 130. Northern Blue	*Plebejus idas*
☐ 131. Anna's Blue	*Plebejus anna*
☐ 132. Melissa's Blue	*Plebejus melissa*
☐ 133. Arctic Blue	*Agriades glandon*
☐ 134. Sierra Nevada Blue	*Agriades podarce*

Family Riodinidae: Metalmarks

☐ 135. Mormon Metalmark	*Apodemia mormo*

Family Nymphalidae: Brushfoots
Subfamily Danaiinae: Milkweed Butterflies

☐ 136. Monarch	*Danaus plexippus*
☐ 137. Queen	*Danaus gilippus*

Subfamily Heliconiinae: Longwings and Fritillaries
Tribe Heliconiini: Longwings

☐ 138. Zebra Longwing   *Heliconius charithonia*
☐ 139. Gulf Fritillary   *Agraulis vanillae*

Tribe Argynnini: Fritillaries

☐ 140. Variegated Fritillary   *Euptoieta claudia*
☐ 141. Silver-bordered Fritillary   *Boloria selene*
☐ 142. Meadow Fritillary   *Boloria bellona*
☐ 143. Western Meadow Fritillary   *Boloria epithore*
☐ 144. Astarte Fritillary   *Boloria astarte*
☐ 145. Freija Fritillary   *Boloria freija*
☐ 146. Arctic Fritillary   *Boloria chariclea*
☐ 147. Great Spangled Fritillary   *Speyeria cybele*
☐ 148. Aphrodite Fritillary   *Speyeria aphrodite*
☐ 149. Coronis Fritillary   *Speyeria coronis*
☐ 150. Zerene Fritillary   *Speyeria zerene*
☐ 151. Callippe Fritillary   *Speyeria callippe*
☐ 152. Great Basin Fritillary   *Speyeria egleis*
☐ 153. Atlantis Fritillary   *Speyeria atlantis*
☐ 154. Northwestern Fritillary   *Speyeria hesperis*
☐ 155. Hydaspe Fritillary   *Speyeria hydaspe*
☐ 156. Mormon Fritillary   *Speyeria mormonia*

Subfamily Limenitidinae: Admirals

☐ 157. White Admiral   *Limenitis arthemis*
☐ 158. Viceroy   *Limenitis archippus*
☐ 159. Weidemeyer's Admiral   *Limenitis weidemeyerii*
☐ 160. Lorquin's Admiral   *Limenitis lorquini*
☐ 161. California Sister   *Adelpha californica*

Subfamily Apaturinae: Emperors

☐ 162. Hackberry Butterfly   *Asterocampa celtis*

Subfamily Nymphalinae: Spiny Brushfoots
Tribe Nymphalini: True Nymphs

☐ 163. American Lady — *Vanessa virginiensis*
☐ 164. Painted Lady — *Vanessa cardui*
☐ 165. West Coast Lady — *Vanessa annabella*
☐ 166. Red Admirable — *Vanessa atalanta*
☐ 167. Milbert's Tortoiseshell — *Aglais milberti*
☐ 168. Compton Tortoiseshell — *Nymphalis l-album*
☐ 169. California Tortoiseshell — *Nymphalis californica*
☐ 170. Mourning Cloak — *Nymphalis antiopa*
☐ 171. Satyr Anglewing — *Polygonia satyrus*
☐ 172. Oreas Anglewing — *Polygonia oreas*
☐ 173. Hoary Comma — *Polygonia gracilis*
☐ 174. Green Comma — *Polygonia faunus*

Tribe Junoniini: Buckeyes

☐ 175. Common Buckeye — *Junonia coenia*

Tribe Melitaeini: Checkers and Crescents

☐ 176. Gillett's Checkerspot — *Euphydryas gillettii*
☐ 177. Edith's Checkerspot — *Euphydryas editha*
☐ 178. Chalcedona Checkerspot — *Euphydryas chalcedona*
☐ 179. Snowberry Checkerspot — *Euphydryas colon*
☐ 180. Anicia Checkerspot — *Euphydryas anicia*
☐ 181. Leanira Checkerspot — *Chlosyne leanira*
☐ 182. Gorgone Checkerspot — *Chlosyne gorgone*
☐ 183. Hoffmann's Checkerspot — *Chlosyne hoffmanni*
☐ 184. Sagebrush Checkerspot — *Chlosyne acastus*
☐ 185. Northern Checkerspot — *Chlosyne palla*
☐ 186. Rockslide Checkerspot — *Chlosyne damoetas*
☐ 187. California Crescent — *Phyciodes orseis*
☐ 188. Pale Crescent — *Phyciodes pallida*
☐ 189. Mylitta Crescent — *Phyciodes mylitta*
☐ 190. Northern Crescent — *Phyciodes cocyta*
☐ 191. Field Crescent — *Phyciodes pulchella*

Subfamily Satyrinae: Satyrs, Browns, and Ringlets

☐ 192. Ochre Ringlet   *Coenonympha tullia*
☐ 193. Common Wood Nymph   *Cercyonis pegala*
☐ 194. Great Basin Wood Nymph   *Cercyonis sthenele*
☐ 195. Dark Wood Nymph   *Cercyonis oetus*
☐ 196. Vidler's Alpine   *Erebia vidleri*
☐ 197. Butler's Alpine   *Erebia epipsodea*
☐ 198. Ridings' Satyr   *Neominois ridingsii*
☐ 199. Melissa's Arctic   *Oeneis melissa*
☐ 200. Chryxus Arctic   *Oeneis chryxus*
☐ 201. Great Arctic   *Oeneis nevadensis*
☐ 202. Macoun's Arctic   *Oeneis macounii*

GLOSSARY

abdomen—the hindmost body segment, behind the thorax and head

aberration—an abnormal organism (or the character that makes it unusual), either genetically or environmentally modified

aestivate—to remain dormant during a hot, dry season; summer diapause

anal—toward the rear

androconia—male pheromone-producing scales, occurring in patches on the wings

antenna, -ae—paired smelling organs protruding from the head

anterior—toward the head

apex—tip; opposite the base

apiculus—pointed tip to the antennal club, especially in some skippers

aposematic—distasteful and warningly colored, like the Monarch

aurora, -ae—the orange-scaled lunules on the ventral hindwings of blues

basal—nearest the body

bi-, trivoltine—double-, triple-brooded

boreal—of cool, northern climes

brood—members of a single generation

cell—space between veins, especially the veinal "loop" on each wing's disc

chrysalis, -ides—the naked pupal stage of a butterfly

circumboreal—distributed around the world in northern regions

circumpolar—distributed around the world south or north of the poles

class—a major subdivision of life forms that branched off long ago (insects, mammals)

cocoon—the silken bag around the pupae of many moths and a few butterflies

compound eye—the optic globe, composed of many clumped lenses that see together

congeners—members of the same genus

conspecific—belonging to the same species

costa—the stiff leading edge of the wing and its large vein

crepuscular—active around dusk or dawn

cryptic—camouflaged; concealed through coloration and pattern

depauperate—impoverished; containing few species

diapause—an interruption of metabolism, usually in winter

dimorphic—possessing two forms, related to sex, season, or other factors

disc—a circular area that may be drawn in the middle of the wing

disjunct populations—occurring widely spaced from one another

diurnal—active during the day

dorsal, -um—the back or upper side; above

eclose—to emerge from the egg or chrysalis, or hatch

ecotype—a variation brought about through local environmental conditions

endemic—occurring only within the area in question, as in "endemic to the high Olympics"

exotic—a species introduced outside its indigenous range (=alien, non-native)

falcate—hooked or curved like a scythe

family—a group of organisms with recognizable features of common descent (cats, brushfoots)

fauna—all the animal species in a defined area, or a subgroup (e.g., the fritillary fauna of Ferry County)

flora—all the plant species in a defined area, or a subgroup (e.g., the grass flora of Grass Valley)

forewings—the anterior pair of wings, or primaries

form—a given appearance or occasional type; not a formal taxon

fulvous—reddish or russet-hued

indigenous—species of native occurrence prior to European colonization

genitalia—the sexual organs and their support structure

genus, -era—a group of closely related species (greater fritillaries, chickadees)

girdle—the silken loop around the thorax that supports a swallowtail or pierid pupa semi-upright from the substrate

glaucous—bluish or foggy gray

head—the first, or forward, of the three body parts

hibernaculum, -i—a rolled and silk-bound leaf in which a caterpillar hibernates

hibernate—to remain dormant during a cold season, or overwinter; winter diapause

hindwing—the posterior pair of wings, or secondaries

Holarctic—distributed around the northern hemisphere

host plant—a caterpillar foodplant

hyaline—transparent or translucent, glassy, as are certain wingspots

hybrid—a sexual cross between two separate species

imago, -oes—the fourth, or adult, stage of metamorphosis

immaculate—unspotted

instar—a stage of larval development between molts

larva, -ae—the second, or caterpillar, stage of metamorphosis

lateral—on or toward the side

lithosol—a rocky soil (often with cryptogam layer intact), or thin soil with many stones on top

local—very limited in distribution to particular places

lunule—a marking shaped like a crescent or partial moon

maculation—spot pattern

margin—the outer edge of the wing

median—in or toward the middle

mesic—wetter, or normal conditions

metamorphosis—the progressive development of an insect through several stages

micropyle—the tiny opening on top of the egg where the spermatazoan enters

mimicry—one species (the mimic) resembling another (the model)

molt—to shed the cuticle between instars

morph—form

natural selection—the preservation of beneficial traits through the survival of fitter individuals who pass these qualities on to their offspring

Nearctic—distributed solely in the northern sector of the New World

nocturnal—active in the night

obligate—biologically required to use a certain food or habitat; not optional

ocellus, -i—an actual simple eye in a caterpillar, or an eyespot on a larva or wing

ommatidium—one of the lenses of the compound eye and the tissue connecting it to the optic nerve

omnivorous—feeding on many foods; polyphagous

order—a higher group of families that have evolved from a common source (primates, Lepidoptera)

osmeterium, -a—a yoke or two-tined "antler" extrusible behind the head of a swallowtail caterpillar, capable of emitting a strong odor

oviposit—to lay eggs

ovum, -a—the first, or egg, stage of metamorphosis

palpus, -i—the furry "arms" along the butterfly face, on either side of the proboscis

phenology—the progression of the seasons as told by plants and animals

phenotype—the traits of an organism as expressed physically; its "looks"

pheromone—a chemical "perfume" emitted by both sexes in courtship for recognition and to stimulate receptivity

polymorphic—a species possessing several distinct forms, often with a genetic basis

polyphenic—a species possessing several distinct forms, seasonally caused

population—a theoretically interbreeding group of individuals within a species

posterior—toward the rear end or tail

primaries—the forewings

proboscis, -es—the fused pair of drinking-straw tubes comprising the butterfly mouthparts, often called "tongue," distinctive to the Lepidoptera

pupa, -ae—the third, or chrysalis, stage of metamorphosis

pupate—to assume the pupal stage

refugium—an ice-free oasis during glaciation

relict, -ual—a species or population left outside the normal range, as by glaciation

scales—many thousands of pigmented or prismatic shingles clothing the wings

scintilla, -ae—the metallic or iridescent silver or turquoise spots near the aurorae on the ventral hindwings of some blues, metalmarks, and satyrs

secondaries—the hind wings

species—a kind of plant or animal, all members of which are capable of interbreeding and producing fertile offspring

speciation—the evolutionary process of the formation of a species

sphragis—a waxy hood deposited over the female's genitalia by the male parnassian during mating, ensuring that his genes alone will be passed to her

stigma, -mata—a dense patch of androconial scales, also called scent pad or sex brand

striated—bearing fine, often parallel lines

subspecies—a geographically differentiated population of a species

sympatric—flying in the same or overlapping ranges

synchronic—flying at the same time

tarsus, -i—the jointed end-section of an insect leg, with claws

taxon, -a—a category of taxonomy, such as a phylum, a family, or a species

"thecla" spot—the bright, often blue and orange, spot complex often found on the hindwings of hairstreaks near the hindwing tornus; with tail, makes "false head"

thorax—the middle of the three body parts, between the head and abdomen, where the wings and legs are attached

tibia, -ae—the second elongated, moveable section of the leg, above the tarsus

tornus—the outer angle of the wing, often drawn out

truncate—shortened; having the wingtip angled so as to look clipped

type locality—the geographic point of origin of the type specimen

type specimen—the original specimen from which a taxon's description was composed

veins—the stiffened tubes that support the membranes of the wing, like kite struts

ventral, -um—the front or underside; beneath

vinous—the color of red wine; maroon or grapey purplish

voltinism—the number of generations or broods

REFERENCES AND RESOURCES

While space will not permit an exhaustive listing of Lepidoptera or even Pacific Northwest butterfly references, this selected list of books and papers quoted or used in the compilation of this book will give readers many entry points to the literature. Each one includes many further citations of relevance to Cascadian butterflies, especially Dornfeld (1980), Guppy and Shepard (2001), Warren (2005), and James and Nunnallee (2011).

Acorn, John. 1993. *Butterflies of Alberta*. Lone Pine Press.
Acorn, John, and Ian Sheldon. 2006. *Butterflies of British Columbia*. Lone Pine Press.
Berkhousen, A. E., and A. M. Shapiro. 1994. Persistent pollen as a tracer for hibernating butterflies. *Great Basin Nat.* 54:71–78.
Bird, C. D., et al. 1995. *Alberta Butterflies*. Provincial Museum of Alberta.
Boyd, Brian, and Robert Michael Pyle, eds. 2000. *Nabokov's Butterflies*. Beacon Press.
Brock, Jim P., and Kenn Kaufman. 2003. *Butterflies of North America*. Houghton Mifflin.
Brower, Lincoln P., and Robert Michael Pyle. 2004. The interchange of migratory monarchs between Mexico and the United States, and the importance of floral corridors to the fall and spring migrations. In *Conserving Migratory Pollinators and Nectar Corridors in Western North America*, ed. Gary Paul Nabhan. Univ. of Arizona Press and Arizona-Sonora Desert Museum.
Brown, F. Martin, et al. 1957. *Colorado Butterflies*. Denver Museum of Natural History.
Burdick, W. N. 1941. A new race of *Plebejus lupini* Bdv. from the Olympic Mountains of Washington (Lepidoptera, Rhopalocera). *Canadian Entomologist* 74:195–196.
Burns, John M. 1964. Evolution of the skipper butterflies in the genus *Erynnis*. UC *Publications in Entomology* 37:1–217.
Christensen, James R. 1981. *A Field Guide to the Butterflies of the Pacific Northwest*. Univ. Press of Idaho.
Collman, Sharon J. 1986. *Butterflies of Lowland King County*. wsu/King Co. Coop. Ext.
Comstock, John Adams. 1927. *Butterflies of California*. Self-published.
Dornfeld, Ernst J. 1980. *The Butterflies of Oregon*. Timber Press.
Douglas, Matthew M. 1986. *The Lives of Butterflies*. Univ. of Michigan Press.
Droppers, David. N.d. *Common Butterflies of the Puget Sound Region and Their Food Plants*. Washington Butterfly Assoc.
Ehrlich, Paul R., and Anne H. Ehrlich. 1961. *How to Know the Butterflies*. Wm. C. Brown Co.
Emmel, Thomas C., et al., eds. 1998. *Systematics of Western American Butterflies*. Mariposa Press.
Ferris, Clifford D. 1972–93. Several important papers on the genus *Colias* in the *Bulletin of the Allyn Museum*.
Ferris, Clifford D., and F. Martin Brown, eds. 1981. *Butterflies of the Rocky Mountain States*. Univ. of Oklahoma Press.
Franklin, J. F., and C. T. Dyrness. 1988. *Natural Vegetation of Oregon and Washington*, rev. ed. osu Press.
Garth, John S., and J. W. Tilden. 1986. *California Butterflies*. Univ. of California Press.
Gilbert, Rod, and Ann Potter. 2014. *A Region Specific Guide to Butterflies of the South Puget Sound, Washington*. Cascadia Prairie-Oak Partnership.
Glassberg, Jeffrey. 2001. *Butterflies Through Binoculars: The West*. Oxford Univ. Press.

Guppy, Crispin S., et al. 1994. Butterflies and skippers of conservation concern in British Columbia. *Canadian Field Naturalist* 108:31–40.

Guppy, Crispin S., and Jon H. Shepard. 2001. *Butterflies of British Columbia*. UBC Press.

Guppy, Richard. 1951–74. Numerous notes on Vancouver Island butterflies, *News* and *Journal* of the Lepidopterists' Society.

Hamilton, Edith. 1942. *Mythology: Timeless Tales of Gods and Heroes*. New American Library.

Hammond, Paul C. Many papers on *Speyeria zerene hippolyta* and its conservation (some referenced in New et al. 1995).

Hammond, P. C., and D. V. McCorkle. 2017. *Taxonomy, Ecology, and Evolutionary Theory of the Genus* Colias. The Franklin Press.

Hardwick, Robert E. 2001. *Butterflies of Washington*. Self-published.

Hardy, G. A. 1947–64. Numerous papers on Vancouver Island butterflies in the *Proceedings of the Entomological Society of British Columbia*.

Hatch, Melville H. 1949. *A Century of Entomology in the Pacific Northwest*. Univ. of Washington Press.

Hewes, Laurence Ilsley. 1936. Butterflies—try and get them. *National Geographic* 109:667–678.

Higgins, Lionel G., and Norman D. Riley. 1980. *A Field Guide to the Butterflies of Britain and Europe*, rev. ed. Collins.

Hinchliff, John. 1994. *An Atlas of Oregon Butterflies*. OSU Bookstore.

———. 1996. *An Atlas of Washington Butterflies*. OSU Bookstore.

Hitchcock, C. Leo, and Arthur Cronquist. 1976. *The Flora of the Pacific Northwest*, rev. ed. Univ. of Washington Press.

Holland, W. J. 1931. *The Butterfly Book*, rev. ed. Doubleday.

Howe, William H., ed. 1975. *The Butterflies of North America*. Doubleday.

James, David G. 2012. Observations on the life history and field biology of an imperiled butterfly *Philotiella leona* (Lepidoptera: Lycaenidae) from South Central Oregon. *J. Res. Lepid.*: 45:93–99.

James, David G., and David Nunnallee. 2011. *Life Histories of Cascadia Butterflies*. OSU Press.

James, D. G., and J. P. Pelham. 2011. Notes on the seasonal biology of *Argynnis coronis* Behr (Lepidoptera: Argynnidae) in central Washington. *J. Lepid. Soc.* 65:249–255

James, D. G., et al. 2015. Beauty with benefits: butterfly conservation in Washington State, USA, wine grape vineyards. *J. Insect Conservation* 19:341–348.

Johnson, Kurt. 1976. Three new Nearctic species of *Callophrys (Mitoura)*, with a diagnosis of all Nearctic consubgeners (Lepidoptera: Lycaenidae). *Bulletin of the Allyn Museum* 43:1–62.

Knopp, Denis, and Lee K. Larkin. 1998. *Butterflies of the North Cascades*. Skagit Environmental Endowment Commission.

Knowles, Kristi M. 2005. *Butterflies of the North Olympic Peninsula*. Trafford Pub.

LaBar, Caitlin C. 2017a. *Butterflies of the Sinlahekin Wildlife Area*. Speyeria Press.

———. 2017b. *Pocket Guide to the Butterflies of Washington*. Speyeria Press.

Layberry, Ross L., et al. 1998. *The Butterflies of Canada*. Univ. of Toronto Press.

Leighton, Ben V. 1946. *The Butterflies of Washington*. Univ. of Washington Press.

MacNeill, C. Don. 1964. The skipper butterflies of the genus *Hesperia* in western North America with special reference to California. *UC Pub. in Entomology* 35:1–130.

McCorkle, D. V., and P. C. Hammond. 1986. Observations on the biology of *Parnassius clodius* (Papilionidae) in the Pacific Northwest. *J. Lepid. Soc.* 39:156–162.

———. 1988. Biology of *Speyeria zerene hippolyta* (Nymphalidae) in a marine-modified environment. *J. Lepid. Soc.* 42:184–192.

McKee, Bates. 1972. *Cascadia: The Geologic Evolution of the Pacific Northwest.* McGraw-Hill.

Miller, Jacqueline Y., ed. 1992. *The Common Names of North American Butterflies.* Smithsonian Institution Press.

Miller, Jeffrey C., and Paul C. Hammond. 1995. *Caterpillars of Pacific Northwest Forests and Woodlands.* USDA (U.S. Forest Service).

———. 2000. *Macromoths of Northwest Forests and Woodlands.* USDA (U.S. Forest Service).

Miller, Lee D., and F. Martin Brown. 1981. *A Catalogue/Checklist of the Butterflies of America North of Mexico.* Memoir No. 2, The Lepidopterists' Society.

Myers, David Lee. 2002. *North Coast Butterflies and Day-flying Moths.* North Coast Land Conservancy.

Neill, W. A. 2001. *The Guide to Butterflies of Oregon and Washington.* Westcliffe Publishers.

———. 2007. *Butterflies of the Pacific Northwest.* Mountain Press.

Neill, W. A., and Doug J. Hepburn. 1976. *Butterflies Afield in the Pacific Northwest.* Pacific Search Books.

New, T., R. M. Pyle, J. A. Thomas, C. D. Thomas, and P. C. Hammond. 1995. Butterfly conservation management. *Annual Review of Entomology* 40:57–83.

Newcomer, E. J. 1964. The Butterflies of Yakima County. *J. Lepid. Soc.* 18:217–228.

North American Butterfly Association. 2001. *Checklist and English Names of North American Butterflies*, rev. ed. NABA.

Opler, Paul A. 1999. *Western Butterflies: A Peterson Field Guide.* Houghton Mifflin.

O'Shea, Colleen. N.d. Mima Mounds Natural Area Preserve Butterfly Guide. DNR/TNC.

Pelham, Jonathan P. 1988. *Ochlodes yuma* (Hesperiidae), a Pleistocene relict discovered in Washington. *Northwest Lepid. Assoc. Newsletter* 2:3–4

———. 2008. *A Catalogue of the Butterflies of the United States and Canada*, rev. 11 March 2016 at butterfliesofamerica.com/US-CanCat.htm.

Pyle, Robert Michael. 1974. *Watching Washington Butterflies.* Seattle Audubon Society.

———. 1976. The status of the valerata arctic. *Atala* 3:32–35.

———. 1981. *Audubon Society Field Guide to North American Butterflies.* Knopf.

———. 1982. Butterfly ecogeography and biological conservation in Washington. *Atala* 8:1–26.

———. 1989. Washington Butterfly Conservation Status Report and Plan. WDFW, Olympia.

———. 1992. *Handbook for Butterfly Watchers.* Houghton Mifflin.

———. 1995. A history of Lepidoptera conservation, with special attention to its Remingtonian debt. *J. Lepid. Soc.* 49:397-411.

———. 2002. *The Butterflies of Cascadia.* Seattle Audubon Society.

———. 2011. *The Thunder Tree: Lessons from an Urban Wildland.* OSU Press.

———. 2013. *Mariposa Road: The First Butterfly Big Year.* Yale Univ. Press.

———. 2014. *Chasing Monarchs: Migrating with the Butterflies of Passage.* Yale Univ. Press.

———. 2015a. Monarchs in the mist: new perspectives on Monarch distribution in the Pacific Northwest. In Oberhauser, Karen S., et al., *Monarchs in a Changing World.* Cornell Univ. Press.

———. 2015b. *Wintergreen: Rambles in a Ravaged Land.* Pharos Editions.

———. 2016. A brief history of Washington butterfly books. wabutterflyassoc.org/wp-content/uploads/2016/11/GnumVol17No4.pdf (and other columns in this series).

Pyle, R. M., and P. C. Hammond. 2018. A review of the Mariposa Copper. *J. Lepid. Soc.* 71.

Rolfs, Don. 2000. *Pictorial Guide to the Butterflies of Chumstick Mountain.* Self-published.

———. 2001. *Pictorial Guide to the Butterflies of Fort Lewis and the Puget Trough.* Self-published.

Sbordoni, Valerio, and Saverio Forestiero. 1998. *Butterflies of the World.* Firefly Books.

Schultz, C. B. 1997. *Ecology and Conservation of Fender's Blue Butterfly.* Ph.D. thesis, Univ. of Washington (and many subsequent papers).

Scott, James A. 1986. *The Butterflies of North America: A Natural History and Field Guide.* Stanford Univ. Press.

———. 1998. New western North American butterflies. *Papilio New Series* 11:1–12 (and many subsequent papers).

Scriber, J. M., et al., eds. 1994. *Swallowtail Butterflies.* Scientific Publishers.

Shapiro, Arthur M. 1974–. Many papers on the biology of western butterflies in *J. Res. Lepid., J. Lepid. Soc.,* and others.

Shapiro, Arthur M., and Timothy D. Manolis. 2007. *Field Guide to Butterflies of the San Francisco Bay and Sacramento Valley Regions.* Univ. of California Press.

Shepard, Jon H. 1964. The genus *Lycaeides* in the Pacific Northwest. *J. Res. Lepid.* 3:25-36 (and many subsequent papers).

Shields, Oakley. 1966–. Many papers on the biology of western butterflies in *J. Res. Lepid.* and *J. Lepid. Soc.*

Singh Bais, Rajiv K. 2016. On the occurrence of Common Baron (Lepidoptera: Nymphalidae: Limenitidinae: *Euthalia aconthea* Cramer, 1777) in the Delhi area and analysis of abiotic factors affecting its distribution in India. *J. Threatened Taxa* 8:9418–9433.

Sperling, Felix A. H. 1993. Mitochondrial DNA phylogeny of the *Papilio machaon* species group (Lepidoptera: Papilionidae). *Memoirs of the Entomological Society of Canada* 165:233–242.

Stanford, Ray E., and Paul A. Opler. 1993. *Atlas of Western USA Butterflies,* and supplements. Gillette Museum, Fort Collins.

Stewart, Bob. 1997. *Common Butterflies of California.* West Coast Lady Press.

Sutton, Patricia Taylor, and Clay Sutton. 1999. *How to Spot Butterflies.* Houghton Mifflin.

Tekulsky, Mathew. 2015. *The Art of Butterfly Gardening.* Skyhorse Publishing.

Tilden, J. W. 1965. *Butterflies of the San Francisco Bay Region.* Univ. of California Press.

Tilden, J. W., and Arthur C. Smith. 1987. *A Field Guide to the Western Butterflies.* Houghton Mifflin.

Tyler, Hamilton, et al. 1994. *Swallowtail Butterflies of the Americas.* Scientific Publishers.

Vernon, Susan. 2005. *Butterflies of the San Juan Islands Checklist.* Archipelago Press.

Warren, Andrew D. 2005. *Butterflies of Oregon.* Gillette Museum, Fort Collins.

Winter, William D. 2001. *Basic Techniques for Observing and Studying Moths and Butterflies.* Memoir No. 5, The Lepidopterists' Society.

Wright, W. G. 1905. *Butterflies of the West Coast of the United States.* Self-published.

Xerces Society. 2016. *Gardening for Butterflies.* Timber Press.

Yip, Mike, and James Miskelly. 2014. *Vancouver Island Butterflies.* Self-published.

Organizations

To become more involved in the enjoyment and study of butterflies and to meet other enthusiasts, we highly recommend joining and attending the open meetings of the organizations listed here, and going along on their field trips. In addition to these, check out the entomological association and native plant society for each state and province.

Eugene-Springfield Butterfly Association (newsletter, field trips, meets monthly in Eugene): naba.org/chapters/nabaes/index.html

Lepidopterists' Society (*News* and *Journal*; annual national and Pacific Slope meetings): lepsoc.org

North American Butterfly Association (publishes *American Butterflies, The Butterfly Gardener*; meets annually): naba.org

Northwest Lepidopterists' Association (for everyone interested in butterflies and moths; meets annually at OSU, Corvallis, late October): mccorkd@fsa.wou.edu

Scarabs (*Scarabogram*; general interest insect group, meets fourth Mondays at Burke Museum, UW, Seattle): tiso@u.washington.edu

Washington Butterfly Association (for all butterfly lovers; newsletter, field trips, meets first Wednesdays at Center for Urban Horticulture, Seattle): wabutterflyassoc.org

Conservation Groups

Monarch Butterflies in the Pacific Northwest (run by David James of WSU): facebook.com/MonarchButterfliesInThePacificNorthwest

Monarch Watch (tagging program, education, seasonal summary): monarchwatch.org

Xerces Society (the premier organization for invertebrate conservation; publishes *Wings*): xerces.org

Internet

Of course there are numerous Internet butterfly resources, but beware: many of the sites merely advertise butterfly profiteers engaged in the deplorable and anti-scientific activity of selling live butterflies for release at events far from their point of origin. The most useful website is butterfliesofamerica.org, where you will find thumbnails and both specimen and live photos of virtually all North American butterflies, as well as Pelham's *Catalogue*.

Several Western lepidopterists maintain websites, Flickr and other accounts of photographs, and butterfly blogs. The one we most recommend, with excellent links, is Caitlin LaBar's northwestbutterflies.blogspot.com.

The best listserver for lepidopterists is LEPS-L (mailman.yale.edu/mailman/listinfo/leps-l) and for Northwest butterfly discussion, groups.yahoo.com/neo/groups/NorWestLeps/info.

Moth lovers will love Pacific Northwest Moths (pnwmoths.biol.wwu.edu) and John Davis's Moths of the Pacific Northwest (mothphotographersgroup.msstate.edu/JDIndex.shtml).

Bug Guide is useful for general insect identification: bugguide.net/node/view/15740.

Other Resources

FOURTH OF JULY BUTTERFLY COUNTS occur in several locations in the region, initiated by the Xerces Society and currently sponsored by the North American Butterfly Association. For locations near you, check with the aforementioned butterfly organizations and naba.org.

BUTTERFLY HOUSES are located in Victoria and Nanaimo, BC, and in the Pacific Science Center in Seattle with one coming in Astoria, OR. Featuring many exotic species, year-round, these are fine places to observe and photograph butterflies up close.

SUPPLIES The most consistent source of nets, rearing equipment, books, and other materials is the Bioquip Company of Gardena, California (bioquip.com). Natural history books on all topics and various other items may be found at the shops of the Seattle Audubon Society and the Audubon Society of Portland.

(by appointment) may be found in the Provincial Museum, Victoria, BC; Burke Museum, University of Washington, Seattle; Department of Entomology, Washington State University, Pullman; and Oregon State Arthropod Collection, Oregon State University, Corvallis. Small public displays are periodically exhibited at these institutions.

Data Banks: Where to Send Your Records

Reliable records of butterfly occurrence in the Pacific Northwest should be turned in to the Northwest Lepidoptera Survey. Send data (species, date, precise location, name of collector or observer, voucher evidence) to the individual state coordinators (Washington: Ann Potter, Department of Fish and Wildlife, 600 Capitol Way N., Olympia, WA 98501; Oregon: Dana Ross, OSAC, Dept. of Integrative Biology, Cordley Hall, OSU, Corvallis, OR 97331); or to the Northwest Lepidoptera Survey co-coordinators: Jonathan Pelham, Burke Museum, UW, Seattle, WA 98195; and R. M. Pyle, 369 Loop Road, Gray's River, WA 98621.

To be reported in the annual Season's Summary of the Lepidopterists' Society, records should be sent to the Zone 2 (Pacific Northwest) Coordinator: Jon H. Shepard, 4925 SW Dakota Ave., Corvallis, OR 97333, (541) 207-3450, shep.lep@netidea.com.

Butterfly findings, accompanied by data and preferably diagnostic voucher photographs, will also happily be received by the following data bases and sharing sites: Butterflies and Moths of North America (BAMONA; "an ambitious effort to collect, store, and share species information and occurrence data"), butterfliesandmoths.org; eButterfly ("an international, data driven project dedicated to butterfly biodiversity, conservation, and education"), e-butterfly.org; and iNaturalist ("a place where you can record what you see in nature, meet other nature lovers, and learn about the natural world"), inaturalist.org.

Always remember that no matter how rich and rewarding the bookshelf and the computer may prove in your search for information, nothing matches the learning experience of actually being outdoors among the butterflies, with your eyes and mind wide open. By all means learn what others say about them; then go out and discover for yourself who these creatures really are, how they live, and what *they themselves* have to tell us about the world.

PHOTO AND ILLUSTRATION CREDITS

Each photograph is identified by its photographer, page number, position, and the county and state (or location and province) in which it was taken.

Sue Anderson, pages 213 (right, Wheeler, OR) and 273 (Wheeler, OR).

Dave Bartholomew, pages 99 (Plumas, CA) and 274 (top left, Big Horn-Sheridan line, WY).

John Baumann, pages 57 (left, Spokane, WA), 75 (Missoula, MT), 98 (middle, Stevens, WA), 211 (left, Spokane, WA), 291 (left, Bonner, ID), 374 (Grant, WA) and 415 (Missoula, MT).

Cheryl Bellin, page 151 (bottom, Okanogan, WA).

Bill Bouton, pages 49 (top left, Madera, CA), 53 (right, Inyo, CA), 87 (bottom right, Ventura, CA), 94 (top right, Boulder, CO), 144 (bottom, Beaverhead, MT), 172 (Kern, CA) and 173 (bottom, Kern, CA).

Ray Bruun, pages 6 (Shasta, CA), 63 (bottom right, Siskiyou, CA), 87 (bottom left, Shasta, CA), 151 (top, Siskiyou, CA), 158 (top right, Shasta, CA), 167 (left, Shasta, CA), 168 (Siskiyou, CA), 184 (bottom left, Shasta, CA), 203 (top, Lassen, CA), 205 (Shasta, CA), 207 (Shasta, CA), 251 (Shasta, CA), 256 (top, Cochise, AZ), 275 (Trinity, CA), 332 (bottom, Shasta, CA), 340 (Monterey, CA), 341 (Shasta, CA), 350 (top, Shasta, CA), 351 (Shasta, CA), 379 (bottom, Trinity, CA), 386 (left, Shasta, CA), 390 (right, Shasta, CA), 396 (Shasta, CA) and 420 (Shasta, CA).

John Christiansen, pages 200 (Kittitas, WA), 256 (bottom, Kittitas, WA) and 309 (right, Kittitas, WA).

Jeanne Dammarell, pages 63 (bottom left, Lincoln, WA), 64 (right, Lincoln, WA), 81 (Lincoln, WA), 84 (both, Spokane, WA), 85 (top, Spokane, WA), 93 (right, Lincoln, WA), 111 (bottom, Spokane, WA), 123 (right, Spokane, WA), 125 (bottom, Lincoln, WA), 135 (top left, Lincoln, WA), 137 (bottom, Spokane, WA), 140 (left, Pend Oreille, WA), 148 (Lincoln, WA), 158 (top left, Lincoln, WA), 162 (left, Lincoln, WA), 176 (bottom left, Spokane, WA), 183 (left, Lincoln, WA), 184 (top, Lincoln, WA), 188 (Pend Oreille, WA), 189 (top and middle, Pend Oreille, WA), 208 (top, Spokane, WA; bottom, Lincoln, WA), 214 (Lincoln, WA), 224 (right, Spokane, WA), 234 (bottom left, Lincoln, WA), 235 (left, Lincoln, WA) 237 (Spokane, WA), 252 (bottom left, Pend Oreille, WA; bottom right, Spokane, WA), 257 (top left and top right, Lincoln, WA), 284 (Spokane, WA), 294 (left, Spokane, WA), 305 (top right, Spokane, WA), 306 (top, Spokane, WA), 311 (bottom left, Pend Oreille, WA; bottom right, Stevens, WA), 313 (both, Lincoln, WA), 314 (top, Lincoln, WA), 321 (right, Spokane, WA), 337 (both, Lincoln, WA), 338 (Spokane, WA), 390 (left, Lincoln, WA), 391 (bottom, Lincoln, WA), 393 (top left, Spokane, WA; bottom two, Pend Oreille, WA) and 401 (left, Lincoln, WA).

John Davis, pages 42 (Klickitat, WA), 95 (top left and bottom, Klickitat, WA), 100 (both, Skamania, WA), 102 (left, Skamania, WA), 120 (left, Klickitat, WA), 150 (top right, Klickitat, WA), 197 (left, Yakima, WA; right, Hood River, OR), 221 (right, Klickitat, WA), 343 (Clark, WA), 350 (bottom, Klickitat, WA), 360 (Yakima, WA), 395 (Yakima, WA), 401 (right, Klickitat, WA), 402 (bottom, Skamania, WA) and 417 (bottom right, Klickitat, WA).

Kim Davis & Mike Stangeland, pages 87 (top, Siskiyou, CA), 89 (right, Mono, CA), 94 (bottom, Apache, AZ), 107 (bottom, Josephine, OR), 113 (top left and top right, Klickitat, WA), 141 (left, Deschutes, OR; right, Lake, OR), 193 (left, Lane, OR), 206 (Jackson, OR), 209 (Jefferson, OR), 239 (Deschutes, OR), 240 (all, Deschutes, OR), 243 (top, Linn, OR), 247 (top, Harney, OR; bottom right, Klamath, OR), 261 (bottom, Deschutes, OR), 263 (left, Jackson, OR), 264 (bottom, Wasco, OR), 267 (all, Deschutes, OR), 268 (Deschutes, OR), 271 (top right, Jackson, OR; bottom, Linn, OR), 319 (top right, Jackson, OR), 322 (right, Wallowa, OR), 328 (right, Mono, CA), 329 (Mono, CA), 368 (Jackson, OR), 369 (Jackson, OR), 382 (top left, Crook, OR; bottom, Wasco, OR), 391 (top, Jackson, OR), 402 (top, Sherman, OR) and 404 (top, Lake, OR).

Dennis Deck, page 178 (top, Lane, OR).

David Droppers, pages 201 (right, Kittitas, WA), 229 (Yakima, WA), 230 (top, Yakima, WA) and 327 (Grant, WA).

Mary Ebenal, page 161 (bottom left, Okanogan, WA).

Candace Fallon, pages 95 (top right, Skamania, WA) and 367 (right, Benton, OR).

Jim Flynn, page 324 (Okanogan, WA).

Rod Gilbert, pages 36 (Pierce, WA), 83 (top right, Clallam, WA), 139 (left, Chelan, WA), 408 (right, Jefferson, WA) and 414 (top left, Jefferson, WA).

Donald Gudehus, page 177 (both, Lane, OR).

David Hagen, page 248 (Klamath, OR).

Tanya Harvey, pages 109 (Lane, OR) and 159 (Lane, OR).

Dennis Holmes, pages 38-39 (Deschutes, OR), 52 (top left, Glenn, CA), 54 (Ferry, WA), 55 (left, Siskiyou, CA), 56 (bottom, Shasta, CA), 58 (left, Ferry, WA), 64 (left,

Colusa, CA), 67 (top right, Valley, ID), 80 (all, Mono, CA), 86 (top, Trinity, CA), 92 (Madera, CA), 93 (left, Lake, OR), 97 (top, Siskiyou, CA), 104 (Napa, CA), 105 (top, Napa, CA), 110 (Mono, CA), 115 (Shasta, CA), 116 (all, Shasta, CA), 145 (top, Park, WY), 155 (left, Lyon, NV), 157 (right, Shasta, CA), 171 (bottom, Shasta, CA), 179 (bottom, Siskiyou, CA), 180 (Siskiyou, CA), 181 (top right, Mono, CA; bottom, Modoc, CA), 195 (Siskiyou, CA), 201 (left, Shasta, CA), 221 (left, Shasta, CA), 242 (top right, Washoe, NV; bottom, Harney, OR), 243 (bottom, Mono, CA), 245 (top, Wasco, OR), 249 (left, Kern, CA; right, Yolo, CA), 255 (Yuma, AZ), 262 (left, Mono-Tuolumne line, CA), 274 (top right, Carbon, MT), 276 (bottom, Siskiyou, CA), 310 (Josephine, OR), 339 (Tehama, CA), 365 (Deschutes, OR), 375 (bottom, Shasta, CA), 381 (Wasco, OR), 385 (both, Mono, CA), 410 (Wallowa, OR) and 411 (both, Lake, OR).

Lori Humphreys, pages 48 (right, Wallowa, OR), 49 (bottom, Deschutes, OR), 50 (both, Deschutes, OR), 111 (top left and top right, Lane, OR), 139 (right, Crook, OR), 176 (top, Lane, OR), 224 (left, Lane, OR), 244 (Lane, OR), 294 (top right, Lane, OR), 355 (bottom left, Lane, OR) and 370 (left, Lane, OR).

David James, pages 29 (Apex Mt., BC), 51 (Benton, WA), 52 (top right, Benton, WA), 60 (both, Okanogan, WA), 77 (right, Columbia, WA), 143 (all, Apex Mt., BC), 161 (bottom right, Yakima, WA), 166 (right, Yakima, WA), 230 (bottom, Yakima, WA), 296 (left, Okanogan, WA), 299 (both, Yakima, WA), 318 (bottom, Pend Oreille, WA), 319 (top left, Pend Oreille, WA; bottom, Shasta, CA), 323 (bottom, Harney, OR), 362 (Solano, CA) and 393 (top right, Columbia, WA).

Sarina Jepsen, page 247 (bottom left, Klamath, OR).

Dakota Kappen, page 259 (bottom right, Harney, OR).

Linda Kappen, pages 56 (middle, Josephine, OR), 61 (Jackson, OR), 63 (top, Jackson, OR), 85 (bottom, Klamath, OR), 88 (Klamath, OR), 103 (bottom left, Jackson, OR), 127 (Jackson, OR), 152 (Jackson, OR), 153 (right, Jackson, OR), 158 (bottom left, Josephine, OR), 166 (left, Josephine, OR), 179 (top, Siskiyou, CA), 189 (bottom, Josephine, OR), 241 (Jackson, OR), 242 (top left, Jackson, OR), 254 (bottom, Jackson, OR), 257 (bottom, Klamath, OR), 270 (Klamath, OR), 315 (Josephine, OR), 330 (right, Josephine, OR), 332 (top, Jackson, OR), 335 (top, Jackson, OR), 348 (Jackson, OR), 366 (bottom, Jackson, OR) and 384 (both, Jackson, OR).

Ken Kertell, pages 57 (top, Tulare, CA), 145 (bottom, Carbon, MT), 165 (top right, Pima, AZ; bottom right, Santa Cruz, AZ) and 169 (Carbon, MT).

Tom Kogut, pages 223 (Yakima, WA) and 235 (right, Yakima, WA).

Norbert Kondla, pages 46 (right, Genelle, BC), 57 (bottom right, Pend d'Oreille Valley, BC), 67 (top left, Pend d'Oreille Valley, BC), 76 (right, Elk River Valley, BC), 94 (top left, Klondike Hwy, YT), 121 (both, near Redwater, AB), 135 (top right, Bragg Creek, AB), 144 (top, Annie Lake Rd, YT), 163 (Frank, AB), 174 (left, Cranbrook, BC), 213 (left, Pend d'Oreille Valley, BC), 269 (bottom, near Radium, BC), 297 (both, Nazco, BC), 305 (top left, Rossland, BC; bottom, Pend d'Oreille Valley, BC), 306 (bottom, Battle River, AB), 307 (Battle River, AB), 325 (bottom, near Keno City, YT), 326 (Milk River Grazing Reserve, AB), 346 (both, Pend d'Oreille Valley, BC), 349 (Rossland, BC), 364 (both, South Castle River Valley, AB), 409 (right, Pend d'Oreille Valley, BC) and 418 (top, near Redwater, AB).

Caitlin LaBar, pages 12-13 (Klickitat, WA), 44 (Okanogan, WA), 46 (left, Cowlitz, WA), 58 (right, Okanogan, WA), 68 (Kittitas, WA),

78 (bottom left and right, Hawaii, HI), 82 (both, Sherman, OR), 89 (left, Okanogan, WA), 103 (top left and top right, Kittitas, WA), 118 (left, Okanogan, WA), 119 (left, Thurston, WA; right, Sherman, OR), 122 (Okanogan, WA), 124 (top, Chelan, WA; bottom, Kittitas, WA), 125 (top, Okanogan, WA), 140 (right, Okanogan, WA), 146 (Wallowa, OR), 155 (right, Kittitas, WA), 156 (both, Kittitas, WA), 158 (bottom right, Cowlitz, WA), 183 (right, Okanogan, WA), 184 (bottom right, Yakima, WA), 186 (Okanogan, WA), 187 (top two, Okanogan, WA; bottom right, Kittitas, WA), 198 (Kittitas, WA), 199 (Okanogan, WA), 217 (left, Kittitas, WA), 225 (Okanogan, WA), 232 (both, Kittitas, WA), 236 (bottom, Lake, OR), 238 (top left, Okanogan, WA; top right, Chelan, WA), 245 (bottom left, Kittitas, WA; bottom right, Sherman, OR), 254 (top, Okanogan, WA), 259 (top two, Benton, OR; middle two and bottom left, Thurston, WA), 260 (Okanogan, WA), 263 (right, Sherman, OR), 265 (top, Kittitas, WA; bottom, Okanogan, WA), 266 (Sherman, OR), 270 (top left, Kittitas, WA), 272 (right, Okanogan, WA), 277 (Kittitas, WA), 294 (bottom right, Cowlitz, WA), 308 (Kittitas, WA), 309 (left, Kittitas, WA), 321 (left, Kittitas, WA), 322 (left, Okanogan, WA), 328 (left, Salt Lake, UT), 330 (left, Sherman, OR), 344 (Kittitas, WA), 353 (Okanogan, WA), 354 (Okanogan, WA), 359 (bottom, Okanogan, WA), 363 (Kittitas, WA), 366 (top, Yakima, WA), 370 (right, Kittitas, WA), 371 (top, Skamania, WA; bottom, Kittitas, WA), 372 (Kittitas, WA), 373 (all, Okanogan, WA), 378 (bottom, Okanogan, WA), 379 (top, Okanogan, WA), 380 (Okanogan, WA), 388 (top, Okanogan, WA) and 419 (Kittitas, WA).

Robin LaBar, page 407 (Okanogan, WA).

John Lane, pages 203 (bottom, Harney, OR), 261 (top, Malheur, OR) and 335 (bottom, Plumas, CA).

Vincent Lucas, page 83 (top left, Clallam, WA).

David Lee Myers, pages 1 (Sherman, OR), 2 (Sherman, OR), 56 (top, Klickitat, WA), 76 (left, Whatcom, WA), 78 (top, Hidalgo, TX), 103 (bottom right, Clatsop, OR), 118 (right, Sherman, OR), 137 (top right, Grant, WA), 153 (left, Jackson, OR), 165 (bottom left, Weston, WY), 212 (Jackson, OR), 218 (right, Clatsop, OR), 234 (top right, Jackson, OR), 278 (left, Klickitat, WA), 281 (bottom two, Jefferson, OR), 320 (Crook, OR), 323 (top, Harney, OR), 342 (right, Clatsop, OR), 345 (Harney, OR), 357 (bottom, Jefferson, OR), 389 (both, Sherman, OR), 397 (Sherman, OR), 398 (bottom right, Jackson, OR), 405 (left, Crook, OR), 406 (Kootenai, ID), 409 (left, near Summit Lake, BC) and 417 (bottom left, Jackson, OR).

Bruce Newhouse, page 252 (top right, Lane, OR).

David Nunnallee, pages 14 (Okanogan, WA), 48 (left, Chelan, WA), 91 (bottom, Okanogan, WA), 97 (bottom, Okanogan, WA), 106 (Grant, WA), 126 (bottom, Okanogan, WA), 149 (top, Okanogan, WA), 150 (top left, Kittitas, WA), 157 (left, Kittitas, WA), 175 (bottom, Garfield, WA), 182 (both, Kittitas, WA), 219 (Mason, WA), 234 (bottom right, Chelan, WA), 236 (top, Kittitas, WA), 238 (bottom, Okanogan, WA), 246 (both, Harney, OR), 252 (top left, Benton, OR), 253 (Kittitas, WA), 264 (top, Clallam, WA), 274 (bottom right, Okanogan, WA), 291 (right, Pend Oreille, WA), 293 (both, Okanogan, WA), 296 (right, Okanogan, WA), 304 (Kittitas, WA), 317 (Pend Oreille, WA), 318 (top, Pend Oreille, WA), 342 (left, King, WA), 355 (top and bottom right, Kittitas, WA), 356 (Okanogan, WA), 382 (top right, Kittitas, WA), 383 (both, Okanogan, WA), 388 (bottom, Okanogan, WA), 403 (Grant, WA), 408 (left, Okanogan, WA) and 412 (Okanogan, WA).

Sue Orlowski, page 114 (Lincoln, WA).

Matt Orsie, page 298 (Clallam, WA).

Mike Patterson, pages 26 (Tillamook, OR), 59 (Clatsop, OR), 123 (left, Clatsop, OR), 231 (left, Clatsop, OR) and 398 (top, Clatsop, OR).

Barbara Peck, page 37 (bottom, Siskiyou, CA).

Jeff Pippen, pages 91 (top left, Watauga, NC; top right, Alleghany, NC), 135 (middle left and middle right, Missoula, MT), 137 (top left, Missoula, MT), 147 (top, Missoula, MT), 162 (right, Missoula, MT), 164 (right, Missoula, MT), 167 (right, Beaverhead, MT), 187 (bottom left, Beaverhead, MT), 193 (right, Monterey, CA), 220 (Missoula, MT) and 269 (top, Missoula, MT).

Thea Pyle, page 5 (Adams, WA).

Bryan E. Reynolds, pages 74 (left, McKenzie, ND; right, Dunn, ND), 77 (left, Cleveland, OK), 96 (Dunn, ND), 98 (top, Green Lake, WI; bottom, Barnes, ND), 101 (McClain, OK), 130 (bottom, Cleveland, OK), 131 (Cleveland, OK), 132 (Cleveland, OK), 133 (Hidalgo, TX), 138 (McKenzie, ND), 161 (top left, Bottineau, ND), 165 (top left, Johnston, OK), 174 (left, Ward, ND), 175 (top, Ward, ND), 283 (both, Hidalgo, TX), 285 (Hidalgo, TX), 286 (Cleveland, OK), 287 (Starr, TX), 288 (Cimarron, OK), 289 (Cimarron, OK), 325 (top, McHenry, ND), 333 (Cleveland, OK), 334 (Cleveland, OK), 377 (Cleveland, OK) and 378 (top, Cleveland, OK).

Rob Santry, pages 8 (Shasta, CA), 47 (Shasta, CA), 49 (top right, Josephine, OR), 53 (left, Inyo, CA), 55 (right, Shasta, CA), 62 (Shasta, CA), 67 (bottom, Siskiyou, CA), 86 (middle, Josephine, OR; bottom, Siskiyou, CA), 102 (right, Shasta, CA), 107 (top left and top right, Siskiyou, CA), 112 (Siskiyou, CA), 113 (bottom, Siskiyou, CA), 120 (right, Shasta, CA), 130 (top, San Diego, CA), 151 (bottom, Modoc, CA), 154 (both, Shasta, CA), 171 (top left and top right,

Shasta, CA), 173 (top, Modoc, CA), 176 (bottom right, Shasta, CA), 178 (bottom, Shasta, CA), 181 (top left, Siskiyou, CA), 196 (Jackson, OR), 204 (Jackson, OR), 211 (right, Jackson, OR), 215 (Josephine, OR), 217 (right, Shasta, CA), 218 (left, Josephine, OR), 231 (right, Josephine, OR), 234 (top left, Siskiyou, CA), 250 (top, San Diego, CA; bottom, Yuma, AZ), 262 (right, Mono-Tuolumne line, CA), 272 (left, Siskiyou, CA), 276 (top, Jackson, OR), 279 (Klamath, OR), 300 (Siskiyou, CA), 311 (top left, Klamath, OR; top right, Siskiyou, CA), 314 (bottom, Jackson, OR), 316 (left, Josephine, OR; right, Siskiyou, CA), 331 (Shasta, CA), 359 (top, Josephine, OR), 361 (Shasta, CA), 375 (top, Shasta, CA), 386 (right, Siskiyou, CA), 387 (Siskiyou, CA), 394 (left, Siskiyou, CA; right, Josephine, OR), 404 (bottom, Modoc, CA), 405 (right, Siskiyou, CA) and 417 (top, Shasta, CA).

David Shaw, pages 149 (bottom, Kittitas, WA) and 164 (left, Kittitas, WA).

John Stuart, page 347 (Pend Oreille, WA).

Richard Szlemp, page 367 (left, Benton, OR).

Idie Ulsh, pages 65 (top, Chelan, WA) and 210 (Mason, WA).

Melanie Weiss, pages 37 (top, Grant, WA), 117 (Okanogan, WA), 126 (top, Okanogan, WA), 190 (Kittitas, WA), 274 (bottom left, Pierce, WA), 278 (right, Kittitas, WA), 281 (top, Grant, WA), 357 (top, Yakima-Pierce line, WA) and 414 (top right, Okanogan, WA).

Alan Wight, pages 52 (bottom, Inyo, CA), 65 (bottom, Tulare, CA), 161 (top right, Sonoma, CA) and 389 (bottom left, Sonoma, CA).

Mike Yip, pages 83 (bottom two, Manning Park, BC), 135 (bottom, Ada, ID) and 147 (bottom, Okanogan, WA).

Kim Zumwalt, pages 105 (bottom, Wallowa, OR) and 170 (Adams, ID).

Illustrations on pages 70, 71, 226, 227 and 367 by **Denise Takahashi.**

Historic photo on page 27 by **A. W. Denny,** negative number UW 501, used with permission from the Special Collections Division, University of Washington Libraries.

All specimens are lodged in either the Burke Museum (BM) at the University of Washington, the Oregon State Arthropod Collection (OSAC) at Oregon State University, the collection of Don Rolfs residing at Washington State University (WSU) or the private collection of Caitlin C. LaBar (CCL). All photos by Caitlin C. LaBar.

Page 45, Dicot Skippers: *T. pylades*, Kitsap, WA (BM); *T. diversus*, Curry, OR (OSAC); *T. mexicana*, Deschutes, OR (OSAC); *E. icelus*, Okanogan, WA (CCL); *E. persius* left and right, Chelan, WA (BM) and middle, Mason, WA (BM); *E. propertius* female, Kern, CA (BM) and male, Klickitat, WA (CCL); *E. pacuvius*, Chelan, WA (BM); *P. centaureae*, Summit, UT (CCL); *P. communis*, Kittitas, WA (CCL); *P. ruralis*, Mason, WA (BM); *H. ericetorum* both, Chelan, WA (WSU).

Page 69, Monocot Skippers, part 1: *O. garita*, Okanogan, WA (WSU); *T. lineola*, Gallatin, MT (WSU); *H. phyleus*, Ignacio, CA (OSAC); *A. campestris* male, Sacramento, CA (OSAC) and female, Polk, OR (OSAC); *O. sylvanoides sylvanoides* both, Clark, WA (OSAC); *O. sylvanoides orecoasta*, Pacific, WA (BM); *O. sylvanoides bonnevilla* both, Grant, WA (BM); *O. yuma* both, Grant, WA (BM); *O. Agricola*, Monterey, CA (BM); *E. vestris* both, Kittitas, WA (BM).

Page 72, Monocot Skippers, part 2: *H. uncas* both, Mono, CA (OSAC); *H. juba* female, Pierce, WA (BM) and male, Franklin, WA (BM); *H. comma manitoba* male, Okanogan, WA (BM) and female, Chelan, WA (BM); *H. comma hulbirti*, Clallam, WA (BM); *H. colorado idaho*, Harney, OR (OSAC); *H. colorado oregonia* both, Thurston, WA (BM); *H. columbia*, Josephine, OR (BM); *H. lindseyi* both, Jackson, OR (OSAC); *H. nevada* all, Kittitas, WA (BM).

Page 73, Monocot Skippers, part 3: *P. peckius* both, Okanogan, WA (WSU); *P. sabuleti* both, Chelan, WA (WSU); *P. mardon mardon* male, Yakima, WA (WSU) and female, Thurston, WA (BM); *P. mardon klamathensis*, Jackson, OR (OSAC); *P. sonora* male, Trinity, CA (OSAC) and female, Siskiyou, CA (OSAC); *P. draco* male, Carbon, WY (BM) and female, Takhini River Valley, YT (BM); *P. themistocles* male, Okanogan, WA (BM) and female, Ferry, WA (BM); *P. mystic* both, Pend Oreille, WA (BM).

Page 128, Sulphurs, part 1: *C. eurytheme* male, Kittitas, WA (CCL) and females, Yakima, WA (BM); *C. philodice* male, Okanogan, WA (CCL) and females, Kittitas, WA (BM); *C. occidentalis* left two males and all females, Yakima, WA (BM) and right male, Chelan, WA (BM); *C. alexandra* male, Wasco, OR (OSAC), yellow female, Harney, OR (BM) and white female, Lake, OR (OSAC).

Page 129, Sulphurs, part 2: *C. christina* left male, Okanogan, WA (CCL) and other three, Pend Oreille, WA (BM); *C. gigantea* male, Deer Lodge, MT (OSAC) and female, Beaverhead, MT (OSAC); *C. interior* left male, Stevens, WA (BM), right male, Okanogan, WA (CCL) and female, Okanogan, WA (BM); *C. skinneri* male and white female, Harney, OR (OSAC) and yellow female, Wallowa, OR (OSAC); *C. nastes* all, Okanogan, WA (BM).

Page 191, Hairstreaks, part 1: *A. halesus* female, Jackson, OR (OSAC) and male, San Bernardino, CA (OSAC); *H. grunus* both, Wasco, OR (OSAC); *S. fuliginosa*, Siskiyou-

Trinity line, CA (OSAC); *S. semiluna*, Okanogan, WA (CCL); *S. behrii*, Chelan, WA (OSAC); *S. californica*, Okanogan, WA (OSAC); *S. titus* both, Yakima, WA (OSAC); *S. sylvinus* left, Deschutes, OR (OSAC) and right, Jackson, OR (OSAC); *S. auretorum* both, Yolo, CA (OSAC); *S. tetra* both, Lake, OR (OSAC); *S. saepium* female, Kittitas, WA (OSAC) and male, Yakima, WA (OSAC).

Page 192, Hairstreaks, part 2: *C. affinis* female, Oizama Lake, BC (OSAC), male dorsal and left ventral, Okanogan, WA (OSAC) and right ventral, Skamania, WA (OSAC); *C. dumetorum* dorsals and right ventral, Klickitat, WA (OSAC) and left ventral, Mason, WA (WSU); *C. sheridanii* dorsal and left ventral, Crook, OR (OSAC) and right ventral, Chelan, WA (WSU); *C. spinetorum* female, Okanogan, WA (CCL) and male, Jefferson, OR (OSAC); *C. johnsoni* both, Mason, WA (OSAC); *C. augustinus*, Kittitas, WA (CCL); *C. mossii*, Crook, OR (OSAC); *C. gryneus*, Harney, OR (OSAC); *C. polios*, Mason, WA (OSAC); *C. eryphon*, Klickitat, WA (CCL); *S. melinus*, Pierce, WA (OSAC).

Page 228, Blues: *C. lucia* male, Yakima, WA (BM) and female, Kittitas, WA (BM); *C. echo* males, Okanogan, WA (CCL) and female, Kittitas, WA (CCL); *E. "heracleoides"* male, Okanogan, WA (CCL) and female, Kittitas, WA (CCL); *E. glaucon* both, Harney, OR (OSAC); *E. baueri* both, Harney, OR (OSAC); *E. enoptes* male, Josephine, OR (OSAC) and female, Klamath, OR (OSAC); *E. columbiae* (Central/N WA) both, Chelan, WA (WSU); *E. columbiae* (SE WA/OR) male, Umatilla, OR (OSAC) and female, Columbia, WA (OSAC).

Page 290, Lesser Fritillaries: *B. selene, freija* and *epithore*, Okanogan, WA (CCL) and *B. chariclea, bellona* and *astarte*, Okanogan, WA (WSU).

Page 301, Greater Fritillaries, part 1: *S. cybele leto* both, Okanogan, WA (CCL); *S. cybele pugetensis*, Marion, OR (BM); *S. aphrodite* both, Elko, BC (OSAC); *S. coronis simaetha* both, Okanogan, WA (CCL); *S. coronis snyderi*, Harney, OR (OSAC); *S. coronis coronis*, Josephine, OR (OSAC); *S. zerene zerene*, Siskiyou, CA (OSAC); *S. zerene gloriosa*, Josephine, OR (OSAC); *S. zerene hippolyta*, Lane, OR (OSAC); *S. zerene bremnerii*, Jefferson, WA (BM); *S. zerene picta*, Okanogan, WA (CCL); *S. zerene gunderi*, Cassia, ID (CCL).

Page 302, Greater Fritillaries, part 2: *S. callippe semivirida* males, Okanogan, WA (CCL) and female, Baker, OR (BM); *S. callippe harmonia*, Harney, OR (OSAC); *S. callippe elaine*, Jackson, OR (OSAC); *S. callippe chilcotinensis*, Riske Creek, BC (OSAC); *S. egleis egleis*, Lake, OR (BM); *S. egleis mattooni*, Jackson, OR (OSAC); *S. egleis oweni* and *moecki*, Klamath, OR (OSAC); *S. egleis macdunnoughi* both, Columbia, WA (BM); *S. mormonia washingtonia* female and left male, Kittitas, WA (CCL) and right male, Okanogan, WA (CCL); *S. mormonia erinna* both, Okanogan, WA (BM); *S. mormonia opis*, Grizzly Creek, BC (OSAC); *S. mormonia artonis*, Harney, OR (OSAC).

Page 303, Greater Fritillaries, part 3: *S. atlantis* all, Pend Oreille, WA (BM); *S. hesperis cottlei*, Modoc, CA (OSAC); *S. hesperis dodgei*, Lane, OR (OSAC); *S. hesperis viola*, Blaine, ID (OSAC); *S. hesperis brico* males, Okanogan, WA (CCL) and female, Okanogan, WA (BM); *S. hydaspe hydaspe* both, Lake, OR (CCL); *S. hydaspe minor* both, Clallam, WA (BM); *S. hydaspe rhodope* all, Okanogan, WA (CCL).

Page 376: *C. leanira*, Harney, OR (OSAC)

Page 400, Wood Nymphs: *C. oetus*, middle, Kittitas, WA (CCL); all others, Okanogan, WA (CCL).

Page 413: *O. melissa* male and female, Okanogan, WA (BM)

Page 414: *O. chryxus* male and female, Okanogan, WA (CCL)

Page 416: *O. nevadensis* male and female, Kittitas, WA (CCL)

Page 418: *O. macounii* male, Lake, MN (BM)

ACKNOWLEDGMENTS

From RMP: A book like this draws its heart and substance from many sources. The author gathers the materials and weaves them together but can in no way be said to have created the whole. I am indebted to so many others over my 60 years of study that have led up to this book that it would take another field guide to properly identify them all. A few stand out—some for several reasons.

First, I thank the late Charles Remington of Yale University, co-founder of the Lepidopterists' Society and fortuitous early acquaintance, for his lifelong mentorship, tuition, and careful critique of my earlier butterfly writings. Other great teachers have included Paul Ehrlich, Melville Hatch, Grant W. Sharpe, Robert Gara, and John Heath. This field guide could not have been written without the knowledge, text review, and overall support of Jonathan Pelham and other Evergreen Aurelians: John Hinchliff, Jon and Sigrid Shepard, Dave McCorkle, Paul Hammond, and later colleagues Andy Warren, Dave Nunnallee, David James, and David Droppers. I am truly indebted to each of them, as well as Norbert Kondla and Caitlin LaBar, for reviewing all or parts of the text and maps. Errors are all mine.

Members of the Northwest Lepidopterists' Association and the Washington and Eugene-Springfield butterfly associations have added greatly to our understanding of Cascadian butterflies. These are too many to name, but among the notables, I must mention Dana Ross (who manages the Oregon records), Ann Potter (who manages the Washington records), Paul Severns, David Lee Myers, Bill Yake, Robert Hardwick, Richard Lindstrom, John Bauman, Jeanne Dammarell, Lori Humphreys, Jeff Miller, Vince Lucas, and J. Alan Wagar.

I especially wish to cite several giants who passed too soon to see the fruits of their work expressed here: John Hinchliff (whose *Atlases* cite many collectors and observers who provided records), Ben Leighton, E. J. Newcomer, John Hopfinger, Ernst Dornfeld, Stan Jewett, J. F. Gates Clark, Don Frechin, Virgil Calkins, Ralph Macy, Ken Fender, Jim Baker, Elmer Griepentrog, Ray Albright, Harold Rice, and the late, great Idie Ulsh. I could not have undertaken this regional review without the publications of Jon and Sigrid Shepard and Crispin Guppy, James A. Scott, Tom and John Emmel, Sterling Mattoon, George Austin, Paul A. Opler, J. W. Tilden, Arthur Shapiro, F. M. Brown, Ray Stanford, Cliff Ferris, and others cited in the text and bibliography. In particular, Andrew D. Warren's *Butterflies of Oregon*, David James and David Nunnallee's *Life Histories*, Jonathan P. Pelham's *Catalogue*, and Jim P. Brock and Kenn Kaufman's *Butterflies of North America* were indispensable.

To all the photographers who have donated their beautiful images: thanks! Additional images were most helpfully provided by Nicolette Bromberg and the University of Washington Libraries Special Collections. Dave Nunnallee kindly undertook the exacting task of recovering the digital files of *The Butterflies of Cascadia*, from which we could work. Caitlin LaBar first agreed to help me wrangle the old transparencies and the new digital images for the book, an enormous job, and ended up doing so much more as co-author, including major work on the maps. The book bears her imprint in many of its best respects. The words *sine qua non* never meant more.

My field studies have been greatly assisted by officals and biologists in Olympic and North Cascades National Parks and San Juan Island National Historic Park, the North Cascades Institute (especially Saul Weisberg) and the former Olympic Institute, The Nature Conservancy, the Sitka Center for Art and Ecology, and, as always, the wonderful staff of the Xerces Society.

Thanks so much to Juree Sondker for urging me to write the book, and to the staff at Timber Press, including Andrew Beckman, Sarah Milhollin, Frances Farrell, and Adrianna Sutton, who have made the work a pleasure and realized the book in such beautiful form. I lovingly thank Florence Sage for her big support throughout the preparation of the manuscript. And of course I owe this and all of my books to my entire extended family, living and gone on, including my original encouragers, Grace Phelps Miller, Helen Bailey Phelps, and Helen Lee Lemmon.

From CCL: I thank the dozens of photographers who have made this book possible, most notably Jeanne Dammarell, Rob Santry, Dennis Holmes, Kim Davis, Mike Stangeland, David Nunnallee, David Lee Myers, Norbert Kondla, Bryan E. Reynolds, Linda Kappen, David James, Ray Bruun, John Davis, Jeff Pippen, and Lori Humphreys. So many other photographers were essential to the success of this book and are listed in the photo and illustration credits: thank you! I also thank Jonathan Pelham for his support and advice, his assistance in proofing species identifications of photos, and for hosting me at the Burke Museum to photograph many of the specimens illustrated in this book. Also many thanks to Christopher Marshall at the Oregon State Arthropod Collection for allowing me to photograph the remaining specimens needed, and to Jon Shepard and Paul Hammond for assisting with finding and selecting the specimens there to photograph for this book. Thanks to Jonathan Pelham, Jon Shepard, Paul Hammond, Andrew Warren, Dana Ross, Ann Potter and David Nunnallee for reviewing the range maps and providing new records and other updates. I also thank my family and friends for their unwavering support and enthusiastic encouragement of this project. Finally, none of this would have been possible without Bob Pyle; I thank him doubly, for inviting me to help with this project and for his support and advice along the way.

INDEX

ABOUT THE AUTHORS

Noted lepidopterist and writer **Robert Michael Pyle** is the founder of the Xerces Society for Invertebrate Conservation and an Honorary Fellow of the Royal Entomological Society. A Yale-trained ecologist and a Guggenheim fellow, he is a full-time biologist and the author of more than 20 books, including *Wintergreen*, which won the John Burroughs Medal, *Chasing Monarchs, Mariposa Road*, and two collections of poetry. His works on butterflies include *The Audubon Society Field Guide to North American Butterflies, Handbook for Butterfly Watchers*, and *The Butterflies of Cascadia*. He lives in Gray's River, Washington.

Pacific Northwest native **Caitlin C. LaBar** was born with a fascination for insects, which has developed into an interest in studying the habitats and life histories of butterflies and moths. A geographer and GIS analyst by training and a conservationist by nature, she enjoys photographing and collecting local butterflies and working on various butterfly projects. She is a member of the Lepidopterists' Society and lives in Kelso, Washington. Visit her at northwestbutterflies.blogspot.com